DATE DUE

The Institutionalized Cabinet

COLLECTION ADMINISTRATION PUBLIQUE
CANADIENNE

CANADIAN PUBLIC ADMINISTRATION
SERIES

Iain Gow, A. Paul Pross,
Co-editors / Co-directeurs

J. E. Hodgetts
Editor Emeritus / Directeur émérite

En publiant cette collection, l'Institut d'administration publique du Canada cherche à promouvoir la
recherche sur des problèmes contemporains touchant
l'administration publique, la gestion du secteur public,
ou les politiques publiques au Canada. Il cherche
aussi à favoriser une meilleure compréhension de ces
questions chez les praticiens, les universitaires, et le
grand public.

This series is sponsored by the Institute of Public
Administration of Canada as part of its commitment
to encourage research on contemporary issues in
Canadian public administration, public sector management, and public policy. It also seeks to foster
wider knowledge and understanding among practi-
tioners, academics, and the general public.

The Institutionalized Cabinet

Governing the Western Provinces

CHRISTOPHER DUNN

The Institute of Public Administration of Canada
Kingston

McGill-Queen's University Press
Montreal & Kingston • London • Buffalo

© McGill-Queen's University Press 1995

ISBN 0-7735-1283-7

Legal deposit second quarter 1995
Bibliothèque nationale du Québec

Printed in Canada on acid-free paper

This book has been published with the help of a grant from the
Social Science Federation of Canada, using funds provided by the
Social Sciences and Humanities Research Council of Canada.
McGill-Queen's University Press is grateful to the Canada Council
for support of its publishing program.

Canadian Cataloguing in Publication Data

Dunn, Christopher J. C., 1948–
 The institutionalized cabinet: governing the Western Provinces
 (Canadian public administration series)
 Includes bibliographical references and index.
 ISBN 0-7735-1283-7
 1. Cabinet system – Canada, Western. 2. Saskatchewan. Executive
 Council. 3. Manitoba. Executive Council. 4. British Columbia.
 Executive Council. 5. Canada, Western – Politics and government.
 I. Institute of Public Administration of Canada. II. Title. III. Series.
 JL198.D86 1995   321.8′043′09712   C95-900295-2

Typeset in Times 10/12 by Caractéra production graphique inc.,
Quebec City.

Dedicated to the memory of
my father, John D'Arcy Dunn;
to Lauren, Kathleen, and Emily,
the next generation;
and to the beautiful ones
not yet born.

Contents

CONTENTS

Tables

Preface

Any acknowledgments in this study must first of all be directed to my doctoral advisor at the University of Toronto, Professor J. Stefan Dupré, a brilliant scholar, for his formative role in the present work. I extend my thanks also to Professors Meyer Brownstone and Albert W. Johnson for participating on my thesis committee. I am grateful to my family as well: to my mother, Patricia Dunn, for inspiration; to my brother, Jeffrey, for current events knowledge; and to my sister, Catherine, for perspective. Thanks go to Robert Coutts, editor of *Manitoba History*, for his valuable proofreading of the last draft. Louise Valentin, my typist, was a pillar of strength throughout the whole process, and I will always be grateful for her cooperation and good cheer. I am indebted to Sharon Wall at Memorial University for her very professional arrangement of the final text. As well, I offer grateful appreciation to the excellent staffs of the British Columbia and Manitoba Legislative Libraries and the Saskatchewan and Manitoba Archives, who allowed me valuable help in this endeavour. Derrick Hynes, acting as research assistant, discovered some very useful biographical material. Appreciation is also extended to the editors of *Canadian Public Administration* for permission to republish chapter 14 of this book, much of which originally appeared in their journal in the winter of 1991. Several anonymous referees, acting on behalf of the Social Science Federation of Canada and McGill-Queen's University Press, have contributed significantly to the professionalism of the manuscript. Sandra Black offered careful and insightful copy-editing on behalf of McGill-Queen's University Press. I would also like to thank Peter Blaney, Acquisitions Editor, for his initial encouragement of this project and his continuing advice during its progress. I, of course, take full responsibility for any errors or omissions.

The Institutionalized Cabinet

Introduction

The subject of this investigation is cabinet decision making in the provincial governments of Saskatchewan, Manitoba, and British Columbia. Specifically, this study attempts to examine the forces that underlie the initiation and persistence of cabinet institutionalization in the postwar period.

The rationale for studying decision making in the provincial executives is clear. Generally speaking, broad and systematic investigations of provincial central executives have been rare. If they do exist, they tend to be premier or function specific.[1] Reviews of western Canadian cabinet government are particularly few. As well, the number and complexity of cabinet-level decision-making structures has grown, and the structures themselves are becoming more difficult and inconvenient to change. This work may therefore help to inform future designs for the machinery of government.

The postwar period has witnessed the replacement of the unaided (or traditional) cabinet by the institutionalized (or structured) cabinet. In other words, unstructured and relatively uncoordinated central executives have given way to those which are more structured, more collegial, and more prone to emphasize planning and coordination. There is not one basic form of institutionalized cabinet, but they all share one characteristic: the premier's role grows from that of mere personnel choice to that of organizational architect with regard to the structure and decision-making processes of cabinet.

The origins of the provincial institutionalized cabinet have not been a subject of great academic interest in Canada. Where such beginnings have been discussed, descriptions have been quite general, usually since the history of the executive has not been the major concern of the author. A few examples from the literature will suffice. Scope and complexity are said to be important factors. The growth in cabinet size, number of cabinet committees, staff assistance, and central policy techniques has been attributed to "increased demands for public goods and services, greater willingness to respond to these demands, and more complex interrelationships among policy areas" in both federal and provincial governments.[2] Another set of writers attribute the strengthening of the central executive to cabinet's desire to reassert a collective power which had drifted away to line department officials or to collaborative networks of federal and provincial functional officials.[3] Still another group sees the development of central structures and processes as the result of the premier's drive for leadership and control.[4] A recent approach is to relate the greater institutional complexity of provincial (and federal) cabinets—namely, the establishment of a cabinet committee system and more impersonal organizational devices—principally to the numerical size of cabinet. "Larger cabinets [more than twenty] become so unwieldy as to require a system of committees."[5]

Although such explanations are not wrong in themselves, they are somewhat misleading. Firstly, they do not distinguish between the factors that promote institutionalization in the first place and those that are responsible for its persistence. The two sets are not necessarily identical. There is always the possibility that an institutionalizing premier will be followed by one, like a Ross Thatcher, who seeks to undo much of the previous incumbent's institutionalization, usually unsuccessfully. It is instructive to know why a structured cabinet persists, especially in an era of rhetoric about government downsizing. Secondly, many of the explanations tend to focus on a single factor, downplaying the complexities of modern government. Thirdly, the explanations do not explicitly consider an analytical distinction between factors internal to government and those that act on it from its environment, nor do they examine the relative balance between these two types of factors. Lastly, with a few exceptions, not enough emphasis has been placed on reviewing the factors that the designers of cabinets themselves felt to be important. This study has sought to avoid all these pitfalls.

One explanation for structured cabinets in the three provinces is dismissed at the outset. The study of these particular cabinet structures reveals that the numerical size of cabinets cannot be considered to have been a factor in their institutionalization. At the time of transition

4

from the unaided to the institutionalized cabinet in the mid- to late 1940s, Saskatchewan had only a dozen cabinet ministers at most. Manitoba had between nine and thirteen, if the whole of the Roblin period (1958–67) is defined as transitional. British Columbia's cabinet hovered around the mid-teens during an extended transition stretching from the late W. A. C. Bennett period, through Dave Barrett's term, to the heightening of institutionalization in the early W. R. Bennett years.

Other explanations have likewise been examined and discarded. The "province-building" theory was in vogue during the author's research, but the relevant literature was too diffuse and contradictory to be of much operational use. The theory also sounded stilted and foreign in discussions with certain types of interviewees — say, finance officials. Other explanations, such as the growth of the welfare state or policy interdependence, met similar fates. More useful information seemed to be forthcoming if respondents and documentary evidence were free to speak for themselves.

The factors promoting initial cabinet institutionalization in the three provinces studied were a mixture of ideology, pragmatism, and historical precedent unique to each province. T. C. Douglas in Saskatchewan was influenced by left-wing ideology from which subsidiary considerations flowed. In Manitoba, Duff Roblin and Walter Weir were subject to a unique blend of ideology, pragmatism, and management factors. In British Columbia, W. R. Bennett began with right-wing ideological premises; his path to institutionalization was made easier by the fact that developments under his two predecessors had foreshadowed it.

There were both endogenous factors (those growing from within government) and exogenous factors (those acting from without) which affected the persistence of institutionalized cabinets. They were common to more than one province, but their relative weight differed between premiers. Endogenous factors included the premier's quest for influence, unsatisfactory aspects of the unaided cabinet, the emulation of predecessors, cabinet's quest both for political and financial control, the urge to simplify decision making, the momentum of past reforms, and ideology. Exogenous factors included the impact of other governments, "semaphore" (or symbolic messages to concerned publics), social science rationalism, and the facilitation of interest group input.

Not surprisingly, the institutionalization of provincial cabinets has had major effects on political actors and functions in the three provinces studied. Cabinet structure has both changed, and been changed by, power relations within cabinet. Full cabinet appears to have been overshadowed as a decision-making centre. It is apparent that central agencies and central departments do not always yield similar political effects.

The research design for this study included a variety of approaches. One was experiential. The author was a planning adviser to the Manitoba cabinet from 1974 to 1977, which involved serving a cabinet committee and becoming involved in a number of planning and budgetary exercises. The preliminary research involved a review of most of the literature on federal and provincial cabinet government as well as several relevant masters theses. The archives of four western premiers and a number of cabinet ministers were examined. The author conducted structured interviews in the early to late eighties with more than two hundred politicians, officials, and academics influential in the development of cabinet systems in the western provinces. He also investigated the cabinet systems of Douglas (Saskatchewan), Roblin (Manitoba), and W. A. C. Bennett (British Columbia), and of all subsequent premiers of those provinces, except Filmon, Romanow, Vander Zalm, and Harcourt. The original focus was to be a comprehensive study of all four western provinces, but this had to be revised when key Alberta officials either refused interviews or would not share information in sufficient detail to allow for useful interprovincial comparisons.

Part One
Introducing Cabinet Structures

Chapter One
Provincial Premiers and Cabinets

The subject of this investigation is cabinet decision making in the provincial governments of Saskatchewan, Manitoba, and British Columbia. Specifically, this study attempts to examine the forces that underlie the initiation and persistence of cabinet institutionalization in the postwar period.

THE DUTIES OF THE FIRST MINISTER

The machinery of government is of special concern to premiers. Like the prime minister, each premier has special duties to perform in the division of responsibilities and the general running of government. The duties of the first minister arise from needs identified in modern organization theory as well as from existing constitutional practice, as the report of the Macdonald Royal Commission noted in a somewhat flawed analogy:

> A chief executive officer (CEO) at the apex of any complex organization is essential if there is to be overall executive control and direction of the organization's activities. Government, like other organizations, can be effective only if it embodies principles of integration and coherence; to promote these, the Prime Minister has assumed characteristics of the CEO function. The expansion of

state activity has made public policies and programs increasingly interdependent. Planning and co-ordination thus assume more importance in the context of executive responsibilities. By constitutional convention, the Prime Minister has the ultimate authority and responsibility for planning and co-ordination at the executive level. Recent Prime Ministers have responded to this challenge in three ways: by reinforcing their authority through a more hierarchical Cabinet structure; by reducing their span of control in working primarily through an inner Cabinet; and by expanding their staff support to assist them in discharging their responsibilities as chief executive officer.[1]

The Privy Council office notes that the prime minister is also charged with the division of responsibilities in cabinet and with the setting of general priorities. "The prerogatives of the Prime Minister include the selection and retention of ministers, and the division of responsibilities among the ministers within the limits prescribed by law. The Prime Minister also indicates the priorities and objectives which he would want the minister to accomplish. These may have political or departmental implications, or both."[2]

The premier, like the prime minister, is responsible for cabinet organization, and as the Brownlow Committee said of the U.S. president, the premier needs help. The quandary is where the premier shall turn for help. The literature on the federal executive is immense but may not always apply to provincial conditions. On the other hand, the literature on the provincial executive is rather slim and tends to be disjointed. This present work is an attempt to add continuity and depth to existing coverage of the provincial executive.

In its structure, this study builds on the logic of the first minister's responsibility: since premiers are responsible for executive organization, the histories of the provincial executive are examined premier by premier. Special attention is given to the main functions for which premiers, and the ministers of finance and Treasury Boards they choose and monitor, have special responsibility. These include the design of cabinet structures, organization of planning and budgeting processes, and selection of decision-making modes. This study also examines the inter-relationships between the various functions: for instance, the complementarity and tension between planning and budgeting. After each premier's record is reviewed in detail, it is summarized in outline form. The study then ends with a review of cabinet institutionalization, focusing on the factors involved in its initiation and persistence, and summarizing its effects.

PROVINCIAL CABINET MODELS

One of the most important (and predictable) findings of the study is that there has been a permanent shift from the "unaided" to the "institutionalized" cabinet model (see Table 1). The term *unaided cabinet* appears to have been first used by Paul Tennant in an article that in passing described the old-style pattern of cabinet government to which W. A. C. Bennett subscribed.[3] His unaided cabinet idea was the inspiration for the first column of Table 1, but it has here been subjected to substantial modifications and adaptations. (Tennant drew a distinction between a traditional and an unaided cabinet: the former has an authoritarian premier, while the latter does not. However, this work uses the two terms interchangeably, unless explicitly indicated to the contrary.) Tennant does not explicitly describe the institutionalized cabinet, but this study does so here in order to highlight in detail the direction that cabinet decision making has taken in the modern era. The term *institutionalized cabinet* in fact derives from J. Stefan Dupré, who contrasted it with the traditional and departmentalized cabinets that pertained at both the federal and provincial levels before and during the rise of the modern administrative state.[4]

It is notable that cabinet institutionalization began at different times in each of the three provinces: Saskatchewan in the late forties, Manitoba in the late fifties and sixties, and British Columbia in the late seventies. Although responsible for the general machinery of government, premiers did not resort to cabinet institutionalization at the same point in history.

Of course, the distinctions between unaided and institutionalized cabinets should not be exaggerated. Institutionalized cabinets are normally more collegial than unaided cabinets. However, they occasionally feature a dominant premier, which is a characteristic usually found in unaided cabinets. Alternatively, institutionalized cabinets will sometimes become fragmented if there are several powerful ministers and a relatively weak premier. There are no facile generalizations about who are the focal decision-makers in unaided and institutionalized cabinets. What can be offered instead are statements of tendency: institutionalized cabinets *tend* to be more collegial, centralist, analytical, and comprehensive in their approach to whereas planning, unaided cabinets *tend* to have dominant premiers, emphasize departmental autonomy, shun staff aid to cabinet, and see planning only as a restricted function of government. However, the one constant difference between the two types of cabinet is that the premier in the unaided cabinet is principally the "architect of personnel choice," whereas in the institutionalized cabinet he is the architect not only of personnel choice but of cabinet structure as well.

Table 1 differentiates between unaided and institutionalized cabinets with specific reference to cabinet structure, central agencies, budgeting and planning, and decision-making modes.

The examination of cabinet structures in the three provinces encompassed by this study is of additional interest because numerical size cannot be considered to have been a factor in institutionalization. Table 2 gives a summary of the size of provincial cabinets and the number of ministries in Saskatchewan, Manitoba, and British Columbia from 1935 to 1986. At the time of transition from the unaided to the institutionalized cabinet, Saskatchewan had only a dozen cabinet ministers. Manitoba had between nine and thirteen, if the whole of the Roblin period is defined as transitional. British Columbia's cabinet hovered around the mid-teens during an extended transition stretching from the late W. A. C. Bennett period through the Dave Barrett era to the heightening of institutionalization in the early Bill Bennett years. Even as late as the mid-seventies, the average size of cabinet in the three provinces was only about twenty members. Saskatchewan, which at one point climbed to an uncharacteristic high of twenty-five ministers, went down below twenty again in 1986. The number of ministers in all three provinces has been consistently below the number of ministries, giving evidence of some measure of self-control exercised by premiers in regard to the size of their cabinets.

Compared to federal cabinets, which were fairly large (and relatively structured) as far back as Lester Pearson, the provincial cabinets in question were relatively small. Table 3 compares Canadian and provincial cabinet sizes from 1935 to 1985. Provincial cabinets, with some exceptions, were usually only half the size of their contemporary Canadian counterparts.

The institutionalized cabinet has come to predominate due to other reasons than size. This study reveals that in Saskatchewan, Manitoba, and British Columbia it initially arose for province-specific reasons, and over time it has persisted for reasons that transcend provincial peculiarities. Subsequent chapters will identify both the peculiar factors that promoted the initiation of cabinet institutionalization and the common factors that affect its persistence.

TERMINOLOGY

Since some terms are central to this study, a few words about terminology are expedient at the outset of this book. There is, first of all, a nominal distinction between the terms cabinet and executive council.

12

TABLE 1

UNAIDED AND INSTITUTIONALIZED CABINET MODELS

The Unaided Cabinet	*The Institutionalized Cabinet*
CABINET STRUCTURE	CABINET STRUCTURE
The premier is principally the architect of personnel choice. His or her main cabinet-building tasks are to choose ministers, to coordinate their actions, and to match ministers with appropriate senior officials.	The premier is the architect of both personnel choice and cabinet structure. He or she has available a varied set of organizational options for adapting cabinet structure to endogenous and exogenous influences.
There is a strong tendency for the premier to hold the Finance (Treasury) portfolio as well and hence to chair both cabinet and the Treasury Board.	The premier seldom, if ever, holds the Finance portfolio. The cabinet is chaired by the premier, and the Treasury Board—with some exceptions—is chaired by the minister of finance.
With some exceptions, there is a general tendency for restricted collegiality (collective decision making) and a dominant premier.	With some exceptions, there is a general tendency for collective decision making and a less dominant premier.
There is a simple cabinet structure.	There is a complex cabinet structure; occasionally an internal hierarchy is established in cabinet.
There are few, if any, cabinet committees (other than the Treasury Board). Those which come into being will generally lack continuing mandates. (The Treasury Board has a continuing mandate established by legislation.)	Extensive use is made of cabinet committees that have continuing mandates and functional representation.
CENTRAL AGENCIES	CENTRAL AGENCIES
There is an absence of central agencies. A Department of Finance is the principal central department.	There are both central departments and central agencies.
There are few cabinet-level staff or staff agencies. Cabinet may obtain rudimentary process assistance from a Provincial Secretary ministry or its equivalent.	Extensive use is made of cabinet-level staff and staff agencies; staff provide aid to cabinet committees or full cabinet, or both.

13

TABLE 1 (continued)

The Unaided Cabinet	*The Institutionalized Cabinet*
Little analysis, planning, or coordination is done for cabinet. However, the premier may come to rely on financial assistance which is provided to him directly. This "fiscally-aided premier" pattern may be an early sign of transition to an institutionalized cabinet.	There is extensive central agency analysis, planning, and coordination provided for cabinet. Two types of analysis are usually given: partisan political input by a PMO-type unit and policy/technocratic input by a PCO-type unit or units.
There may be or may not be a clerk of the executive council; even if there is, no staff are allowed to attend cabinet meetings on a regular basis.	There is a clerk of the executive council who attends all meetings and keeps detailed records, not only of Orders in Council, but also of cabinet decisions.
BUDGETING AND PLANNING	BUDGETING AND PLANNING
Budgeting is an essential priority setting function and is, with some exceptions, centralized. A central figure—the premier or finance minister (who are sometimes the same person)—usually exercises detailed centralized budgetary responsibilities, but maintains a nominal Treasury Board through which to exercise control. Where political influence is spread evenly around cabinet—and this is unusual—budgeting will be collective in nature.	Budgeting is an essential priority setting function of the central executive. It is generally collective in nature, but occasionally it will be individualized under the premier (or finance minister) if he or she is a dominant enough politician. Collectivization of budgeting means that responsibilities in the annual budget process are widely spread to cabinet committees and the Treasury Board as well as to full cabinet. The degree of collectivization is flexible and dependent upon perceptions of fiscal or political contingencies.
The *aims* of budgeting are predominantly financial control—that is, effective control over expenditure growth—and the close relating of revenues to expenditures.	The *aims* of budgeting are broader than mere financial control; they include, for example, planning, management, and policy choice objectives.
The *means* of budgeting involve intervention in the annual budget making process and the in-year vetting of financial allotments.	Since there are multiple aims for budgeting, some of the *means* include command or political controls taken in an off-budget context: eg. public

14

TABLE 1 (continued)

The Unaided Cabinet	*The Institutionalized Cabinet*
	sector compensation controls, public service reductions, government reorganization, reform of financial administration legislation, reform of central agency roles, and so forth. These amount to "budgeting by other means." Traditional means of financial control continue, as in the unaided cabinet, but with a wider array of actors.
Planning is seen as optional, rather than as an essential function of the central executive. Where planning in government does take place, it appears to develop along a continuum. In the unaided cabinet, planning is sporadic, project oriented, and personalistic; outsiders are sometimes involved. There may next evolve a transitional type of planning, with outsiders performing both project and comprehensive planning.	Planning is seen as optional, rather than as an essential function of the central executive. There is, however, a tendency for institutionalized cabinets to move towards the end of the planning continuum. The institutionalized variant of planning tends to be collegial in nature and comprehensive in regard to public and/ or private objects.
The premier or finance minister can usually only be expected to achieve short-term coordination of policies.	Where planning and budgeting do coexist, they will do so in either complementary or competitive fashion. The two are usually seen as complementary functions (which this study calls the "planning-budgeting nexus") but occasionally they are balanced off against each other, creating planning-budgeting tension.
DECISION-MAKING MODES	DECISION-MAKING MODES
Flow of policy advice tends to be through discrete hierarchical channels. Senior departmental officials provide policy advice to cabinet ministers, and occasionally to the premier directly, and do not usually face alternate sources of policy advice in the full cabinet context.	There are alternative sources of policy advice on issues, the most notable being officials of central agencies or central departments, who provide policy advice to full cabinet and cabinet committees.

15

TABLE 1 (continued)

The Unaided Cabinet	The Institutionalized Cabinet
Cabinet decision making is, with some exceptions, decentralized. (Decentralized decision making is that which favours departmental autonomy over the power of central executive.) Ministers have broad policy latitude in non-budgetary matters and face few trade-offs between funcitonal areas of government. (However, one variant of the unaided model features a dominant premier who, in effect, weakens departmental autonomy.)	Cabinet decision making becomes, with some exceptions, more centralized. (Centralized decision making is that which favours the power of the central executive over departmental autonomy.) Ministers are obligated to make functional area trade-offs, aided by cabinet committees and other mechanisms of collective desicion making. There is, however, a fairly constant tension between centralization and departmental autonomy, and the premier may find it politic to try to achieve balance in central/departmental relations.

Cabinets are the "efficient" executive in that they are the main policy-initiating and administering bodies and operate on constitutional conventions that are more or less similar in all Commonwealth countries. The *executive council* is the formal or "dignified" executive. This distinction between the *efficient* and *dignified* executive—terms first coined by English essayist Walter Bagehot (1826–77)—was made in his important book, *The English Constitution*, published in 1867. That same year, the Canadian Constitution Act stated that The lieutenant-governor in council "shall be construed as referring to the Lieutenant Governor of the Province by and with the Advice of the Executive Council thereof" (S.66).

The Constitution Act of 1867 does not refer to cabinets by name at either the federal or provincial levels, as is consistent with constitutional convention. The Act does, however, provide for executive councils in Ontario and Quebec (S.63); the executive authorities in Nova Scotia and New Brunswick were to continue as they existed at the Union (S.64). The latter arrangement was duplicated in instruments admitting British Columbia, Prince Edward Island, and Newfoundland. Statutes creating Manitoba, Saskatchewan, and Alberta established executive authorities in those provinces.[5]

There are a host of other terms which are given specific meanings. *Cabinet-level planning* is the systematic, purposeful attempt to improve the discharge of collective and individual responsibility by means of

TABLE 2
SIZE OF PROVINCIAL CABINETS AND NUMBER OF MINISTRIES, WESTERN CANADA, 1935–86

Year	Saskatchewan		Manitoba		British Columbia	
	Ministers	Ministries	Ministers	Ministries	Ministers	Ministries
1935	9	13	9	12	8	14
1936	9	12	8	12	8	14
1937	9	13	9	12	8	14
1938	9	12	9	13	9	14
1939	9	12	9	13	9	14
1940	8	13	10	12	9	14
1941	8	13	13	13*	9	14
1942	9	13	12	13*	8	13*
1943	9	13	10	13*	8	14
1944	9	13	10	13*	8	14*
1945	12	16	11	13*	8	14*
1946	11	16	10	13*	8	14*
1947	12	16	11	13*	12	15*
1948	12	15	11	13*	10	15*
1949	11	13	12	13*	10	15*
1950	12	14	10	12*	11	15*
1951	12	14	9	13	11	15*
1952	12	14	10	13	7	15*
1953	13	14	10	13	11	15
1954	14	16	10	12	10	14
1955	14	16	10	13	10	15
1956	14	16	10	13	11	15
1957	15	15	10	13	12	16
1958	15	15	10	13	12	16
1959	15	16	9	13	12	16
1960	15	16	9	12	12	17
1961	15	16	9	13	12	17
1962	15	16	11	14	12	17
1963	15	16	9	14	11	17
1964	15	16	13	14	10	17
1965	12	14	13	14	13	19
1966	12	14	13	15	13	17
1967	13	16	12	16	15	17
1968	13	17	12	16	15	18
1969	13	17	13	17	16	18
1970	13	17	13	16	16	18
1971	15	19	14	13	16	18
1972	12	17	13	17	17	18
1973	15	20	14	18	14	18

TABLE 2 (continued)

Year	Saskatchewan		Manitoba		British Columbia	
	Ministers	Ministries	Ministers	Ministries	Ministers	Ministries
1974	18	21	15	18	18	20
1975	18	21	17	18	19	20
1976	17	22	17	19	15	19
1977	19	22	17	18	18	19
1978	19	23	15	19	17	19
1979	19	23	15	17	16	20
1980	20	25	17	20	16	17
1981	19	25	18	22	20	21
1982-83	16	25	18	22	20	21
1984	25	26	20	24	19	20
1985	24	26	19	24	19	20
1986	19	26	21	24	21	22
% growth	111%	100%	133%	100%	163%	57%

Source: For 1935–85, the annual *Canadian Parliamentary Guide* for British Columbia, Toronto *Globe and Mail* of February 12, 1986 (re February 11, 1986, cabinet shuffle); for Saskatchewan in 1986, the Saskatchewan Information Services *News Release* of December 16, 1985, regarding changes that day to the provincial cabinet; for Manitoba in 1986, Toronto *Globe and Mail* of April 15, 1986 (on the new Pawley cabinet, sworn in on April 17, 1986). Note: With the *Canadian Parliamentary Guide*, the practice has been to list ministers and departments as of January of the upcoming year or December of the preceding year. For instance, British Columbia was surveyed in December 1934 for the 1935 *Canadian Parliamentary Guide*.

Key: 1. The table includes the premier as a minister and counts the Executive Council Office as a ministry.

   2. Not counted as having ministries are: (a) ministers of the executive council without portfolio; (b) commissioners (e.g., commissioner of northern affairs or provincial lands commissioner or railway commissioner); (c) deputy premiers; (d) ministers in charge of Crown corporations; (e) ministers responsible for certain policy areas; (f) ministers responsible for Dominion-Provincial relations.

   3. Provincial secretaries are counted as having ministries.

* A coalition government (as listed in *Canadian Parliamentary Guide*). In fact, the B.C. coalition lasted from 1941–52, and Manitoba's served from 1940–50. An earlier political union in Manitoba, called the Liberal-Progressive Party, had been formed in 1932; it made an arrangement with the Social Credit in 1936. In 1940 World War II prompted an all-party coalition in Manitoba, comprised of the Liberal Progressive, Conservative, CCF, and Social Credit Parties. The CCF abandoned the coalition in 1942, and the Conservatives did the same in 1950.

TABLE 3

CANADIAN AND WESTERN PROVINCIAL CABINET SIZES, 1935–85

Canadian Prime Minister	Canadian Ministry	Saskatchewan Ministry	Manitoba Ministry	B.C. Ministry
King (1935–48)	16–19	9–12	9–11	8–10
St Laurent (1948–57)	20–21	11–15	10–12	10–12
Diefenbaker (1957–63)	17–23	15	9–11	11–12
Pearson (1963–68)	26–25	12–15	12–13	10–15
Trudeau (1968–79)	27–33	13–19	13–17	16–19
Clark (1979–80)	30	20	17	16
Trudeau (1980–84)	32–37	16–25	18–20	19–21
Turner (1984)	29	25	20	21
Mulroney (1984–)	40	25	19	21

Source: For Canadian ministries: Ian Clark, *Recent Changes to the Cabinet Decision-Making System* (Ottawa: Privy Council Office, December 3, 1984), p. 4; for provincial ministries, data derived from Table 1.

central intervention in the structure and processes of several sectors of government. Such a definition implies a direct planning role for the premier, cabinet, and central agencies, and also important involvement for the budgetary and management bodies of government. In the context of this study, *budgeting* means the "expenditure budget process." This is to distinguish it from the "revenue budget process," which is the series of steps leading to the presentation of tax and assorted revenue matters by the minister of finance. Broadly speaking, the purpose of the expenditure budget process is to prepare the Main Estimates of Expenditure which are submitted for the legislature's approval, but there are important sub-purposes as well.[6]

Cabinet decision making, the subject of this work, is a general descriptor referring to the amalgam of activities that cabinets are supposed to perform. To Govern is to Choose goes the old maxim, and cabinets are called upon to make choices arising from a wide variety of planning, budgeting, coordinating, and partisanship activities. *Central agencies* are organizations that fulfil service-wide facilitative and control roles in government.[7] The term *PMO/PCO model* is occasionally used to describe provincial central agency roles: as in Ottawa in the 1970s and 1980s, there was a division between executive council officials who gave partisan political input (the PMO model) and those who gave policy and technocratic input (the PCO model). The *central executive* refers to the collectivity of political and non-political elements of the executive who are engaged in central policy

19

generation and coordination. It can be said to include the cabinet, its committees, the Executive Council Office, the Department of Finance, the Treasury Board Secretariat, and other relevant central agencies and central departments.

This study differentiates between central departments and central agencies. A *central department* is a department that performs a service-wide facilitative and coordinative role but is headed by a minister other than the premier. (Occasionally the study refers to part of a department as a central department, as in the Treasury Board Secretariat in Finance.) *Central agencies*, on the other hand, are those service-wide facilitative and coordinative bodies directly responsible to the premier. (In spite of this distinction, central agency is occasionally used as a generic term in titles and in overview sections.) It is uncommon, in Canadian political science, to draw a distinction between central agencies and central departments. The distinction is useful, however. As shall be seen, there are implications arising from the fact that unaided cabinets have only central departments and institutionalized cabinets have both central departments and central agencies.

At its inception, this study ambitiously set out to include Alberta, thereby offering a panorama of cabinet institutionalization in all four western provinces. The panoramic overview was precluded, and the already egregious length of this study contained, because of the reluctance of key Alberta sources in the 1980s to participate fully in interviews and information sharing.

What follows, then, is a foray into the structural history of the executives of three western provinces. It deals with the provinces in the order in which their central executives developed the modern characteristics of the institutionalized cabinet: Saskatchewan, then Manitoba, and lastly British Columbia. Saskatchewan led the country in development of the machinery of government; Manitoba after much experimentation followed with its own designs. British Columbia somewhat later developed a unique brand of political and administrative machinery at its centre.

Just as there has been no standard pattern of cabinet institutionalization, there has been no standard process of initiation. Mixtures of ideology and pragmatism unique to each province have been operative during the period of initiation. However, cabinet institutionalization owes its persistence to internal and external factors common to more than one province. Changing the structure of cabinet changes how power is wielded and who wields it. The premier's responsibilities, for example, have become substantially more elaborate. It now remains to examine the ways in which premiers have exercised these broadened responsiblities.

Part Two

Cabinet Decision Making in Saskatchewan

Part Two

Cabinet Decision Making
in Saskatchewan

Saskatchewan has a definite tradition as far as the central executive is concerned; it is, in fact, a tradition of institutionalized cabinets. Structured cabinets have persisted, in greater or lesser degree, through the regimes of five premiers. Cabinets have been institutionalized to the extent that they have featured multiple functional cabinet committees, ✓ highly developed analytic support from both central agencies and central departments, collective budgeting and planning along with attempts to interrelate the two, and some attempt at achieving balance between departments and the central executive. The initiation of institutionalization derived from ideological factors, but the factors leading to its persistence were more complex.

One might be tempted to attribute the persistence of institutionalization solely to the effects of ideology. The province has experienced more than three decades of socialist government since World War II. Yet Tommy Douglas, Woodrow Lloyd, and Allan Blakeney also shared a commitment to ensuring cabinet's political control, a belief in social science rationalism, and a fondness for the symbolism inherent in structural reforms. These factors contributed to the durability of the institutionalized mode, even though Blakeney also had intergovernmental and financial control pressures impinging upon him.

Even Ross Thatcher, who came closest to a return to the unaided cabinet, persisted in some facets of institutionalization. He retained the Treasury Board, Budget Bureau, Government Finance Office, and certain ECO officials. The desire to extend his own influence and to ensure financial control quite simply gave him no realistic alternative. Some aspects of institutionalization also carried over from the CCF era.

As well, it appears that Devine respected certain aspects of the past tradition of institutionalization, and in some ways he even extended it. There was, for example, a sizable cabinet secretariat serving cabinet *per se*, whereas before only the committees of cabinet were aided, and there was much progress in attempting a balance between the centre and the departments. Devine continued institutionalization to extend his own influence and to promote financial control by cabinet. Appealing to interests, using symbolism, and pursuing social science rationalism were additional factors favouring the structured cabinet.

Meyer Brownstone, a Douglas-era senior official, has stated that the CCF experience of 1944–64 in Saskatchewan had shown a model of government "innovation and bureaucratic adaptation."[1] Brownstone suggested that a successful adaptation process, enabling a new regime to redirect government and break new ground, consists of two elements: "innovations in the structure and process of government," and "bureaucratic adaptation."[2] Thus, he enunciated one of the clearest philosophies of cabinet institutionalization at the provincial level in Canada.

According to Brownstone, the structure and process of government had seen many ideologically-driven innovations in the CCF years. Among these were the creation of an Economic Advisory and Planning Board to articulate CCF ideology in the governmental context, a Cabinet Secretariat to aid decision making, and a Budget Bureau to provide centralized budget review and administrative management.

Brownstone also made it clear that ideology had been fundamental to the initiation of CCF institutionalization, and that transformation of the bureaucracy was just as much a concern to the CCF as innovations in governmental structure and process. There was a definite strategy for eliciting a bureaucratic response, since Premiers Douglas and Lloyd realized that ideology was meaningless if a traditional bureaucracy resisted cabinet's efforts at change. To quote Brownstone directly, the strategy consisted of five elements:

1. Strong involved political leadership and support;
2. A centralized planning and advisory system linked to an improved Cabinet operation;
3. Innovating programs with new structures and new bureaucrats where these are necessary. The non-innovative elements in the

system can be left unchanged until a response becomes necessary;

4. Diffusion of new methods and processes through a combination of direction, persuasion, and training, and competent staff;

5. Installation and maintenance of central devices for evaluating and developing individual sectors of the system, and with central agencies receptive to strengthening decentralized initiatives.[3]

Brownstone's list of structural innovations and bureaucratic adaptations is largely but not completely synonymous with what can be called the "CCF tradition" or the "CCF strategy" regarding the machinery of government. A summary of the CCF tradition should also include insights from the writings of A. W. Johnson and others, and these shall be reviewed in due course. One must be conscious that these writings by participants had an element of idealism to them. They should thus be seen as outlining only the tentative directions that had been set for the cabinet and central agencies of the Saskatchewan government as well as for the processes that they employed.

The CCF premiers aimed to establish an institutionalized cabinet for the first time in Canada, although they would not have used that particular term. Subsequently, future premiers modified but essentially maintained large elements of the institutionalized cabinet tradition. Part 2 will review the directions that were set for cabinet structure, central agencies, planning and budgeting, and decision making modes, first during the Douglas-Lloyd era and then for succeeding governments. Some were successfully accomplished; others were not.

Chapter Two
The Douglas-Lloyd Era

The CCF tradition of institutionalized cabinets was initiated as a result of social-democratic ideology. Premiers Thomas (Tommy) C. Douglas and Woodrow S. Lloyd (1944–61 and 1961–64, respectively) elaborated a decision-making system which suited the needs of a ground-breaking, interventionist government. Their version of institutionalization included specialized cabinet committees, the use of both central agencies and central departments, detailed theories of collective budgeting, attempts to relate planning and budgeting, an early emphasis on organization and management studies, a growing reliance on policy analysis, and a faith in the educative function of central agents.

One offshoot of this educative function was an annual series of seminars on government operations. The records of seminar presentations and other material allow us to trace the major outlines of the CCF approach to the machinery of government in the forties and fifties. Rather than reviewing the personality of the premiers and the historical development of the machinery of government, as is done for subsequent premiers, this chapter will instead review the actual shape of the Douglas-Lloyd institutionalized cabinet. The CCF era has no lack of historical reviews of its politics and government already.[1]

CABINET STRUCTURES

The installation of specialized cabinet committees was one sign of a developing system of institutionalization in Saskatchewan. There were three elements to the postwar cabinet framework—economic planning, budgetary procedures, and crown corporation management—each of which had a special committee structure erected to serve it. While there was significant overlap conceptually, separate cabinet committees and secretariats developed to allow for greater specialization.

Economic planning was performed by the Economic Advisory and Planning Board (EPAB); budgetary procedures were overseen by the Treasury Board; and corporate management of the Crown agencies was the responsibility of the Government Finance Office (GFO). These were functionally-oriented cabinet committees with continuing mandates. The EAPB, and the GFO in a *de facto* sense, were cabinet committees with a few civil service members; the Treasury Board included ministers only. Each had its own secretariat (which, confusingly, was sometimes referred to by the same name as the cabinet committee). This was the era of high profile bureaucrats: T. K. (Tommy) Shoyama made his name as secretary to the EAPB, A. W. Johnson was deputy treasurer, and Allan Blakeney was GFO secretary.

Planning, and especially planning of a collective and comprehensive nature, is a tendency of institutionalized cabinets. Shoyama described Douglas-era planning relationships in collective terms.[2] The collective institutions included the Legislative Assembly, caucus, and cabinet. Cabinet was, of course, the focus. Its internal committees included the EAPB, the Treasury Board, the GFO, and the Industrial Relations Committee. The EAPB provided an advisory and planning research function. The Treasury Board advised cabinet on how financial resources should be allocated. The GFO controlled Crown corporation capital expenditure decisions and saw to the consistency of their administrative policies. The Industrial Relations Committee ensured the consistency of governmental labour relations.

Most of the cabinet structures were in place by the end of the forties. The EAPB was set up at the end of 1945 by an order in council, replacing a body of outside economic experts called the Economic Advisory Board. The EAPB was meant to collect and analyze basic data on the economy, the budget, and the "Crowns"; to do economic planning; to evaluate policy; and, at first, to control the Crown corporations.

Participants seem to differ as to the reasons for the EAPB's creation, but ideology seems the dominant motive. "The need for a central

27

planning agency with permanent staff grew out of the rapid growth of government functions following the war, combined with the sudden venture of government into a number of Crown Corporation enterprises,"[3] wrote Tommy Shoyama. However, T. H. and Ian McLeod implicitly deny this postwar growth explanation and have instead explained the EAPB as a product of prewar socialist thinking (eg. the 1936 League for Social Reform planning document *Social Planning for Canada*) and wartime party literature. "All sides understood that the board would play a central role in designing the socialist state: it would provide a fresh analysis of the Saskatchewan economy, examine new ideas for expanding industry and raising capital and develop new government management methods. Judging from party literature, setting up the board might be the most important single step the Douglas Government would take."[4] The actual form the EAPB took was the result of a battle between those wanting grassroots planning and those wanting concentrated expertise. The latter faction, with the premier's decisive input, won.[5] George Cadbury, a committed Fabian socialist and member of the English family of chocolate manufacturers, was the first chairman of the EAPB. He offers only a technical explanation for the Board's creation—the need for an advisory body independent of the civil service—but this does not preclude an ideological basis for planning.[6]

Other cabinet structures and central bodies followed soon after, as the logic of institutionalization unfurled. Out of the original EAPB cabinet committee and secretariat grew important organisms: a central department called the Budget Bureau was created in 1946, as was a cabinet committee (with a secretariat) for overseeing Crown corporations. These were followed by the GFO, created in 1947 under Secretary George Tamaki. Surprisingly, the Treasury Board seems to have been resurrected only near the end of the first term of the new government, shortly after the creation of the Budget Bureau in 1946. "In 1947–48, because of the growing importance of centralized financial controls, the government found it necessary to reactivate the Treasury Board."[7] The industrial policy bodies were late arrivals, too: "Somewhat later [after the Treasury Board], industrial development activities were separated from the Planning Board and assigned to a new agency— the Industrial Development Office."[8] Analogous planning and coordinating bodies at the departmental level evidently grew in prominence during the fifties.[9]

In this flurry of organization, the government had to be careful about the party's role in the planning process. It was, after all, an idealistic Tommy Douglas who had opted for a populist approach to planning, arguing the year before his government was first elected that the participation of workers' and farmers' organizations could help save a government economic planning regime from the "blight of regimentation."[10] However, the EAPB did not include any citizen representatives and was answerable to the cabinet alone. The reason, according to T. H. McLeod, was pragmatic: "Saskatchewan was already building one of the most complicated government structures in Canada, and had no need to multiply committees and centres of power."[11] Activists from the party and labour and agricultural groups were instead given appointments on the boards of Crown corporations to focus their activism. Party activism dwindled, however, in part due to the lack of a high-profile party role in central policy making.

CENTRAL AGENCIES

The Douglas-Lloyd governments were the first in Saskatchewan (and probably in Canada) to have staff aid in the institutionalized mode to both the full cabinet and to its committees. However, it was aid to the committees which predominated. There were now sources of policy advice to cabinet bodies other than the departments: there were central agencies as well as central departments, and both performed analysis, planning, and coordination on behalf of cabinet.

For cabinet's use, there was a cabinet secretary and a small staff who prepared agendas, recorded minutes, and monitored the implementation of cabinet decisions. Cabinet secretaries in Saskatchewan had not always existed. In fact, the Province and cabinet functioned without a secretary for over forty years after joining Confederation. Formal minutes were only taken when cabinet met as the Executive Council. In 1948 Tim Lee was transferred from the Planning Board to become the first secretary to cabinet.[12] The cabinet secretariat was established in 1948, but it was not until 1950 that the cabinet secretary, in true institutionalized fashion, attended all cabinet meetings to record discussions and decisions.[13]

The analysis provided to cabinet's committees was important. The EAPB's secretariat worked on the preparation of briefs for royal commissions, parliamentary committees, and public speeches. It also assisted the full cabinet occasionally on particular policy problems.[14] The secretariat to the GFO provided assistance to Crown corporations in the areas of investment, industrial relations, and business strategy.

There was also a special central department for the purpose of budgeting. The CCF government of T. C. Douglas had given early emphasis to budgeting as an instrument of planning. As noted above, it had created the EAPB at the end of 1945 to perform the tasks of planning, policy evaluation, and control of Crown corporations.

Budgeting soon came under the EAPB's purview as well. In September 1946 the cabinet decided that the EAPB would "advise and coordinate the budgeting practices of the various departments of the government and . . . provide the basic facts for the preparation of the provincial budget."[15] The placement of budget responsibilities with a Budget Bureau within the EAPB, a central agency, raised some questions.

"It stripped the Treasury Department of its major responsibility. [Clarence] Fines, the Provincial Treasurer, accepted the system at first, possibly because he was a member of the EAPB himself. As time went on, however, Fines and the rest of the EAPB increasingly looked upon the *Budget Bureau* as being Fines' advisors." Therefore, the budgeting function returned to its traditional central department home. "In January 1948 responsibility for the Budget Bureau was transferred to Fines. In 1950, the Director of the Budget Bureau, Tommy McLeod, became Deputy Provincial Treasurer, at which time the Budget Bureau formally became a branch of the Treasury Department."[16]

Cadbury described the rationale for the Bureau as follows: "The concept of the [Budget] Bureau was derived largely from the United States and was based on the notion that drawing up a budget involved more than the mere compilation of figures once a year. Budget-making and evaluation should be continuous; it should encompass a longer period than an annual budget, and should be based on work programs from which financial requirements could be derived."[17]

However, Saskatchewan's Budget Bureau found it necessary to place a higher operational priority, at least in terms of manpower, on administrative management than on budget review. Some of the more esoteric aspects of government—policy analysis and intergovernmental affairs—did not have many persons attached to them. Wes Bolstad, at the time a junior official of the Budget Bureau (and later a Blakeney cabinet secretary), has described his general impressions of the Bureau in the early fifties:

Most of the action at that time, at least from a junior analyst's point of view, was in the Administrative Management Division. [The other part of the Bureau was the Budget Division.]

I suspect that a lot of policy and program analysis was done by the deputy Provincial Treasurer and the Director of the Budget Bureau in those days. The Budget Division had one person keeping track of details of approved budgets and exercising budget control, one *trying* to do program analysis and one part-time revenue analyst—who was also the government's expert on federal-provincial relations. [The total Budget Bureau staff was

10–12 people, most of them in the Administrative Management Division.][18]

One's expectations of what the budget process actually accomplished must be tempered by the realization that the resources available to it were actually quite modest.

Most of the Budget Bureau's early efforts were devoted to what A. W. Johnson called "Organization and Methods work."[19] Organization and Methods work was dedicated to the objectives of identifying policy inconsistencies; improving organization; facilitating communication between government, the civil service, and the public; and lessening public inconvenience and administrative costs. The main vehicle for achieving these objectives was the "administrative survey," which showed the effects of early social science rationalism. The administrative survey studied the extent to which the procedures of an agency were related to its objectives. The Bureau would analyze the policies and programs of the department, gather facts on its procedures, analyze the facts, and draw conclusions, usually acting in concert with departmental officials.[20]

In 1960 the Administrative Management/Budget Division distinction was erased. Instead, there were to be groups of analysts, responsible for the overview of specific departments, who would provide both administrative analysis and program analysis. This was done to avoid wasted expertise and heighten promotional opportunities.[21]

PLANNING AND BUDGETING

Douglas and Lloyd fostered approaches to planning and budgeting which were in the classic institutionalized mold. Planning was to be comprehensive and collegial; budgeting was to feature an expanded number of aims and be a collegial exercise; and there was to be an explicit connection, or "nexus," between planning and budgeting. Both planning and budgeting were obviously affected by the social science rationalism current at the time.

Several characteristic themes ran through CCF planning and budgeting. D. Levin, then the director of research and planning in the Department of Social Welfare and Rehabilitation, defined planning in rationalist terms:

In its simplest terms planning is a systematic method of arriving at a rational decision. It is the application of the determination of a course of action . . . I call it a rationalist approach because it

31

uses reason and the instruments of reason, such as research, as opposed to approaches which can be called "intuitive," or "giving into pressures," or "following the line of least resistance." Its chief characteristics are: its impersonality, in the sense that the method exists independently of the person pursuing it; its logic, in that its conclusions follow from its premises and not from some extraneous interest; and its objectivity, in the sense that the same results would be arrived at by anyone pursuing the method who started at the same point.[22]

Levin also quoted with approval a similarly rationalist definition from John D. Millett, which described planning as "the process of determining the objectives of administrative effort and of devising the means calculated to achieve them."[23] T. K. Shoyama, the secretary to the Economic Advisory and Planning Board, used both definitions as well; they were probably the central working definitions for government planning at the time.[24]

Government seminar documents usually portrayed planning as a rational activity encompassing a wide range of sequential stages with successively more technical and more specific tasks:

philosophical $\rightarrow$ policy $\rightarrow$ program $\rightarrow$ techniques of $\rightarrow$ program
goals   decisions   design   implementation   execution

Scope of the Planning Activity

Elected officials and the civil service both shared planning responsibilities. Levin placed a high degree of emphasis on the bureaucratic role in planning, which he situated at the levels of "program design" and "techniques of implementation," as did Shoyama.[25] Levin's description of planning practices[26] is generally similar to the outlines of CCF budgeting practices, showing how much the two overlapped.[27]

The record of planning in the Douglas government was mixed, but generally favourable, according to T. H. and Ian McLeod. They have seen the comprehensive nature of CCF planning and the evaluatory activity of planners as strong points:

> The Planning Board never achieved the Olympian heights that Douglas had mused about before the election. For one thing, many of the levers of economic control—monetary policy, the income-tax system, trade policy, and so on—rested in the hands of the federal government. Just as important, the various ministers

regularly borrowed the board's staff for fire-fighting duty when they needed research support in coping with immediate problems. Despite these limitations, the board managed to hold a position apart from, and in a sense above, the daily routine, and to maintain a long-term view. One of its early works was a four-year plan, which outlined where the government could get the best results for its economic development dollars. From its vantage point, the board could also observe the overall pattern of government activities, assess their effectiveness in the light of the cabinet's declared objectives, and speak before being spoken to.[28]

The other successes of planners in the Douglas era were said to include: emphasizing the productivity of the provincial economy, braking unrestrained social and economic spending, and achieving a more collegial sharing of information from the premier and finance minister with full cabinet.[29]

CCF politicians and administrators understood that budgeting was an important function of the central executive since it involved the "determination of the propensity for community expenditure."[30] Such expenditure, especially involving redistribution of wealth, is ideologically important to a left-wing government.

A. W. Johnson reviewed the role played by budgeting in the policy-making process in a 1958 seminar lecture (which appeared the next year as an article in *Canadian Public Administration*). In his description, one sees the broadening of the aims of budgeting, in the fashion of institutionalized cabinets, to include management and policy choice in addition to the traditional aim of financial control. "[Budgeting] has a fourfold job: to ensure that the required resources are made available for implementing the government's programmes; to ensure that the most economical administrative methods are employed in program execution (thus minimizing the resources required); to advise the government as to whether the most effective (and efficient) combination of programs is being employed for achieving the government's objectives; and to assist the government in appraising alternative proposals for new programs—both tax and expenditure programs."[31]

Johnson noted that the first two jobs of budgeting had been satisfactorily developed. Ensuring appropriate methods of program execution, for example, included analysis of program expenditure history, comparison of inter-regional expenditure costs for the same program, and Organization and Methods studies. These short-term matters had been dealt with already, but the latter two jobs were less satisfactorily developed. With regard to matters of program mix, the budgeter needed a broad background in social science rationalism. In other

33

words, the budgeter had to understand the existing programs of his or her own and other governments; possess knowledge of germane social and scientific theory; review the thinking of departmental personnel as to superior program alternatives; and keep abreast of relevant social, economic, and technological developments.[32] These were longer-term matters, some of which fell under the aegis of the planner, and needed to be better developed. Such was the state of provincial budgeting in the late 1950s.

Budgeting practices were better elaborated by the end of the decade. D. D. Tansley, director of the Budget Bureau (and another familiar name from the era), described the process in a training seminar.[33] His general description of the procedure, which showed the inner workings of institutionalization, covered three aspects. The first was the development of work plans in the departments. These were overall plans that outlined departmental objectives and proposed both the methods and the estimated expenditures necessary to achieve them, classified both as to purpose and object.[34] The second aspect of budgeting focused on the three-to-five-year projections sent to the EAPB. The third aspect was a review by cabinet and the Treasury Board, aided by staff of the EAPB and the Budget Bureau. The Planning Board prepared an Economic Outlook to guide cabinet, whereas both the departments and the Bureau prepared revenue estimates to cross-check each other and to aid planning.

Tansley's description highlights some important institutionalized aspects of CCF budgeting, acknowledging that budgeting and planning were interconnected, that both featured collective responsibilities, and that the planning involved was comprehensive in nature. The Treasury Board appears as the workhorse at the collective ministerial level, with cabinet used mainly to set initial targets and to settle matters in dispute.

The CCF administration, in a weak gesture towards central/departmental balance, aimed for a mixture of flexibility and control in budgeting matters. Flexibility was achieved by the use of "virements" (transfers between subvotes by the Treasury Board), special warrants (funding by order in council, later approved by the legislature in supplementary estimates), and supplementary allotments (transfers of funds beyond quarterly allotments by Budget Bureau approval). Flexibility was thus built in at the level of the politician, but individual ministers were subjected to collective cabinet or central agency checks.

Control, however, seemed to pervade the budgeting process. The Budget Bureau was given wide latitude in ensuring adherence to the estimates. Art Wakabayashi, a Social Welfare Department budget officer (and later deputy treasurer/deputy finance minister in the

Thatcher and Devine governments) outlined the levers available to the Budget Bureau: quarterly allotments, isolation of requests for new programs, quarterly follow-up meetings regarding cabinet decisions, establishment control, and space control.[35] Wakabayashi's description demonstrates that the traditional aim of financial control continued in the CCF government alongside the other aims. Moreover, traditional budgeting means—that is, intervention in the annual budget process and in-year vetting of financial allotments—were employed as well.

The evaluation of CCF-era budgeting is mixed, but generally positive. According to Cadbury, "When the CCF came to power in 1944, Saskatchewan had the highest per capita debt of any province. After five years the province's credit rating was as high as any, the debt was under control, and was progressively reduced over the years."[36] Anthony Careless has noted that during the CCF years "the province acquired the technique of designing and living within budgets." However, the coordination was not expanded to lower levels of the administration. "Provincial budgets remained aggregative and policy was primarily formulated at the departmental level upon whatever criteria seemed appropriate."[37]

The Complementarity of Planning and Budgeting

The CCF-era premiers also advocated the institutionalized cabinet when they insisted on the interconnectedness of planning and budgeting functions. This theme (alluded to briefly in the previous section) received its classic enunciation in Canada in A. W. Johnson's 1959 *Canadian Public Administration* article. In it, the problem Johnson set for himself was to identify the conceptual and operational linkages between planning and budgeting. Budgeting, he observed, does not merely begin where planning leaves off, only concerning itself with the most economic delivery of programs. "The concern of the budget official . . . is the same as the concern of the planning official: to facilitate the formulation and selection of policies and programmes which are most likely to achieve the goals of the government."[38] Budgets, like plans, are policy documents; both contain implicit evaluations and relate the use of scarce resources to policy objectives.

Conceptually, the linkage between planning and budgeting is a close one, and Johnson has given a lucid explanation of what must have been current Saskatchewan administrative thought on the subject:

> Budget analysis proceeds on the assumption, ideally, that the government's goals have explicitly been identified, and elaborated in meaningful terms. It assumes that alternative policies—both

general and specific—have been examined and weighed, and those which most closely embody the government's goals selected. It assumes that the initiative for evolving policy vehicles—specific programmes—rests with the department, and with the central planning agency. The budget official, in other words, takes the goals and broad policies of the government as given data. And, so far as programmes are concerned, his principal task is to ensure that all the alternatives and alternative combinations have been elicited in order that they and their probable consequences can be evaluated. He takes the initiative in evolving alternative programmes only when it seems to him that there are undiscovered possibilities—and this will usually occur in the course of his systematic review of "old" programmes.[39]

The job of planning, then, is to make more explicit the government's political goals and to identify broad alternative policies, which in combination are likely to achieve these goals. The planner examines trends and the general costs of program alternatives and uses both inductive and deductive methods as appropriate.

The budget official, on the other hand, works *within* the framework provided by the planners—be they central or departmental. The more clearly the goals of government have been elaborated, the more positively the policies have been stated, and the more critically policy alternatives and policy conflicts have been evaluated, the more sensibly can the budget official examine the programmes proposed in the annual budget . . .
The meeting point between budgeting and planning perhaps becomes clearer after looking at the policy-formulating process in this way, and after examining the respective roles of the planning and budgeting officials. The meeting point, it seems to me, is this: the evaluation of programmes in relation to the policies implied by the government's goals. This evaluation the planner may perform when he has completed the task of elaborating and evaluating goals and policies, and this the budgeter may perform from the opposite end of the policy formulating spectrum, when he has completed his task of evaluating the resources required to implement the programmes proposed from the past.[40]

There was, then, a "spectrum" approach to Johnson's conceptual linkage. Evaluation of goals is at one end of the spectrum, and evaluation of resources is at the other. The planner evaluates goals; the budgeter evaluates resources.

Organizationally, the linkage between planning and budgeting functions is simple: through such customary techniques of coordination as organizational integration and having planning and budgeting personalities join together in committees and working parties. So, organizationally, cross-links were important. The personalities that were so combined in fact included Thomas K. Shoyama and A. W. Johnson.

In 1952 Johnson became deputy treasurer and Douglas became chairman of the EAPB, replacing George Cadbury, with Shoyoma remaining as secretary. "Shoyama sat on the Treasury Board while Johnson sat on the EAPB. The Budget Bureau took over the preparatory work for the annual planning conferences [of cabinet], although the EAPB continued to participate in Treasury Board review of this preparatory work. The EAPB also became responsible for preparing an economic review and forecast, which served as the basis for revenue estimates prepared in Finance and for ministerial evaluation of the budget."[41] Other civil servants appeared as needed. Both the EAPB secretary and the deputy treasurer would attend the Cabinet Conference on Planning and Budgeting. The name itself was an indication of the importance attached to the planning-budgeting nexus.

The allocation of civil servants seemed to echo the element of cross-membership in the two cabinet bodies themselves. In 1960, for example, the EAPB had as members the premier (chair), provincial treasurer, minister of education, minister of mineral resources, Speaker, and backbenchers Thorson and Brown. The Treasury Board included the provincial treasurer (chair), premier, minister of education, minister of public works, and attorney-general.[42]

George Cadbury's comments about advising cabinet are germane here. He was later to articulate what must then have been conventional wisdom about the need for planning-budgeting balance. Cadbury ruled out the alternatives: the Treasury option, or giving Treasury control over all economic matters, because of its traditionally negative and overwhelming influence; and a Department of Planning, since it is difficult for a line department to serve cabinet as a whole.[43]

Perhaps the harmony of planning-budgeting relationships was helped by the fact that the personnel involved were not numerous and remained in their posts, or in the central agencies, for many years. Directors of the Budget Bureau in the CCF era were few: Paul Byers (of the U.S.), 1947–48; Thomas H. McLeod, 1949–50; A. W. Johnson, 1950–52; and Don Tansley, 1953–60. Deputy provincial treasurers were Thomas Lax, 1938–50; Thomas H. McLeod, 1950–52; and A. W. Johnson, 1952–64. Officials of the EAPB were Thomas H. McLeod, secretary, 1946–49; George Cadbury, chairman, 1946–51; and

Thomas Shoyama, secretary, 1950–64. The premier chaired the EAPB from 1952 on.

Perhaps the combination of years of experience, innate talent, and a remarkable *esprit de corps* borne out of personal friendships explains the effect that Saskatchewan senior officials were to have on the world of Canadian public administration. The "Saskatchewan Mafia" helped popularize the new rationalism in government with a effect far out of proportion to their numbers. Al Johnson went on to Ottawa to become an assistant deputy minister of finance (1964–68), constitutional advisor to the prime minister (1968–70), secretary of the Treasury Board (1970–73), deputy minister of the National Health and Welfare Department (1973–75), and president of the CBC (1975–82). A Harvard M.P.A. and Ph.D., Johnson helped introduce the Planning-Programming-Budgeting System (PPBS) in the federal government and was never far from the front lines in new intellectual developments in public management in his later career as professor at the University of Toronto and Senior Fellow at the Canadian Centre for Management Development. Tommy Shoyama had a similarly high-profile Ottawa career, including stints as senior economist with the newly formed Economic Council of Canada; as assistant deputy minister (1968–74), then deputy minister of finance (1975–79); and as chairman of the board of Atomic Energy of Canada Limited. He went on to teach public administration at the University of Victoria. His status as a public policy expert was recognized in his appointment to the Macdonald Commission by Prime Minister Trudeau.

Others from the Douglas years made their mark as well. Several, like Don Tansley and Jim MacNeill, moved into deputy positions in Ottawa, while others—notably Al Davidson, Del Lyngseth, and Art Wakabayashi[44]—became assistant deputies. Much economic development work in New Brunswick, beginning with the Robichaud government, was undertaken by Saskatchewan expatriots working in senior positions. Meyer Brownstone, the deputy in municipal affairs, established a remarkable legacy in the Winnipeg city government (nicknamed "Unicity"), which he redesigned on the precepts of participatory democracy. Allan Blakeney, of course, became minister of education, provincial treasurer, and minister of health in the embattled Lloyd government and later formed his own NDP government as premier from 1971 to 1982.

Douglas and Lloyd brought about the advent of institutionalized cabinets in the Canadian setting. For the first time there was a structured system at the cabinet level: specialized cabinet committees (other than the Treasury Board) with continuing mandates, staff aid to cabinet and especially to its committees, an emphasis on comprehensive cabinet planning, collective budgeting with a variety of aims, a commitment to planning-budgeting complementarity, and some attempts at central/departmental balance.

An ideological foundation underpinned the initiation of Saskatchewan's institutionalization. Postwar social democratic interventionism, a proactive planning approach, and a certain technocratic impulse marked the CCF's approach to the social sphere. As Brownstone noted, ideology informed certain measures in the public administration context: central planning to help design a socialist state, diffusion of new administrative techniques, and a dual emphasis on central evaluation and strengthened departments. Yet other factors ensured the persistence of the new forms. The symbolic function of an economic planning unit, for example, was substantial in a province that had been so buffeted by economic forces, and this helped to ensure its continued existence.

The activities of the new central agencies originated for essentially ideological reasons. Central planning was an article of faith with the CCF. The planning function, however, began to be described in social science rationalist terms, ie. as a means to achieve cabinet's goals and evaluate the effectiveness of government programs. The GFO's function was also essentially ideological; it helped to translate the socialist goal of nationalization into action. The Budget Bureau's job, as described by Johnson, was ideological in nature and sought to ensure the optimum program mix to secure the socialist goals of cabinet. The task of budgeters also came to be described in rationalist terms, as a budgeter was said to need a wide background in the social sciences.

Because of the ideologically central role of planning, it seemed natural that budgeting be situated in close proximity to it. Planning had, of course, been the first concern of goverment, as witnessed by the early creation of the Economic Advisory Committee and the Economic Advisory and Planning Board. However, creation of the Treasury Board and Budget Bureau came soon after, in the late 1940s, and henceforth planning and budgeting matters were closely linked.

The collective nature of budgeting responsibilities indicated a concern that full cabinet exercise political control over the direction of government. A detailed review of the annual budget cycle reveals that important roles were played by the cabinet, Treasury Board, Budget Bureau, and EAPB, and by hybrid bodies such as the Cabinet-Planning Board Conference (later called the Cabinet Conference on Planning and Budgeting). This collectivization of budgeting contrasts rather starkly with the practices of other contemporary provincial governments, which centralized the process under the premier and finance minister, and only occasionally under cabinet in a meaningful sense.

As well, the aims of budeting went beyond those of traditional financial control to include those of management and policy choice.

In the drive to reshape government along ideological lines, it seemed inevitable that some departmental/corporate autonomy would be lost to the central agencies. This was doubtless the case with the GFO's activities and with the social science influenced Organization and Methods work and the predominance of administrative analysts in the Budget Bureau. Planning bodies set up in some departments may have reflected central biases.

The principles of democratic socialism therefore had a wide effect in Saskatchewan, touching on aspects as diverse as the organization of cabinet, the activities of central agencies, and the roles of departments. Ideology was the single most important but not the only factor behind the persistence of institutionalization. The rationalist approach of the new social scientists being hired by the government dovetailed neatly. The wish to have cabinet exercise political control explains why planning and budgeting continued to be joint exercises. Moreover, the symbolic value of high-profile economic planning in a province that had been economically ravaged during the Great Depression must have been important indeed.

Chapter Three
The Thatcher Interlude

One of the hardest things to achieve in a political history is a sense of nuance. The general impression that most academics foster regarding the Thatcher years (1964–71) is that Thatcher was both a break from the pattern of the previous twenty years and a practitioner of the traditional or unaided cabinet style. Yet such a view tends to downplay the persistence of institutionalized cabinet characteristics in the Thatcher years. The signs of such persistence were: the continuation of cabinet structures such as the Treasury Board and the Government Finance Office, albeit in weakened form; the return of a semblance of collective decision making in the Treasury Board after 1968; and the keeping of some central agency forms, such as the Budget Bureau and a skeleton ECO (with a cabinet secretary and clerk). Thatcher, of course, differed from his CCF predecessors (and was in the unaided or traditional mold) when he centralized decision making as the premier's role, depended heavily on a central department (Treasury), neglected planning as a basic function, stressed financial control to the exclusion of other aims in budgeting, and abandoned the joining of planning and budgeting. The point, however, is this: he did not completely abandon the stuctured cabinet.

The motives that moved Thatcher to retain some vestiges of institutionalization were few but significant. The most potent were the premier's quest for aggrandizement and influence, coupled with a strong desire for financial control. The two motives tended to be indistinguishable until 1968, when the premier ceased to carry the portfolio of treasurer, and Davie Steuart became both treasurer and chairman of the Treasury Board. Some aspects of institutionalization may also have continued simply due to sheer momentum from the CCF days.

The dominant metaphor of the Thatcher years was that government could be run as if it were a small business. It was a hard-headed, no-nonsense approach to the art of governance that was not out of place in the contemporary scene: for example, W. A. C. Bennett, also shaped by a small business background, had been advocating it for years. It came naturally to Ross Thatcher. His father, whose frugality during the lean Depression years "bordered on obsession,"[1] was a thriving hardware merchant in Moose Jaw. Returning to Saskatchewan with a Queen's University commerce degree, Thatcher combined a political career with co-management of the family business, ranching, and real-estate investment. Paradoxically, Thatcher was elected as a CCF M.P. for Moose Jaw in the general elections of 1945, 1949, and 1953. Predictably, he left the party in 1955 (over welfare state policies) and unsuccessfully attempted to seek office as a Liberal in the general elections of 1957 and 1958. He became the leader of the moribund provincial Liberals in 1959, went on to form the government in 1964 and 1967, and finally lost power in the election of 1971.

Throughout, Thatcher's characteristic views shaped the party and the government it came to inherit. "As much as his hardware business and cattle ranch occupied Thatcher, politics was his passion. His hardware and ranching businesses solidified his belief that personal inititiative and the work ethic were the basics for individual success. The same principles had to be applied to government if the economy was to prosper, and for Thatcher that made his political goals obvious. In Saskatchewan, Thatcher believed the principle of private initiative, which had originally built the province and been replaced by the CCF doctrine of government involvement in business and personal affairs, was suffocating development."[2]

Thatcher not only had characteristic views, but also character traits that sometimes militated against his own political interests. He fought a long and bitter series of battles with the federal Liberals over provincial political control and social and constitutional policy. He insisted on absolute control of financial affairs from day one of the new government, he brooked little opposition within the party itself, and he was not afraid to stand up to interest groups making demands on the provincial purse. The net result was that by the time of the 1971 election, as Davie Steuart has remarked, "if there was anybody we hadn't alienated, it was because we hadn't got to them yet."

CABINET STRUCTURE AND CENTRAL AGENCIES

A fair amount of continuity characterized both cabinet structure and the central agencies. There were not complete similarities, but the overlaps between the Douglas-Lloyd and Thatcher eras were apparent in some important areas. MacLean notes that the Government Finance Office continued throughout the period.[3] Eager mentions some elements of persistence—namely, the retention of the forms of the Treasury Board and the EAPB (renamed the Economic Development Board)—but she stresses that the premier was dominant and loath to share responsibility. Thatcher was the "boss at the top," a fact which was accepted (and expected) by his cabinet members.[4]

Among the central departments and agencies, there were continuities such as the Budget Bureau and the economic secretariat. Under Thatcher, the Budget Bureau continued to play a central role. A former deputy has noted that "In some terms, Budget Bureau [in the Treasury Department] was even more important [than in the CCF years]. Under Lloyd, it provided checks and balances on departments. Under Thatcher, the Budget Bureau became an advocate for departments because Thatcher was so ruthless."[5]

Some ECO cabinet officials, such as the secretary to cabinet and the clerk of the executive council, continued as well. Either would prepare the cabinet agenda, as circumstances dictated, but they were more an extension of the premier's power than a means to aid collective cabinet decision making. There were also a few executive assistants serving the premier directly.

Central agencies and central departments had been a favourite target of Thatcher's before the 1964 election; his contention that they were peopled by "kooks, eggheads and friends of the government" was well known. Ironically, however, a central department—the Treasury Department, and especially its Budget Bureau—became the only source of input to a premier who did not have many confidential advisors. The Bureau was especially useful to Thatcher, and later to Steuart, in writing budget speeches and reviewing some expenditure plans.

A former deputy treasurer has observed that "the role of the Budget Bureau remained the same: to get out the annual budget. However, it ceased doing studies of efficiency and effectiveness [as under the CCF]. It became a financial watchdog, a trouble shooter. [In addition] one of its tasks became getting economic development going . . . It represented the government at the bargaining table with industry."[6] Thatcher would set the major parameters of business deals, and the Budget Bureau would tidy the loose ends. The Bureau did lose its "brains trust" image but maintained a central role. As in the unaided pattern, Thatcher's principal *aim* in budgeting was financial control; the Budget Bureau assisted him in the principal *means* to achieve this, which was intervention in the annual budget-making process.

The Budget Bureau's fate was better than that of a key CCF-era government central agency, the EAPB Secretariat in the Executive Council Office. Tommy Shoyama left the secretariat, and the Saskatch-ewan government, in 1964. J. J. (Jim) Moore became Shoyama's Liberal government counterpart, heading the Economic Development Board (EDB), a body also situated in the Executive Council Office and oriented to economic review and statistics. It was hindered by a lack of mandate and ended in 1969. Saskatchewan *Public Accounts* records show that the 1964–65 expenditures of the EAPB were $78,285, whereas expenditures on the EDB were somewhat higher, varying between $97,452 and $163,224 in the next four fiscal years.[7] Thus, the EDB was not really disadvantaged fiscally. Its main problem was that Moore had been hired because of his impressive electoral expertise, but the premier could not figure out what to do with him once he was in place in the EDB.[8] The *Public Accounts* show that $101,710 was budgeted for the EDB for 1969–70 but not expended.[9] A central agency had been almost totally eclipsed by the Budget Bureau, part of a central department, mainly because the premier could not decide on a use for it. However, the fact that it remained for so long, even as a shell, is testimony to the persistence of institutionalized forms.

The predominance of one strong central department—Treasury, with its important Budget Bureau—and the lack of strong central planning agencies had a few effects. It put the Treasury in anomalous situations: it was both "fiscal inspector" of departments and the protector of their interests. This may have exacerbated the existent trend in the central executive toward the "budgeter's mentality" (an over-preoccupation with fiscal responsibility to the detriment of policy planning and development), which A. W. Johnson tried to escape.

If one is to believe Allan Blakeney, this situation also shifted the locus of power in the Thatcher government to the Treasury. "Without meaning to be overly critical I believe that at least in its latter days, the previous government operated what I would call too tight a ship in the sense that they had an inadequate number of central planning people. I think it put a great deal of additional pressure on deputies and particularly on ministers and a couple of key ministers, principally the Premier and the Provincial Treasurer. I think that what were essentially *ad hoc* arrangements developed whereby the Deputy provincial treasurer undertook a fair number of these duties."[10] Here Blakeney reveals one of the factors that led him to persist in the institutionalized cabinet format: ie. the unsatisfactory aspects of the unaided mode.

BUDGETING

Budgeting was an area in which both continuities and discontinuities were evident: similarities occurred in basic budgeting philosophies and cycles, but dissimilarities were also apparent since Thatcher did not believe in the concept of institutionalized cabinet budgeting.

The basic budget philosophy of the Liberals, like the budget format, was largely the same as that of the CCF. There was a dislike of deficits, a tolerance for Crown corporations, and a relative emphasis on social expenditures. The dislike of deficits was a long-standing Saskatchewan tradition. "Between 1948 and 1971, the province produced 22 balanced budgets in 24 years."[11] Each year the government would produce a budget with a small surplus. In part, this was accomplished by judicious reporting of revenues in years other the ones they were received. Special trust accounts allowed Thatcher to siphon off general revenue from years with potentially large surpluses and to report that revenue in "rainy day" years. Two such trust accounts were established, for the South Saskatchewan Base Hospital (now the Plains Hospital) and for the University of Saskatchewan Hospital. Liquor Board profits also served as a reserve source of revenue. The government could control the amount that was transferred to consolidated revenue and determine what would be retained as Board profits, available for use in another year.

Tolerance of Crown corporations, despite a professed free market orientation, turned out to be another Thatcher trait. This was doubtless because of the corporations' revenue-generating capacity. Return on investment, service, and employment potential were identified by Thatcher as criteria by which to decide on the continued existence of Crown corporations. It was return on investment that Thatcher concentrated upon year after year in his budget addresses; a touch of pride in Crown corporation performance even seemed to be evident on occasion. When a corporation's operation involved a loss to the taxpayer (as was the case with Saskair, Saskatchewan Guarantee and Fidelity Company, Estevan Clay Products, and the Wizewood plyboard plant), it was sold to the private sector. Davie Steuart has noted that Thatcher entertained offers from the private sector to privatize the

Saskatchewan Government Insurance Office (SGIO) and the Saskatchewan Transportation Company (STC). However, he declined them because of the inability of the private firms to ensure low insurance rates in the former case, and because of Greyhound's unwillingness to maintain uneconomical rural routes in the latter.[12] In 1961 there were twelve Crown corporations with assets of $577 million; in 1971, there were *thirteen* Crown corporations with assets of $915 million.[13]

Thatcher was not set against social spending. He railed bitterly against welfare expenditures, but generally healthy revenue growth allowed him to keep providing a steady supply of demanded social infrastructure.

The budget cycle continued much as it had before, but minus the Cabinet Conference on Planning and Budgeting and other manifestations of collective, comprehensive decision making. The role of cabinet and, from 1964 to 1968, the Treasury Board were virtually ignored. The role of nominally responsible individual ministers might also have been overlooked, had there not been strong pressure from the Treasury Department ensuring that the minister be present when his own estimates were discussed. The cycle was short as the call for estimates came in July. The targets for each department were essentially set by the deputy treasurer and the Budget Bureau, and were largely guided by "what was done last year" and the forecast fiscal framework. Departmental spending packages were received by the Budget Bureau in October. The Bureau would do a summary of major policy and expenditure proposals for the premier (Treasury Board), analyzed within the general parameters of the fiscal framework. The review process would take until mid-November. Following this, each minister and his staff would appear before the premier to argue for his own expenditures. The review stage of the process would end by Christmas time. Finance officials would work on the final draft of the expenditure plans and the budget speech over the holidays. The budget speech was delivered much later, usually at the end of February.

The Waning of Institutionalized Cabinet Budgeting

Thatcher did not continue the institutionalized form of budgeting that had characterized the CCF years. Instead, he partially adopted the unaided pattern, wherein the premier, who for much of the period was also the treasurer, exercised detailed centralized budgetary responsibilities; the aim of budgeting was predominantly financial control; and there was no planning-budgeting connection.

The premier did indeed exercise centralized budgetary control. Thatcher's mind would be made up before the ministers and their staffs appeared before him during budget review. It was changed only if a minister was particularly powerful (as was Public Health Minister Gordon Grant) or if a minister could convince Thatcher that spending cuts might place him in political trouble. Davie Steuart has described the central role of Ross Thatcher in preparing the Budget:

> The budgetary process under Ross was . . . brutal. They [the departments] would come in with a request for new programs and try to give him all the reasons they should go ahead. But Ross would say, "I don't want to hear about it! What's the bottom figure? O.K. You can have so much." He had a figure in his head. He wouldn't go through line by line, department by department. He figured . . . if you go through line by line you get sold, that budgets end up much higher than before . . . He was convinced that there was a smaller figure that departments could live with. The problem was to find that figure. They [Ross and the departments] would fight back and forth.
>
> Ross knew what they had last year. He didn't like to hear them try to pull tricks on him like asking for more than they knew they would get. That would really make him mad.
>
> For a time I [with the Budget Bureau] was advising the departments on how to present arguments to Ross . . . The keys to success with him were these. First, get a meeting with Ross privately. It is difficult for a premier to back down in public. You would say, "Have you got five minutes to talk? There are a couple of things I want to get advice on." Second, you [cabinet ministers] would say "No way they're [department] going to get that" — give him the bad news [high budgets] before Ross saw it . . . Say they wanted $12 million, you would ask him if $11.5 million sounded better. But not just walk in with inflated demands, with departments giving advice. This made Thatcher mad.[14]

Thatcher also broke with the institutionalized approach by implicitly holding that the aim of budgeting was merely financial control; he did not include the broader aims of planning, management, and policy choice. He also neglected to honour the earlier CCF institutionalization in the areas of planning and budgeting.

Ross Thatcher's Liberals were elected on April 22, 1964, having enunciated "a simple platform which emphasized relief from high taxation, Saskatchewan's relative lack of industrialization, and her slow population growth."[15] This platform was evidently taken seriously: it was the main guide to action of the provincial Treasury Department throughout the late sixties. Once ensconced in power, Thatcher sought

47

to discredit the record of the party that had not only held power for the previous twenty years but had also pioneered modern expenditure budgeting in Canada.

The instrument chosen by Thatcher to demolish the CCF image of budget expertise was the Royal Commission on Government Administration. The Royal Commission was created by an order in council on July 7, 1964 and was chaired by Frederick W. Johnson. Its terms of reference ensured a critical stance. It was to report on "organization and administrative problems" and matters of general concern to all departments and agencies. One of its several areas of investigation was budget control.[16] A senior Treasury Department official of the day has suggested that financial control was one reason for the creation of the body. "The stated reason for the Johnson Commission was that the Socialists didn't know how to manage. [The report of the commission] was to be a review of waste and extravagance in government. My own cynical view is that Ross wanted a cover. He wanted to cut staff and to privatize certain activities."[17] The commission's report would perhaps develop compelling reasons to do so. That Thatcher refused to take major action on its recommendations is a sign that they did not jibe with his traditional view of the role of budgeting.

The report of the Royal Commission was highly critical of the preceding government's record of program planning, management information systems, and financial management in general. The analysis and recommendations of the commission aimed pointedly toward an institutionalized cabinet concept of budgeting. In fact, the report seemed to extend the concept of institutionalized cabinet budgeting previously followed by the Douglas-Lloyd governments. Readers will recall that the institutionalized cabinet approach to budgeting holds that planning and budgeting should be interrelated and that planning, management, and policy choice aims should be pursued in budgeting along with the traditional aim of financial control. Table 4 shows how certain recommendations of the report corresponded to the tenets of the institutionalized cabinet model.

Thatcher's inaction was, in effect, a rejection of these premises and marked a discontinuation of the CCF's institutionalized cabinet budgeting. When one examines the rationalist social science language of the report, which extends and modernizes the logic of CCF approaches in planning,[18] management,[19] and finances,[20] it is no wonder that Thatcher did not like it. The foregoing recommendations were not accepted.

The report of the Johnson Commission achieved only limited effect. The 1965 Treasury Department Act did in fact remove the pre-audit responsibility from the provincial auditor, in keeping with a Johnson

TABLE 4

CORRESPONDENCE BETWEEN THE INSTITUTIONALIZED CABINET MODEL
AND SASKATCHEWAN'S 1965 JOHNSON ROYAL COMMISSION REPORT

Institutionalized Cabinet Model	*Corresponding Johnson Recommendations*
Institutionalized cabinets attempt to interrelate planning and budgeting as complementary functions to create a planning-budgeting nexus.	The report of the Royal Comission proposed a "program-planning, program-budgeting" framework which would consist of three elements: • a *program framework* consisting of aim statements, program structures, and measurable objectives • a *program basis for management* consisting of comparisons of objectives with expenditures and achievements • freedom for managers to make decisions within specific budget constraints.
The aims of budgeting include planning, management, and policy choice as well as budgetary control.	The report of the Royal Commission outlined a variety of budget forms to be used in conjunction with new management and choice techniques such as cost-benefit analysis. It also suggested a multi-level management information system. These measures would open communication channels, promote objective setting and resource planning, and make possible coordinated interdepartmental project management.

recommendation.[21] Most of the achievements were minor, however, involving matters such as procedures employed in Highways, government services, and contracting out. Thatcher's treasurer, Davie Steuart, was later frank in his assessment of the Johnson Commission report:

It wasn't what Ross wanted; he probably didn't make it clear what he wanted. To our detriment we didn't use it more. Ross had in mind that the Johnson people [Fred Johnson, Lloyd Barber, and

John Rowand] would go to it and identify unneeded people and indicate places to cut the budget. Well, when the Johnson people got into the departments they found that things were not as inefficient as first thought. In putting programs into effect, officials were doing their jobs . . . relatively effectively. There was of course some effect from the report. We started a car pool agency — the Central Vehicles Agency. But mostly it was a case of the Liberals having campaigned for years on "waste" and "big government" — the inefficiencies in government. We found some programs to do away with, but not a great number.

Rather than cut programs, we decided to cut every department's expenditures by ten per cent. Ross's first idea was that he would resign if the cuts hadn't been achieved by a certain date, but this was later modified to say that we would do our best. Immediately the civil service set out to oppose us. There is no question the civil service had been politicized by the CCF.[22]

Noticeably absent from the list of Johnson Report results is any change in the broadly defined financial administration. The commission had provided a snapshot of financial affairs and a comprehensive reform package. Yet Murray Wallace, Budget Bureau director and deputy minister of finance in the subsequent NDP government in the 1970s, would later note that the Thatcher budgeting system retained the traditional unaided cabinet line-item orientation with few bows to planning or management. There was little description of program objectives and activities, and none at all relating to program outputs and accountability measures.[23]

In ignoring the Johnson Report suggestions, Thatcher was in effect closing off the possibility of continuing the interrelating of planning and budgeting begun under the CCF. The 1965 Johnson Report recommendations were obviously a continuation of the logic described by "the other Johnson," A. W. Johnson, in his 1958 lectures.

Thatcher's aims in budgeting matters were thus limited to financial control only. His methods during the annual budget-making process were inelegant but effective. One approach was simply to cut programs in an arbitrary fashion, as was done in August 1969, saving a total of $12 million.[24] Another was to target cuts in percentage terms so that expenditures would be cut to the targeted figure, and the Budget Bureau would allocate what the departments had left to work with. Another useful method was to be extremely cautious in estimating revenues, year after year; this Thatcher saw as a way to control the expenditure side of the budget.

50

Still another method was to "jawbone" departmental people. A former deputy treasurer has recalled that estimates review was done at "mammoth meetings, with budget estimates presented to Ross, as Treasury Board . . . Minister and staff would be present. Ross could be extremely rough on both: insulting the minister, having shouting matches and tantrums. Thatcher would sometimes leave the meetings . . . He could be a great showman, especially with the University. With Health it was blind rage. But he was effective! Blakeney was too, but he achieved it through mind power."[25]

Thatcher's effectiveness could be gauged by these facts: "he got smaller government . . . the rate of spending growth, at around 2%, was the lowest in Canada. There were smaller taxes, and no deficits."[26]

The preoccupation with financial control continued with Davie Steuart as treasurer. Steuart favoured using Budget Bureau people as fiscal inspectors to achieve economies: "When I was the Treasurer I reformed the Budget Bureau and broadened its scope. We would send out Budget Bureau people to Departments as they were preparing their budgets. Departments hated it . . . Budget Bureau would report back [to the Treasury Board] areas of padding, areas where departments were falling down. It would give ministers a way to go after the departments—to see where they were hiding mistakes and to expose where they were not saving money."[27]

One method which Thatcher attempted to use in financial control turned out to be a major embarrassment for the government. In his review of the university funding crisis of 1967–68, Michael Hayden noted that "Thatcher decided that a victory at the polls on 11 October 1967 gave him the security to say something to keep party members happy. He did [on October 8 and November 8] . . . Thatcher said that there was concern because the university spent so much money while the legislature had little information on the spending after it was authorized . . . His plan, as he elaborated it, was to replace one vote for university funds with a series of sub-votes so that the legislature and the public would have more information and so that the government would have control over the actual sums spent on such items as salaries and equipment."[28]

Many saw this attempt at line-item budgeting as a forerunner to treatment of the university like a government department and as an affront to university autonomy. Faculty, student, and administration groups raised strenuous objections. As a result, "when the budget was presented in the Legislative Assembly in March, there were several informational sub-headings, but only two items to be voted on, one sum for operating expenses, one for the capital grant."[29] Detailed scrutiny did not in fact take place; the same pattern as before prevailed—quick passage of a general sum. Generally ignored in the discussion was the fact that the cabinet had always had detailed information and some control regarding university spending.[30]

DECISION-MAKING MODES

One variant of the unaided cabinet features a dominant premier who, in effect, weakens departmental autonomy. This was essentially the case with Thatcher, but some perspective should be brought to the question of his alleged dominance of the Liberal cabinet and government. Academics have portrayed him as autocratic and oriented to one-man government. Although there is a strong element of truth to this, Thatcher was more consensual than as generally described and did in fact share power with his latter-day treasurer.

Ross Thatcher's government has been generally described as premier-centred, unsophisticated, and lacking in planning capability. Dyck's book on provincial politics has observed only that Thatcher "reverted to a more personal dominance of cabinet operations."[31] Richards and Pratt have noted that "his style of administration was autocratic, and he was personally responsible for virtually all substantial policy initiatives within his government. Most, but not all, of these initiatives concerned the furthering of private investment."[32] In a similar observation, Eager has stated that the Thatcher style was a departure from the general practice of collective decision making. He was loath to share responsibility to an extent unequaled by earlier Liberal premiers and did not believe in the team approach of the CCF-NDP governments who preceded and succeeded him.[33]

Unlike Thatcher, the CCF had stressed the collective aspect of political and financial decision making. Consider their approach to planning. At the political level, an annual planning conference had set the basic direction for the budget cycle. At the bureaucratic level, the Budget Bureau and the Economic Planning and Advisory Board staff had provided documentation to aid a top-down planning process and, incidentally, collective decision making. Thatcher ended the practice of annual planning conferences. A former deputy treasurer to Thatcher has observed that "instead of a collective decision-making process there was a one-person type of the decision-making process. The Premier and Provincial Treasurer made the decisions . . . You got a series of *ad hoc* decisions rather than planned ones."[34]

Another relative difference in collegiality was manifested in Treasury Board operations. During his early years in office, Thatcher dominated the Treasury Board as a means to reduce government size and inefficiency. Basically, the Board was a rubber stamp.[35] One of Thatcher's former deputy treasurers has noted that "under [Woodrow] Lloyd Treasury Board consisted of 3–5 members of cabinet, who took their role very seriously. Thatcher appointed a full Treasury Board, and the other ministers never came to meetings, but they signed the minutes. This was up until Davie Steuart came to the Treasury post. When I questioned Mr Thatcher about it, he said "What do I need them for"? He had no respect for ministers as policy planners. Ministers didn't rank in meetings. The officials ranked higher in budget priorities meetings."[36]

Treasury Board meetings were abbreviated not only in membership, but also in the time taken for decision making. A former deputy treasurer has observed that "Ross was ahead of the times in bringing a businesslike approach to government. For example, before Thatcher [ie. in the CCF-NDP government] ten to twenty items would take the whole day [for the Treasury Board to decide]. Thatcher would take half an hour to deal with the same number of items. He was just like a chairman of the board or CEO, except that he was running a government."[37]

In 1968 Davie Steuart became treasury minister, and such extremes were mitigated. A former deputy Treasurer has noted that "Steuart brought back many of the attributes of the Budget Bureau and the planning process, such as: Treasury Board actually met, there were longer deliberations, there were officials present, and there were now some planning mechanisms."[38] In other words, an element of collective decision making had returned. This is generally overlooked in reviews of the Thatcher years.

Even Executive Council Office staff, who nominally gave aid to full cabinet, ended up actively or passively bolstering the pattern of domination by the premier. Eager gives a detailed description of Thatcher's use of information and central staff:

The development of structured cabinet organization was halted with the accession of Premier Thatcher in 1964. His personal inclinations as well as Liberal Party tradition harked back to the pre-1940s method of having cabinet direction stem entirely from the premier. No formal minutes were kept of Cabinet meetings. Thatcher reportedly had gained access to at least some CCF cabinet minutes, and he had no inclination of providing a reciprocal opportunity. Furthermore, it was in line with his general approach to maintain personal scrutiny over areas of particular interest to him. Decisions tended to be implemented as a result of personal communication or of reminders sent to ministers from notes made by the premier or the secretary at Cabinet meetings.

Little attention apparently was given to separation of duties among personnel in the premier's office, although specific titles were assigned. Part of the time, for example, the positions of secretary of cabinet and clerk of the executive council were separate, but separate in name rather than fact. The respective incumbents worked together without appreciable distinction of powers, with either of them preparing the cabinet agenda. At other times, the jobs were combined, and perhaps other duties would be added, such as those of assistant to clerk of the legislature. An administrative innovation was to give the clerk of the executive council the status of a permanent head. He was to act in effect as a deputy minister for the agencies which reported directly to the premier, and during Mr Thatcher's administration such agencies became numerous.[39]

The "one-man government" image of Thatcher and the Liberals is challenged by Senator Steuart, the former provincial treasurer:

On some issues, Thatcher would intimidate the [cabinet] meeting. If it was him for and twelve against, the consensus would be "for." Cabinet meetings were short and to the point. But in most cases, Ross would lay the groundwork, expecting that a certain number [of ministers] would get the implications of what he was saying . . . He would bring up matters casually two or three times — "Anybody feel strongly about this," he would say — then he would make a decision and would say, "You can't back out now." He was like Trudeau; Trudeau would set out the steps he wanted to take in caucus [and repeat them several times]. Two months later he would say, "You were aware this is my choice, don't back down now." Then he would give them the date, time, and place he had informed them of his plans, saying, "You didn't object then." All leaders do this.

Thatcher would back off on occasion. I never saw him run roughshod over ministers. He would work them. He wasn't a one-man government, but he was the boss. The prime minister and premiers in this country have far more power than U.S. presidents and governors. He would *really* battle when cabinet decided something and then wanted to back down . . .

Ross liked to be seen as a decision-maker — to have the guts to say no. He was totally convinced you were doing no one a favour by wasting money.[40]

Thatcher liked to cultivate the image of a central authority, but it seems likely that this was essentially for fiscal reasons. "If you could get Ross to come out and look at a problem, you were halfway home. For example, the Prince Albert Jail: he went there and was told there were no exercise facilities at all . . . A $75 grand gymnasium resulted, on his own initiative. "I'm as softhearted as anybody," he would say. He was the person to institute conjugal visits to the jail . . . However, he said someone has to have an overall view and not get emotionally involved. He expected ministers to get involved with their responsibilities and to argue with him on them."[41]

Thatcher's central authority image is also mitigated by the fact that Davie Steuart shared some of the authority with the premier. "When the departments would come to Treasury Board, Ross would show up and would sometimes try and take over the meeting. I had to remind him he wasn't chairman any more."[42] As well, Steuart enjoyed a certain amount of influence with Thatcher as his lieutenant in the Liberal caucus. He had been influential in paving the way for Thatcher's leadership bid in 1959, was president of the provincial Liberal Party in the crucial organizing years of 1959–62, and was Thatcher's surrogate in Party affairs. Although not always successful, he was not afraid to argue over government policies he did not like.[43]

In many ways, Ross Thatcher seemed sympathetic to the return of the unaided cabinet. This was evident in his approaches to budgeting, planning, collective decision making, central departments, and departmental autonomy. Yet he did not completely depart from the institutionalized model.

Thatcher did not accept the institutionalized cabinet version of budgeting that was made available to him. He sent clear signals that the aim of budgeting was merely financial control. He rejected both past practice and Johnson Committee recommendations that favoured expansion of the purposes of the budgeting process.

Another sign of the unaided cabinet was the lack of planning-budgeting complementarity; in fact, planning quite simply ceased as a central function (outside the premier's mind). The cabinet planning conference was not reactivated by Thatcher, nor was the EAPB. The Economic Development Board, which replaced the EAPB in the ECO, ceased to function in 1969, starved for a mandate.

As well, Thatcher seriously weakened the institutionalized tradition of collective financial decision making, which had prevailed previously under Douglas and Lloyd, in order to heighten his own power. From 1964 until 1968, he effectively *was* the Treasury Board, like his counterpart W. A. C. Bennett in British Columbia. Under the Saskatchewan Liberals, the institutionalized cabinet pattern of the CCF years was replaced by a fiscally-aided premier and treasurer. This, we have posited, was one sign of an unaided cabinet. Displaying another unaided characteristic, Thatcher relied on a central department—the Treasury Department and its Budget Bureau—to run government.

A dominant premier who restricts departmental autonomy is one variant of the unaided cabinet model. Under Thatcher, departmental autonomy seemed to be even more restricted than it had been under the CCF. Indicators such as the hectoring of ministers, the centralized estimates process, Budget Bureau fiscal inspectors, and the university issue all suggest that departmental autonomy was weakened under Thatcher. The civil service was there not to generate ideas, but to obey.[44]

In the final analysis, Ross Thatcher's Liberal government did not feature a complete departure from the institutionalized cabinet model. Key cabinet committees such as the Treasury Board and the Government Finance Office were kept in operation, albeit with less influence in the face of a powerful premier. There was a partial return of collective decision making to the Treasury Board after 1968. The Budget Bureau and the Economic Secretariat continued to exist, although the latter was largely an emply shell. A secretary to cabinet and a clerk of the executive council continued to serve. On paper at least (viz. the Johnson Commission's mandate and report) the Thatcher government was, like the previous governments, committed to improvements in the policy development process. Effectively, the two parties in government had the same general budget philosophy towards the deficits, the social welfare infrastructure, and the Crown corporations. Their budget cycles even featured similar key characteristics.

What transpired, then, was the persistence of some institutionalization, with a premier definitely sympathetic to the unaided cabinet model. That some elements of institutionalization survived can be attributed to three factors. Firstly, the premier's quest for influence promoted the retention of key cabinet officers and made him use Treasury officials as expenditure police. Secondly, having mere financial control as the principal aim of the budgeting process contributed to the extremely high profile of the Budget Bureau and rendered superfluous the recommended multiple budgeting aims of the Johnson Report. Thirdly, the momentum of past reforms led to the retention of the GFO, the Economic Development Board Secretariat (the revised EAPB), and the general budgeting format. It was left to the next government to return to a more full-fledged institutionalization.

Chapter Four
The Blakeney Years

When the New Democrats assumed power in 1971, they bore with them the inheritance of the earlier CCF experiment in institutionalization. The key aspects of the CCF tradition were: multiple cabinet committees, staff aid to cabinet from both central agencies and central departments, a dedication to collective planning and budgeting, an emphasis on their interconnectedness, and some attempt at balancing central and departmental influence. While it is clear that Blakeney's government (1971–82) was very attentive to the need to modify central structures and processes, it was less so with regard to the decentralized initiatives of which Brownstone wrote. Even the premier found evidence of a certain amount of overcentralization in budgetary matters. Merely getting central structures to operate effectively was a daunting challenge for the NDP administration as government grew and became more complex.

One striking difference between the CCF and NDP eras was the broader range of factors affecting the persistence of institutionalization under Blakeney. Douglas and Lloyd were spurred by ideology to initiate many of their institutionalized arrangements. Ideology was also a factor in explaining the persistence of planning structures under Blakeney, but it was only one of many. Unsatisfactory aspects of certain of Thatcher's unaided practices put too much pressure on deputies and key ministers; this promoted the trend to collective decision making and the growth of central agency personnel. The NDP cabinet's quest for political and financial control led to the reintroduction of a regularized budgetary process and the cabinet planning conference. When the Treasury Board became too much of a "heavy operation," however, the urge for decongestion led to a streamlined Board agenda. The fondness for social science rationalism could explain the preoccupation with detailed procedures, the role of the Bureau of Management Improvement, and Blakeney's basically proactive planning stance. Supplementary factors such as intergovernmental relations, symbolism, and momentum also came into play.

The Blakeney style of institutionalization was similar, but not identical, to that of Douglas and Lloyd. While there was now the beginning of a priorities committee, the status of planning slipped somewhat, and there were weaker organizational links for planning and budgeting—characteristics that set the two socialist eras apart. Yet the *grandes lignes* of the institutionalized tradition remained.

A sense of apprenticeship often accompanies great traditions. At least, such was the case with Allan Blakeney. The new premier had been intimately involved with the Saskatchewan CCF administration for many years. A Dalhousie law graduate, Nova Scotia Rhodes Scholar, and interested CCFer, Blakeney combined political vision with a administrator's sense of the achievable. In 1950 he became secretary and legal advisor to the Government Finance Office, the *de facto* cabinet committee (with a few non-ministerial members) that oversaw provincial Crown corporations. From 1955 to 1958 he was chairman of the Saskatchewan Securities Commission. An important member of the social circle formed by the best and brightest of the new CCF bureaucratic elite, Blakeney was elected to the legislature in 1960 and was successively minister of education, provincial treasurer, and minister of health. In all, he had had close to a decade-and-a-half to absorb key aspects of the CCF tradition of institutionalized cabinet governance.

Blakeney's political career was what might be expected from one schooled so extensively in the Saskatchewan Left. He made some daring economic and constitutional stands but never lost his characteristic need to have balanced analysis of the options before him. His imagination flowed effortlessly from one aspect of government to another, and he placed his mark on most of them. Blakeney was chosen leader to replace Woodrow Lloyd in 1970. Elected in 1971 on the basis of the activist manifesto, *A New Deal For People*, his government successfully sought new mandates in 1975 and 1978. During this time, he orchestrated a Crown-corporation-led development strategy and encouraged the design of a generous social welfare net. However, the technocratic side of the Blakeney government became its undoing, and it lost to the more populist Devine Conservatives in the general election of 1982. In 1986 another attempt to regain power was unsuccessful, and in 1987 Blakeney resigned as leader. This enabled another apprentice, Roy Romanow, to assume leadership. Thereafter the former leader accepted academic appointments and collaborated on a series of legal and administrative analyses.[1]

The Blakeney era was, predictably, different things to different people. Rather than praising Blakeney's achievements in administration, J. F. Conway had criticized the preeminence given to them over the task of coalition building. What experience he had, Conway notes, was almost entirely legal and bureaucratic. "His approach to all political problems was that of a technocrat who believed in administrative rather than political solutions . . . [He] was never able to convey the stirring vision that Williams, Douglas, Lloyd and to a lesser extent, Coldwell, all in their different ways could convey."[2] On the other hand, Blakeney biographer Dennis Gruending has praised the pragmatic and efficient government that Blakeney ran, adding that if the NDP waned under his tutelage, "it was certainly waning before his time."[3] Perhaps the most germane comment comes from Blakeney himself, who stated that "what I find I am the bearer of is a great Saskatchewan tradition of public administration."[4]

CABINET STRUCTURE

Like his institutionalized CCF predecessors, Allan Blakeney saw the need to structure cabinet itself. He reintroduced as his main cabinet committees the familiar trio of economic planning and budgetary and corporate bodies. A Planning Committee of Cabinet was created, somewhat in the image of the old Economic Advisory and Planning Board. In keeping with the times, central planning included a social as well as an economic element. Under Blakeney, the Treasury Board continued as a budgetary review mechanism. The Government Finance Office, which had survived the sixties despite Thatcher's anti-Crown corporation rhetoric, was renamed the Crown Investments Corporation in 1978.

A comprehensive, collegial planning approach was an integral part of the Saskatchewan tradition of institutionalized cabinets. Blakeney gave several indications of his commitment to the idea of planning, culminating in the establishment of the Planning Committee of Cabinet and the creation of a special central agency for planning, called the Planning Bureau. The Planning Committee of Cabinet was inaugurated in the fall of 1972, more than a year after the election of the New Democrats and after the restructuring of the Treasury Board. The late creation of such a cabinet committee did not mean that planning was absent as a concern, but merely that designing appropriate structures was unexpectedly difficult.

The administration's earlier concern with planning had been publicly demonstrated on October 27, 1971, when the premier announced the formation of an Advisory Committee on Policy, Planning, and Program Development, known as the Mitchell Committee. At that juncture, Blakeney dedicated the administration to planning, stating that "my government is committed to a 'planning approach' in developing programs and dealing with emerging problems, instead of being in the position of always having to react to situations resulting from planning done by others."[5] (It is interesting to note that this proactive terminology was very similar to that enunciated by previous CCF officials, such as Levin, and hence is suggestive of a common ideological source.)

In fact, the Mitchell Committee had already existed unofficially for a couple of months, and its preliminary thinking was already well known to the premier. The committee, a group of senior advisors, was mandated to examine central agency structures and to look at the coordination of both planning and management in the government. Grant Mitchell and his co-researchers, Wes Bolstad and Roy Lloyd, had been impressed by the McLeod Report on central organization in Manitoba (see the chapter on Schreyer's cabinet). Their indebtedness to the McLeod Report, and to the Manitoba model in general, was evident in a number of recommendations. These included the following recommendations:

1. There should be a senior planning committee of cabinet, chaired by the premier.
2. There should be a secretariat to aid cabinet planning.
3. Cabinet-level control procedures should be eased to allow maximum administrative discretion to permanent heads.
4. A management committee and secretariat should replace the Treasury Board, allowing the secretariat to oversee budgeting, personnel management, organization and methods, and coordination of computers.[6]

As described below, the Mitchell design was only partially implemented.

The second public indication of the administration's concern with planning was an outgrowth of Mitchell Committee recommendations. On April 13, 1972 the premier announced the appointment of a chief planning officer in the Executive Council Office, Hubert A. Prefontaine. At the same time, a director of policy analysis and research, Gerry J. Gartner, was appointed. The announcement of these events mentioned another planning rationale: the creation of a competent, informed government.[7]

The third public indication of the importance that the administration attached to planning was the creation of a planning committee. This too reflected the Mitchell recommendations but was also in keeping with a Saskatchewan tradition, the Economic Advisory and Planning Board. At its first meeting in September 1972, the Planning Committee to the Executive Council reviewed its responsibilities (presumably accorded to it by cabinet). Policy coordination and priorization were to be among its major functions: it was to play a creative role in new program development as well as in prioritizing proposals to effect a rational approach to implementation.[8]

The fourth public indication of the emphasis on planning was that legislation clearly identified the instrument to perform it. The Executive Council Act of 1972[9] had for the first time in Saskatchewan created a planning committee, although cabinet could have created it under its own authority. (The practice in many provincial Acts is to identify only the Treasury Board explicitly, as in Saskatchewan's Treasury Department (or Finance Department) legislation of 1907, 1917, 1931, 1934–5, and 1983.) The use of legislation presumably allowed the government to semaphore—send a symbolic message to the public—about its dedication to planning and its semi-permanent status. Moving a second reading of the Act, Premier Blakeney said the Planning Committee would essentially "perform the same functions as the Planning Committee [EAPB] of some years ago or the Industrial Development Board of a few years ago, each of them part of and responsible to the Executive Council."[10] The legislation specified that the premier was a member of the six-person committee, which would also be served by a chief planning officer.

Paradoxically, the Legislative Assembly and Executive Council Act of 1979, later introduced by the Blakeney government, made no mention of a planning committee. It said only that the lieutenant-governor in council could "establish one or more committees to the Executive Council."[11] The duties of the committees would be established by cabinet. This return to normal practices signalled a decreased profile for planning and provided a mechanism for flexibility.

One Mitchell recommendation that did not succeed was that which called for a management committee and secretariat. The premier's intentions for the Treasury Board had, in fact, been set from the beginning. Blakeney designed a role for the Treasury Board before he did so for any other committee of cabinet. His views were made known to ministers and deputies in a memo dated September 15, 1971.[12] The Treasury Board was to be a powerful financial control body active in scrutinizing, costing, and evaluating the financial implications of departmental policies. It was to maintain a complementary relationship to cabinet, and to the proposed Planning Committee of cabinet, and to strike a purposeful balance between centralized and decentralized administration. The Board would have both budgetary review and organizational review duties.[13]

We have noted that budgeting in an institutionalized cabinet is generally collective in nature. Blakeney not only reinforced the Treasury Board as a collective exercise but also made certain that it considered its responsibility in relation to the greater collectivity — cabinet. The relationship of the Board to the departments may have appeared overly restrictive, wrote Blakeney, but there were actually elements of flexibility in it. Treasury Board decisions could be appealed to cabinet, and resources were allocated to sub-votes and not "objects of expenditure."[14]

In a presentation made years later to a staff seminar, Deputy Minister of Finance D. M. Wallace reviewed what happened to the Treasury Board in practice. The presentation summarized quite succinctly the unsatisfactory aspects of whatever remnants of unaided cabinet budgeting had remained by 1972. It also showed the importance of cabinet political and financial control as factors in the reform of budgeting in the Blakeney era.

In 1972 there were significant shortcomings in most aspects of the [Treasury Board] process. The information being provided to the Treasury Board was relatively poor. It was input-oriented, devoid of tough analytical content, and forced the Treasury Board to take decisions with incomplete reconnaissance of the issue having been done on their behalf. Finally, the nature of the Treasury Board operation itself had some obvious flaws. Budget Review was compressed. Late submissions from departments combined with lack of attention to early scheduling by the Treasury Board itself led to twelve and thirteen hour meetings for a period of over two months. This led to relatively ineffectual decision-making due to the obvious effect that long meetings had on Treasury Board members and certain Treasury Board staffers.

A, B and X budget items were improperly defined. A program which had been run in a previous year was automatically granted "A" budget status which exempted it from tough review with respect to its core concepts. "B" budget programming was simply defined as new programming, regardless of the level of government commitment to that programming. "X" budget programming was virtually non-existent.

The mid-term meetings of Treasury Board were absorbing nearly two days per week in every week and the meetings ran as long as ten hours.

The absence of good information and high quality staff work meant that the Treasury Board tended to focus on trivia rather than key issues.[15]

The steps taken to alleviate these shortcomings were also attempts to heighten cabinet's political and financial control. First, the problem of information quality was tackled by searching for a new program budget system that would focus attention on outputs rather than inputs; this resulted in the beginning of the PMIS (Program-based Management Information System). The budget submission format was altered to ensure that departments provided cabinet with broad analysis of issues and gave it a realistic range of alternatives to consider. Second, Saskatchewan began a national recruiting campaign in 1972 to upgrade the quality of Treasury Board staff. Third, the Treasury Board streamlined its decision-making process into three levels and elongated its annual budget review so that discussions would be more relevant to the political needs of cabinet. Fourth, the Treasury Board tried to enlarge the pool of discretionary revenues open to it by defining X items (of the ABX system) early in the 1974–75 budgetary review and in subsequent years, so that they could compete vigorously with new programs to which cabinet was uncommitted (B items).[16] However, a preoccupation with financial control not typical of institutionalized cabinets was soon to result in an overloaded Treasury Board.

The final cabinet structure needing mention is the Crown Investments Corporation of Saskatchewan (CIC) which was the old Government Finance Office, renamed and reordered. Created by The Crown Corporations Act of 1978, which updated original GFO legislation of 1947, the CIC provided a more detailed means of assessing Crown corporation capital plans, operating performance, and broad policy. The basic motive for re-creating a cabinet committee for Crown corporations was to clarify the concept of political control by cabinet. Gordon MacLean has noted that as of 1981 there were two basic tenets in the Saskatchewan government's approach to Crown corporations.

The requirement for a holding company or a corporate head office through which capital budgets are channeled follows directly from a basic tenet of the approach taken to Crown corporations in Sas-katchewan—*that the prime instrument for exercising policy control is [Cabinet's] control over new capital investment.*

A second basic tenet of the Saskatchewan approach is that the corporations are to have a large measure of operating independ-ence. *This is independence from the usual personnel and adminis-trative procedures of the public service but not independence from the influence of the Cabinet.* Boards of directors chaired by Cab-inet ministers formed the mechanism initially decided upon to meet the requirement of operating flexibility combined with a policy link to the government.[17] (Emphases added.)

This political control role was of course a controversial one, soon to be altered by the Devine government.

DECISION-MAKING MODES

By the mid-seventies the Treasury Board had still not established an efficient balance in its relations with the departments. Apparent over-centralization was to be the recurring decision-making problem, espe-cially in the area of budgeting, during much of the Blakeney era. Increasing centralization is generally a characteristic of institutional-ized cabinets. As many other premiers did in similar circumstances, Blakeney attempted to mollify departments by establishing greater central/departmental balance. However, it was not merely goodwill towards departments which provoked this reaction. There were several indications that decision points were clogged or overloaded; Blakeney was trying to decongest them. This process would lead to some pro-cedural changes.

By 1977, despite complaints from the finance minister[18] and the director of the Budget Bureau[19] about departmental endruns, it was becoming obvious to Blakeney that the Treasury Board was centralizing decision making and that departments were chafing. Minutes of a confidential July 1977 meeting[20] between Blakeney and one of his closer cabinet confidants noted that there was a need to "politicize [the] budget process." The Treasury Board had become "a very heavy operation" whose "fancy formulas" should be replaced. There had to be "political perceptions of the budget." The minister wanted to know why the premier was "allowing Finance to raid everyone" and sug-gested that what was needed was a "major decentralization process (if not at the deputy minister level, then at the administrative officer level)." Some of these themes were to show up a week later in some of the premier's comments to the Treasury Board Seminar of July 14, 1977.

That seminar had been organized to achieve a retrospective evaluation of six years of Treasury Board experience and to review future directions indicated for it by cabinet. Participants included the premier; Board members Byers, Robbins, Whelan, and Vickers; staff from Finance and the Budget Bureau; and some deputy ministers. Comments made at the seminar indicated that Finance felt relatively comfortable with the existing Treasury Board process, but the premier and departments were less sanguine. They also showed that the premier was taking his responsibilities as organizational architect seriously; he was a major force pushing for central/departmental balance.

The premier's prepared remarks[21] highlighted problems of balance and congestion. Overall, he noted, the process had become more rational, a familiar CCF-NDP theme. Balance, however, was a problem. Treasury Board approval was becoming necessary even for very detailed matters. This "control agency syndrome" was wasting managerial ability. Blakeney felt that the Budget Bureau should instead offer training courses for departments and help them improve administrative procedures that were frequently performed poorly.

The deputy minister of finance echoed the overload theme in his remarks on the overcharged nature of Board responsibilities. "Increasingly," he observed, "Treasury Board has been asked to provide advice and to examine complex issues with respect to tax policy, borrowing and legislation. I am sure that each branch can think of examples of matters of which they are dealing with Treasury Board, which were handled outside the central process two years ago [in 1975]."[22]

The director of the Budget Bureau agreed that the weaknesses were indeed volume, bottlenecking, late staff analysis, and centralization. Even the introduction of different levels of approval authority had not reduced the volume of decision making required of the Treasury Board. On the other hand, he pointed out, there were certain benefits to centralization:

> The process clearly works. As an agency charged with review, evaluation and decision making in a resource optimizing context, the Treasury Board does its job.
>
> The *single review agency approach* has produced a *focus* for co-ordination, *for priority assignment*, and for broad management in relation to the vast range of decisions a government must make—decisions regarding funding and activity levels for existing and new programming, all competing for a limited revenue

resource; decisions regarding investment policy, taxation, resource management, and administration of a complex administrative mechanism—that most other provincial jurisdictions have not achieved. In terms of other provincial structures, there appears no better way of reviewing and relating the broad policy as well as the dollar implications of a decision in one area to the *full range of government programming and priorities*.[23] (Emphases added.)

Here it is interesting to note the use of "priority assignment" language to describe the function of the Treasury Board. Apparently, it had been long forgotten that the Planning Committee had been given this explicit responsibility in 1972.

The decentralization option also had its attractions. Later that year, the Department of Finance undertook a review of the Treasury Board process. Its author was Finance Analyst Michael Costello (later to be deputy minister of finance in the early 1980s). The reforms that resulted from this review were in keeping with the general themes of decongestion that had been discussed at the 1977 seminar. They included a general role for the Treasury Board in keeping with the nature of its membership as well as decentralization of staff reclassification and resource reassignment powers to permanent heads. The 1979–80 and 1980–81 Estimates guidelines, previously established by the Treasury Board alone, were now prepared in conjunction with departmental officials.[24]

Changes were also implemented in the PMIS system, incorporating some of the Anderson Report suggestions (to be discussed in the next section). The commitment of senior management personnel was actively sought, and the model was simplified.

Financial control and central/departmental balance were budgeting aims in the Blakeney administration, but they were to some extent incompatible. There were just too many initial reforms to the central budgeting machinery that had centralizing implications. For instance, the Blakeney mandate for the Treasury Board was heavily oriented towards control; Treasury Board analysts were more widely recruited, better trained, and made to present much more budget material for the central executive to analyze; and the Treasury Board became the single review agency for a very wide array of public policy decisions. Faced with this fact of life, departments began to opt out of the decision-making process. This in turn led to new attempts to honour the decentralization objective: the Treasury Board rid itself of more trivial items, leaving departments freer to reassign financial resources and to design their annual budgets, within guidelines.

COMPREHENSIVE PLANNING

That the Blakeney cabinet was devoted to institutionalized comprehensive planning is evident both in the variety of matters considered
by the Planning Committee and the attempt to interrelate various policy
areas in planning. The Planning Committee seems to have been quite
active in the first term of the NDP government (1971–75); thereafter
it reduced the level of its input both in policy terms and in time spent
by the committee.

Institutionalized planning persisted due to various factors. Blakeney,
like his CCF predecessors, was affected by democratic socialist ideology. He had, after all, been a senior official and then a minister in
the Douglas and Lloyd governments. Supplementing the ideological
factor was the influence of social science rationalism. This revealed
itself in the Planning Committee's basic approach, which involved a
long-term focus, the setting of broad objectives which departments
were expected to augment, and a general willingness to subject public
policy to intense analytical scrutiny. The intergovernmental factor was
also important in both the workload of the committee and the progressive elevation of this policy area to central department status. The
fact that planning persisted, however, did not mean that its profile was
as high as under Douglas; for various reasons (to be discussed later),
it was not.

The frequency of Planning Committee meetings varied over time.
The committee met twelve times between September 1973 and June
1974 and considered twenty-three items, ranging from comprehensive
policy papers to brief proposals. Several ministry submissions resulted.
Between September 1, 1974 and March 7, 1975 the committee met
four times and considered six papers, which it converted into cabinet
proposals. A 1980 document noted that the Planning Committee met
on the average once every two months.[25] While some of the landmark
NDP legislation of the early seventies seems to have originated with
the Planning Committee, in later years the committee became more
of a think-tank or brainstorming mechanism, with little direct impact
on legislation.

In 1973–74 the Planning Committee undertook an objectives-setting
exercise for the resource sector and emerged with an emphasis on
exploration, in-province processing, proper economic return, and a
coherent stance *vis-à-vis* industry. The committee had major input into
oil and gas legislation that was introduced in December 1973. The
government's potash strategy began a period of gestation in the Planning Committee from October 11, 1973 to March 20, 1974 as the

67

committee explored ways of controlling "what it considered excessive industry profits and allowing government participation in the industry." The Planning Committee also studied the creation of a new Crown corporation for northern mineral development; this would emerge later that year as the Saskatchewan Mining Development Corporation (SMDC).

From 1973 to 1975 the Planning Committee was also involved in setting social and economic objectives. During 1973–74 it studied communications policy, water supply, programs for the disadvantaged, service centre evolution, rural transportation alternatives, and general tourism policy. It delayed the introduction of health programs for eyeglass and ambulance coverage and considered health service questions in general. The committee was instrumental as well in forming an interdepartmental committee on the cost of living. Because of the cost-of-living initiative, a comprehensive housing policy study was begun, the minimum wage was increased, and a personal income tax cut was approved. Many other measures were sidelined or not encouraged.

Intergovernmental affairs also shaped some of the committee's work. For example, the Planning Committee considered the federal-provincial aspects of energy policy, industrial development, and GATT negotiations.

As the seventies wore on, departmental planning capacities increased dramatically and the Planning Committee came to react to long-range departmental plans as well as to initiate specific projects itself. From November 1979 to June 1980, for example, the committee responded to the five-year plan of the Saskatchewan Housing Corporation, proposals to expand environmental protection powers of the Department of the Environment, options for long-term parks policy from the Department of Tourism and Renewable Resources, and a review of medium and long-term K–12 education policies from the Department of Education.

The committee was directly involved in sensitive issues such as the staging of uranium development and held joint meetings with the special cabinet committee on uranium. (The latter was established to let involved departments "fight it out" on the uranium question; the Planning Committee would act as the impartial arbiter from time to time, largely between the Crown Investments Corporation and the Department of the Environment.)

While it retains collective responsibility, an institutionalized cabinet occasionally retreats from collegiality, or collective decision making, for strategic reasons. Perhaps surprisingly, many of the major decisions of the late seventies were taken without direct involvement by the

Planning Committee. Smaller *ad hoc* committees of cabinet, some involving as few as two ministers, sketched the most important details of what were ultimately cabinet decisions. Smaller committees were active in the cases of potash, gas, and constitutional policy. One can conjecture that the particular circumstances surrounding intergovernmental relations at the time encouraged the retreat to this pattern.

The decision to provide for nationalization of potash was ultimately made by full cabinet, who debated the question from June until August of 1975. Actual details, however, were worked out by a committee of two: Elwood Cowley, the minister of mineral resources, and Roy Romanow, the attorney-general. Cowley handled the financial, personnel, and administrative aspects of the expansion of the role of the Potash Corporation of Saskatchewan (which had been established in February 1975), and Romanow handled the statutory and constitutional aspects of expanded PCS powers. Cowley and Romanow were at various times aided by a number of top Saskatchewan officials: John Burton, David Dombowsky, Garry Beatty, Roy Lloyd, Don Ching, and Kenneth Lysyk. This collective body of ministers and officials met from August to September in a small Legislative Building office which they nicknamed "the bunker." The secrecy of the discussions is evident from public and political reaction to the Speech from the Throne of November 12, 1975. The announcement of planned provincial control of potash resources was a total surprise to all but the NDP cabinet and caucus, who had been kept apprised of the committee's work all along.[26]

Policy making in oil and gas pricing, and subsequent legal challenges, also showed a drift towards smaller decision-making bodies. Bill 42—The Oil and Gas Conservation, Stabilization and Development Act of 1973—and associated legislation had been developed as a result of Planning Committee guidance and work by lead minister Kim Thorson (minister of mineral resources, 1972–75). However, when the Supreme Court CIGOL decision—*Canadian Industrial Gas and Oil Ltd. v. Government of Saskatchewan*—came down in 1978, invalidating the acts, a smaller committee composed of ministers Romanow, Messer, and Smishek was given responsibility for drafting Bill 47 to protect energy revenues. In this they were chiefly aided by Roy Lloyd, at the time chief planning officer.[27]

The third and last example of restricted collegiality was the pattern of Saskatchewan participation in the constitutional negotiations of 1979–82. In this series, Premier Blakeney and Roy Romanow constituted an *ad hoc* committee on the constitution. The premier was lead person and Romanow was the "delegated minister" from Saskatchewan operating under a mandate from the premier. Cabinet was involved to the extent of participating in weekly discussions and providing suggestions on public relations exercises, but they were not responsible for any specific changes. A small number of officials, largely centred in the newly created Department of Intergovernmental Affairs, aided the Blakeney-Romanow committee.[28]

Despite many accomplishments, the Planning Committee (together with its servant, the Planning Bureau, covered later in this section and the next) never really lived up to Blakeney's expectations. He had at least wanted planning to achieve the same stature as it had in the CCF years. This it could not do for a number of reasons.

One reason for the obscurity of the planning role was the importance of personalities. Elwood Cowley has observed that "Many ministers were unsure of its [Planning Committee's] role. Even Al's [Blakeney's] view of the role changed with the people [who served on and reported to Planning Committee]. Prefontaine stressed long-term planning and long-term problems. He was interested in bringing about a guaranteed Annual Income. Gerry Gartner followed in Hubert's steps; he stressed long-term research. Roy Lloyd was a one-at-a-time problem solver. Murray Wallace was both . . . Blakeney was not really sure what he wanted from Planning Committee. What for sure he wanted was for them to cover a topic and move on to new ones. But at the next meeting they would still be discussing the same one."[29] The premier seemed to be constrained by the necessity for teamwork.

Another reason for the ambiguous role of planning in the Blakeney regime was the academic nature of the exercise. Roy Romanow has noted that "Planning Committee was involved [in major issues] but not as a problem solver. For that [problem solving] the premier would strike special committees or task forces. Planning Committee had more of a forward look at things; it was more of a think-tank. It would do ten-year projections, for example. It did forward planning."[30]

As Elwood Cowley has pointed out, Planning Committee was seldom used as a decision-making body. Generally, things would go directly to Cabinet if a decision was needed. Planning Committee was a review agency. It didn't do priorities setting [like its Planning and Priorities counterpart in Ottawa] but instead was more of a facilitator, a research coordinator, a second look."[31] Although its original mandate had explicitly mentioned a priority-setting function, the Planning Committee ultimately did not establish priorities among the whole range of government programs. The committee's work involved picking and choosing a restricted range of items to investigate and doing long-term policy projections. The Treasury Board (and of course cabinet) effectively exercised the prioritization function, especially after the 1975 fiscal contraction.

Roy Lloyd, former chief planning officer, attributes the tendency to generalize in planning matters to central/departmental balance. "Planning and Research [the former name for the Planning Bureau] and Planning Committee would establish research policy across the government. They would be the first cut. They would provide a conceptual framework for specific problems. My own attitude is that the only role of the Planning Office was to establish conceptual bases. It is not proper for a central agency to become involved in program planning. It is important to have people think they invented the program in the line agency."[32]

Another reason for the status of the Planning Committee and Planning Bureau was the fluid pattern of bureaucratic postings. One insider described the Blakeney government as involving an old boys' network that made bureaucratic affiliations less important than personal relationships, especially among those having served in Finance. In fact, the Planning Bureau at times seemed to be an alternative posting for Finance officials. Roy Lloyd had worked in the Treasury in the sixties, then went to Mineral Resources, and later was chief planning officer. Jack McPhee, a deputy secretary in the Planning Bureau, had experience in Finance and in the Alberta government. D. Murray Wallace had been a high flier in Finance (assistant deputy minister, 1972; director of the budget bureau, 1972–76; and deputy minister, 1976–79) before becoming chief planning officer. Several other planning officials had Finance Department backgrounds. While this doubtless gave Planning Bureau a valuable personnel pool, it may have hindered the development of a distinctive planning *esprit de corps*.

Planning officials had been relatively stronger in the 1950s and 1960s because the Treasury Department and the Government Finance Office had been relatively smaller operations than their counterparts in the 1970s. The strengthened staff allotments and roles of the GFO (CIC) and the Treasury Board/Finance Department in the Blakeney era were seen as necessary in an era of expenditure growth and heightened use of Crown corporations. The strengthening of planning would have meant lessening ministerial interest in TB/CIC roles, another reason planning remained weak.[33]

A final reason for planning's weak performance was the siphoning effect of departmental working groups and new departmental forms. Treasury Board staff and CIC staff in general tended to have more effect than planning staff because of greater staff numbers. However, what few staff Planning Bureau did have were being continually seconded to work on cross-departmental working groups under the general authority of a minister other than the premier (who was the Planning Bureau's responsible minister). In addition, the creation in 1979 of a

Department of Intergovernmental Affairs (IGA) siphoned staff and jurisdiction away from the Planning Bureau. Intergovernmental Affairs had, in fact, been the weak sister in the Executive Council Office for most of the seventies, with junior heads and revolving staff. The step up in the pace of constitutional negotiations seemed to require a distinctive competence in the area. Roy Romanow became the first minister of a new, more specialized department and Howard Leeson became his deputy.

CENTRAL AGENCIES

As is the case with most institutionalized central executives, Blakeney's cabinet organization featured both central agencies and central departments who provided planning, coordination, and analysis. Blakeney increased the resources devoted to cabinet administration in general. Ideological and intergovernmental factors seemed instrumental in the growth of such aid.

Blakeney thought Thatcher had overburdened deputies and ministers. He thus made more extensive use of cabinet-level staff—staff situated not only in central departments but also in central agencies and secretariats. He installed a central agency section called Planning and Research in the Executive Council Office (ECO) to aid the Planning Committee. The Budget Bureau, the familiar central department section in the newly renamed (1972) Department of Finance, expanded its scope. A new central department, the Department of Intergovernmental Relations, was created using some staff from the ECO. A number of secretariats for special purposes appeared and were subsequently dissolved. The premier's personal staff, as Blakeney would be at pains to point out in the ensuing years, did not grow very much larger than Thatcher's had been.

The ECO was not the same under the two premiers. Thatcher's ECO performed mainly cabinet record-keeping functions and was eclipsed by the Treasury Department. Blakeney's ECO contained "political" officers, at first called special or executive assistants; after 1979–80 the post of principal secretary to the premier was institutionalized. There were also "policy" or "process" officers: a deputy minister to the premier, a secretary to the executive council (cabinet), a clerk of the executive council (to process cabinet documents), and several other officers. The cabinet secretary and the clerk were mentioned in legislative form as early as 1972,[34] but legislative mention of a deputy minister to the premier came only in 1979,[35] presumably in order to heighten the status of the premier. The secretary to the executive council oversaw a small cabinet secretariat specializing in cabinet documentation and legislative liaison and was the superior to the clerk of the executive council. The clerk/assistant cabinet secretary served as secretary to the Legislative Review Committee. There was also an assistant cabinet secretary for the Saskatoon Cabinet Office. There was thus, at least by the end of the Blakeney era, a PMO-PCO split in the ECO.

Within the ECO, the Planning and Research body which aided the Planning Committee of Cabinet was plainly the focus of activity and interest. In the latter part of the NDP administration, Planning and Research was renamed the Planning Bureau. The evolution of the Planning Bureau demonstrates the problematic nature of the planning function in the NDP government. The Planning Bureau was a central agency which attempted to make its mark alongside older, more established central departments such as the Finance (Treasury) Department and the Government Finance Office. This was not always easy to accomplish.

In early 1972 chief planning officer Hubert Prefontaine drew up organizational proposals for what was simply called Planning and Research. Premier Blakeney strongly objected to the vague and overly technical statement of responsibilities and the proposals were redrafted. The new draft offered a more philosophical rationale for the new central agency. It also revealed the factors that were encouraging Blakeney to persist in having a central planning agency: intergovernmental relations and the desire to have cabinet exercise political control.

The rationale for creating Planning and Research, Prefontaine argued, included both external and internal aspects. The primary issues external facing the government involved the federal government and industry. Economic development trends were such that a "dynamic shift in [the] overall provincial position" was necessary if Saskatchewan was to avoid "specializing in raw material exports and depopulation." Departmental responses *per se* would not produce this dynamic shift. Regarding internal issues, Planning and Research could also play a role in ensuring cabinet political control, argued Prefontaine (echoing the earlier Brownstone and A. W. Johnson), by helping resource allocation to match political priorities.[36]

Later that year cabinet approved Prefontaine's proposed organization of Planning and Research. As in the external-internal split in Prefontaine's conception of planning needs, the new central agency would have an intergovernmental-internal policy split. The general duties of Planning and Research would be to provide general aid to the Planning Committee, to coordinate interdepartmental activities, to provide provincial development research and analysis, and to act as a focus for intergovernmental affairs. There were three sections: Policy Analysis and Research, Coordination, and Intergovernmental Support.

Reflecting the importance of the intergovernmental factor, Planning and Research tended to stress federal-provincial issues in its first year. Research activities covered oil policy; DREE, ARDA, and special areas programming; telecommunications; cost sharing on mental health and manpower policy; and an inventory of intergovernmental programs. However, an in-house history of central planning structures notes that during this time the bureau was largely dismissed as comprising "a bunch of dreamers" lacking in political sensitivity.[37] A year later Blakeney would announce the appointment of a new chief planning officer. Prefontaine was to go to the Department of Social Services, where in 1974 he became deputy minister.

Dr G. J. Gartner became the new chief planner on June 15, 1973. He had previously been director of policy analysis and research and before that had been both a federal and Saskatchewan civil servant. In a news release, the premier emphasized economic growth as the desired end that Planning and Research should now target.[38] Gartner would be head planning officer for three years.

The revised organization of the Planning and Research Branch of the Executive Council, as it was now called, would reflect the economic development thrust. Perhaps the most important part of the Branch for development purposes was a new Resource Policy Section. (The other sections of the Branch were revised versions of the original organization.) Resource questions—for example, oil taxation and nationalization of the potash industry—were to dominate Saskatchewan politics in the mid-seventies, and it was the Resource Policy Section which would handle the initial bureaucratic arrangements. Mac-Donald's planning history notes, however, that the Resource Policy Section occasionally antagonized the departments when undertaking interdepartmental coordination.[39]

During the mid-seventies Planning and Research pioneered an unusual type of central agency organization called the secretariat. Central secretariats in the Blakeney government were mixed central agency/departmental entities answering to a specific minister. They were housed in Planning and Research and charged with the coordination of interdepartmental policy in a broad policy area. The secretariat form allowed for quick, flexible response to a public policy area of pressing necessity, while at the same time allowing for equal flexibility in dismantling the initial bureaucratic elements of the response. The secretariat form was an *ad hoc* response to a problem—a mechanism that gave a first approximation of a solution, the details of which could

74

later be accomplished by line departments. The main examples of the secretariat form in the 1970s were the Manpower, Energy, Potash, and Cultural Policy secretariats.

The Manpower Secretariat was established in the fall of 1974 at the suggestion of Planning and Research. It carried out day-to-day work for the Interdepartmental Committee on Manpower. Blakeney has noted that "The Manpower Secretariat had as one of its roles the resolution of a continuing low-level conflict between the Department of Education and the Department of Labour with respect to manpower policy."[40] An Energy Secretariat, working with an Interdepartmental Committee on Energy, and a Potash Secretariat were also created in the first term. They served many of the purposes pursued in earlier days by the Economic Advisory and Planning Board.[41] In the late seventies a Cultural Policy Secretariat was also established.

Sources suggest that the secretariat mode was a two-edged sword. As MacDonald has observed, "considerable disagreement exists over the utility of these bodies [secretariats]. Their proponents point out that they provided flexibility, a chance to assemble the best people, ease of termination, and were particularly applicable to cross-cutting issues. Their detractors feel that they undermined the ability of departments to operationalize and to gain confidence and allege that they took all of the glory and none of the responsibility."[42]

Blakeney noted that the good outweighed the bad: "I liked the secretariat model because it was easy to establish, easy to marshall high level talent and easy to terminate. It was much easier to terminate a secretariat than it would have been to retrieve the top positions from either the Planning and Research staff or from departmental staff. This is important not only as a saving of top talent who may be under-used if they are sited only in a single agency of government. Admittedly this did serve to reduce the talent directly available to the Planning Bureau."[43]

By 1980 the structure of the Planning Bureau (as it was now called) had become even more simplified.[44] Reflecting the even greater importance of the intergovernmental factor, the Intergovernmental Affairs Branch had in 1979 become a separate central department, the Department of Intergovernmental Affairs. There were now only three major sections to the Planning Bureau: the Social Policy unit, the Resource Policy unit, and the Economic Policy unit. A deputy secretary to the Planning Committee headed each unit, with three planning analysts each. The deputy secretaries answered to the secretary of the planning committee, who was also the deputy minister to the premier. The position of deputy, as previously noted, had been added by legislation in 1979.

In general terms, the responsibilities of the half-dozen Planning Bureau staff were to provide assistance to the Planning Committee and to act as independent initiators of policy questions. The Planning Bureau assured the completeness of Planning Committee agenda documents, prepared critiques of departmental analyses, and monitored the implementation of Planning Committee decisions. The Bureau would also undertake independent analysis of socio-economic trends and problems.

Planning may be an important part of the institutionalized cabinet, but its presence does not always guarantee its primacy among central functions. All things considered, planning enjoyed an ambivalent status in the Blakeney era. It was said by the premier to be a focal point of Saskatchewan public administration. Planning infrastructure appeared in the form of a cabinet committee (the Planning Committee), a central agency (the Planning Bureau), short-term secretariats overseeing functional-area planning, and increasingly energized departmental planning. Yet planning primacy was not a given, as witnessed by the siphoning-off of planning personnel, the domination of Finance officials in the Planning Bureau, and the ambiguous mandate of the Planning Committee. One success seems to have been the involvement of departments in planning exercises.

The central/departmental balance evident in planning at the bureaucratic level was not as apparent in budgeting matters. As the principal central department, the Department of Finance continued to exert strong policy influence, partly because of the quality of its staff appointments and partly because it influenced ministers and departments through its Budget Bureau. A list of instructions given to new Budget Bureau analysts in the early eighties was symptomatic of the extent of Finance/Budget Bureau power. It noted that a wide variety of information was to be provided by the departments to the Treasury Board. With all major Treasury Board requests, departments were to provide the following: an executive summary, background, policy implications, a problem statement, target group identification, intent/objectives, output measures, an analysis of alternatives, cost data, and correct style. Apparently, Budget Bureau analysts were to assure that this information was available in suitable form to the Board; this amounted to substantial leverage by the Treasury Board staff over departmental officials.

Even Premier Blakeney was to observe that Treasury Board and Finance *staff* had eroded central/departmental balance and that normal decision points had atrophied. Too much was being referred to the Treasury Board instead of being decided at the official level, perhaps even by meetings of deputies, the Premier told a seminar in 1977. Too many referrals meant there were too many demands on ministerial time. Ministers had to be more "reasonable" with their time, seeing that an election was two or so years away, and they were going to have to spend more time "politicking." Finance was attracting talent from the departments rather than the opposite, which was preferable. There was a tendency toward excessive reliance on official channels—eg. the need for a Treasury Board Minute or cabinet Minute before doing anything. In an implied criticism of the power of Treasury Board staff, Blakeney saw a need for them to "recognize that active ministerial participation [is] important and that Ministers bring to deliberations [a] perspective at times different from staff. To maintain credibility, Treasury Board must exercise independent judgement."[45]

The effect of social science rationalism was apparent in the ambitious management information system established in Blakeney's time. The NDP experiment in systematic budgeting consisted of two aspects: a new approach to documentation (the PMIS statement) and a new approach to budget review (the latter to be reviewed in a later section). The PMIS (Program-based Management Information System) was a voluntary middle-management information system which aimed to generate material which was useful in, but not restricted to, budget review. In general, similarities to the PPBS were noticeable. More paperwork and more time were needed, but the program itself was voluntary for departments. The benefits of the new system were expected to outweigh the costs in time and effort. Of course, the Finance Department did its best to persuade potential users of the benefits.

The PMIS was not administered by the Budget Bureau but by a separate, complementary office within Finance called the Bureau of Management Improvement (BMI). The BMI was a complement to the Budget Bureau in the sense that it supported the annual program evaluation process that was part of the budget review (of which the Budget Bureau was the lead agency). Using the PMIS, the Budget Bureau could make informed recommendations to the Treasury Board and cabinet. In addition to the PMIS Unit, there was also an Operational Review Unit in the BMI. The latter was a consulting service to departments, which provided services similar to the old Administrative Management Division of CCF days. Its job was to suggest improvements in financial and personnel management, communications, and planning and program evaluation, as well as to analyze the efficiency, economy, and effectiveness of program delivery. The social sciences orientation was evident here as well.

77

PLANNING AND BUDGETING

Blakeney sought to establish links between planning and budgeting at both the cabinet and central agency levels. The links were not always easy to obtain, given electoral exigencies and the ambivalent status of planning in the government. Yet, even though they were weak links, they were notable continuations of the institutionalized cabinet's planning-budgeting nexus, experienced under the CCF government.

As previously seen, planning and budgeting had been integrated during the early fifties in the CCF government. This had been accomplished by the expedient of bureaucratic cross-memberships. The EAPB secretary was made a member of the Treasury Board and the deputy treasurer likewise became a member of EAPB. This arrangment continued until the Ross Thatcher years (1964–71). The planning-budgeting nexus was effectively dissolved by the appointment of the Economic Development Board (EDB) as a replacement for the EAPB Secretariat in the Executive Council Office; with only a vague purpose to the EDB, central planning ceased to exist in a meaningful sense. Premier Thatcher tended to use his central staff, especially Treasury staff, as aides in a drive to bring specific industries to the province. Premier Blakeney wanted to reinstate the planning-budgeting balance that had existed before in 1964.

To understand how he tried to achieve this, first let us look at the cabinet level and then proceed to the bureaucratic level. Planning-budgeting linkages at the cabinet level were to be achieved by fostering complementarity between the Treasury Board and Planning Committee, and by developing the possibilities inherent in Cabinet Planning Conferences.

As one way of working out balance at the cabinet level, senior officials delineated areas of responsibility for cabinet committees and their staff. A joint memorandum from the Department of Finance and the Executive Council Office which would house the planning group, set out some of the guidelines in August of 1972:

It is clear that we are both concerned with much the same questions, but from substantially different perspectives. The Planning group will focus in on the overall policy thrust of government programs, the overall framework for resource allocation and the related policy and program evolution of departments and agencies. The Treasury Board will focus in on the implementation of government policy, the organizational and operational aspects of program administration, and the management of staff and fiscal resources within the overall framework. It is obviously impossible to separate the roles of the two central agencies, or even to try to define them in a mutually exclusive way. We will have to work together on most issues, in a mutually reinforcing and complementary way.[46]

Here one finds central actors attempting to implement the planning-budgeting conceptual link that A. W. Johnson and others had struggled with some years earlier.

Another cabinet-level method for achieving balance was the joint Planning Committee and Treasury Board meeting. Held most years, the joint meeting enabled the two committees to achieve a common list of priorities to present to the Cabinet [Budget] Planning Conference. The usual agenda for the joint meeting was to review five-year economic and demographic forecasts, fiscal frameworks based on the economic forecasts, and Crown corporation plans, in the light of provincial investment and employment needs. The rough shape of government and Crown corporation programming and priorities would then be established.

The second major instrument in developing the planning-budgeting nexus was the Cabinet Planning Conference. This conference took place in the context of a budget preparation system which was roughly similar to that of the CCF era. It usually took place in the early part of the year's budget review process.

The planning-budgeting link was not always effective in practice, although it may have appeared to be on the surface. Budget Bureau Director J. E. Sinclair noted in 1979 that much of the early agenda of the Cabinet Planning Conferences (from 1971–75) was devoted to implementing the 1971 campaign program called the "New Deal for People." Sinclair explained that there were, in essence, two processes operating:

These Cabinet Planning Conferences were not, therefore, sources of detailed information about what Cabinet wanted to see in subsequent budgets. The first term of office was a period of rapidly increasing revenues such that budgets could be put together by Treasury Board without forcing major confrontations between various members of the Cabinet and Treasury Board concerning resource allocation decisions that took away from one initiative to fund another initiative. In effect, there were two processes; on the one hand, Treasury Board staff and the line departments jointly produced the budgets for ratification by Cabinet every January at the annual Cabinet Budget Finalization meeting; on the other hand, Cabinet, senior officials of Executive Council's Research and Planning and the Department of Finance, and senior line department officials jointly participated in the Cabinet Planning process which focussed on the three to five year time frame.[47]

Cabinet's desire to exercise financial control was to prove a potent factor in the reunification of planning and budgeting. Expansionary pressures on the expenditure budget manifested themselves after the 1975 election; public sector input costs had escalated due to the effects of the energy crisis and poor national economic performance. Despite this, program managers continued to develop the new programs as they had been encouraged to do in the first term. Cabinet reacted by refusing to allow planning and budgeting to continue to develop on separate tracks.

The preparation of the 1976–77 budget brought these conflicting trends into sharp focus. On the one hand, line departments had submitted another in a series of very ambitious work programs for approval by Treasury Board. On the other hand, Department of Finance officials were indicating very clearly that the slow growth in revenues predicted over the next several years meant that expenditures plans would have to be curtailed.

More importantly, Cabinet interpreted the situation to mean that fiscal restraints were being put in the path of its strategy for economic, social and cultural re-development of the province. It became very clear during the 1976–77 budget that Cabinet was simply not about to countenance this kind of situation. That is, whatever the micro objectives of line departments, and whatever the financial restrictions identified by the Department of Finance, Cabinet was not about to see its program of economic, social and cultural development for the province sidetracked. It became clear, further, that steps would have to be taken to ensure that Cabinet got its way in this process.

The solution that was developed by Department of Finance and Cabinet officials was a revival of the Cabinet Planning Conference, which had not been held for two years. Instead of [as in] the first term Cabinet Planning Conference on broad objectives and blue sky thinking, the new version of the Cabinet Planning Conference would recalibrate to consider budgetary objectives. This was not inconsistent with the subtle change in the approach taken by Cabinet to the development of the Province. During the first term in office, a number of major separate initiatives had been established across the entire range of government activity. Accordingly, the second term in office involved a more selective filling-in of that program framework. Working on this assumption, Cabinet was thus willing to focus its attention on budgetary planning for the duration of the second term.[48]

Reasserting cabinet financial control was thus a major factor promoting the resurrection of the Cabinet Planning Conference. With the conference now dedicated to providing more explicit objectives for the Treasury Board, there was a reunion of planning and budgeting. In the NDP era, the Treasury Board would conduct budget review in light of directions set forth by the Cabinet Planning Conference.

A comparison of the budgeting cycles of the CCF and NDP years reveals a few differences. One was that economic forecasts in the Blakeney years would be done by Finance rather than the Planning Bureau, cabinet's equivalent of the EPAB. In the CCF era, two cabinet-level meetings immediately preceded the Budget Bureau review of estimates; this was not the case in the NDP era. These arrangements were possibly more efficient, but they seem on the surface to indicate less concern with planning and objective setting in a budget context. Planning had an ambivalent status in the Blakeney government, as the above section on planning has already demonstrated.

Nonetheless, a high degree of collective decision making went into both budgeting and planning in the Blakeney years. Institutionalized cabinets tend to perform this way. Budgeting matters intimately involved the cabinet, Treasury Board, Budget Bureau Tax and Fiscal Policy Branch, and interacting departments over a ten-month period. Meanwhile, the full cabinet, the Cabinet Planning Conference, Treasury Board, and departments were involved in the planning side of the cycle.

A planning and budgeting balance was aimed for on the bureaucratic level as well. Early in the Blakeney years, officials sought to assure it. The 1972 Finance-ECO joint memorandum, referred to earlier, covered aspects of balance.[49] The respective staffs of Finance and the Executive Council Office agreed to meet to discuss paper flow and cabinet committee jurisdiction. The functioning of the Planning and Treasury Board committees was to be aided by regular meetings between G. H. Beatty, deputy minister of finance; Hubert A. Prefontaine, the chief planning officer; and Keith O. Saddlemeyer, the cabinet secretary.

Despite these efforts, the bureaucratic planning-budgeting link failed to become more than a weak echo of past CCF practice. In the CCF era, A. W. Johnson had warned about conducting budgeting solely with the short-term, finance-oriented perspective of the budget analyst. Such a perspective seemed to dominate the Budget Bureau nevertheless. Wes Bolstad, a senior officer who had seen action in both the CCF and NDP eras, informed the 1977 Treasury Board Seminar that at both the personal and the organizational level "there was a closer relationship [in the CCF era] between the Budget Bureau and the Economic Advisory and Planning Board than there is now between the Budget Bureau and Planning and Research."[50]

There was, of course, some degree of structural overlap in the bureaucracy with regard to planning-budgeting matters. The Planning and Research team of the Executive Council would offer a critique of the fiscal framework at the Cabinet Planning Conference; the Board of the Crown Investments Corporation (CIC) and the staff of the Treasury Board would also be represented and have an opportunity to contribute. Planning staff and the CIC generally did not contribute to the line-by-line analysis of the later Treasury Board review; however, the presidents of the CIC and the Planning Committee got all the Treasury Board's agendas and had a standing invitation to send staff to the meetings if they so wished. Yet despite the overlap, the budgetary process tended to stress a one-year budgeting perspective rather than a multi-year planning outlook.

In retrospect, then, the Blakeney government's central structure was influenced by a broader range of factors than the Douglas-Lloyd governments had been. Not surprisingly, Blakeney adopted much that his CCF predecessors had pioneered, but he was not a slavish imitator. The CCF institutionalized cabinet model persisted as far as the basic cabinet structure, central agencies, planning and budgeting, and decision-making modes were concerned, but contemporary factors led to some changes.

Blakeney had three major cabinet committees to cover planning, corporate, and budgetary responsibilities, as had Douglas and Lloyd. Moreover, there was, in the guise of the Planning Committee, the beginning of a priorities-setting committee of cabinet. Ideological, rationalist, and intergovernmental factors ensured the persistence of a comprehensive planning approach. The Douglas-Lloyd Cabinet Conference on Planning and Budgeting evolved into the Blakeney Cabinet Planning Conference, and a new planning mechanism, the secretariat, was born.

A multiplicity of factors affected the Blakeney cabinet. The terminology that the premier used when establishing the planning framework was similar to that used by his CCF predecessors, indicating the continued importance of the ideology factor. The fact that the Planning Committee was given legislative form early in the first term betrayed a felt need to semaphore the planning message to the public. The constant adjustment to Treasury Board operations shows that Blakeney and his cabinet were determined to establish political and financial control over the machinery of government but were sensitive as well to the problem of overloaded decision making.

Both central agencies and central departments assumed more prominence than they had in the less institutionalized Thatcher years. The persistence of committee staff aid, situated in central departments and agencies, was in part a reaction against the unsatisfactory, less institutionalized aspects of Thatcher's cabinet bureaucracy. The Planning Bureau in particular reflected the importance of intergovernmental and political control factors. Social science rationalism led Finance to establish new management improvement bodies and processes applicable throughout the public service.

The explicit philosophy of joining planning and budgeting, an institutionalized cabinet tendency with ideological roots, spanned the two eras of social democratic government. Cabinet's desire to reassert financial control led to the resumption of the planning-budgeting nexus in 1975, after it had weakened somewhat in the first term. The financial control factor affected central/departmental relations. The premier's troubles with designing appropriate decentralization were clearly a result of his overwhelming emphasis on cabinet financial control as the principal aim of budgeting. (This was, of course, a notable exception to the institutuionalized model in Blakeney's government.)

Although planning and management were also considered important in the Blakeney financial administration, they were not as integrally tied to budgeting as was the control aim. Blakeney's message of balance was sometimes lost in the drive to modernize the province's antiquated financial system. The budget process came to be seen as one that fostered centralized control. Yet it was not unalloyed centralism that characterized the NDP years. Rather, the planning wings of the departments had, owing to the Planning Committee's encouragement, become self-starting entities. Departments were not forced into accepting the PMIS.

Reforms undertaken by the succeeding Progressive Conservative government of Premier Grant Devine showed that more decentralization was possible under normal circumstances. They also demonstrated that in some ways the logic of institutionalization could be extended.

Chapter Five
The Devine Government

On assuming power in the April 26, 1982 provincial general election, Progressive Conservative Premier Grant Devine would persist in the Saskatchewan tradition of the structured cabinet. Devine's government slashed the Blakeney-era policies related to nationalized industries, social affairs, and public employment. Nevertheless, the premier maintained much of the characteristic cabinet institutionalization of the past decades. Understandably, some differences emerged.

The elements of such persistence were wide-ranging. The same basic trio of cabinet committees for planning, budgeting, and corporate affairs were retained. The staff aid component was substantial: compared to Blakeney, Devine provided even more assistance to the full cabinet. There was a PMO-PCO split in the operation in the ECO. Collective planning occurred, but it was more project oriented. Planning-budgeting connections existed, but they were based on tension rather than complementarity. The budgeting format had many similarities to NDP practices, and there were uneven attempts at establishing a balance between the centre and departments.

Devine felt the considerable weight of many factors as he decided to continue cabinet institutionalization. The first was emulation of the NDP pattern; as a novice to government, he found the framework systematic and convenient. Another was a desire to exercise personal influence as premier. One can induce this from a series of modifications he made to cabinet and central agency machinery. Devine, a university agricultural economist, was not immune to social science rationalism; early in his tenure the ECO did a major study on productivity and Finance inaugurated a Zero-Base Budgeting system. He was prone to conveying messages to important public groups through changes in cabinet operation, as was the case with private-sector membership on the Crown Management Board. Cabinet's desire to exercise political control resulted in the waning of most cabinet committees in the first term. At the beginning of the second term, financial control became a major factor in cabinet decision making as Saskatchewan inaugurated a Bill Bennett-style restraint program.

Devine accomplished something next to impossible in Saskatchewan politics, if not in Canadian politics: he united the personæ of the academic and populist in one man. Portraying himself as "just a farmer who happened to get a PhD in economics,"[1] he never failed to remind listeners that he was "the only premier in the country with a Canadian Wheat Board quota number."[2] Devine was born on a farm near Moose Jaw, Saskatchewan, and attended the University of Saskatchewan in Saskatoon, where he received his B.Sc. in 1967. He then obtained a Master's degree in agricultural economics from the University of Alberta in 1970, followed by a Ph.D. in agricultural economics from Ohio State University in 1976. From 1976 to 1979 Devine both farmed and taught agricultural economics at the University of Saskatchewan. The academic and manager in him accepted with ease the NDP bureaucratic forms and in some cases expanded them.

The populist politician in Devine had a somewhat harder time. Encouraged by the new strength of the provincial Progressive Conservatives, Devine had sought election in Saskatoon's Nutana riding in 1978, only to lose by a wide margin to a Blakeney cabinet minister. In spite of this, he won the party leadership the following year, replacing the mercurial Dick Collver, who had inexplicably left the Party to form a new one advocating union with the United States. Collver had helped build the Conservatives from a virtual nonentity in provincial politics to the status of Her Majesty's Loyal Opposition. It looked briefly as if the party had been entrusted to the wrong hands because Devine promptly lost once more, this time in a 1980 by-election in Estevan.

However, in the general election of 1982 Devine and his party rode a wave of anti-big government sentiment into office. In 1986 he avoided repeating the unfortunate one-term example of another Saskatchewan Conservative leader, J. T. M. Anderson (1929–34) and squeaked back into office with a rural-based majority but with slightly less of the popular vote than was held by the NDP. In the final analysis, it appeared that the populist tag had been chimerical. The 1986 victory had in fact been bought as a result of a promise by Prime Minister Mulroney to pump $1 billion into an agricultural sector hard hit by a commoditities slump. In 1991 Roy Romanow, himself playing something of a populist card, would lead the New Democrats to power with a convincing fifty-five-seat win, compared with ten for the PCs and one for the Liberals.[3]

CABINET STRUCTURE

With some modifications, the same basic trio of planning, budgetary, and corporate cabinet committees continued into the Devine years. New cabinet committees emerged, but they were clearly of secondary importance. Emulation was clearly a factor in the new premier's organizational design.

Devine continued with the basic NDP planning committee model after the 1982 election, despite the fact that he was not obliged to do so. (As mentioned above, legislation regarding the Executive Council became non-specific as to the names and functions of cabinet committees in 1979.) If anything, the committee's purposes became even broader than before. Like its predecessors, the PC Cabinet Planning Committee eschewed the setting of priorities. Instead, defined its tasks as developing policy and preparing proposals for cabinet reviews. The Planning Committee acted as a screening or "decongestion" device, shielding cabinet from too much policy detail. It also placed a fair amount of emphasis on devising ways to attract industry to Saskatchewan.[4] The purposes of the committee, as will be seen shortly, changed somewhat in 1986.

The Planning Committee contained a core group of five members, but meetings were relatively open. A representative caucus member routinely attended, but any caucus member or minister was entitled to attend the meetings. Invitations were occasionally extended to individuals from both the public and private sectors if ministers desired information on specific topics.

Late in the first term cabinet's desire to exercise political control manifested itself in a drift away from committee decision making. As the election came closer at the end of the first PC government, use of the Planning Committee declined. Because of the relative inexperience of its members, the Conservative cabinet preferred to plan for the future *en masse* rather than in committees.

This affinity for full cabinet political control was also apparent in the demise of the early policy committees of cabinet. The October 1983 "priorities exercise" had led to the creation of three subcommittees of the Planning Committee, named Social Policy, Economic Development, and Resource and Regulatory. (Various officials later referred to these as committees of cabinet.) These subcommittees were largely inactive after two years, however, confirming that cabinet-level planning activities were largely considered a job for full cabinet, especially with an election looming. The urge to send a symbolic message to the important Conservative agricultural constituency was evident in the creation of the hybrid (ministerial/MLA) Special Cabinet Committee on Farm Input Costs, which was established in January of 1986 and reported to cabinet six months later.[5]

At the beginning of the second PC term, a change in planning arrangements took place, marking a move to a more hierarchical approach to planning. Order in Council 1061/86 of November 12, 1986 changed the name of the Planning Committee to the Planning and Priorities Committee. (The 1986 Government Organization Act would continue the practice of not naming specific cabinet committees.) Membership on the new committee was to consist of the premier—perhaps an indication of his search for influence—as well as the provincial secretary and the ministers of Finance, Justice, and Tourism. The Planning and Priorities Committee was to review submissions to ensure that political priorities were suggested to full cabinet to balance the financial considerations presented by the Treasury Board. Planning once again returned to its pre-election status as committee work, rather than being a task of the full cabinet, with the difference that a priorities function was now added. Yet, as will be noted in the case of the 1987 restraint program, cabinet would show no compunction about swinging back to political control. When political crises loomed, whether real or manufactured, there was a tendency for planning control to move to full cabinet.

The second major committee in the Devine cabinet was the Treasury Board. It continued much as before, except for a legislative clarification of its powers. The Department of Finance Act, 1983[6] outlined in detail the organization, management, and evaluation duties of the Treasury Board, which had previously been only summarily described. The minister of Finance would be chairman and the Finance deputy would serve as the Board's secretary.

The last major cabinet committee was the Crown Management Board (CMB), a renamed and reordered version of the Crown Investments Corporation. Cabinet had decided that it wanted new directions and new control mechanisms for the Crown corporation sector. It established the Crown Investments Review Commission under the chairmanship of Regina chartered accountant Wolfgang Wolff, F.C.A., to review the objectives, administrative structure, and financing arrangements of Crown investments in Saskatchewan. The commission's report stated that Crown corporations had unclear objectives, too much political control, and no fixed dividend policy.[7]

The Devine government did not make major changes to the mandate of the cabinet committee involved. Yet, it would later initiate an ambitious program of "public participation" (ie. privatization) and selective selling of Crown corporation bonds. In 1983 the role and mixed composition of the Crown Management Board was announced. "While functioning as a Crown Corporation holding company [the CMB] will operate as a Cabinet Committee analogous to its government-side counterpart, the Treasury Board. The Crown Management Board will report directly to Cabinet and also receive major policy and some central direction from the Cabinet Planning Committee . . . The Crown Management Board is composed of at least eight Ministers of the Crown and four non-ministerial appointees. There will be a Chairman and Vice Chairman who will both be ministers, together with a Board of Directors composed of at least six additional ministers and at least four civilians."[8]

This mixed public-private make-up of the Board—together with the new provision that Crown corporation boards would henceforth be chaired by private-sector individuals, with ministers as vice-chairs—was a symbolic message. It indicated to the private sector that practices in the Crown sector were henceforth to be more business oriented. The new control mechanism would implicitly bring new directions.

CENTRAL AGENCIES

Devine continued the essential elements of institutionalization at the cabinet staff level through both central agencies and central departments (minus the Department of Intergovernmental Affairs). The Executive Council Office enjoyed a steady rise in prominence, partly to reflect cabinet's collective drive for influence and partly to give the premier more leverage. There was a PMO-PCO split in the Executive Council Office and the ECO provided more aid to full cabinet. Some alterations were also made to the structures and mission of the Department of Finance.

From the time of the 1982 election until Dr Norman Riddell became deputy minister to the premier in 1984, a power vacuum existed at the top of the ECO. From 1982 to 1983 Derek Bedson (from Manitoba) had been clerk of the executive council, the top position, but the Devine/Bedson personality match was bad, and Bedson left for a provincial trade position posting. Gren Smith-Windsor, by profession a hospital administrator, then became acting deputy minister to the premier as well as acting secretary to the cabinet. Elizabeth Crosthwaite became clerk of the executive council, answering to the deputy. Smith-Windsor held his acting deputy position from 1983 to 1984. Norman Riddell, a long-time Ottawa mandarin then working for External Affairs in Brazil and a former rural schoolmate of Devine's, was hired for the deputy's position in 1984. Smith-Windsor operated as cabinet secretary temporarily until this position was also assumed by Riddell.

The net effect of this movement at the top was to leave an unsettled understanding as to what role the premier wanted the ECO to assume. Premier Devine seemed quite anxious to make the Riddell ECO more assertive. He believed that politicians should be more involved in policy making, with the ECO as their surrogate. Norman Riddell—like Michael Pitfield, his previous superior in the Privy Council Office in Ottawa—believed in the importance of staking out a position in central agency politics.

The Devine ECO also followed the PMO/PCO model found in many institutionalized cabinets. It had both political and bureaucratic actors, the former giving partisan advice and advancing the premier's influence with the party and the latter giving policy development advice. As the principal aide to the premier in his role as chairman of cabinet, the deputy minister to the premier headed a cabinet secretariat and oversaw the work of all officials except the principal secretary. There was a regular turnover of principal secretaries during the Devine era. All provided partisan political advice and were rumoured to have links with the B.C. Social Credit and Ontario Conservative Parties.

Unlike Blakeney's ECO, there was less division of labour among officials under Devine. Whereas Blakeney had a deputy to the premier, a cabinet secretary, a clerk of the executive council, a principal secretary, and a director of executive programs, the deputy and secretary positions were now filled by one person, Riddell (until December 1987).

The ECO provided more staff for full cabinet in the area of secretariat services. In the review of estimates for his Executive Council Office discussed by the Committee of Finance on June 17, 1985, Premier Devine gave a useful review of the divisions of the ECO and their various achievements.[9] The review indicates that Devine acknowledged the basic soundness of Blakeney's belief about central agencies, namely, that there should be extensive use of cabinet level staff to serve cabinet and its committees. The elaboration of the ECO's roles was an indication of the growing importance of a major central agency alongside an important central department, the powerful Department of Finance. The ECO's growth also reflects cabinet's desire for political control.

There were five divisions in the ECO: Public Affairs; Intergovernmental Affairs (headed by an associate deputy); Protocol; the Cabinet

Secretariat; and the Policy Secretariat, which was the Planning Bureau renamed (also headed by an associate deputy minister).[10] Devine had carried over the cabinet secretariat and policy secretariat (Planning Bureau) formats from the Blakeney years. The numbers of staff involved were, however, appreciably higher. The creation of the Inter-governmental Affairs division was essentially a change from a central department to a central agency format, since a Department of Inter-governmental Affairs had existed under Blakeney from 1979–82.

The recruitment of Executive Council officials and some senior Finance staff was increasingly from line departments, a nod to the concept of central/departmental balance. Cabinet secretariat officers were nicknamed the "crown princes" by ECO officials because they were identified as upwardly mobile high-fliers who, with a year or two of training in the secretariat, would be able to assume senior departmental positions. Some officials disputed the crown princes image, noting that Finance officials were still a most favoured recruiting source for senior government jobs, even if there had been a conscientious effort to reduce this emphasis. Policy Secretariat and Intergovernmental Affairs staff were likewise recruited from depart-mental posts and returned after a few years, usually at a more senior level than they had previously held.

As if to symbolize its openness to social science rationalism, the Executive Council Office launched a productivity study early in the life of the new government. This study involved a voluntary survey of employees in the departmental and Crown corporation sectors, to which several thousands purportedly replied. It recommended the cre-ation of a Cabinet Council on Productivity, which would implement the study's findings, but cabinet did not follow through.

Possibly because of the high degree of similarity in their functions, the Budget Bureau and the Bureau of Management Improvement were amalgamated into a new body called the Treasury Board Division (TBD) in 1983. The TBD was to be composed of three branches, each concerned with expenditure matters. The Programs Branch performed budget preparation similar to that previously performed by Budget Bureau; the Planning Branch analyzed longer-term expenditure impli-cations; and the Management Services Branch was the analogue of the Operational Review Unit.

PLANNING THEMES

Premier Devine continued the basic structure of institutionalized cen-tral planning but with his own distinctive changes. As in the Blakeney government, planning activity took place at both the cabinet and central agency levels. At the cabinet level, planning was said to take place in the context of the Planning Committee (changed to the Planning and Priorities Committee in 1986). This has not always been the case, however, because when major controversies or "regularized crises" (such as elections) occurred, Devine switched to full cabinet decision making. With the crisis over, the premier returned to planning by committee.

Compared with the government of Blakeney, central planning was less philosophical and comprehensive but more program and project oriented and was slanted more to accomodate planning-budgeting tension. In his predilection for project planning, Devine was displaying the unaided planning style to some extent. His emphasis seemed to be on developing programs rather than on devising comprehensive plans for government action. One senior analyst in the Planning Bureau (Policy Secretariat) described the Bureau circa February 1984 as a "rent-a-brain/fix-it/serve-cabinet sort of body" which viewed planning as just "a bag of tricks" for different settings.[11]

The project-oriented work of the Policy Secretariat is apparent in Premier Devine's summary of its activities before the Committee of Finance in 1985. The Policy Secretariat (headed by Larry Martin) designed the government priorities exercise process; participated in mixed government and private sector committees; advised on the terms of reference for the consultations and project team that preceded the establishment of the Saskatchewan Water Corporation; designed and advised on the Rural Development Task Force; and helped design the Employment Development Agency, an information clearinghouse and coordinator of provincial employment programs.[12]

The Executive Council Office subsequently continued its involvement in specific projects and programs. One of the most notable was participation with Finance in the development of the innovative, money-purchase Saskatchewan Pension Plan, introduced in 1986.[13] The ECO helped develop proposals for rural development corporations and extended rural television delivery. It participated in department-specific zero-base budget reviews. The especially active Intergovernmental Affairs Division helped prepare National Agricultural Strategy proposals in the areas of emergency relief, farm finance, trade, research, and resource development, which were presented at the Annual Conference of First Ministers in Halifax in November 1985. The ECO also had the job of coordinating provincial input for federal initiatives in the new round of GATT talks that got underway in November 1985.

Another change to planning in Saskatchewan was the introduction of the notion of planning-budgeting tension or competition. The PC

government was less intent on keeping planning-budgeting complementarity alive as an operative guideline for the central executive. The
quest for influence by both the premier and cabinet appeared to be at
the root of this development. There were several signs of planning-
budgeting tension. For one thing, the recruitment patterns of the ECO
and Finance did not involve the interchange of officials as was the
case in the Blakeney years. For another, there was now a structural
tension between the ECO and Finance that was seen as normal and
acceptable. In effect, ECO activities reduced the power of Finance.

A senior ECO official explained matters this way in February 1984:
"Finance is having trouble with keeping power. Cabinet Planning
Committee has taken up some policy power that Treasury Board or
Cabinet used to exercise [in the NDP years]. Planning Bureau is doing
what Finance used to do—for example, the ten-year economic scenario.
There is a long-term shift on the planning side on capital issues . . .
The Budget Process has changed. Cabinet [as before] will provide
direction as the first step. Planning Bureau helps with annual Cabinet
planning sessions, say, analyzing twelve major planning initiatives.
Finance now has the job of revenue raising."[14]

Of course, this was somewhat simplistic: Finance reviewed expenditure options as well as undertaking "revenue raising" and continued
to plan. The change was that the Planning Bureau (and its successor,
the Policy Secretariat) was doing some of the planning that Finance
used to do. By 1986 the emphasis in Finance was on long-term
planning, the role of the secretariat to the Treasury Board, and research
on the fiscal effects of changes in the Crown corporation sector (such
as privatization).

The tension was elevated to official status when Norman Riddell,
new deputy minister to the premier and cabinet secretary, addressed
Treasury Board officials during a 1985 seminar. He informed them
that he desired friction between the Policy Secretariat and the Treasury
Board Division as far as policy analysis was concerned. One would
be chiefly concerned with ideas and the other with dollars, but neither
should be expected to predominate over the other.

The dual routing of departmental submissions, with comments from
both Planning and Priorities and the Treasury Board being considered
by cabinet, was an expression of the structural tension foreseen for
the ECO and Finance. A senior official said in 1987 that "Riddell has
inaugurated the parallel decision-making process because he feels that
Finance has been too centralist on some issues. He wants to insure
that the political agenda is as well served as the financial agenda."[15]

Dr Riddell described the procedures as follows: "The establishment
of the Planning and Priorites Committee of Cabinet has resulted in a

change in Cabinet procedures and hence a change in Executive Council's functions. All documents submitted for Cabinet consideration will now be simultaneously forwarded by the Cabinet Secretariat to the Planning and Priorities Committee and Treasury Board for their comments. Comments from both committees will be attached to the submissions which will then go before full Cabinet. The Policy Secretariat's role has been expanded to provide organizational and analytical support to the Planning and Priorities Committee."[16]

A senior government official suggested in November 1986 that the "Planning and Priorities Committee will do much the same as before, but will review some matters that only Treasury Board would look at before. The role of Treasury Board will be to ensure financial control, value for money accounting and so forth. Planning and Priorities will establish the political context. Now if line departments have ideas they will be routed through Planning and Priorities."[17]

Charts gave a simplified version of the dual decision-making process in the Devine cabinet as of October 1986. They showed that, at the crucial "review and recommendation" stage of the process, both the Treasury Board and Planning and Priorities were to provide input to cabinet in parallel fashion. The central staff of the two committees—the Treasury Board Secretariat and Policy Secretariat—were to engage in a certain dualism at the proposal preparation stage, when both consulted with the departments drafting the proposals.

The terminology used by the participants indicates that planning-budgeting tension, especially at the committee level, was meant to enhance the political control of cabinet. The fact that the basic design came from the premier's deputy minister, and that a central agency reporting to the premier stood to gain much by the changes, seem to indicate as well that enhancement of the premier's influence may have been a factor leading to the new design.

BUDGETING PRACTICES

Devine's budgeting practices were characteristic of institutionalized cabinets. His government's actions demonstrated a flexible degree of collective budgetary decision making, a balance between centralized and decentralized administration, and an occasional use of political controls taken in an "off-budget" context (meaning outside the regular budget process). Much of this pattern can be traced to a single factor: the desire of cabinet to exercise financial control.

Devine maintained the general outline of Blakeney-era budgeting, but put new processes in place and altered the balance of power. In order to grasp the entire range of the Devine government's budgeting practices, one should distinguish between its normal budgeting cycle and its financial control in a restraint situation.

The Normal Budget Cycle

The normal budget cycle of the Devine government demonstrated institutionalized collective budgeting and a developing central/departmental balance. The cycle was essentially the same as it had been in the NDP era, except that owing to the 1986 pre-election and 1987 post-election restraint program considerations, it took place in an abbreviated fashion for two years.

There were similarities to Blakeney's institutionalized budgeting, one of which was collective decision making. At the political level, full cabinet, the Treasury Board, and the Cabinet Planning Conference were involved. The Cabinet Planning Conference was roughly modelled on past NDP and federal practices. The premier and chief ministers outlined political objectives and cabinet provided guidelines for the Treasury Board, drawn from its long-term strategy. At the staff level, there was involvement by the Department of Finance (the Treasury Board and Tax and Economic Policy Divisions), the Executive Council Office, and line departments.

Departments had an even greater budgeting role beginning in the 1988–89 fiscal year; this effectively promoted central/departmental balance. Instead of Treasury Board staff summarizing and presenting budget exhibits to the Treasury Board in the departmental budget review phase, the departments themselves fulfilled this role, with Treasury Board staff acting in a support role and offering critiques of the departments. When interviewed in February 1986, Minister of Finance Gary Lane provided the rationale for the change: "By this procedure we hope to achieve a better assessment of the managers in the departments. Between the two presentations we will get an idea of who is best able to manage."[18]

In July 1984 the PMIS experiment—a management information system useful for budgeting and dating from the early seventies—came to an end. It was replaced by the Budget Preparation portion of the Computerized Financial Management System.

Social science rationalism often finds a natural home in the budget process. The Conservatives had established a rationalist precedent by introducing a modified form of zero-base budgeting early in the fiscal year 1984–85. As is often the case with institutionalized budgeting, there were multiple objectives: program prioritization, evaluation, reorganization, and downsizing.[19] The methodology used in ZBB was also an attempt at central/departmental balance. As in most other ZBB systems in use, an actual zero base was not used, but the Province adhered to the concept that all programs must justify their existence. Reviews were to be transacted in a three-year rolling plan under the general direction of a ZBB Committee consisting of the deputy minister of finance and other deputy ministers. Study teams varied depending on the nature of the department under review but typically included in their membership some representatives from the Treasury Board Division and the Executive Council Office. The reports went to a Deputies Committee first, where some initial trade-offs are possible, then to the Treasury Board and finally to full cabinet.

By the beginning of the second Devine government (after the election of October 20, 1986), it was becoming evident that ZBB had not had a major impact in Saskatchewan. The plethora of new spending programs in the pre-election year was evidence that the *political* will for restraint had not existed. The budgeting model was also lacking in incentives. The basic concept had been to group deputies together in order to force trade-offs, but there was nothing in the model to force them to make these decisions together. In fact, there was a movement away from expecting committees of deputies to implement restraint; in 1987 politicians were instead cast in that role.

Central/Departmental Balance

The balance of power between the centre and the departments favoured the latter somewhat more in the Devine government than during the Blakeney era. (The word *somewhat* is used because the 1987 restraint exercise had centralizing implications.) Finance's power was partially restricted, and there were more joint management ventures between central agencies and the departments.

The Department of Finance had some day-to-day operations taken away from it and given to the departments. In February 1986 Finance Minister Gary Lane noted that the general trend of reform revealed a new, more modest understanding of Finance's role in government: "We have changed Finance's role from a strictly adversarial one vis-à-vis departments to a more cooperative arrangement. We have had terrific responses regarding the [modifying of] the centralization of power in Finance. Finance in some cases was running the departments."[20]

Although Finance was not literally running the departments in the NDP era, the avenues of influence open to it were more numerous during the NDP years. Now it had to share the review of cabinet submissions with the Policy Secretariat and coordinate the review of Treasury Board submissions with the departments; even its program evaluations were shared duties. The Conservatives sincerely believed, at least in the early Devine years, that they had introduced a new era of central/departmental collegiality and interaction in financial administration. The ZBB Committee was an example. The interactive stance was also said to be apparent in two other bodies, one called the Management Committee and the other named the Executive Forum.

The Management Committee was a subcommittee of the Treasury Board, established in April 1984, whose function was to conduct broad financial and administrative evaluations and to serve as a debating forum for selected ministers and deputies with finance-related responsibilities. It consisted of two Treasury Board ministers, selected deputies, and the deputy minister to the premier (ex officio), with the assistant deputy minister in charge of the Treasury Board Division as its secretary. The committee had its own secretariat in the Finance Department, called the Program Evaluation Unit (formerly the Program Review Group). The Treasury Board secretariat maintained project management responsibility, but the review teams usually contained relevant departmental representation.[21]

The Executive Forum partially owed its existence to cabinet's quest for political control. Deputy Minister to the Premier Norman Riddell had originally meant it to be the administrative equivalent of the Management Committee, but it began to take on the vestiges of a control mechanism. The Executive Forum, meeting monthly, was a management committee for general policy matters. It consisted of deputy ministers and associate deputy ministers. Deputies were informed about the policies cabinet had established, discussion ensued as to how to translate political directions into administrative policies, and feedback to cabinet would result. The Executive Forum was not quite as cooperation oriented as the Management Committee; it did not generally examine cross-governmental matters and served largely as a conduit for "top-down" messages.

A senior Finance official summed up Finance's status in 1986: "In the past, Finance was used as a training ground to go on to bigger and better things. It was closely tied into the Premier's Office. But now that's not the case . . . Collegiality is the modern way of doing things." Presumably, the abandonment of Finance's responsibility to train the province's administrative elite helped to make collegial relationships work. One should hasten to add that Finance was not a training ground in an institutional sense in the NDP era; Finance merely hired highly qualified individuals who happened to have generalist skills that made them valuable to various other government departments.

Financial Control in a Restraint Situation

Perhaps the Conservative administration's early collegial approach was made possible by the fact that financial restraint had not been a significant concern of the new government. After a restraint situation did in fact materialize, the financial control factor turned the degree of collective cabinet decision making and central/departmental balance into flexible matters indeed. The restraint dynamics were roughly similar to those that British Columbia had experienced in 1983–84: government reorganization by legislative means, civil service reductions, and various on- and off-budget reduction exercises. Political controls taken in such circumstances are, of course, thoroughly in keeping with the institutionalized cabinet model.

Finance Minister Gary Lane indicated in early 1986 that the momentum for restraint had only recently been increasing:

> There have been several restraint methods used. But the political decision that was taken when the government took office was that education and health would not become political issues in the next election. These were "NDP issues" and they [the NDP] have a high degree of credibility on them. It would be unwise to tinker with them or change them to a significant degree . . . So any restraint in those areas has been very modest. In the first years we concentrated on hiring freezes, reductions in purchasing and various across-the-board reductions.
>
> In January of 1986 there was a major restraint program in government "program operations" and I expect that will continue. [These are programs that the government itself carries out without involving third party operations.][22]

A Finance official reviewed the strategy for involving the bureaucracy in this relatively modest restraint program (modest, since attrition seemed to be the main route to employee reductions). The strategy also included an attempt at central/departmental balance: "We're trying for a more participative model—to get CEOs to share in deficit control and to share cabinet's concerns—to 'buy into' financial problems . . . We want them to be careful about implementing restraint, to be careful about negative fallout re: interest groups. They should be convinced of the need to sell restraint, and be committed to implementing it.[23]

It was, however, premature to talk of both central/departmental balance and restraint in 1986. That year a widespread perception existed both within and outside the provincial government that electoral cycle considerations had made any restraint attempts chimerical: restraint measures were not severe before the mid-term of the government, so they were not to be severe afterwards. The plethora of new programs in the 1986 pre-election Throne Speech (with its veiled references to restraint)[24] and in the Budget Speech were further indications of the lack of a restraint atmosphere. Not until the budget cycle after the provincial election would the political impact of the structural deficit make itself felt; until then the government's honeymoon with the bureaucracy would continue.

However, restraint was to become a publicly apparent central concern of the Devine cabinet in 1987, when it was shown that the degree of collective decision making and central/departmental balance depended on perceptions of the impending financial crisis. In March 1987 fiscal alarm bells were sounded by the "Saskatchewan Economic and Financial Report." Whereas the 1986 budget had forecast a deficit figure of $389 million for 1986–87, the Report put it at $1.2 billion, a threefold increase.[25] Evidently, the problem was not merely a cyclical or temporary downturn in the economy. The Report forecast an annual deficit of over $1.5 billion by 1987–88 and of over $2 billion by 1990–91 if nothing were changed. One of the "new realities" it mentioned were long-term declines in resource prices.[26] The Report targeted a balanced budget by 1991 and a deficit reduction figure of $800 million for 1987–88.[27]

To achieve the $800 million deficit reduction figure, the Report outlined both expenditure and revenue measures. On the expenditure side, the Report targeted the size of the bureaucracy. From 1982–83 to 1986–87 the public service was thinned by one thousand workers; it would now lose an additional two thousand. The report also suggested capping the budgets of third parties—that is, municipalities, schools, hospitals, and universities. There were to be no wage increases for government or Crown sector employees for two years. The revenue options—user fees and tax hikes—were more vaguely enunciated.[28] Economic Development and Trade Minister Bob Andrew, a senior member of cabinet, later revealed the ideological underpinnings of the drive for financial control.[29]

When it actually came time to implement restraint—in other words, to achieve the budgetary aim of financial control—the Devine government turned to both traditional financial means and to political controls taken in an off-budget context. The traditional means included the "0–25% exercise," whereas the political controls involved activities outside the regular budget process: legislatively mandated reorganization, management studies, and public service reductions.

98

The first explicit restraint move was reorganization. Legislation was to give cabinet an unusually broad power to reorganize the public administration. Bill 5, The Government Organization Act, was introduced on December 16, 1986 by Deputy Premier Eric Bernston. Its key provision was S.5, which would permit the disestablishment of departments without recourse to the legislative process to change individual department acts.[30] The legislation was both introduced and passed in December of 1986, but not without strenuous objections from the Opposition, who suspected that it was unconstitutional.[31] The government maintained that it had precedents for such legislation.[32] Whatever the technical or constitutional arguments, the instrument was used relatively often in 1986–87. Between December 1986 and March 26, 1987 a total of nine departments and agencies were dismantled.[33] The aim was obviously financial control, as Finance Minister Lane indicated when announcing reorganizations in March of 1987.[34]

The second major restraint action was a management study which grew logically from the reorganization effort. Just as reorganizations had been suggested internally, the government now turned to external bodies to suggest further reorganizations. On January 30, 1987 Premier Devine announced the hiring of the national firm of Coopers and Lybrand to conduct an independent and comprehensive review of proposals for reorganization of government departments and agencies. Again, financial control was said to be a motivating factor, along with the aim of privatization.[35]

A third level of restraint action within the provincial government was partly on-budget and partly off-budget: the program of public service reductions forecast in the March 1987 "Saskatchewan Economic and Financial Position Report." On March 20, 1987 Lorne Hepworth, minister responsible for the Public Service Commission, announced a series of measures aimed at reducing the provincial government workforce by two thousand people.[36] Hepworth repeated the financial control theme, noting that "it is anticipated that the initiatives will result in savings to the government in excess of $100 million over the next five years."[37] In fact, the Provincial Budget of June 17, 1987 contained estimates of savings that were higher than first forecast and layoffs that represented a higher proportion of the staff reductions than was first stated.[38] The Regina *Leader-Post* also cited more elevated government staff losses.[39]

The last level of restraint action within the government was what one might call the "0–25% exercise." This was in fact the decision-making process that had allowed the staff reductions to take place, but it also allowed cabinet to become involved in the larger question of program deletion and modification. In mid-January Finance Minister Lane sent directives to the departments, asking them to generate expenditure reduction scenarios of zero, five, fifteen, and twenty-five per cent. It must be added that this request was *supplemental* to the Call for Estimates, which had already gone out in September 1986, and was hence considered off-budget. In February, as requested, the departmental submissions were sent to the Finance Department, where the Treasury Board Division did a written analysis and critique of them. The next step was full cabinet discussion, which took place in late February and through most of March, ending with a wrap up in late April. Finance was then free to put the provincial budget together in May.

It is interesting to note a few facts about the 0–25% reduction exercise. One is that there was a short-circuiting of the regular decision-making process; a crisis situation had engendered maximum collective decision making. The Treasury Board and Planning and Priorities Committee were bypassed in favour of full cabinet. Indeed, the original intent in early 1987 had been that there would be a joint Treasury Board/Planning and Priorities Committee vetting body totalling eight cabinet members, with the premier in attendance. However, the feeling grew that the other eight cabinet members would also have to be involved if they were to become fundamentally committed to protecting what was a politically difficult package. The dual decision-making process outlined late in 1986 was temporarily sidelined in favour of full collegial cooperation. Full cabinet was now more involved in the budgetary process than at any other time since forming the government in 1982. Cabinet intended to return to the regular format in the Fall of 1987.

The dynamics of staff involvement were also somewhat different than had been planned. The Policy Secretariat in the ECO gave its comments not to cabinet or to Planning and Priorities members during this exercise but to the premier directly. Devine had apparently used his central agency to increase his own influence. Unlike Lane's original plan, the departments did not both summarize and defend their budgets. The Treasury Board Division, answerable to the minister of finance, summarized them. Cabinet discussion of the expenditure reduction scenarios involved three stages: the responsible minister gave a presentation, the assistant deputy minister for the Treasury Board Division presented a written critique, and full cabinet discussed the issues. The result was a plethora of program alterations or deletions in health, education, and direct services. Central/departmental balance had also been temporarily derailed due to the crisis situation. The

100

immediate winners in the power stakes were full cabinet and especially the premier and finance minister, together with their own departments.

The ostensible result of the various levels of financial control was a reduced deficit. Finance Minister Lane stated in his June 1987 Budget Speech that the main impact of restraint had been felt in the expenditure budget process: "By reducing government expenditures and by introducing the revenue-generating initiatives just announced, the deficit for 1987 will be reduced to $577 million, a decrease of 60 per cent, over $900 million from the projected deficit of $1.5 billion. *This substantially revised deficit target has been achieved primarily through expenditure control.*"[40] (Emphasis added.)

In a pre-budget document, the Saskatchewan Government Employees Union (SGEU) contested the original 1986–87 $1.2 billion deficit figure, saying that it had contained $400 million worth of one-time expenditures, and hence the original $1.5 billion figure for 1987–88 had also been overstated.[41] Finance officials pointed out that they had not based the 1987–88 projected deficit on the previous year's deficit figure but on actual expenditures.[42] Whatever the figures, it was evident that not just deficits *per se* but ideology and the slowly growing political will of the premier and cabinet to exercise financial control had generated the 1987 restraint program.

Central/departmental balance had accordingly been dislodged for the time being as an aim of the government. The combination of a late-starting estimates process (hindered by an election), a major reduction in staff and programs, and a comprehensive review of programming by a consultant firm — all happening simultaneously — engendered a bunker mentality in many departments. One disgruntled former Saskatchewan deputy minister argued in June of 1987 that departmental autonomy had been savaged by three polices: a drastic paring of research and planning wings (they harboured "socialist" planners), an early retirement program that left departments shorn of highly specialized personnel, and an increased politicization of the civil service resulting from the introduction of departmental chiefs of staff to circumvent deputies who identified too closely with their programs.[43] Whatever the opinions of deputies, the significant reductions in departmental staff were mute but more eloquent testimony to the relative powerlessness of departments. The Executive Council Office, on the other hand, barely suffered any reductions in the 1987 restraint exercise.[44]

Ultimately the degree of central/departmental balance proved to be flexible, as were the degree of collective decision making and the proclivity for off-budget political control measures. The normal budgetary process was to feature input by the planning and treasury committees as well as by full cabinet, but when a drastic restraint program was deemed necessary only full cabinet was used. Off-budget measures—reorganization and management studies in reducing the public service—were used when on-budget measures were not sufficient. When quick responses to deficit crises are required, governments cannot wait until the next budget cycle begins. Yet even though there were variations in degree, the variations were a matter of having more or less institutionalization in cabinet.

The original design formulated by Douglas and Lloyd had thus persisted. The Progressive Conservative government shared but modified some of the approaches favoured by the New Democrats (and the CCF before them). There were functional cabinet committees, staff aid to cabinet, collective planning and budgeting with connections between the two, and an initial willingness to have departments play important roles. As the 1987 restraint program would demonstrate, the two parties could be miles apart on policy content, but with regard to policy-making structures they could be quite alike. Emulation was thus a factor in Devine's basic cabinet design.

The premier continued the basic Saskatchewan cabinet model of three major committees for planning, financial, and corporate affairs. The Crown Management Board became the new name for the board of the Crown Investments Corporation, and Devine semaphored his opening of the Crown corporation sector to business influence by appointing a third of the CMB Board from the private sector. Symbolism was no doubt also important in the creation of a special cabinet committee on farm input costs. As well as the familiar triumvirate of cabinet committees, the PC cabinet created new committees for social, economic, and regulatory affairs. However, cabinet's drive for political control led to underutilization of the committee system before elections and during fiscal crises.

The premier's quest for influence and cabinet's quest for political control appeared to be twin factors in the development of the Executive Council Office. One can deduce what Devine's motivation must have been from a series of interrelated changes he made to the ECO. First he established a PMO-type section in the ECO, which served to increase his leverage in party affairs. His ECO, in combination with the departments, began to exercise powers that were once the preserve of Finance. With a turnover of ECO heads, he launched a search for someone both influential and *sympatico*, and hired Riddell, a longtime acquaintance, making him his surrogate—more powerful than anyone previously in the policy/administration (PCO) side of the ECO. Then a new priorities committee was formed within cabinet, with the premier as chair, and a "dual cabinet submission" procedure began,

102

which put the premier's committee in some respects on an even footing with the Treasury Board. The "planning-budgeting tension" approach that Riddell pioneered also gave the ECO a higher profile. Cabinet's quest for political control was strong enough to increase the size of the ECO and to prevent it from becoming an entrenched and threatening bureaucracy. The practice of rotating appointments for ECO officers became the standard *modus operandi*.

There was both change and continuity in budgeting. The changes were ones that increased the level of institutionalization in PC budgeting and reflected the importance of the financial control factor: for instance, ZBB, collective decision making, and off-budget measures. Continuity in the budgeting cycle was assured by the use of a wide variety of political and bureaucratic actors and by the "front-ending" of policy matters by a Cabinet Planning Conference.

Central/departmental balance is an aim that many institutionalized cabinets ultimately seek. While the PCs seemed sincere in their attempts to achieve it, many of their attempts at balance also reflected the impact of social science rationalism. Yet the degree of balance was also flexible, as the restraint situation showed.

The persistence of institutionalization in the Devine government was indeed a notable trend. It ended the automatic identification of structured cabinets in Saskatchewan with the CCF-NDP approach to governing. Devine continued and even elaborated on some past arrangements, allowing them to become firmly rooted in the province's political governance.

Part Three

Cabinet Decision Making in Manitoba

Part Three
Cabinet Decision Making in Manitoba

MOMENTUM IN MANITOBA

Manitoba stands as a contrast to its neighbour, Saskatchewan, as far as development of the central executive is concerned. The two provinces differed in regard to both the initiation and pace of cabinet institutionalization. Yet similar forces aided its persistence in both cases.

The pace of institutionalization in Manitoba lagged far behind that of Saskatchewan. The Saskatchewan CCF pioneered the use of cabinet committees for special purposes; until the late 1950s Manitoba preferred full cabinet as the decision-making focus. Whereas Saskatchewan surrounded its cabinet in the post-1944 period with advisors to give planning and budgeting advice, Manitoba subscribed to the unaided cabinet model until the late fifties (and thereafter began a slow transition to full institutionalization). A dedication to planning was part of the CCF intellectual baggage and manifested itself clearly early in the Douglas government, but not until sometime into the Roblin era was there a conscious planning approach in Manitoba government. The planning-budgeting nexus was an article of faith in Douglas's public administration almost from the beginning and continued to be so under both Lloyd and Blakeney. Yet only in the 1980s was there a consistent attempt to meld planning and budgeting at the cabinet level in Manitoba.

Different factors lay behind the initiation of institutionalization in the two provinces. In Saskatchewan, ideology played a major role in structuring cabinet; but in Manitoba, ideology was joined by pragmatism and the simple desire for better management in government.

Cabinet institutionalization persisted in Manitoba, as it had in Saskatchewan, due to a variety of factors. It continued under Roblin and Weir because the premier and cabinet sought financial control through structural experiments and were responding to the perceived imperatives raised by social scientists and intergovernmental relations. The influences affecting Schreyer were similarly diverse. He emulated Roblin and Weir when establishing his initial machinery of government, and a more left-wing ideology was readily apparent in the emphasis on planning and intervention practised by his central executive. Lyon was obviously nostalgic for the days of the unaided cabinet, but cabinet pressure and momentum, intergovernmental factors, and his own desire for influence provoked a partial return to institutionalization. Pawley seemed influenced by a quite disparate set of factors. He was unsatisfied with the unaided aspects of Lyon-style government, most notably the lack of planning, yet he initially emulated the cabinet committee design of his predecessor. Political and financial control were important factors, but so was ideology. Pawley respected social science rationalism, but he was also sympathetic to interest group input when designing the machinery of government.

The recent history of the Manitoba cabinet is indeed a varied and interesting one. Part Three studies a thirty-year span, beginning with an in-depth investigation of the Roblin and Weir years (1958–67 and 1967–69, respectively) and ending with an analysis of the Pawley New Democratic government (1981–88).

Chapter Six
The Roblin-Weir Governments

The Manitoba Liberal-Progressive cabinets of premiers Bracken, Garson, and Campbell (1922–58) were, by and large, unaided cabinets. There were occasional deviations, like short-term planning exercises and policy advice to cabinet in the Garson era, but these did not change the essentially traditional, unaided nature of cabinet's operations.[1] The contrast between them and the more institutionalized cabinets of Roblin and Weir was to be quite dramatic. In fact, it would be more accurate to call the latter "transitional cabinets". Initially they displayed a combination of unaided and institutionalized cabinet characteristics, but they shifted unmistakably to the institutionalized camp at the end of the sixties.

ROBLIN AND MODERNIZATION

Progressive Conservative Dufferin Roblin (1958–67) was a modernizing premier. His impatience with the status quo and desire for decisive action were apparent both in his public persona and in his private correspondence to ministers and officials. Perhaps his impatience came from the combination of a strong political pedigree, a family name to resurrect, and many years spent chafing under the relatively quiescent Liberal-Progressive governments. Members of the United Empire Loyalist Roblin family had sat in the assemblies of Upper Canada and the united Province of Canada in the pre-Confederation years. His grandfather had been the premier of Manitoba from 1900 to 1915, but was tarnished by scandal at the end of his time in office. First elected to the legislature in 1949, Roblin had joined politics partly to hasten the end of the coalition in Manitoba. The Conservatives abandoned the coalition in 1950. Personal ambitions then beckoned: Roblin defeated incumbent Errick Willis in a bitter fight for the PC leadership in 1954 and went on to form a minority government in 1958 and successive majority governments in 1959, 1963, and 1966.

He was a reserved and formal man (he once even described himself as "a bit of a dry stick") yet he was progressive enough to earn the reputation of being a left-wing radical among the old guard of his party.[2] The rest of the population did not share this image; Roblin's most popular newspaper cartoon portrait was that of a boy scout, and it was hard to fear a man who practised the bagpipes in his legislative office.

Manitobans with a long memory will recall many concrete results of Roblin's stewardship: the Red River Floodway, the Centennial Concert Hall, the Pan-American Pool in Winnipeg, and several new government educational facilities. He created two new universities and consolidated the archaic system of small school divisions, even at considerable political cost to himself and his Conservative Party. Transportation routes grew, and for the first time in its history, Manitoba had a premier with a northern vision. Like his federal counterpart, John Diefenbaker, Roblin had a special interest in the exploitation of chronically underdeveloped northern natural resources.

A 1967 personality profile of Roblin, in retrospect quite prophetic, typified the premier as "a political animal who deep down wants out of politics. That's the contradiction that has long confused his friends and made his public success at times almost unbearable to him."[3] He continually sought the relative comfort and respite from public life that business life could bring but was always drawn back, irresistibly, into the political fray.

Roblin left the government in 1967, after much cautious introspection, in an unsuccessful bid for the national Progressive Conservative leadership. He then ran unsuccessfully in Winnipeg South Centre in the general election of 1968. Roblin served as president of Canadian Pacific Investments Limited until 1974, at which time he left the firm for an extremely ill-advised attempt at federal politics in the election of 1974, this time in Peterborough. He emerged from this episode "rueful, unemployed, casting about for something to do with the rest of his life, and determined to have nothing whatever to do with politics ever again."[4] Luckily, business opportunity beckoned and he became president and majority owner in a national security firm, Metropolitan Investigation and Security (Canada) Limited, based in Winnipeg. Roblin was appointed to the Senate in 1978 and later served in the Mulroney cabinet as government house leader of the Senate from September 1984 until June 1986. He retired from the Senate at the statutory retirement age of 75 in 1992.

Premier Walter Weir (1967–69) basically carried out what Roblin had started. Weir, a personable, cigar-chomping mortician from Minnedosa, was outwardly a rather lacklustre politician. He had first been elected in the Roblin sweep of 1959 and subsequently served as minister of municipal affairs and then as minister of highways. Weir did not share his predecessor's genius for activist government but seized upon his cabinet reforms as a way of entrenching restraint. His restraint and socially conservative attitudes were out of keeping with mainstream opinion, and he lost the early election he called in 1969.

To make his vision manifest, Roblin had to consider new, more institutionalized machinery for government. In doing so, the importance of ideology, pragmatism, and good management weighed heavily. Starting from ideological premises, Roblin and his cabinet put together an interesting balance of coordinated public- and private-sector economic planning and development bodies. Although there was indeed a partnership, there was little doubt (except perhaps for the 1963–66 period) about who was the senior partner. Ideologically, the Conservatives were economic interventionists with a clear will to dominate the direction of economic development.

As Harold Chorney has suggested, their interventionism consisted of several factors. "The Conservative policy . . . can be seen as a policy of modernization. In their attitudes toward economic growth, government participation in stimulating the economy, the level and importance of government expenditures and the importance of foreign investment to the economy, the Conservatives were 'progressives,' free enterprise revisionists rather than traditionalists . . . The apparent discrepancy between their policy with regard to the importance of direct government intervention on behalf of business and their stated endorsation [sic] of the mythology of 'free enterprise' simply reflected current capitalist ideology."[5] This trio of growth, investment, and economic stimulation were indeed the core of the Conservative party's ideology and proved a guiding force in the development of Roblin's machinery of government.

The Roblin Conservatives tried to induce appropriate responses from the private sector in a variety of areas. They founded a Manitoba Development Fund in 1959 to foster industrial growth. In 1961 they established a public/private task force called the Committee on Manitoba's Economic Future (COMEF) to plan public- and private-sector roles in economic development. In 1963 they created a Manitoba Economic Consultative Board (MECB) to set up a pipeline for private-sector policy advice, reporting direct to cabinet. In 1967 they established a new task force, Targets for Economic Development (TED), which was somewhat analogous to what COMEF had been in the early sixties. This private-sector emphasis affected the design of cabinet structure, central bodies, and planning procedures.

In defining the specific form of public-private partnerships and financial management, Roblin and Weir were pragmatic. COMEF, TED, and the MECB reflected European, and especially French, influences. In seeking to improve the operation of the Treasury Board, his main vehicle for pursuing good management, Roblin borrowed heavily from domestic jurisdictions.

CABINET STRUCTURE

Cabinet structure featured dual cabinet committees in both the Roblin and Weir governments. This made them somewhat more structured than the Liberal-Progressive cabinets, which essentially had only a Treasury Board, but not quite as structured as successive cabinets, which comprised a multiplicity of committees. The Treasury Board was the financial committee of Roblin's cabinet. There was also the Manitoba Development Authority (MDA), whose job was to oversee economic development and industrial growth. Although cabinet was somewhat structured, for nearly half of its existence it was the smallest Executive Council since the late thirties. At first composed of nine ministers, from 1964 on it hovered at about thirteen.

Premier Roblin held dual portfolios for most of his time in office — those of premier and treasurer. He was acting treasurer from 1958 to 1959 and treasurer from 1959 to 1966. Despite his contributions as Manitoba's first institutionalized premier, Roblin maintained this dual portfolio practice, which had long been a tradition with the province's unaided cabinets.[6] Roblin enjoyed a great deal of power. Not only was he premier and treasurer — the two most influential Cabinet posts — but he was also chairman of the only two cabinet committees formed in his government, the Manitoba Development Authority and the Treasury Board. In 1966 Roblin gave the Treasury Board chairmanship to Gurney Evans along with the Treasury portfolio.

The Treasury Board had its own staff, consisting of the personnel of the Budget and Research Branch of the Treasury Department. The Manitoba Development Authority was served from 1959 to 1963 by a statutory board of deputy ministers known as the Manitoba Development Board, and from 1963 to 1968 by a statutory private-sector board known as the Manitoba Economic Consultative Board. The Manitoba Development Fund Board, a quasi-independent economic development grant agency, which functioned like a "quasi-central agency" to the Roblin cabinet, will be described later.

In the Weir government of twelve to thirteen ministers, there was also a dual structure, but the roles of committees and of their staff had changed. The Treasury Board was replaced by the Management Committee of Cabinet (MCC) which had responsibilities going well beyond those of a regular Treasury Board. The Manitoba Development Authority was replaced by the Planning and Priorities Committee of Cabinet (PPCC) whose mandate exceeded that of narrow economic development to the more institutionalized task of planning and global priority-setting.

These new configurations were actually a direct result of a Roblin-era initiative, the Operation Productivity studies, which had first been commissioned in 1967. Unlike Roblin, however, Weir headed neither cabinet committee. Management Committee Secretariat staff were placed in the Executive Council Office rather than in the Treasury Department. Policy input to Planning and Priorities now came, not from deputy or private-sector boards, but directly from another body within the Executive Council Office, the PPCC Secretariat. The growth of central agencies to supplement central departments is, of course, one sign of an institutionalized cabinet.

The Manitoba Development Authority

The real break from the past came with the Manitoba Development Authority (MDA), a cabinet committee with a clear mandate for planning and analysis and with access to significant staff assistance. As shall later be seen, the type of planning involved was transitional to fully institutionalized cabinet planning. Its initiation stemmed from an essentially ideological source, economic interventionism. The MDA phase was preceded by what might be called the "consultant phase" and was followed by the Planning and Priorities phase in which the MDA was dismantled.

The Manitoba Development Authority actually owed its genesis to developments in the preceding Campbell administration. In 1956 the Manitoba Department of Industry and Commerce hired Arthur D. Little, Inc., a leading American industrial research firm, to undertake a series of three economic surveys of natural resources in northern Manitoba.[7] Thus began Manitoba's long reliance on outside consultants and experts to help design the machinery of government. In 1958–60

113

A. D. Little consultants established a general plan for northern economic development, advised on a structure for cabinet, and helped organize the detailed implementation of the original plan. Much later, they were also to help in evaluating government forestry ventures.

The main Arthur D. Little report led ultimately to the creation of the MDA in Roblin's government. The two-hundred-page *Economic Survey of Northern Manitoba, 1958* released to the public on October 16, 1958 reviewed hydro, transportation, and natural resource opportunities in what had been a chronically underdeveloped and ignored area of the province. Its interventionist economic philosophy, which the minister responsible regarded as "in tune with stated government policy," was based on that of the recent *Report* of the Royal Commission on Canada's Economic Prospects (the Gordon Commission). The latter had stated that "in the future as in the past, government action will be needed in certain areas of activity to supplement the role of private initiative and enterprise."[8]

The *Economic Survey* recommended creation of a Northern Manitoba Development Board (in essence, a cabinet committee) to formulate and coordinate northern development policy, with a development fund at its disposal. The Board was to be a planning-oriented, functional cabinet committee with staff assistance, clearly in the institutionalized mold.[9] Integral to the Board's effectiveness would be its access to a development fund enabling it to intervene economically in northern development. It would finance special infrastructure projects and development subsidies.[10] The Board would not necessarily be a permanent group; as development occurred, its role would become less important.[11]

On August 25, 1958 Premier Roblin met with ministers, officials, and James Langley of A. D. Little to begin implementation of the *Economic Survey*'s recommendations.[12] Langley was asked to develop his proposal for an Authority in time for the regular Spring legislative session. As for the development fund, Langley and a provincial official were instructed to prepare a development corporation Act featuring an appointed board of directors who would establish both general and operational policy. The previously unified A. D. Little proposal was now in effect divided into two parts: an Authority and a corporation that was quite independent of the former. The previous northern focus had shifted to a more inclusive interventionist theme with a major new emphasis on economic development.

A. D. Little consultants presented a more detailed outline of the proposed Development Authority to the government on November 26, 1958.[13] The new draft took it for granted that there would be significant government expenditures in the pursuit of economic growth. This fact had implications for a cabinet-level Authority. Government could not delegate its authority, yet it should not smother its creation either. Here were planted the first seeds of the relative independence of the MDA *vis-à-vis* the full cabinet:

> Much of the Authority's activity would be in the field of natural resource development which is an important responsibility of the Provincial Government; substantial expenditures of government funds would also be involved. It is therefore clear that the Government cannot delegate its authority in this area to an independent or semi-independent agency. On the other hand, *the administration and execution of the projects agreed upon should be free from the day-to-day pressures that face the members of the Manitoba Cabinet*. To some extent, this can be achieved through the Government Departments and the semi-independent Boards and Commissions. At the present time, however, there is only a very limited degree of cooperation between the various agencies concerned. Further, *apart from the Cabinet itself, there is no focal point of authority and direction. A mechanism is therefore needed to establish development policies and to coordinate and direct their execution.*[14] (Emphases added.)

The reader might dwell for a moment on the words "apart from the Cabinet itself." One gets the impression that cabinet and the "mechanism" were not meant to interact a great deal.

The Authority would have a two-level structure. A council consisting of cabinet ministers concerned with resource development would have responsibility for policy formulation and implementation. (In practice, the council was later called the Manitoba Development Authority instead.) A Board of deputy ministers and the heads of semi-independent government agencies (later called the Manitoba Development Board) would recommend new policies to council and implement council decisions. The planners hoped to ensure coordination between the council and Board by establishing an executive director to council who would be the chairman of the board as well.[15]

The planners were also careful to think through the relationship between the Authority, the provincial treasurer, and the Treasury Board. Their advice was to keep the provincial treasurer off the Development Authority and not to establish formal Authority/Treasury Board links. Justifying this with the argument that the "historic conservatism" of a Treasury would be opposed to the necessary large-scale development expenditures, they presupposed large government expenditures for the purposes of economic growth.[16]

After the consultant phase, the MDA experienced three stages of evolution, each one arising from a new legislated base. From 1959 to 1963 the newly created Authority established a track record of economic intervention in all areas of the province, not just the North. From 1963 to 1966 it was less interventionist and leadership oriented and was more sharply focused as a conduit for business communications to cabinet. The pragmatism of Roblin and his cabinet was starting to emerge, with European indicative planning models being adapted to the Manitoba setting. A Manitoba Economic Consultative Board (MECB)—composed of business representatives, lesser numbers of government, and labour spokesmen—replaced the Manitoba Development Board (the second-tier officials level of the MDA). The cabinet subsequently grew disenchanted with the consultative mode, and from 1966 to 1968 the Authority experimented with new interventionist powers of program implementation. In 1968 Premier Weir decided to discontinue the MECB. The MDA concept was folded into that of a Priorities and Planning Committee, and a new stage of Manitoba cabinet development began.

In practice, the MDA's activities favoured the central executive over the departments[17] and, according to Careless, led to departmental bitterness. Roblin ruled with a "dictatorial hand," arbitrating the interdepartmental feuds which arose as departments lost their traditional functions or had them merged due to MDA initiatives.[18] An internal management study called Operation Productivity noted in 1968 that "Experimentation with the central planning device has included allowing the planning agency to coordinate the activities of the various program departments. This, as we have seen in the case of the Manitoba Development Authority, has met with failure when it has been tried."[19] Even a Schreyer-era study was to comment on the spillover bitterness engendered by the intervention of central agents and agencies in the Roblin-Weir era, noting that line agencies called the latter "White House arrangements" run by "super-deputies."[20]

Throughout the 1958 to 1968 period, full cabinet appears to have been rather distant from direct participation in economic policy making, serving instead as a final reviewer, a settler of interdepartmental disputes, and a disseminator of general economic guidelines. In establishing the MDA, planners thought through its relationship to the provincial treasurer and the Treasury Board but not its relationship to full cabinet. In provincial structural arrangements for managing the Agricultural Rehabilitation and Development Act of 1961 (ARDA), the MDA figures heavily but full cabinet does not. The MDA, not full cabinet, is referred to as the "high command" for economic development in the early Roblin years. On paper the Manitoba Economic

Consultative Board reported to the MDA, not to cabinet, and the various MDA/MECB working relationships established in 1963 did not include full cabinet. The role of full cabinet was mentioned only peripherally in the legislation of 1966 that established the Growth Account, the Youth and Manpower Agency, and the Nelson Agency. When Manitoba was negotiating the arrangements for an integrated forestry complex in The Pas, it was not full cabinet which was involved but an informal cabinet committee. Presumably, Premier Roblin served as the intermediary between the MDA and cabinet, perceiving this to be the most efficient arrangement of ministerial time and energy.

Before turning to the Planning and Priorities phase of the evolution of Manitoba cabinet planning, it is important to discuss the rise of Manitoba's Treasury Board in the Roblin years. This is because the Operation Productivity Report of 1968 was to suggest closely interrelated modifications to both the MDA and the Treasury Board, with the government accepting many of them. It therefore makes sense to approach the changes from a knowledge of each of the committees' histories.

The Treasury Board

The second pillar of Roblin's cabinet committee structure was the Treasury Board. The mandate of the Board continued but was broadened. Roblin, the first chairman of the Board, was a pragmatic borrower of the best in contemporary financial administration practices across Canada.

The Manitoba Treasury Board dates back over a hundred years to The Treasury Department Act of 1887.[21] Such was the pace of reform in Manitoba that it was not until nearly fifty years later that the structure and functions of the Treasury Board were further clarified. In The Treasury Act of 1936[22], the treasurer was specified as chairman over the other two members, and a secretary was provided who could be either the deputy treasurer or assistant deputy treasurer (s.13). The Board appeared to have limited, almost tribunal-like powers.

It was the 1936 legislation that saw the Treasury Board through the Liberal-Progressive years and right up to 1969. The legislative description in the Act is an accurate guide to what actually transpired in the Bracken, Garson, and Campbell Treasury Boards, to judge by Donnelly's comment.[23] Yet within the confines of this antiquated legislation, Roblin fashioned an activist and wide-ranging Treasury Board.

Roblin told the author in December 1983 that collective financial decision making was a conscious policy of his: "The main job of [my] Treasury Board was to review departmental spending plans and to relate them to the government's ability to spend . . . Treasury Board consisted of three ministers who were rotated every year or so to ensure a good knowledge of government and to ensure collective responsibility . . . [This rotation] gave them experience and perspective."[24]

The process of establishing cabinet committees was not, however, an easy one: "We had to 'reinvent' things when we formed the government. Only one member had been in a Cabinet before. We had to find out what the machinery was, and what were the limits of our own experience."[25] To assist him in designing the Treasury Board, Roblin relied on correspondence and visitors from other jurisdictions. In no other area would his pragmatism be quite so pronounced.

The jurisdictions by which Manitoba was most influenced were Ontario, Saskatchewan, and the federal government. When he held his first Treasury Board meeting on July 16, 1958, Roblin had the description of the newly redesigned Ontario Treasury Board passed to the other members, Gurney Evans and Stewart McLean. Manitoba's role statement for the Treasury Board was to be somewhat similar to that of Ontario's. Unlike Ontario, however, Manitoba's Treasury Board was to have responsibility for superannuation policy, establishment control, and staff policy.[26]

Ottawa and Saskatchewan officials were also tapped for information.[27] The Saskatchewan emphasis on Organization and Methods (O&M) work, which A. W. Johnson reviewed for the Board on July 29, 1958, appears to have influenced Roblin; a special O&M unit was later established in the Treasury Department, and its work figured heavily on the agenda of the Treasury Board throughout the sixties. J. S. Anderson, deputy treasurer under both the Liberal and Conservative governments (and later finance deputy under Schreyer) has observed that the federal influence reinforced the conviction that, as in Ottawa, Treasury Board staff should be part of the Finance Department, and all expenditure programs should pass through the Treasury Board screen both at budget time and throughout the year.[28]

"Treasury Board Direction #1" of March 18, 1959 outlined Treasury Board staff arrangements.[29] There was to be a Budget and Research Branch of the Treasury Department, split up into three divisions: the Budget Research Division, the Organization and Methods Division, and the Economic Research Division.[30]

The range of Treasury Board activities was wide indeed. In fact, the Board covered matters which in later eras would have been referred to specialized cabinet committees for evaluation: water policy, health plan premiums, "Roads to Resources," urban renewal, and alcohol education.[31] Of course, it dealt with matters of a more financial and less political nature as well.

There appears to have been relatively more interaction between the Treasury Board and cabinet—effectively promoting collective decision making—than there was between the MDA and cabinet. Roblin, as mentioned, rotated ministerial membership on the Treasury Board. As well, cabinet was integrally linked with the Board in the process of reviewing annual estimates.

To put some perspective on the extent of collective decision making, one should consider the matter of general premier-cabinet relations. Roblin has been called a dictatorial premier, a martinet.[32] He himself does not give this impression and neither does Derek Bedson, his clerk of the executive council. As Roblin has explained, "My technique [in Cabinet] was to ensure that each minister had a chance to state his opinion. After that I would declare what the consensus was. I was careful not to act if there was determined opposition. Each [minister] shared decisions equally."[33]

Bedson has elaborated on the premier's style, noting that "Roblin was a good chairman and administrator. He was quite unusual in getting the best out of his ministers. By quietening the loquacious he was able to get the brighter lights in Cabinet to contribute . . . He was not domineering. He left his ministers fairly autonomous but contacted them weekly to keep in touch with affairs."[34]

OPERATION PRODUCTIVITY AND ITS AFTERMATH

In November 1966 concerns over financial control forced cabinet to begin a confidential internal efficiency review of the processes and machinery of government. By the time the study was over, the groundwork had been laid for one of the most wide-ranging changes in the history of the Manitoba central executive. Roblin and his cabinet had crossed the threshold to greater cabinet institutionalization. The development of central agencies and central analytical capacity would follow.

Gurney Evans's submission to cabinet in March of 1967 outlined the financial urgency for the administrative productivity study later called Operation Productivity: "The spiraling costs brought on by the growing significance of, and emphasis placed on, education and other bold Provincial programs requires the Government of this Province to concern itself with two key requirements. First is the need to ensure that effective decisions are made in the allocation of funds to programs—that proper costing of priorities is established. Second is the

119

need to ensure the maintenance of a high level of manpower productivity and efficiency."[35]

Gordon W. Holland, who in 1968 became the first secretary of the Management Committee of Cabinet, has cast the reasons for creating the review in both political and financial control language: "Operation Productivity was Roblin's idea . . . Roblin was concerned about the growth in the bureaucracy. He was concerned about decision-making. He was concerned about the ability of elected officials—ministers—to actually take decisions [and make them effective]."[36]

A special cabinet committee directed the study. Continuing the characteristic melding of governmental and private-sector personnel, cabinet chose as research director A. R. Aird, the partner in charge of the Winnipeg office of the consulting firm, P. S. Ross and Partners. A public-private senior advisory committee was established. There were seven projects included in the study, each with a project director.[37] It would be Roblin's successor, Walter Weir (1967–69), who would actually receive and implement Operation Productivity recommendations.

Of the many organizational problems identified by the government organization project team,[38] expenditure control considerations weighed most heavily. Ultimately they formed the basis for the reorganization of departments and for the dual cabinet committee structure recommended in the team's report. The authors maintained that certain responsibilities should be delegated to two cabinet committees as a means to achieve expenditure control. Each minister would "ideally sit on at least one of these Committees and thereby ensure total cabinet involvement in the general management process."[39] One committee would control expenditures by setting priorities among government programs; the other would control expenditures by controlling current costs and maintaining management efficiency. The first half of the expenditure control design would be called the Planning and Priorities Committee of Cabinet (PPCC) and would be a reconstituted version of the Manitoba Development Authority. In contrast to the MDA's interventionist style, the new planning committee would make decisions about program mix and direction without becoming involved in program execution.

The second half of the expenditure control design would "be viewed in its proper role as the Management Committee of Cabinet [MCC],"[40] a reformed version of the Treasury Board. The language of the report seemed to indicate that the proposed Management Committee Secretariat would be structurally independent of the Department of Finance and, presumably, would be placed in the Executive Council Office.

120

The secretariat was to have three functional areas of responsibility. The first was budgeting; a Budget Group was to introduce the rationalist program budgeting concept.[41] The second responsibility was management improvement. The third would encompass personnel administration, collective bargaining, and establishment control. The Civil Service Commission would continue to be the central recruiting agency for the government and would protect the merit principle and review grievances.

Changes to the Manitoba cabinet and modifications of departmental responsibilities were announced on September 25, 1968.[42] As Operation Productivity had recommended, all cabinet ministers except the premier belonged to either the Planning and Priorities Committee or the Management Committee. Each of the committees had six members, while cabinet itself had a total of thirteen ministers. Finance Minister Gurney Evans chaired the Management Committee and Labour Minister C. H. Witney chaired Planning and Priorities. Why the new premier, Walter Weir, did not chair Planning and Priorities, as Premier Roblin had chaired the MDA, is not clear; observers suggest that it was his nature to delegate tasks. There were major shifts in departmental duties, and many departments were renamed to reflect their new responsibilities. In all, about three hundred programs were regrouped on the basis of function and objectives. News releases of the time mentioned a variety of functions for the new committees, but they all reflected the financial control factor and the legacy of Operation Productivity.[43]

At its first meeting the Management Committee of Cabinet acknowledged the three functions outlined for it in the Operation Productivity report.[44] The third responsibility—a wide-ranging control of many aspects of personnel administration along the lines of changes brought about in Ottawa in 1967—was a departure for Manitoba. Whereas previously the powers had been shared in a de facto sense between the CSC and the Treasury Board, they were now unambiguously in the MCC's court. As Operation Productivity had seemed to suggest, an MCC Secretariat was created in the Executive Council Office. Gordon W. Holland was chosen as secretary to the MCC, a position he held until 1974, when he was replaced by Hans Schneider, a former deputy in the Health and Social Development Department.

The terms of reference of the Planning and Priorities Committee of Cabinet were sent to all ministers and deputies on October 10, 1968 by PPCC chairman C. H. Witney. The duties were largely the same as those suggested by Operation Productivity, although cabinet added objectives relating to the review of federal-provincial cost-sharing and the coordination of special interdepartmental studies. Robert A. Wallace was chosen as secretary to Planning and Priorities, a position he held from 1968 to 1970.

Cabinet began to fulfil its new program budgeting and priorization responsibilities. Respectable progress was made in the next few months in implementing the Planning-Programming-Budgeting System (PPBS).[45] Even though the productivity report had not mentioned a priority-setting role for the committee (despite including the word *priorities* in its proposed title!), the premier obviously saw the PPCC as performing such a role. Planning and Priorities did in fact come to recommend the priorities for consideration by cabinet in the budget process.

The first priority-setting exercise was a hurried affair; during the fall of 1968 the PPCC had had its secretariat prepare a three-level statement of the relative priority of government programs.[46] The PPCC minutes of November 29, 1968 record that the committee accepted many of the secretariat's suggestions for the budgetary process, which was about to start in three days, but that the rush had prevented thorough consultation and analysis.[47]

As for the politics of cabinet reorganization, Careless has maintained that interdepartmental squabbles continued relatively unabated. There were two new committees and three new secretariats, but they were run by the same politicians with the same old turf problems as had existed before.[48]

CENTRAL AGENCIES/CENTRAL STAFF

Although the growth of central agencies and central staff was less dramatic than that of cabinet committees, there were some definite movements towards an institutionalized cabinet. For instance, there were progressively more central staff. A clerk of the executive council, Derek Bedson, actually sat in on cabinet meetings. Alternative sources of policy advice grew, and there was more analysis, planning, and coordination. A strong central agency—the MDA's successor, the Planning and Priorities Secretariat—as well as a strong central department—the Treasury Board Secretariat's successor, the Management Committee Secretariat—developed. Generally, the same factors that had engendered the creation of committees of cabinet and Operation Productivity were operative in the establishment of central agencies.

The Premier's Office

One of Premier Roblin's first needs in office was for an official who could help him organize the administrative side of cabinet affairs. On

August 1, 1958 Roblin hired Derek R. C. Bedson as clerk. Bedson came with impeccable Tory connections. His grandfather had joined the Wolseley expedition against Riel and stayed on in Manitoba. Educated at Manitoba and Balliol, Bedson had served as a foreign service officer with the Department of External Affairs, spending two-and-one-half years with the permanent Canadian mission to the United Nations.[49] In 1955 he had been hired by federal Conservative Leader George Drew. From 1956 he was private secretary to John G. Diefenbaker, when the latter was leader of the Opposition and then later prime minister. Bedson had known Roblin earlier through a family relationship.[50] Contemporary CCF Leader Lloyd Stinson called Bedson "Duff Roblin's most influential friend and advisor."[51]

Bedson performed a variety of functions. His diplomatic background was useful in his Manitoba post, as he handled all matters of protocol, arranged federal-provincial conferences, informed Manitoba External Affairs ministers travelling abroad, and arranged meetings between international political figures and Manitoba politicians. He processed Orders in Council (O/Cs) and was the custodian of O/Cs dating back to 1878. He kept cabinet minutes; unlike the practice in contemporary Ottawa, he would not record the discussion but only the actual decisions.[52] He also followed up on departments in certain circumstances to see if cabinet directives had been followed. Bedson was to serve as clerk under four premiers from 1958 to 1981.

He was not average. A journalist who knew him described Bedson as having "a wide brow and receding hairline, suggesting an obvious sagacity, a Spanish cardinal perhaps, come again as a Manitoba civil servant."[53] An avid historian, he had forceful opinions on a stunning array of controversies in world history and kept a painting of a personal hero, Charles I, in his legislative building office. "He added to Manitoba something few governments ever possess, namely historical perspective. Every issue was the outgrowth of something else. This made for maturity of decision. Ministers are less inclined to be rash when they can see the day's controversies in the light of centuries."[54]

It was not all serious, however. "He would sit behind me in Cabinet," Duff Roblin has recalled, "and when he really objected to something being said, he would make these rude noises. Sometimes he would moan." It was a disconcerting trick, Bedson said, that he had learned from a mentor, his Oxford tutor of Saxon literature.[55]

Besides Bedson, the premier relied on assistance from other sources. Roblin was enough like a premier of an unaided cabinet not to insist on a major build-up of personal staff (beyond his executive assistant). Because he was his own treasurer from 1958 to 1966, Roblin had no trouble getting staff assistance from the Treasury.[56] In a way, Treasury

Board staff were also the premier's staff. When he gave up supervision of the Treasury, however, there was a slight increase in staff, and Roblin hired an assistant to handle political affairs.

Manitoba Development Authority Staff

Staff aid to the Manitoba Development Authority began modestly and in a line department. By the end of the Roblin-Weir era, the number of staff had increased, and they were now housed in the Executive Council Office. The MDA had gone from the unaided cabinet phase, which involved assistance to cabinet from a central department, to the institutionalized cabinet pattern of cabinet aid from a central agency.

Industrial advisor Rex Grose outlined what he saw as MDA staff needs to Industry and Commerce Minister Gurney Evans, and through him to cabinet, in November 1958; this was the period when the second Arthur D. Little MDA draft was being considered as well. Grose wanted a group of "top flight specialists . . . with practical operating experience in their respective areas."[57] He suggested that there be a joint executive director of the Manitoba Development Council (later called the MDA Directorate or simply the MDA) and a chairman of the Development Board, together with economics, mining, and forestry specialists. He saw A. D. Little staff as assisting in development efforts for the next few years.[58] Grose was unsuccessful in the short run, but later on he achieved a measure of what he had been requesting (see Table 5). To some extent, intergovernmental relations affected the job descriptions and activities of the MDA staff.

Rex Grose himself was the major staff person on the MDA; in fact, along with Deputy Provincial Treasurer J. Stuart Anderson, he was one of the province's most powerful civil servants. Grose, a Manitoban by birth and education, had become Executive Assistant to federal Deputy Minister of Mines and Resources Hugh Keenleyside after serving as an ordnance officer with the Canadian army in World War II. In 1948 he returned to Manitoba and entered the provincial civil service, eventually becoming deputy minister of industry and commerce. For the next two to three decades, he was to make northern resource and industrial development almost a personal crusade, beginning with the *Economic Survey of Northern Manitoba* in the late 1950s. There was a short hiatus from the provincial service in 1957, but after the Conservative victory Grose acted as a consultant to Gurney Evans[59] and shortly afterwards was back in his old deputy position.

In the Conservative administration, Grose's levers of power multiplied. He was to keep his deputy position until 1966, but in 1958 he also became general manager and vice-chairman of the Manitoba

TABLE 5
LIST OF MANITOBA DEVELOPMENT AUTHORITY PROFESSIONAL STAFF, 1959–68

INDUSTRY AND COMMERCE PHASE

1959–60	economist
1960–61	economist, industrial development engineer, freight rate consultant, executive assistant
1961–62	same as 1960–61
1962–63	economist, industrial development engineer
1963–64	executive director, Manitoba Economic Consultative Board (MECB), executive assistant
1964–65	same as 1963–64
1965–66	executive director (MECB), two senior officers, executive assistant
1966–67	executive director (MECB), three senior officers, executive assistant

EXECUTIVE COUNCIL OFFICE PHASE

1967–68	two deputy ministers, eight senior staff

Source: Manitoba. *Public Accounts*, 1959–60 to 1967–68. Staff earning below a certain amount (earlier in this decade it was $5,000, then $7,500, per annum) were not recorded under "salaries paid" in the *Public Accounts* past 1958–59.
Information from 1959–60 to 1962–63 does not reveal the fact that the MDA was served by an executive director who was the deputy minister of industry and commerce; hence, he is not listed under the Manitoba Development Authority.

Development Fund (MDF), a newly created industrial development lending agency. When the Manitoba Development Authority came into being, Grose was its first executive director and chairman of the board. He was primarily responsible for the report of the Committee on Manitoba's Economic Future (1963) and the report of the Commission on Targets for Economic Development (1969). In the mid-1960s the government asked the MDF to take on a heavier workload, and the MDF Board in turn asked for more of Grose's time. The result was that in August of 1966 Grose resigned all his other posts and became the full-time chairman of the MDF. This is the position from which he resigned on March 31, 1970.[60] Needless to say, Grose's influence extended far beyond what a civil servant usually enjoys.

The Manitoba Development Authority Act of 1959 spelled out the bare framework of MDA staff arrangements.[61] It specifically mentioned an executive director and an executive secretary and allowed for other assistants and employees (s.7). The executive director was also chairman of the board of the Manitoba Development Authority and was expected to manage the operations of the Authority and to have general supervision of the employees of the directorate or of the Board (s.12). S.10 of the Act gave the Board the ability to have permanent staff as well.

At the beginning Roblin did not place his cabinet committee staff in central agencies. The modest staff component of the MDA Directorate, despite the lack of legislative directives to that effect, was housed in the Department of Industry and Commerce. (The Board itself seems to have had no staff other than the director and secretary.) Rex Grose, of course, became the executive director. The executive secretary (and economist) from 1959 to 1963 was Samuel Trachtenberg. As Table 5 indicates, Grose and Trachtenberg were the major professional staff of the MDA during its first year of operation and were joined by only one or two other professionals over the next three years. Grose was able to act as executive director only on a part-time basis due to the exigencies of his other positions as deputy and MDF vice-chairman.

Early MDA staff responsibilities appear to have been dominated by the necessity to react to federal studies. Requesting more help in November 1959, Grose wrote to Gurney Evans, saying that the crush of federal business was detracting from the real job of the MDA, which was industrial and northern development; more personnel were therefore essential.[62] Later evidence indicates that much work originally conceived to be within the purview of the MDA staff ended up being parcelled out by Grose to regular Industry and Commerce staff and A. D. Little consultants, with himself as the master orchestrator.[63]

With the passing of The Development Authority Act of 1963, a new stage in the Authority's staff evolution was reached.[64] An increase in staff serving the MDA resulted from the new "indicative planning" role that was thrust upon the Authority. The Authority itself (the ministerial component) was to appoint a secretary and other staff as considered necessary (s.4[4]). The Manitoba Economic Consultative Board (MECB) was also to have a staff capacity; the Board could hire its own or it could request departmental staff from ministers (s.17).

Again acting on the advice of Rex Grose, cabinet decided to combine the posts of a research director to the MECB and secretary to the MDA in one person.[65] The continued placement of MECB/MDA staff in the Industry and Commerce Department was apparently due to the designation of the industry and commerce minister as the responsible minister under the Act.[66] Economist Dr Baldur H. Kristjanson, who a government news release said had won "a continent-wide reputation in the field of agriculture, economic development and natural resources"[67] became the MECB's executive director (as the research director was now called). In 1967 Gordon Lawson became acting MECB executive director.

The initiation of the third wave of changes[68] to the MDA in 1966 marked a period of decline for the MECB and its staff. Baldur Kristjanson ceased to be involved with the MECB and became one of the Manitoba Development Authority's deputy ministers. Following this, other staff members gradually left the employ of the MECB, and eventually Premier Weir disbanded the MECB altogether.

The legislative changes made to the MDA in 1966 were only amendments; the general MDA framework of 1963 was left intact. This meant that the ministerial MDA could hire its own staff, which it proceeded to do with alacrity. The new staff doubled between 1966–67 and 1967–68. After 1967, however, MDA staff were placed in a central agency, the ECO. This was a mark of institutionalization and foreshadowed the development of a PPCC Secretariat in the ECO. There were two MDA deputy ministers in the ECO, Baldur H. Kristjanson (Economics) and B. Scott Bateman (Youth and Manpower) as well as eight or nine professional staff. These ECO staff were phased out in 1968 to make room for the new PPCC Secretariat staff.

A PPCC Secretariat came into existence in October of 1968. The PPCC had a secretary, as the Operation Productivity report had suggested;[69] however, contrary to its suggestions[70] the deputy treasurer and Treasury Board secretary were not to be the other members of the secretariat. The secretary was R. A. Wallace, and the other staff were G. R. Anderson, the assistant secretary, as well as a senior economist and an economic research analyst. Both Wallace and the senior economist had worked on the MDA staff earlier.

Treasury Board Staff

Ultimately the Treasury Board staff of Roblin's era would be replaced by the Management Committee Secretariat of the Weir and Schreyer years. This development—the placing of the financial management function in a new analysis-oriented central department (along with other central functions)—can itself be considered a heightening of institutionalization. Yet even in the Roblin era, Treasury Board staff were showing the tendencies for centralized decision making and increased central staff levels that are often associated with institutionalized cabinets.

Treasury Board staff in the Campbell era had been composed essentially of two people: Deputy Treasurer J. Stuart Anderson (as secretary) and Budget Research Analyst C. N. Rowse. These Treasury officials appeared at virtually every Treasury Board meeting. Doubtless, they could rely on the rest of the Treasury Department for additional aid beyond the scope of their own resources; but since the Treasury Board had a fairly modest workload, this was probably not often necessary. Anderson worked briefly with the new Conservative administration; then in 1959 he left to pursue a succession of other appointments, serving as assistant treasurer, International Nickel; treasurer, Metropolitan Winnipeg; and deputy, Manitoba Department of Mines and Resources. From 1966 to 1976 he was back as Manitoba's deputy minister of finance; but despite his significant personal status and experience, he was unable to resist the diminution of his department's profile.

As a result of the Roblin administration's initiatives to expand the role of the Treasury Board, changes were wrought in the structure of Treasury Board staff itself. The Budget and Research Branch of the Manitoba Treasury acted as the secretariat to the Treasury Board for the entire Roblin era. With more than a dozen officials, it was about four or five times as large as the staff of the early MDA. A chief budget analyst (under the director of budget and research) was responsible for the formulation, presentation, and execution of the budgetary program.[71] The chief Organization and Methods analyst controlled a division which evaluated and developed organizational structures, work methods, and new program innovations.[72] The chief of the Research Division headed a group whose public finance duties included preparing overviews of policies relating to taxation, public borrowing, spending, budgeting, revenue estimating, and federal-provincial-municipal relations.

With the installation of the new staff network for the Treasury Board, the number of personnel from the Treasury Department appearing at Treasury Board meetings increased modestly. However, Anderson and Rowse, the staff of the Campbell era, were also the early mainstays of the Roblin Treasury Board. Rowse was now the Budget and Research director and assistant secretary to the Treasury Board. When Anderson left the provincial civil service, R. M. Burns became the deputy treasurer and new Treasury Board secretary for the early 1960s.

The basic design for Treasury Board assistance held for most of the next decade. By 1968 J. S. Anderson was once again deputy provincial treasurer and secretary of the Treasury Board. The Budget and Research Branch had been replaced by the Treasury Research Division, headed by Lance Partridge, the assistant secretary of the Treasury Board and assistant deputy minister (Treasury) in charge of research and budgets. The Treasury Research Division had three branches: the

128

Economic and Federal-Provincial Research Branch; the Budget Branch; and the Treasury Board Secretariat, which handled the administrative management of Treasury Board. The only major change was that Organization and Methods was moved away from its former soulmates and over to the Finance and Administration Division.[73]

The secretariat to the Management Committee of Cabinet, which replaced the Treasury Board Secretariat in 1968, was apparently structured roughly along the lines suggested by Operation Productivity. Staff numbers appear moderate—the public accounts for 1969–70 list only five professionals in the MCC Secretariat—but they were fairly senior government personnel. The installation of program budgeting was an early priority of the secretariat.

BUDGET REFORM

There were both unaided and institutionalized budgeting characteristics in the Roblin-Weir cabinets. For much of the Conservative era, the traditional emphasis remained on the financial control aim; cabinet then moved tentatively toward the type of budgeting characteristic of institutionalized cabinets. In the latter case, analysis forms a large part of budgeting procedures, and the *aims* of budgeting extend beyond financial control to include planning, management, and policy choice objectives. The *means* of budgeting expanded toward the end of the Roblin-Weir era to include off-budget measures such as the Operation Productivity efficiency study, the reform of financial administration legislation, and the installation of new central agency roles. Roblin and Weir were influenced in budgeting matters principally by the financial control factor, but a subsidiary factor was at work as well— social science rationalism.

From 1959 to 1967 preparation of the estimates under Roblin had been marked by what might be regarded as traditional Treasury Board approaches. There was an emphasis on input categories in departmental budget requests, and there were arbitrary reductions of requests in the sense that cabinet and the Treasury Board did not act in a systematized way.[74] Analysis did not seem to be at the forefront of estimates review. As late as 1966 and 1967 reminders to the Treasury Board from Stuart Anderson hinted at hasty and incrementalist reviews.[75]

Gurney Evans became the new minister of finance in 1966. The pace of government growth soon became an issue. Between 1958 and 1968 provincial current expenditures expanded rapidly from $80.8 million to $335.9 million.[76] In 1967 the Treasury Board acknowledged that the financial control factor was rendering imperative the need for changes in budgeting; the Board cited inadequate budget controls as having necessitated major new taxation for the province.[77] The Treasury Board accordingly suggested program budgeting, and Deputy Treasurer Anderson reviewed the advantages of such a system in a memo to Premier Roblin.[78] The implementation of program budgeting was to occur in two stages, beginning with examination by the currently ongoing Operation Productivity study and progressing to implementation.

Operation Productivity was itself influenced by factors other than mere financial control. The organizational problems identified by the government organization project team reflected the typical concern of social scientists in the sixties with rationalism in government. The identified problems included: lack of expenditure control; insufficient planning and priority setting; lack of adequate information flow to cabinet, the Treasury Board, and the departments; insufficient attention to improving management effectiveness; and poor control of establishments.[79] This social science rationalism resulted in a broadened array of aims for the budgeting recommended.

The report recommended budgeting as a major area of responsibility for the new Management Committee of Cabinet. It further recommended that the budget group in the MCC Secretariat introduce program budgeting. What the authors understood by program budgeting was never made clear, but it appeared to be synonymous with the currently popular PPBS. The PPBS clearly involved the injection of other aims such as planning, policy choice, and better management into the budgeting sphere alongside the traditional financial control aim. Concern over financial control had joined with social science reform trends to produce a budgeting system with multiple aims.

The multiple aims of budgeting could be seen in the recommended functions for the budget group. This group was to perform policy analysis, interpret program outcomes, recommend ways to measure program effectiveness, review potential trouble spots in the departments, and arrange interprogram transfers of funds.[80] These functions implied policy choice and better management objectives.

The second stage, of course, was departmental implementation of program budgeting. Here broadened budget aims were also apparent. Departments were instructed in October 1968 to begin converting their estimates to the program budgeting concept. In May 1969, in what was a clear attempt to introduce planning, departments were instructed to institute five-year budget projections.[81]

It would be left to Schreyer to implement many initiatives begun under Roblin and Weir. For example, NDP central agencies would oversee the implementation of program budgeting (PPBS) in the early seventies. Also, an NDP-controlled legislature would pass the new Financial Administration Act, which had been prepared by the Weir government, and which put into effect many of the recommendations of the Operation Productivity report.

In the Roblin-Weir governments, planning derived from ideological and, to a lesser extent, pragmatic factors and might best be described as transitional in nature. It was not exactly unaided cabinet planning, which tends to be sporadic and perhaps personalistic in nature. With two major comprehensive planning efforts (as well as intensive efforts on a project basis), Conservative initiatives of the 1960s went far beyond the unaided stage. Yet their was it planning was not typical of an institutionalized cabinet, which often involves the collegial participation of cabinet and the use of extensive staff resources in planning efforts.

The Roblin-Weir planning efforts, save for one, were done at one remove from cabinet, either by what one might call public-private development agencies (quasi-central agencies) or by temporary planning structures which were disassembled after being used. Such agencies and structures apparently obviated the need for a more intensive build-up of central planning staff. What transpired was planning without a fully institutionalized cabinet, albeit in a transitional mode between unaided and institutionalized planning. The Conservatives' intended Northern Development Plan of 1968–69, which featured direction from Planning and Priorities and involvement from both a central agency (the PPCC Secretariat) and departments, put the transitional nature of earlier efforts in relief. The northern plan was halted, however, by the 1969 provincial general election.

Not surprisingly, the transitional mode of planning featured aspects of both unaided and institutionalized cabinet planning which were juxtaposed in new and unfamiliar ways. As in unaided cabinets, the Roblin-Weir governments had their planning done to a great extent by outsiders, that is, personnel from the non-governmental sector. One class of outsiders consisted of public-private development agencies, or quasi-central agencies as this work also terms them. Analogous to central agencies, which coordinate and help cabinet plan the activities of departments, the quasi-central agencies helped cabinet plan the activities of private-sector organizations and firms which were cooperating with or dependent upon government.

There were, however, indirect rather than direct links between cabinet and these quasi-central agencies. One such indirect link was provided by the premier himself; Roblin had instigated one such agency, the Manitoba Development Fund (MDF), in 1958. He had been responsible for its initial "banker's approach" to lending; and when permission was sought to change this to a "development approach," it was to Roblin rather than to cabinet that the responsible minister and Rex Grose came. The premier appeared to use an "arm's length" rationale for the cabinet/MDF relationship when it suited his purposes. Grose provided another indirect link; he was secretary of the MDA cabinet committee and a leading member of the executive of the MDF. After him, Baldur Kristjanson provided still another indirect link, serving from 1963–66 as MDA secretary and as executive director of the MECB, another quasi-central agency.

Another class of outsiders were the temporary planning structures—COMEF, the Committee on Manitoba's Economic Future (1961–63) and TED, the Targets for Economic Development Commission (1967–69)—which used cooperative techniques to involve labour and business in planning. Again Grose, as lead offical in both COMEF and TED, provided an indirect link to cabinet. COMEF and TED, as far as the private sector was concerned, were examples of "self-planning," which was somewhat analogous to self-regulation.

The decision-making style of the Conservatives tilted toward central domination: a few politicians, central departments, agencies, and officials seemed to determine the direction of policy development. The premier apparently did not set out to dominate the scene, but history has so judged him. As W. L. Morton has observed, "The Roblin government, as thoroughly as it tried to embody the will and aspiration of a new and dynamic society, was in fact a *tour de force*, attempted by one lonely and devoted man."[82]

Roblin pledged non-interference by the central departments and agencies he had structured to aid cabinet, but ultimately they were perceived in the opposite way, as examples of a Manitoba "White House." Rex Grose's imprint was all over the Roblin-Weir era: few major economic development decisions were taken without his input. Even his own departmental staff noticed that he was a loner who kept the details of major projects to himself.[83] The policy results of the Conservative years were unmistakably impressive, but they were achieved at the cost of a central/departmental enmity which was to impede future premiers and cabinets.

Chapter Seven
The Schreyer Era

If the Roblin era constituted the transitional phase on the way to establishing an institutionalized cabinet, the Schreyer era culminated its development. The Schreyer cabinet was heavily institutionalized. It demonstrated a tendency for collective decision making with its use of cabinet committees and its later creation of a Planning Committee of the whole cabinet. The premier became the unabashed architect of cabinet form, experimenting broadly during his tenure. The Schreyer gouvernment had central agencies as well as central departments, and extensive use was made of cabinet-level staff, central agency analysis, planning and coordination, and intensified cabinet record-keeping. Budgeting had multiple aims, and there was a comprehensive, collegial planning approach to public policy out of which an elementary planning-budgeting balance began to evolve. Alternate sources of policy advice, other than ministerial resources, were sought. Cabinet decision making became more centralized, but there were some nods to departmental autonomy. In fact, under Schreyer, Manitoba would have one of the most structured cabinets of the day in Canada.

Cabinet institutionalization persisted, and indeed expanded, due to many factors. Not the least of them was emulation. Like the Progressives a half century before them, the New Democrats were surprised to find themselves in government after the election of June 25, 1969.[1] They did not have an administrative element in their platform and in general tended to consider matters of process to be of secondary importance to specific policy results.[2] As a result, the NDP was responsive to what appeared to be a well-designed administrative framework put in place in the year preceding the 1969 election. The net effect of adopting Conservative administrative forms was to make Roblin and Schreyer appear similar in many respects.

The Schreyer machinery of government indeed contained echoes of the experiments of the sixties. Until 1973 (and to some extent afterwards), there was a dualism in the structure of the central executive; the planning and management committees would continue, along with their respective secretariats. (Planning and Priorities ceased to exist in 1973.) As before, development agencies harnessed business and labour officials in the pursuit of the economic development dream, but the partnership theme which had originally sparked them did not continue. Conservative-era senior officials continued to staff many central agency and deputy minister positions, only gradually to be complemented by New Democratic appointees.

Emulation was, of course, not the only factor behind the persistence of the structured cabinet. As this study's section on planning will show, CCF-NDP ideology was heavily steeped in the tradition of central planning. The New Democrats engaged in comprehensive planning, as the Conservatives had done, but it was more public-sector oriented and was accompanied by far more intensive sectoral planning efforts. Schreyer, a former university political science teacher, was a firm believer in social science rationalism, and consequently his central executive bore the marks of contemporary trends in management theory. As the regime matured, fiscal control became more of a concern, and this too came to affect the design of the machinery of government. Other factors affecting the design of decision making were intergovernmental affairs and the desire for political symbolism.

Emulation, ideology, and modern techniques were perhaps natural attributes of a young premier in a progressive era. Schreyer was, however, a paradox: a young achiever with a sense of tradition and rootedness. The unofficial slogan his party handlers chose for the youthful Ed Schreyer in the 1958 election in Brokenhead riding seems, in retrospect, to say it all: "better to have a kid who acts like a man than a man who acts like a kid."[3] He seemed to be the youngest at everything: at twenty-two, he was the youngest person then elected to the Manitoba Legislature; later he was the youngest premier in the history of Manitoba; and when chosen to be governor general in 1978, he was the youngest in Canadian history, at forty-three.[4] At first, Schreyer had a young man's awe of his ideological and political predecessors, enough not to stray from the accepted orthodoxy, but later he would place his own stamp on government.

Yet he never forgot his roots. Schreyer was born of second-generation Austro-German parents in Beausejour, Manitoba, a small town eighty kilometers to the north of Winnipeg, and grew up in an ethnically mixed environment. He was the first premier to be at home in the German and Ukranian languages, and he gradually built up his facility in French. These language skills allowed Schreyer to symbolize in his own person the "Manitoba mosaic." He was unusually sensitive to ethnicity in the construction of his cabinets: his first, for example, included two Ukrainians, a French Canadian, an Icelander, four Anglo-Saxons, and three Jews.[5]

Schreyer imbibed the social democratic ideology informally from family discussions about the Depression; joined the CCF at nineteen; and at twenty-one, served as the campaign manager for Jake Schultz, founder of the Manitoba Farmers Union (and later his father-in-law). As the first Catholic premier since Marc A. Girard in 1871, he had a special sensitivity to the educational costs borne by separate schools—enough to try, unsuccessfully, to extend public funding to them in the early 1970s. A surprisingly shy, laconic man, he often returned to Beausejour and the family farm to rediscover his roots and escape the bureaucratic grind. On the eve of his elevation to the position of governor general, a reporter would find him "still unsophisticated, still closely tied to his prairie roots; still more at home with Ukrainian farmers than with bureaucrats."[6]

Unsophisticated but not unaware, Schreyer had absorbed much by the time he occupied the premier's office. At twenty-two, he had four degrees (a B.A., B.Ped., B.Ed., and M.A.) and was teaching political science and international relations at the University of Manitoba. He was, according to his mother, "always studying the lives of Laurier and Mackenzie King."[7] By the time he became premier, Schreyer had become familiar with the broad corpus of western liberal and social democratic thought.[8]

An easy facility with social and economic theory enabled him to easily turn aside the accusations hurled at him about betraying social democracy after Manitoba adopted the Trudeau wage and price controls regime. Schreyer's intellectual bent led to some similarity of views and mutual respect between the two men, and Trudeau appointed him governor general (1979–84) and Canadian High Commissioner to Australia (1984–88). He developed a missionary zeal regarding policy about non-renewable energy, which enveloped his last years as premier, his time as the Queen's representative, and his life as a private citizen after his diplomatic sojourn.

CABINET STRUCTURE

Premier Schreyer's cabinet was institutionalized to the extent that it had multiple cabinet committees, collective decision making, and at first, an internal hierarchy. Initially the emulation factor determined the structure, which then became open to influences such as ideology, social science rationalism, and the desire for fiscal control.

Cabinet structure was largely dualist for the first four years of the Schreyer government and thereafter became relatively more complex. Schreyer at first accepted the Operation Productivity model of cabinet. Shortly after assuming office, he committed himself to it with only minor changes and found it basically workable until 1973. As in Weir's day, there were two main anchor committees, the Planning and Priorities Committee of Cabinet (PPCC) and the Management Committee of Cabinet (MCC), as well as *ad hoc* and more minor committees. The evolution of cabinet decision making resulted in the dissolution of the PPCC in 1973, its replacement by a committee of the whole Planning Committee of Cabinet, and the creation of specialized cabinet sub-committees for planning purposes. The initial cabinet comprised thirteen ministers; by 1977 the number had grown to seventeen. Schreyer did not look anywhere but to himself and to Manitoba sources in making cabinet structure decisions.

> I had no precedent to give me direction. I had some experience from academe. I didn't want to consult widely . . . to avoid the situation that many people would be annoyed if their advice were not taken. I went incommunicado for three days, matching personalities to portfolios . . .
>
> I didn't take a look at Saskatchewan [and the CCF-NDP cabinet machinery]; by the time we came to power there had not been an NDP government in Saskatchewan for five years. We were on our own for a few years [until the Blakeney New Democrats were elected in 1971].
>
> I was reasonably satisfied . . . with the Operation Productivity model . . . We did accept it on the basis that it could be adapted later if it proved ineffective.[9]

Emulation proved to be a determining factor for Schreyer's early cabinet. The legacy of the Conservative era was clear when the New Democrats introduced financial administration legislation which the previous government had not had time to pass. Two notable bills were the Financial Administration Act and the Provincial Auditor's Act, shepherded through the legislature the same summer as the election.

Finance Minister Saul Cherniack made only minor changes to the original Conservative bills, and the Acts received royal assent on September 19, 1968.

The Financial Administration Act[10] is germane to a review of cabinet structure because part of it dealt with the financial committee of cabinet. The Act replaced the venerable Treasury Department Act. Under it, references to the treasurer and the Treasury Board were replaced by general references to cabinet (the lieutenant-governor in council) and to "the member of the Executive Council charged by the Lieutenant Governor in Council with the administration of this Act." This formula was meant to allow for flexibility in cabinet's design of financial management. Contrary to the pattern of most administrations, there would be no automatic designation of the finance minister as the chief financial minister. S.83 and S.84 granted authority to exercise the Act's enumerated powers and to make regulations through the lieutenant-governor. In fact, the de facto locus of financial decision making became the Management Committee of Cabinet. The Department of Finance became the new name of the Department of the Provincial Treasurer.

The legacy of the Conservative era was also evident in 1970 when the New Democrats introduced Bill 40, the Executive Government Organization Act, which was given royal assent on June 1, 1970.[11] The Act repealed both the Executive Council Act and the Development Authority Act. Moving a second reading of Bill 40,[12] Schreyer said that its main effect would be "to formalize a number of practices already in use."[13]

So flexible was the Executive Government Organization Act that its provisions remain largely intact to the present day. It is filled with general phrases and enabling clauses which have allowed it to adapt to the needs of successive governments. The Act gave indirect legislative recognition to the existing planning and management cabinet committees, the latter of which had been functioning under the authority of the old Development Authority Act.[14] It was not explained why the government felt it necessary for cabinet committees to have a legislative base.

The McLeod Memoranda

With so many NDP members being neophytes in the details of administration, one of Schreyer's first concerns was to hold a series of orientation sessions on the machinery of government for cabinet and caucus.[15] The concern for self-education also impelled Finance Minister Cherniack to hire a special consultant to get a reading on the usefulness of the Conservative cabinet design. The consultant's report was largely in agreement with the basic Operation Productivity design but sounded warnings about a few of its elements. While the report did not affect the legislation on executive government (Schreyer said it was the same as Weir's) its contents were circulated among ministers and helped cabinet to make better use of the two main committees and secretariats.[16] The report demonstrates that social science rationalism came to influence many specific NDP government practices: the size of committees, the various roles to be played in planning, the formal links between planners and budgeters, and the bolstering of departmental managerial resources. It also shows the strong promotion that the notion of consolidating an institutionalized cabinet was getting right from the start.

Advice from a representative of Saskatchewan's institutionalized cabinet tradition was sought during the formative phase of the new government; not surprisingly, he recommended more institutionalization for Manitoba's cabinet. The consultant was Dr T. H. McLeod, an academic and ex-deputy treasurer of Saskatchewan, whom the Schreyer government would unsuccessfully court to fill a position in 1970.[17] In August and September of 1969, he submitted a series of lengthy memos to Cherniack, who passed them to other ministers.

Three main points about cabinet institutionalization were made in McLeod's memos. First, collective decision making must be protected, even though the size of the two main committees would hinder the development of the necessary uncommitted cabinet majority.[18] Second, a commitment to planning is important, since a government is judged by the quality of its policies; this implies a reorganization of the traditional cabinet to include a small planning committee served by a planning secretariat, which would review policy proposals within a decentralized planning system. Third, planning and budgeting should be complementary, implicitly along the Saskatchewan CCF model, including overlapping staff attendance at the main meetings of the two chief cabinet committees and budgeting conducted within the broad indicative views of the planning committee.

As well as enunciating a number of general themes, the McLeod memos made specific recommendations about the further institutionalization of the central executive and departments (see Table 6). A "strong Treasury" theme is evident in the suggestions that the minister of finance chair the MCC and that the fiscal and expenditure aspects of the budgetary process be considered a unity under the minister of finance. Table 6 lists the McLeod recommendations with comments about their subsequent implementation by the Schreyer government. The extent of follow-up shows the effect that the McLeod memoranda

TABLE 6

SPECIFIC RECOMMENDATIONS BY T. H. MCLEOD REGARDING MANITOBA
CABINET STRUCTURE AND SUBSEQUENT FOLLOW-UP BY THE SCHREYER
GOVERNMENT

Recommendation	Implemented	Comments
MEMO #1—STRUCTURE		
Cabinet committees should not be statutory entities.	no	S.7 of the Executive Government Authority Act created planning and management committees.
There should be small committee sizes to allow for an uncommitted majority in cabinet. Rotate ministers.	yes	Except for the Planning Committee of the whole cabinet, this suggestion was followed.
The premier should belong to the Planning and Priorities Committee.	yes	
Fiscal management should be under the finance minister.	no	Program auditors and effective control of the annual budget process were under the Management Committee minister, who was not finance minister for most of the Schreyer period (1972–77).
MEMO #2—PLANNING		
The premier should be active in planning and policy formation.	yes	Schreyer's own tendencies were towards activism.
There should be a senior planning officer in each department, who would maintain liaison with the PPCC.	yes	Phased in gradually.
There should be a research director position created in the Planning Secretariat, with about half-a-dozen staff.	yes	No specifically designated research director was appointed, but the Economic Analysis Group and RED Secretariat performed analogous functions.
A provincial research plan should be developed and submitted to the PPCC.	yes	Done in a micro sense.

139

TABLE 6 (continued)

Recommendation	Implemented	Comments
MEMO #3—MANAGEMENT COMMITTEE		
The MCC should be a committee of three, not half the cabinet.	yes	Followed literally at first; thereafter, the MCC was always a small percentage of the cabinet size.
The minister of finance should be chairman of the MCC and head of the MCC secretariat.	no	See memo #1, fourth point.
Fiscal and expenditure planning should not be considered separate functions, as under Operation Productivity.	no	
Government should regard the MCC Secretariat and Department of Finance as parallel structures, each reporting to the minister of finance through an associate deputy minister (in order to make the budget process a unity).	no	See memo #1, fourth point.
MEMO #4—DEPARTMENTAL ORGANIZATION		
The immediate priority was to recruit from outside the civil service for new talent.	yes	Done not immediately, but gradually.
The development and promotion of existing staff was only a secondary, fall-back priority.	yes	
Cabinet should create specialized bureaus of administrative services in the departments, comprising planning, personnel and training, budgeting, and operational services.	yes	Done not in name, but in effect.
MEMO #5—GENERAL		
The Manitoba Economic Consultative Board should be retained in some form.	yes	The MECB metamorphized into the Economic Development Advisory Board; functions broadened.

TABLE 6 (continued)

Recommendation	Implemented	Comments
The Development Authority Act should be repealed.	yes	Repealed in 1970 and superceded by The Executive Government Organization Act.
There should be planning and budgeting cross-memberships between the planning and the management groups.	yes	Such cross-memberships were installed at several points.
Cabinet should create machinery for evaluation at the departmental, MCC, and planning levels.	yes	Evaluation capacities were expanded at all levels of the government, but as part of the general improvement in management, not in isolation from other aspects.

MEMO #6—FEDERAL-PROVINCIAL RELATIONS SECRETARIAT

An intergovernmental (i.e. federal-provincial-municipal) body should be created, rather than a federal-provincial relations central body.	no	An Intergovernmental Relations Subcommittee of cabinet was established, but it dealt only with aboriginal matters.
The IGR Secretariat should be put under the PPCC.	no	The Federal-Provincial Relations and Research Division continued in the Finance Department.
The premier should be responsible for the IGR Secretariat placed in the ECO.	yes	

Source: T. H. McLeod, "Planning Organization," memoranda, September 12, 1969; text.

(and social science rationalism) had on the mind-set of the premier and the rest of cabinet.

THE FIRST PHASE OF SCHREYER CABINET DEVELOPMENT

By the end of his first term in 1973, Premier Schreyer had clearly placed his own stamp on the structure of the Manitoba cabinet. There now existed not only the Planning and Priorities Committee and the Management Committee but also what Schreyer called "cluster committees": the Health, Education, and Social Policy Committee; the

Urban Affairs Committee; and an informal Churchill Forest Industries (CFI) Committee. The "decongestion factor"—the wish to free the time of the premier and cabinet—had clearly weighed on the premier's mind in creating the cluster committees:

> Another innovation was that we set up in Manitoba, almost in lock step with Ontario (but not in consultation with it) "cluster groups" for policy analysis purposes in Cabinet. These were Cabinet Committees that grouped together ministers from departments performing similar functions—like Health, Education and Social Policy, Resources and Economic Development . . .
>
> I like to think that the idea came from myself; the idea recommended itself. It was time-saving for Ministers. Time was a seemingly intractable problem. Deputy Ministers who had an affiliation of interest would also be able to communicate more easily and to offer better advice [to Ministers].
>
> It did work fairly well. It did not save some time for certain Ministers, but it did save time overall for Cabinet and for the Premier. And quite candidly, in Cabinet when you have one half competent ministers and one half uncertain, tentative, unsure of foot, it relieves some anxiety from the Premier to have submissions dealt with by a policy cluster of ministers. It is important to ensure that the mix is such that you do not have all the uncertain ministers in one group and all the experienced and aggressive ministers in another one.[19]

The Planning and Priorities Committee was re-created by Order in Council 932/70 on September 17, 1970. In a memorandum Schreyer outlined differences between the MDA and PPCC concepts, at the same time implicitly admitting that emulation was the original factor in his design of cabinet:

> The Planning and Priorities Committee of Cabinet is the Manitoba Development Authority renamed. The differences are that the Manitoba Development Authority is under the Chairmanship of the first Minister whereas under the Planning and Priorities Committee of Cabinet concept the first Minister is neither the Chairman nor a member of the Planning Committee. Another difference is that the PPCC concept calls for a somewhat broader approach to planning and includes a review and priority establishment of all major programs of government. The Manitoba Development Corporation did not review all programs and tended to

concentrate on economic development programs with lesser emphasis on social development programs.[20]

The PPCC concept was continued under Schreyer until 1973. The mandate in the 1970 Order in Council, as in the legislation, was "to study and advise on the planning of government programs and projects and their relative priorities." As Tommy McLeod had suggested, the PPCC was restricted to five ministers. Schreyer—following recommendations by Operation Productivity, by McLeod, and finally by a cabinet seminar held November 21–22, 1969—became chairman. Sidney Green, minister of mines and resources, was made vice-chairman.

The PPCC became extremely active in the first four years of the Schreyer era. It was here that most of the innovative programs of the government were first discussed at the cabinet level. The PPCC displayed a keen interest in northern development and in manpower and education policy, recommending programs that often straddled the latter two. These programs were essentially aimed at serving the dispossessed of Manitoba society. In its four-year life, the PPCC also covered items dealing with housing policy, economic development, foreign ownership, land banking, communications policy, public infrastructure at Churchill and Leaf Rapids, student aid, consumer protection, fisheries, natural resource policy, and related matters. The PPCC helped to create and gave policy guidance to a number of central/departmental working groups. It reviewed the various chapters prepared for the Guidelines exercise discussed later in this chapter. It was clearly the intellectual dynamo of the early Schreyer government and was its cutting edge of innovation.

As for the Management Committee of Cabinet, its actual operation differed in several respects from the role that had been suggested for it by Operation Productivity. These aspects shall be discussed later in this study. For the moment it is sufficient to point out that one departure from Operation Productivity, and indeed from McLeod's advice, involved the chairmanship of the Management Committee. Previous to the 1969 election, the provincial treasurer had been the Chairman of the Management Committee. This had been standard practice among the provinces and had been an implicit assumption in the productivity report. Yet throughout the Schreyer era, two of the three Manitoba finance ministers (Schreyer and Saul Miller) did not head the Management Committee. Finance Minister Saul Cherniack did indeed head it from 1970 to 1972 (taking over from Youth and Education Minister Saul Miller, who had chaired it briefly in the Fall of 1969), but even then he did not devote much time to the job, since he was involved in time-consuming Unicity negotiations. Most of the de facto chairmanship duties fell to A. R. (Russ) Paulley, who was vice-chairman from 1970 to 1972. Ben Hanuschak, minister of education, was chairman from 1972 to 1975, and Education Minister Ian Turnbull chaired from 1975 to 1977.

As one Manitoba NDP finance minister put it, "NDP finance ministers were revenue-raisers only," and at the outset "there was a fair amount of antagonism [in the Finance Department] . . . Finance was bitter over the loss of control."[21] Finance's traditional role as keeper of the purse was muted at the cabinet table. So, in essence, the tradition of the strong treasury was lost to Manitoba for the duration. The Finance Department did not stage-manage expenditure planning, nor did the finance minister usually chair the primary financial committee of cabinet.

Emulation was also at work in the establishment of duties for the Management Committee. Its functions were the same ones Operation Productivity had foreseen a few years before. They included budget and estimates preparation, personnel administration, management advisory services, and operation of the computer centre.

The Cabinet Committee on Urban Affairs, later renamed the Housing and Urban Development (HUD) Subcommittee, originated due to the necessity for policy coherence vis-à-vis local government. The main tasks of the Urban Affairs Committee and its successor were to initiate reviews of city government in Winnipeg, to recommend relevant policy, and to monitor the attendant changes. The stages leading to the creation of the committee are set out in Meyer Brownstone and T. J. Plunkett's exhaustive and masterful study, *Metropolitan Winnipeg*.[22] In June 1970 cabinet established a Cabinet Committee on Urban Affairs to conduct a promised policy review of Winnipeg's two-tier metropolitan government. It prepared a White Paper incorporating cabinet's consensus about the amalgamation of area municipalities and citizen participation. This was released on December 23, 1970 and served as a basis for extensive public hearings. Legislation was passed on June 24, 1971, and the Unicity, as it was colloquially known, came into being on January 1, 1972.[23] The need for coherence in provincial-municipal relations continued to shape cabinet committee development.[24] The HUD Subcommittee was to continue the work of the Urban Affairs Committee implied in the White Paper.[25]

Another informal committee that was formed early in the Schreyer years was the Churchill Forest Industries (CFI) Committee. Cabinet's desire for financial control was the factor that led Schreyer to create this committee, which consisted of the premier and the ministers of Finance, Industry and Commerce, Resources, and on certain occasions, the attorney general.[26] The CFI Committee was formed after the new NDP government realized that it had not been given clear information by Rex Grose regarding the costs of an integrated forestry complex at The Pas, Manitoba. Articles by Philip Mathias in the *Financial Post*[27] revealed that the cost estimate for The Pas Forestry Complex had risen seventy per cent to $135 million. In a showdown on March 22, 1970, Rex Grose was unable to provide the NDP cabinet with a satisfactory explanation for this increase, he resigned the next day.[28] The NDP had assumed that regular MDF controls were still applicable to The Pas Complex loans, when in fact Grose had approved the loosening of them soon after the NDP were elected.[29] From August 1, 1969 to May 21, 1970, loan payments of $59,707,897 were made by the MDF to the Kasser Companies (of which $24,689,600 ended up in Swiss bank accounts).[30] Cabinet ordered a special audit by the provincial auditor as well as a special engineering audit of the companies by Stothert Engineering Ltd. of Vancouver. Stothert was unable to get technical information to which the MDF was entitled.[31]

It was around this time that Cabinet became more directly involved in the supervision of the complex. An informal cabinet committee removed effective control of the CFI project from its nominal board of directors.[32] As a result of the failure of the private companies to honour their obligations, the Province deemed it necessary to place The Pas complex under receivership in January of 1971. The complex was turned into a provincial Crown corporation called Manitoba Forestry Resources Limited (MANFOR) in October of 1973. (Both the Pawley and Filmon governments sought to privatize MANFOR in the late eighties. In March of 1989 it was sold to Repap Enterprises Corp. Inc. of Montreal.)

The last of the early cabinet committees formed under Schreyer was the Health, Education, and Social Policy (HESP) Committee. HESP was a formal cabinet committee created by Order in Council 1146/71 on October 27, 1971. It was composed of three members under the chairmanship of Saul Miller; Jay Kaufman became the secretary to HESP in October 1971. HESP also originated as a financial control measure; it was meant to make more effective use of resources for the large projects foreseen in the social policy field.[33] Looking back in 1988, Schreyer noted that "I was of course concerned about cost containment. Some ministers if left alone have a tendency to jack up expenditures. Others do not. I had some ministers like this [the latter], but not enough. I was hoping to get early preliminary help from HESP [in cost containment]."[34]

Two early policy reviews associated with HESP were the White Paper on Health Policy and the Post Secondary Review. The former document, released in July 1972,[35] was the product of a departmental working group answering to HESP. Appropriately, it had been engendered by alarming increases in health costs and the unequal distribution of health benefits.[36] The principal financial control innovation suggested by the White Paper was the installation of district health systems.[37] The Task Force on Post-Secondary Education was established by cabinet in February of 1972, and its report was published in November of the following year.[38] Its principal recommendations, which included making universities, colleges, and non-institutional adult education part of a single post-secondary system, were vetted by HESP in 1974 and 1975.

The Second Phase of Schreyer Cabinet Development

Further institutionalization came with the re-election of the Schreyer government on June 28, 1973. The second phase of Manitoba's cabinet structure development lasted from 1973 until electoral defeat in October of 1977. Cabinet became somewhat more complex in its structure and, in planning matters, more collegial and less hierarchical. Order in Council 938/73 of September 5, 1973 dismantled the PPCC and provided that all major policy and planning matters be dealt with by the entire cabinet in Cabinet Planning Sessions. Other orders in council created a new subcommittee on Economic and Resource Development (later called the RED subcommittee for short) and a new subcommittee on Health, Education, and Social Policy.

Premier Schreyer enunciated the new cabinet procedures to ministers, deputies, and cabinet committee secretaries on September 6, 1973. Major policy questions would continue to be referred from the major subcommittees to cabinet. Regular cabinet meetings would ordinarily consist of morning and afternoon sessions, with the morning sessions being devoted to "legal instruments" and the afternoon sessions set aside for planning and policy deliberations. In effect, the afternoon sessions would become a planning cabinet with committee-of-the-whole meetings at which submissions would be received from the cabinet policy subcommittees, the Management Committee, and the departments.[39]

The reasons for the changes were interwoven but essentially reflected cabinet's desire to extend the collective aspects of cabinet political control. Cabinet pressure was one reason; some disaffected ministers were suggesting that every minister should be a part of the planning process. Schreyer was also becoming more sensitive to the dynamics of ministerial peer relationships and sought to avoid the implication that certain members were "junior ministers" because they

146

had not been part of the Planning and Priorities Committee.[40] Both Schreyer and Green thought that it was better to link ministers who were working on similar subjects.[41] The changes were premeditated, having been contemplated at least since December 1971.[42]

The Cabinet Planning Committee was thus a broad planning mechanism which shared the planning function with other committees. It considered economic and social development plans, monitored achievements relative to objectives, set the public policy research agenda, and dealt with legislative proposals and expenditure estimates.

The HESP Subcommittee mandate did not change appreciably; the expenditure containment motivation did not appear to be a driving force. The RED Subcommittee's work reflected the impact of governmental relations. It was active in negotiating and vetting agreements between Manitoba and the federal Department of Regional Economic Expansion (DREE), especially the DREE General Development Agreement and its various subagreements, such as the Manitoba Northlands Agreement and the Manitoba-Canada ARDA agreement. The two subcommittees became three in 1976 when cabinet created the Manpower and Employment Cabinet Subcommittee (MECS), effective December 1, 1976. It had actually existed informally for a few years. The work of the MECS would also reflect the importance of intergovernmental relations, due to the nature of labour market policy making in Canada.

Another full committee came into being in December 1975 when an Order in Council created the Provincial Land Use Committee (PLUC). It owed its existence to provisions in the new Planning Act of 1975. A deputy minister-level committee called the Interdepartmental Planning Board (IDPB) existed by virtue of the Act to make recommendations to the PLUC. Unlike the pattern for other cabinet committees, the staff support for PLUC/IDPB was situated in a line department, Municipal Affairs. This basic arrangement would last far beyond the Schreyer government.

Informal subcommittees of cabinet continued or were created anew; most reflected the need for policy coherence in the intergovernmental realm. HUD became involved in the study of joint transportation projects with the City of Winnipeg and in 1977 participated in the Development Plan Review process that had been mandated by the new City of Winnipeg Act. The Provincial Employment and Winter Works Subcommittee of Cabinet coordinated the often bewildering array of job creation projects labelled by an assortment of acronyms. As well, an Intergovernmental Relations Subcommittee of Cabinet was created to plan aboriginal policy in concert with aboriginal groups.

The contrast in the degree of cabinet institutionalization between the Roblin-Weir and Schreyer eras was, in short, striking. Roblin had two main committees in cabinet; Schreyer had more than half a dozen. Roblin's planning was done by one committee, whereas Schreyer's was done by full cabinet as well as by a number of committees and focused on more than narrow economic planning.

CENTRAL AGENCIES

Another important element in the institutionalization of cabinet under Schreyer was the intensive build-up of central agency staff. The Planning Secretariat and Management Secretariat—in essence, two central agencies within another central agency (the ECO)—grew quite dramatically and assumed aggressive roles in furthering the wills of both premier and cabinet. The main central department, Finance, wielded some influence due to the status of personalities involved, but was basically eclipsed for the Schreyer period.

Some clarification is necessary regarding the structure of the Executive Council Office (ECO). Technically, the ECO consisted of three parts: the Premier's Office, the Planning Secretariat of Cabinet, and the Management Secretariat of Cabinet. By the end of the Schreyer years, the Premier's Office numbered only a few professionals; the Planning Secretariat numbered about forty; and the Management Secretariat, the largest by far, comprised about eighty people (or double this number before its Computer Centre component was removed).

The Premier's Office housed the clerk of the executive council and the premier's executive assistants. The clerk was Derek Bedson, continuing in this role from the Roblin-Weir years. In a way, his continuation as institutionalized clerk was a metaphor for what was happening in the broader administrative picture, with Roblin patterns being repeated by Schreyer. Bedson attended the morning sessions of cabinet that were devoted to legal instruments, whereas the planning secretary attended the afternoon planning sessions. There were two executive assistants who, in a nascent PMO function, performed various political tasks for Schreyer.

An affinity for comprehensive planning is often associated with institutionalized cabinets. The Planning Secretariat was Schreyer's major bureaucratic planning mechanism; significantly, it engaged in both micro (sectoral) and macro (comprehensive) planning. As well, it was something of a high-powered personnel agency for Schreyer. The basic unwritten but understood strategy was for the secretariat to hire highly qualified personnel, let them plan and dream, and then send them to departments to make the dreams operational. This is the reason why Schreyer's planning officials had such short durations in office in the seventies.

148

There were four planning secretaries in the Schreyer era, and they all stengthened cabinet's capacity for central planning. Robert A. Wallace was the first secretary to the PPCC under Schreyer. Wallace, an ex-Agriculture deputy, had held the same position under Walter Weir since June 1968 and was to remain until November 1970. Schreyer had a distaste for firing personnel of the former government. Wallace, for example, was kept on when a more deeply partisan premier might have routinely dismissed him; he was later given a lateral transfer at the deputy level. Nevertheless, it was during his tenure that the secretariat took on new personnel with distinctive NDP backgrounds: Lionel Orlikow (education), Saul Schubert (housing), and Wilson Parasiuk (later to be secretary himself).

The first clearly NDP appointee to head the Planning Secretariat was a forty-eight-year-old Cherniack recruit, J. C. (Jack) Weldon, head of the McGill University Economics Department.[43] Weldon was recruited by Cherniack upon consultation with the premier. He was a very attractive candidate because of his reputation as an intellectual god-father of the New Democratic Party,[44] as an advocate of social demo-cratic planning,[45] and as a solid academic. A teacher at McGill since 1949, he had been the chair in Economics since it was created as a separate department. He was a long-time economic advisor to the non-operating railway unions and had a solid reputation as a friend of labour.

For his part, Weldon must have found the prospect of a stint in the halls of power to be an intriguing one. The concept of political will as fundamental to the realization of the twin goals of full employment and redistribution of income pervaded his economic writing.[46] Now he had the opportunity to help stiffen the resolve of specific actors. He had, however, specified from the beginning that his stint with the Manitoba government was a temporary one and that he would soon return to his teaching duties. Accordingly, his period as planning secretary lasted from November 1970 to September 1972.

Weldon built the basic planning structure of the early NDP govern-ment. It consisted of a short- and long-range planning orientation, the use of policy reviews, the installation of working groups, and the division of the secretariat into two parts. Weldon's planning orientation and sense of mission involved long-term policy planning and the discovery—no surprise this—of the government's will.[47] Departmental policy reviews began in the Spring of 1971. They were meant to be a continuously revolving process of analyzing various departments' pol-icies far enough ahead of time that expenditure estimates could be prepared in light of cabinet policy guidelines. The policy review process focused on what departments did, what they should do, and what issues needed clarification. The secretariat was the lead agency in charge of the analytical side of the reviews. The PPCC scheduled half-a-dozen reviews for 1971–72, most of them involving smaller (and easier-to-do) departments.

Planning Secretariat working groups were another Weldon contribution. As Ernie Petrich explained, "The notion is that as policy issues appear . . . the Planning Secretariat takes on an *entrepreneurial* role in organizing research and planning on the issues in question, usually interdepartmental in character. The groups are small so that they are indeed working groups. They are gathered from within the system from wherever expertise is available. They usually have a Secretariat Member, but are not dominated by the Secretariat, and more often than not have a line-department chairman. They report through the PPCC mechanism. They have a limited life, being disbanded when their report has been dealt with by PPCC."[48]

There were seven such early interdepartmental working groups by 1971: Northern, Manpower, Employment, Urban Affairs, Energy, Housing, and Tourism and Recreation. The Northern Working Group was both a support group for the all-party Northern Task Force of the Legislative Assembly and an early planning mechanism used by the PPCC.[49] One working group in particular—on Manpower—provided recommendations which were later used in the further restructuring of cabinet and its secretariat.[50] Soon after its report, cabinet created the informal Manpower and Employment Cabinet Subcommittee, which achieved formal status in 1976.

The last element of the Weldon planning structure was the division of the Planning Secretariat into two bodies, the Planning Secretariat and the Continuing Programs Secretariat. The latter was a way of gingerly separating off the traditional planners of the old regime from the activist social democratic planners of the new one. For a year or so Continuing Programs (the old regime planners) managed the negotiations with Ottawa on DREE programs and The Pas Special Area agreement, while the Planning Secretariat geared up for the major macro-planning exercise, *Guidelines for the Seventies*. The secretariat could now also concentrate on setting guidelines for innovative programming, such as the provincial (rather than private) development of the Leaf Rapids townsite to service Sherritt Gordon's Ruttan Lake mining project.[51] In September 1972 the PPCC decided to recommend the transfer of the Continuing Programs Secretariat to appropriate departments such as Agriculture, Finance, and Industry and Commerce. It hoped by this to achieve economies and to establish clearer lines of authority.[52]

Marc Eliesen was the next planning secretary. A mixture of political strategist and government technocrat, he offered a useful combination of skills in the early Schreyer years. As an economist, Eliesen had served with the federal departments of Finance and Industry; from 1968 to 1971 he was the federal NDP director of research. His tenure was on the short side (September 1972 to June 1974) largely because he was lured away early by Premier Barrett of British Columbia to become planning advisor to cabinet in Victoria. (It was to be an apparently easy and personable shift; four months later a *Globe and Mail* article had him dancing an impromptu hora with his new boss in a Chinese restaurant while the other attendees at the Western Premiers' Conference looked on.)[53] Some interviewees remember him as largely a political advisor, but it was Eliesen who carried through to completion one of Weldon's original projects, the *Guidelines for the Seventies* comprehensive planning exercise.[54]

The last Schreyer planning secretary was Wilson D. (Willie) Parasiuk. Parasiuk exemplified the Manitoba social democratic experience. He was born in Stenen, Saskatchewan, and moved with his family at the age of five to Transcona, a working-class suburb of Winnipeg. The family ran a grain farm while the father supplemented its income by working on the railroad. Education was valued, so the family supplemented the services of the local one-room schoolhouse with a series of correspondence courses. The persistence paid off; Parasiuk became the Manitoba Rhodes Scholar in 1966. He came back two years later with a special degree in sociology and, based on his British experiences, a deeper concern about the injuries of class.

In 1970 he left a development planning position in the Department of Regional Economic Expansion for the more activist Schreyer government. In rapid succession, he served as a town planner, assistant secretary to the Planning and Priorities Committee of Cabinet, and secretary to the Economic and Resource Development Subcommittee before assuming the post of planning secretary of cabinet. A one-time member of the Oxford University hockey team delegation to the U.S.S.R. and an old-timers' hockey regular, he was regarded as a team player in politics, too.[55] He capped off a career in the public service by serving as the minister of energy and mines in the Pawley government. Many considered him a potential leader for the provincial NDP, but he turned aside such suggestions.

During Parasiuk's tenure the Planning Secretariat expanded to forty individuals (and well over that during the Northern Plan exercise of 1975–76). It extended its influence widely throughout the civil service by the expanded use of working groups and by the sheer force of

151

expertise of its more prominent members. Parasiuk quit the secretariat in 1977 in a successful bid for the Transcona seat, leaving Senior Planning Analyst Michael Decter as acting secretary.

The Management Committee Secretariat, the other central agency, dwarfed the Planning Secretariat with its large number of employees. Part of the explanation for its size was that the Management Secretariat performed functions that in other provinces would have been performed by a Civil Service Commission: personnel administration, staff relations, and development and training.

There were a number of clashes between MCC and PPCC senior personnel in the early years, despite McLeod's warnings that their relative jurisdictions should be clearly marked. In fact, the possibility of a clear delineation was a doubtful proposition in many areas. Premier Schreyer saw some utility in what he called the "creative tension" between the two secretariats: "I saw there was some [hostility] at first, but it was a logical way to proceed, and as long as the rivalry was carried out with civility, it was useful . . . It was a kind of checks and balances situation, but not to the extent of duplication of effort"[56] If one secretariat had a better idea, the premier would take it. (In this respect, Premier Schreyer reminds one of U.S. President Franklin Roosevelt, who was famous for promoting what he saw as constructive rivalry between federal agencies.)[57]

Some tension remained between the two secretariats for the duration of the NDP administration. The final cabinet review of estimates would typically involve officials of the PPCC secretariat (later the Planning Secretariat) arguing for expansion of programs, and MCC program auditors suggesting cutbacks or no growth. In practice, this resulted in a high degree of competitiveness in the planning subcommittees of cabinet with regard to program approval. The intermingling probably staved off challenges on a more macro-political level. McLeod's recommendation to have planning and management staff sit on counterpart cabinet committees was, however, followed.

PLANNING TRADITIONS IN THE SCHREYER GOVERNMENT

Schreyer and the NDP cabinet inherited two different planning traditions and tried, somewhat unsuccessfully, to accommodate both of them. On the one hand, they took possession of a government which had grown accustomed to the transitional mode of planning. This, it will be recalled, featured a blend of unaided and institutionalized cabinet planning characteristics. The major unaided characteristic involved planning "at one remove" by two classes of outsiders, namely, development agencies with private-sector-dominated boards or else temporary planning structures consisting largely of private-sector representatives. The planning was at one remove because cabinet used indirect links between it and the outside groups. Either the premier or cabinet officials cross-appointed to the boards of the outside groups provided the linkage. The object of the planning was to promote desirable economic development activities in both the public and private sectors. The major institutionalized aspect of the transitional mode involved the use of both project and comprehensive planning exercises.

On the other hand, there was a strong tradition of comprehensive central planning that had pervaded CCF-NDP ideology for more than a third of a century. The "Regina Manifesto" closed with a call for a full program of socialized planning, and the Douglas government in Saskatchewan made planning a high-profile activity. Planning was, as Wiseman has said, the "cornerstone of the CCF's thinking."[58] Because of the Saskatchewan example and that of federal postwar Keynesianism, social democrats began to perceive planning as a job mainly for institutionalized cabinets and governmental functionaries rather than for some quasi-independent planning commission, as the League for Social Reconstruction had first perceived it.[59]

If the machinery of government inherited by the Manitoba New Democrats had not already included a mechanism for central planning, it would thus have been necessary to invent it. As it was, the nascent institutionalized cabinet planning mode of 1968 to 1969, with its collegial cabinet involvement and some central agency analysis, fit neatly with the mind-set of New Democratic decision makers.

Time would prove the central planning tradition to be the strongest. The planning activities that received the highest profile in the Schreyer government were comprehensive central plans such as *Guidelines for the Seventies* (1973) and *The Northern Plan* (1976). The Schreyer brand of planning tilted heavily towards public-sector-oriented central planning. In a way, this tendency was a matter of practical necessity. The private sector was too wary of the so-called socialist tendencies of the government to allow itself to be brought into a really intimate partnership with it.[60] Premier Schreyer even felt compelled to become the initial NDP industry and commerce minister to allay widely felt business fears of radicalism in cabinet. The government itself found private sector groups uneven in their capacity to dialogue: Schreyer has said that the NDP cabinet found the Manitoba branch of the Canadian Manufacturers' Association realistic to deal with, but the Manitoba Chambers of Commerce were just the opposite.[61]

Still, the government's familiarity with the transitional mode resulted in some carry-over between the Roblin-Weir and Schreyer years. Schreyer continued to use quasi-central agencies (development agencies) for planning, coordination, and communication purposes. As before, the boards of these agencies were dominated by personnel from the private sector who were expected to serve public purposes. There were two development agencies, the Economic Development Advisory Board (EDAB) and the Manitoba Development Corporation (MDC).

The MDC was the Manitoba Development Fund as reconstituted by the NDP government. Cabinet appeared uncertain about how close a relationship it wanted with the MDC. Originally it signalled an interest in using the MDC as a development planning tool which would feature the cabinet and responsible minister interacting with the MDC under Part II of The Development Corporation Act. Consideration was even given to making a cabinet minister chairman of the MDC in order to enhance the government's policy control of the corporation, but this change never took place. Cabinet reconsidered getting too close to a politically dangerous entity, and the MDC Board seemed increasingly to make its own way as far as policy making went.

The EDAB was an NDP version[62] of the Manitoba Economic Consultative Board (MECB) of Roblin's day. It was created by Order in Council 1461/69 on November 19, 1969. Composed mostly of businessmen, it was chaired by Baldur Kristjanson.[63] An intended emphasis of the Board was to assess the annual operations of the MDF (later the MDC) and, if requested by cabinet, its individual loans. Its founding Order in Council also called upon the EDAB to recommend to a legislative committee how best to stimulate and coordinate public and private economic development activities and to recommend priorities in provincial development plans.[64] This made the EDAB an adjunct planning body, at least in theory.

In practice, the EDAB was energetic but not terribly effective. Premier Schreyer found some utility in the Board,[65] but felt that its effectiveness was hindered by the generally poor health of Kristjanson.[66] In 1975 Kristjanson was replaced by Len Remis, who had been the deputy in Industry and Commerce from 1970 to 1975. A long-time Board member has pointed out, however, that the EDAB was hindered by a number of flaws: it never had much in the way of real independence and personnel resources; matters referred to it were generally inconsequential; the Planning Secretariat was resentful of it as an outside body and only shared information if ordered by a minister; and it was said to be generally viewed as a public relations gesture, a way of selling the government to the private sector.[67] Of course, the EDAB's greatest flaw was that it represented a former government's transitional planning mode, and it co-existed with a much stronger central planning style.

Central Planning

CCF-NDP ideology made it inevitable that central planning would be a centrepoint of the Schreyer government. Our review of Schreyer's cabinet structure and central agencies has already made allusions to several planning ventures undertaken by the NDP government. The most notable, of course, were the comprehensive plans of the early and late seventies called *Guidelines for the Seventies* and *The Northern Plan*. Consultants' plans were also used in order to guage public response to planning ideas. With its emphasis on collegiality and comprehensiveness, Schreyer's framework was the very model of institutionalized planning, McAllister's comments about the premier's lack of economic planning,[68] regional planning,[69] and Planning Secretariat success[70] notwithstanding.

One planning technique used by the Schreyer government involved commissioning a well-known consultant to make an independent report in an area where the cabinet intended to act. Whether by design or by happenstance, the report would typically recommend reforms from which the government could move back and thus appear to be moderate rather than radical.[71] The irony was that often the government then moved in a fairly radical direction regardless. This was plainly the case with the reforms that followed on the heels of the more radical Kierans Report on resource policy[72] and the Barber Report on welfare policy.[73]

The most important comprehensive planning initiative under Schreyer was *Guidelines for the Seventies* (1973). Sidney Green has stated that the *Guidelines* exercise stemmed from an ideological attraction to central planning: "Planning was part of our theory . . . it is a part of socialist rhetoric . . . Some people thought macro-planning, the setting of objectives, was important. It was also important to measure a government by its ability to measure up to a portion of these objectives. It was definitely a feature of the ideological commitment of several people like Evans, Cherniack, Gonick and myself. Schreyer would have less tendency toward macro-planning, and I say this as a compliment, because he was more realistic than the rest of us . . . We talked about having a central plan all the years we were out of power; we talked about it from day one, 1969."[74]

Schreyer has admitted that he was initially reticent about the *Guidelines* effort: "I thought that any attempt to publish a plan would be interpreted as 'master-planning,' a definitive blueprint for the future, and would be a political problem for me. I did not consider it a waste of time, but I thought it would create a level of expectations [that may or may not have been met]."[75] Nevertheless, the premier allowed himself to be talked into the exercise.

In retrospect, Schreyer has regarded the episode a good example of the premier's role in modern provincial cabinets: "Contrary to public opinion, a premier cannot always have his own way in terms of causing things to be done. A premier can however almost always stall things or sideline things he doesn't want to see happen. . . The power of the office lends itself to preventing [negative] things to be done . . . more than causing good things to be done. This is of course in the absence of colleagues' consensus and providing constitutional jurisdiction exists [for the action]."[76]

Guidelines for the Seventies[77] was a three-volume comprehensive planning framework intended to present the public with alternative policy principles and objectives for consideration. Volume three of the plan, entitled *Regional Perspectives*, outlined proposals for urban, rural, and northern Manitoba. For urban Manitoba, the document suggested provincial assumption of certain responsibilities, provision of new sources of municipal taxation, increased land banking, and "critical repair" in housing policy. For rural Manitoba, it proposed land lease options to allow a focus on production resources, use of the Manitoba Development Corporation to promote industrial development through small loans, organization of district health boards to allocate global budgets and equalize health resources in the province, and decentralization of government administration and planning. For northern Manitoba, it recommended greater public involvement in mineral exploration and development, a manpower policy based on dual labour market analysis, and community-oriented economic activity such as cooperatives and municipal development corporations.

The *Guidelines* plan was regional, economic, and social in its emphasis. It was never accepted *in toto*, but many of its recommendations were ultimately put into effect. This was largely because they amounted to extrapolations of what was already being planned or put in effect by various ministers. McAllister is correct in his assertion that NDP planning was mainly directed to public sector objects.[78] One has to search hard in *Guidelines* to find mention of the private sector. This, of course, brings the Schreyer planning style into marked contrast with that of Roblin and Weir.

Planning and Budgeting

For all its elaborate structure, the Schreyer cabinet deviated from the standard institutionalized cabinet model in its lack of attention to a planning-budgeting nexus, as well as in its reliance on the premier as

156

the central actor in the annual budget process. However, the role of the Management Committee on a day-to-day basis brought back some of the collective aspects to financial decision making.

Planning and budgeting wings of the Executive Council Office were somewhat competitive for much of the Schreyer era. Thereafter, they came to occupy separate universes, thus obviating the possibility of a meaningful planning-budgeting nexus. Careless has captured the sense of hostility between the governr ent's planning and budgeting groups at the beginning of the seventies

> The Cabinet committees and secretariats took considerable time to work out their respective jurisdictions; they tended to clash in their policy, framework and priority directives to departments. Continuing difficulties centred about a stalemate between the Management Committee (Treasury Board) and the Priorities and Planning Committee [sic] whereby the Treasury Board's concern with departmental conformity to the PPBS format prevented the flow of funds to departments, although the Priorities and Planning Committee had previously authorized the priority expenditure and departmental program. In short, by attempting to implement PPBS in one sweep the Treasury Board effectively set its own priorities by delaying funds, although, strictly speaking, it was supposed to perform only a positive management service to departments empowered to carry out authorized development responsibilities.[79]

The struggle between the PPCC and MCC over the PPBS format went on for two years. In January 1970 the PPCC noted with unease the existence of possible duplication and agreed that the roles and functions of both committees should be clarified in regard to PPBS.[80] Such was not to be the case, however. Marc Eliesen, who assumed the role of cabinet planning secretary after J. C. Weldon, has explained why not: "It was partly strategy. MCC politicians and officials would appear at PPCC or Cabinet and then attempt to countermand the decision at the Management [MCC] level if they didn't like it. They used the program budgeting to stall departmental plans they were opposed to. It was also a matter of personalities. MCC Secretariat contained officials from the previous administration . . . like Gordon Holland . . . and there was a bit of friction. Finally we asked the Premier to intervene in 1972 and succeeded in getting the [program budgeting] function away from MCC.[81] Schreyer has described the PPBS dispute as "rivalry expressing itself in esoteric language."[82]

The irony of the victory was that, once it won, the PPCC and its secretariat did comparatively little program budgeting, thus losing a remaining opportunity to solidify a planning-budgeting nexus. One reason was that many of the prerequisites for program budgeting were not in place. One such measure was accurate and meaningful budget and program forecasting. For forecasting to be meaningful, for it to be something other than a mere mechanical extension of existing trends, departments had to have clear indications of government goals. The goals, however, were still in the process of being defined. Another reason was that the PPCC Secretariat was undergoing a change in direction. By 1972–73 it saw its major function as the enunciation of global plans, which were not closely tied to the budgeting process.

A last reason for the decreased emphasis on PPBS was the character of the premier. Originally he had been convinced of the need to reorient expenditures in order to give cabinet more political control. To this effect, the departmental estimates information forms were redesigned to highlight program history, objectives, and descriptions; interrelationships with other programs; geographic/regional impacts; and indicators to measure program effectiveness. Financial summary data would follow this more narrative information. In spite of this plethora of information, over time Premier Schreyer came to prefer concentrating on MCC secretariat analyses of incremental increases to program budgets, especially in his second term (1973–77), when he perceived the state of the economy to be worsening.[83]

By the end of the Schreyer era, MCC financial analyses and restraint exercises had become the focus of attention, rather than the departmental planning information. Departments, not surprisingly, came to devote only token attention to supplying this planning information. PPBS remained mainly as a vestigial element, for the forms were still designed in the PPBS format. (Zero-base budgeting assumptions, if not methodology, were adopted for the 1976–77 expenditure budget process, but the premier was not intimately involved with this rather ephemeral exercise.)[84]

Institutionalized cabinets usually feature collective budgeting, but the premier came to dominate the annual estimates preparation. Schreyer began to absorb the expenditure budget function himself because he could not interest other cabinet members in accepting it. Cabinet review of estimates would begin with several ministers in attendance but would dwindle down to only a few—indeed, often to the premier alone—as the hours grew long. Schreyer saw himself as a protector of the integrity of financial control:

I found it [the estimates process] to be the single most time-consuming matter of the year. The matter did not lend itself to sharing with other ministers. Ministers have a certain tendency to log-rolling: "I won't question your estimates if you won't question mine . . . " But I thought the estimates process had to be a serious one because of [the danger of] an exponential growth of personnel and of level of expenditure . . .

One reason the [Lyon] Conservatives were not able to bring a "hiccup" or downward change in Manitoba expenditures is that it [the estimates] is something I personally slaved over, line by line, item by item. This is unorthodox, that the Premier of a province should quibble with ministers and line officials, regardless of whether the matter concerned twenty thousand or a million dollars . . .

I found it . . . time-consuming but effective.[85]

From about the middle of October until December 21 (significantly, Schreyer's birthday), cabinet would go into an extraordinary session every night during the week, save for when the Legislature was in session. For this two-month period the premier effectively (as he put it) "hijacked" the Management Committee and its secretariat, the latter being used to generate summaries of departmental estimates, and the former restructured as a committee of the whole cabinet. Departments would appear and defend their budget submissions. The MCC would then formally make recommendations to full cabinet, which would consider them, and the estimates would then be tabled in the house in January or February.

There was, however, a measure of collective financial decision making in the year-round operation of the Management Committee. Whatever the prospective benefits of the "dual model" of Operation Productivity, the MCC itself came to play the dual role by default when the Planning and Priorities Committee disappeared in 1973. The quest for financial control resulted in a very detail-oriented MCC.[86]

DECISION-MAKING MODES

In an institutionalized cabinet, there is a tendency for decision making to become more centralized under the cabinet and central agencies. This was the case in the Schreyer government, despite precautions to prevent excesses. As Meyer Brownstone has alleged was the case for Douglas' regime in Saskatchewan,[87] Schreyer had an adaptation process in mind for the Manitoba bureaucracy. In fact, Schreyer himself maintains that his decision-making modes amounted to a slightly modified version of the Brownstone schema (see Chapter two). That is, he believed in strong cabinet leadership, central planning, not forcing innovation on non-innovative elements, and coupling central evaluation with decentralized initiatives.[88] In other words, like the Blakeney government, the Schreyer regime was sensitive to departmental needs in theory; yet in practice, it tended to be somewhat centralizing.

Schreyer left non-innovative elements of the bureaucracy relatively intact and made things happen by hiring a new breed of civil servants. Contrary to the practice of succeeding premiers, Schreyer directly fired only one deputy minister and governed largely with a complement of Conservative-era staff. McAllister found that "a large majority, almost two-thirds of those employed as deputy ministers or assistant deputy ministers or at similarly high levels [in the civil service] in 1975–76, had been employed by the Manitoba government prior to the 1969 election . . . the bureaucracy continued to be controlled, for the most part, by individuals hired by previous Conservative and Liberal governments."[89]

The NDP bureaucracy, then, was an "add-on" one. If innovation was deemed necessary, new officials sympathetic to the government's views would be hired. Schreyer found the civil service he had inherited to be politically neutral.[90] The matching of minister and deputy was itself an interactive process; although the premier had the prerogative to hire deputies, he frequently sought the input of the minister involved or even of a small *ad hoc* committee of cabinet.

Despite the care taken to assuage departmental sensitivities regarding tenure, the Schreyer administration ended up with a reputation for centralized administration. This reputation stemmed largely from what was generally called the "control orientation" of the Management Committee and its secretariat. The MCC's reputation for control was evident in confidential departmental answers to a survey on government decentralization done in 1973.[91] The Planning Secretariat also earned for itself a reputation for elitism and insensitivity to departmental policy concerns.

Unheedful of warnings made by McLeod, the Management Committee became bogged down in the minutiae of government.[92] Meetings lasted six or seven hours and often dealt with forty or more items; attendance consequently suffered, leaving on average one or two ministers (of a total of five) at MCC meetings at any one time.[93] When an analyst suggested removing some personnel duties from the MCC and raising the cut-off point to lessen the number of items on the MCC agenda,[94] his advice was not taken.

Things did not change because the premier was satisfied with the status quo. Schreyer found that the secretariat delivered "a useful element of prudence and caution"[95] to financial deliberations, and he was glad to have a consistent element of cost constraint in the administrative structure. The general complaints about the alleged control orientation of the MCC carried less and less weight with the premier. "By 1973–74 the psychology had changed and the public was beginning to show impatience about the cost syndrome in government. So I felt totally justified in putting on more of a 'control orientation.' I gave short shrift about these kinds of comments [critical of the MCC]; it was a matter of necessity."[96] The premier, in short, had come to value small tax bills over officials' feelings. The fact that the he filled in for Cherniack when the latter could not handle Finance for personal reasons (November 13, 1972 to May 2, 1973 and January 8, 1975 to September 22, 1976) may have helped Schreyer become extra sensitive to fiscal matters and their implications.

The Planning Secretariat itself became the target of some departmental hostility, although to a lesser extent than with the Management Committee. The normal, day-to-day task of Planning Secretariat personnel was to dispense short-term policy evaluation advice, usually in a cabinet committee context with departmental personnel present—a situation which was guaranteed to generate conflict. Some departmental personnel resented the elitist airs taken on by the several M.A.s and Ph.D.s in the secretariat. Also, the highly strung personalities of some of the secretariat principals generated animosity on occasion.

In retrospect, then, Schreyer continued the process of cabinet institutionalization because many factors favoured it. They were essentially the same factors as those that had influenced Roblin and Weir. One essential difference was that Schreyer initially emulated his predecessors' cabinet structure. The Planning and Priorities Committee and the Management Committee were directly borrowed from the dualist design of the previous government. Using private officials for public purposes, development agencies from the previous era coexisted with central planning bodies of the CCF-NDP variety. Another factor involved was the impact of contemporary social science with its rationalistic emphasis on the directive machinery of government. The McLeod memos encouraged and extended the NDP cabinet's tendencies to increased institutionalization, extending the logic of analytic work done in the Roblin-Weir years.

The desire to heighten the role that Cabinet played in financial control led to the rise in stature of the Management Committee, the establishment of the CFI Committee and HESP, the eclipse of departmental autonomy, and a decrease in status of the Department of Finance. Finance's profile slipped during the period of MCC hegemony because its minister did not usually serve as MCC chairman, as he had before Schreyer (an exception was Cherniack, who served in 1970–72). Because the MCC Secretariat continued to be in the ECO, not in Finance, revenue-raising for policy vetted elsewhere became the main concern of Finance. The premier did in fact serve as finance minister on two occasions during the seventies. However, this was due more to the temporary incapacity of the natural choice for Finance, Saul Cherniack, than to any unaided cabinet characteristics reappearing in the new government.

The effect of ideology was manifested in the eventual triumph of the CCF-NDP central planning tradition over the transitional planning style of Roblin and Weir. The indicative planning of Roblin and Weir had certainly had a wider scope—including both public and private sectors—but Schreyer's public-sector-oriented central planning was deeper, much more detailed, and more ambitious. Schreyer continued the use of quasi-central agencies but did not make them as much a centrepiece of planning as Roblin had done.

Despite the prevalence of institutionalized characteristics on other fronts, there was not as much progress in budgeting matters. A planning-budgeting nexus failed to materialize, and the premier returned to line-item scrutiny in order to effect financial control. Yet Schreyer had grasped the elemental importance of providing cabinet with a broadly institutionalized framework. A multiplicity of factors had been instrumental in promoting cabinet institutionalization in his government. His successor initially resisted the trend to a structured cabinet, but even he came to appreciate some elements of it.

Chapter Eight
The Lyon Interlude

Sterling Lyon, the only one-term premier in the history of Manitoba (1977–81), was genuinely nostalgic for the days of the unaided cabinet. He abolished most of the Schreyer-era cabinet committees as well as the central agencies for planning and management. He made do with the minimum number possible, two statutory committees. The authority structure of cabinet, which favoured the premier, and the relative autonomy that Lyon accorded to ministers both indicated Lyon's fondness for traditional unaided decision making modes. He even disregarded the rationalist recommendations for reform of the central executive, made by a task force which he himself had established. However, the premier was to discover that he had limited freedom to return to the traditional style. Yet pressure from within cabinet, momentum from past reforms, intergovernmental imperatives, the wish for financial control, and his own desire for influence caused him to reinvent or persist in some of the aspects of institutionalized governance.

Lyon's nostalgia may have had something to do with his political roots in the previous generation; certainly his style—solitary, combative, and self-assured—derived from a lifetime of self-reliance. Born in Windsor in 1927, his parents separated when Lyon was an infant, and he was brought up in his mother's family home in Portage la Prairie, Manitoba. He never knew his father and relied instead on his maternal grandfather, Sterling Roy Cuthbert, to act as a father figure.[1] Lyon's mother was obliged to take in boarders to make ends meet. Her son financed much of his own university education by doing highways work, and then worked as a Winnipeg *Free Press* reporter from 1948 to 1949 to make enough money for law school. He graduated from law school in 1953 and worked as a Crown attorney from 1953 to 1957.

Roblin recruited Lyon, who then ran successfully in Fort Garry, a Winnipeg suburb, in the 1958 provincial election. Lyon had intimate roots in the party: one of his personal heroes was Arthur Meighen, who had, like him, lived on Dufferin Street in Portage la Prairie; his political mentor, former Conservative M.P. Cal Miller, lived across the street; and he had been a student Conservative in university.[2] Lyon served as Roblin's chief lieutenant in a long succession of cabinet portfolios, including the highest-profile post of attorney-general, which he held consistently for years (except for the period of 1963 to 1966). He was re-elected in the elections of 1959, 1962, and 1966.

Lyon was also the heir apparent to Roblin. However, in its 1967 leadership convention, the Conservative Party instead opted for a rural candidate, Walter Weir, who could appeal to its traditional backbone of voter strength in southern and central Manitoba. Weir had the added advantages of possessing a more affable personality and a keener team-player attitude than the more aggressive Lyon. The latter left politics before the general election of 1969 and worked until 1974 as corporate counsel to General Distributors, a large Manitoba retail merchandising firm. Yet his aggressive tendencies served Lyon well in 1975, when he deposed the reigning leader, Sidney Spivak, whose easier ways had not been conducive to winning the 1973 provincial election. A harder edge was now seen as an electoral advantage, especially in contrast to Premier Schreyer, who appeared progressively less interested in the day-to-day governance of the province and was apparently giving up policy determination by default to minister and deputy minister policy entrepreneurs.[3]

A harder edge was indeed what Lyon brought to the provincial scene. As one reporter put it, "in the Roblin government, it was his attorney-general Sterling Lyon who did the gutter fighting and spoke the strong words . . . When Lyon returned as premier, he had to be his own street fighter."[4] Lyon regularly called social democrats "the handmaidens of communism." In one notable legislature encounter in 1980, he accused NDP M.L.A. Saul Cherniack and a number of his colleagues of representing Karl Marx.[5] His intransigence in constitutional negotiations—he opposed an entrenched Charter of Rights— was instrumental in effecting the S.33 "override" included in the Constitution Act of 1982. He opposed the idea of French as an official language of Manitoba, despite the wording of the Manitoba Act of 1870, and half-heartedly complied with Supreme Court directives on the matter.

Lyon began a policy of government restraint and public-service downsizing. His hard edge was also evident in cabinet. As one observer noted: "He runs a tight ship as premier. He sets the tone and gives his 14 ministers their heads to run their own departments, though he wants to know if they're getting into trouble before it hits. His staff says he's tops at delegating responsibility, but he's also demanding and hard on failure, with a tightly controlled anger. In his office, as in the legislature, he's adept at the quick quip."[6]

A sense of self-assuredness lay behind Lyon's demanding nature. He had proven himself in the demanding worlds of the Crown attorney, the politician, and the corporate lawyer and expected others to challenge themselves as well. He was a premier who would seek advice from a trusted band of advisors, but because of a lifetime of experience "would go against all advice to follow his own instincts and intuition."[7] His self-assuredness was not inflexibility, however. "You have to remember he's primarily a trial lawyer," one contemporary said of his style as premier, "it may look as if he's totally against [your position], but he's just probing to see if your position holds up."[8]

REPORT ON GOVERNMENT ORGANIZATION AND ECONOMY

The Progressive Conservatives returned to power with thirty-three seats, compared to the NDP total of twenty-three and the Liberals' one, in the general election of October 11, 1977. (At dissolution, the rankings had been: NDP, 31; PCs, 23; and Liberals, 3.) A large part of the Conservative appeal had been their emphasis on fiscal reform. The instrument chosen to map the new organizational and process approach was a task force consisting of middle management public officials and representatives of business and industry. The Task Force on Government Organization and Economy was co-chaired by Conrad Riley, a senior executive officer with the Great West Life Assurance Company, and by Sidney Spivak, a prominent Winnipeg businessman and ex-leader of the Manitoba Progressive Conservatives, who was re-elected in October 1977. Asked to re-evaluate the role and structure of the provincial government, the Task Force reported in April 1978. Its "Report on Government Organization and Economy" concentrated on two objectives: central and departmental reorganization, and trimming an allegedly overgrown public service.

The Riley-Spivak Report's recommendations were not totally adopted by the new government, but the document itself is instructive.

It demonstrates graphically that the advice that the new Government received about the structure of the central executive was not as carefully thought out as that which had been given to Roblin and Schreyer. Roblin had benefitted from an in-depth economic review with coherent recommendations prepared by A. D. Little Consultants and had borrowed artfully from the Treasury Board experience of other provincial governments. Schreyer had had his own experience to rely on as well as the advice of T. H. McLeod, a seasoned veteran of cabinet structuring. By contrast, Lyon's advice came from a committee of private-sector-oriented individuals who were preoccupied with a management perspective, which in this particular case seemed to ignore past traditions of responsible government. The report included, for example, a fundamentally flawed departure from the historic mission of Treasury Boards.

Not surprisingly, the government rejected the main thrusts of the report, chose to rely on traditional cabinet practices, and consequently had a central executive which was somewhat underdeveloped. Lyon initially had a decentralized approach to cabinet structure, which left most of the initiative with individual ministers and comparatively little with collective entities in the cabinet context. However, not even a premier genuinely nostalgic for the simpler government of the unaided cabinet era could avoid the intergovernmental, momentum, and influence factors which favoured the persistence of at least a measure of institutionalization. Most importantly, when the development program of the government grew complex and was in need of constant attention, the premier succumbed to pressure within cabinet for more cabinet committees. There were even some indications of a nascent planning-budgeting nexus.

Since an unspoken motive in appointing the Riley-Spivak Task Force was the desire for it to act as an indictment of the past practices of the NDP government, one of its thrusts was a critique of Schreyer-era institutionalization. Predictably, a significant part of the report was devoted to an attack on the perceived lack of financial control in the NDP years, and the document marshalled a parade of indicators to demonstrate its point. Provincial government expenditures had grown by 319 per cent from 1968 to 1978, and public-sector department and agency employment rose by 43 per cent. These increases were seen as unjustified when referenced to the growth of gross provincial product or growth in provincial population. The combined deficit for 1977–78 was forecast at $225.1 million, but the report warned that the situation could be exacerbated by the current practice of fifteen to twenty per cent expenditure overruns beyond the Main Estimates figures—this in a province with sluggish revenues. Without effective expenditure restraint, warned the report, a slowdown in the economy and further deterioration in revenue growth could result in an even larger deficit.[9] Detailed restraint measures were outlined on a department-by-department basis in the second volume of the report. It offered varied and inventive ways to reduce program budgets and trim public and personnel rosters.

The Riley-Spivak Task Force de-emphasized the need for institutionalized cabinet planning. In the report, management concerns eclipsed planning concerns, and even cabinet structure reflected a management orientation, not one which would facilitate planning or a balance between planning and management. The Task Force report contained a critique of previous institutionalization. It disapproved of Schreyer-era centralism and control, by which it meant the overcomplexity of cabinet and its central bureaucracy. The dualism of cabinet had been ended, but a dual secretariat structure remained, breeding bureaucratic competition at the centre and thus hindering departments. According to the Report, cabinet's complexity (there had been eight cabinet committees) made for a cumbersome policy process. "To receive approval for new or revised policy or program initiatives, departments sometimes had to go through two or more Cabinet Sub-Committees and Cabinet. After they received policy approval they had to go to Management Committee for approval. Similarly, on-going programs required annual line by line estimates review, periodic program audit, approval over $25,000 and so forth. The authority of the line department manager was thereby undermined. In this situation, accountability for achieving program objectives tended to break down."[10]

The only discussion of cabinet structure in the report concerned the Management/Treasury Committee. There was almost no discussion of the role of full cabinet or of what institutionalized committees it should have, if any. This was a curious gap in a report studying government organization. To replace the central structure, the Task Force proposed a less institutionalized central management structure with a Treasury Committee composed of six non-departmental ministers. (With cabinet at about fifteen members, presumably this would imply a kind of cabinet hierarchy.) That the Task Force would use the term *central management* is probably telling. There was to be no explicit planning body of cabinet, although with effort one can read some quasi-planning implications into the unusual functions described for the Treasury Committee ministers. These ministers were not to have departmental responsibilities *per se*, although each of the six would have his or her own staff. Six functional areas for Treasury ministers were outlined: Crown corporations, government administration, finance and intergovernmental relations, personnel administration, legislation and policy development, and northern affairs. "The proposed Treasury Committee would be made up of Ministers with 'staff' responsibilities. Essentially their time would be devoted to their assigned staff functions. In this way, sufficient time and attention would be directed to the overall management and supervision of government, while responsibility and accountability for line department operations are assigned to departmental ministers."[11] The policy process would involve Treasury Committee review of most matters requiring decision before they went to cabinet. Cabinet would thus be spared a preoccupation with minor items; it would deal only with major issues referred to it by the Treasury Committee. The committee would be kept informed by a management information system, "management indicators," and economic and policy updates.

The Treasury Committee idea has a distinct air of unreality to it. There are many indications that the authors were unfamiliar with basic constitutional theory and the philosophy and nuances of cabinet institutionalization. It is difficult, nay impossible, to distinguish between the corporate responsibilities of the committee and those performed by individual committee ministers. The report says that *line* ministers will have responsibility and accountability for line department operations. Yet terminology such as *staff* minister responsible for Crown corporations or for finance and intergovernmental fiscal relations or for Northern Affairs coexists with the foregoing. It seems difficult to fathom the exact meaning of the responsibility if "line" and "staff" responsibility could intersect. Moreover, some descriptions of staff minister responsibilities seem unrealistic. The mandates for the staff ministers of Legislation and policy development[12] and of finance and intergovernmental fiscal relations[13] were significant departures from ministry designs as they have been traditionally known in Canada.

The Task Force was relatively more coherent concerning the role of central departments, the Department of Finance, and the Civil Service Commission, recommending that Finance should regain its old budget role and CSC its old personnel role. The report stated that the Department of Finance's responsibilities should include expenditure planning. It clearly implied that the divorce of expenditure planning from other Department of Finance functions should end. It also suggested that a Treasury Committee be given responsibility for budget review and approval of departmental estimates. The staff function would be largely provided by the Department of Finance.[14]

The Task Force preferred that expenditure planning now be done on the basis of Zero-Base Budgeting. Within this context, the Treasury Committee would allocate resources and monitor results. The report seemed to opt for the purist or unadulterated version of ZBB. Interestingly, despite its critiques of institutionalization on other fronts, in advocating ZBB the report was opting for an institutionalized style of budgeting. Its description of ZBB emphasizes planning and policy choice aims as well as the traditional financial control aim of budgeting.[15]

The Task Force found personnel responsibilities split between the Management Committee of cabinet and the Civil Service Commission. This, of course, was faithful to the original design by Operation Productivity. The arrangement in 1977 is outlined in Table 7.

The Riley-Spivak Task Force recommended that independence be restored to the Civil Service Commission but that a Treasury Committee minister overseeing personnel administration should have some responsibilities as well.[16] One minister would be the "focal point for all personnel matters."[17]

The Task Force had suggested, in essence, a lessening of the institutionalized nature of the Manitoba cabinet. By mentioning only a proposed Treasury Committee, it implied that there would be no planning committee of cabinet, or any other cabinet committees for that matter. The Treasury Committee (collectively) would not in future handle personnel policy to the same extent as had the Management Committee. The report was at best ambiguous on the need for central staff reporting to Treasury ministers; but it was clear that its authors disapproved of the previous levels of activism by central staff.

THE LYON CABINET STRUCTURE

In practice, the Lyon cabinet was to be even more shorn of institutionalized trappings than the Riley-Spivak Report had suggested. With his reliance on the bare minimum of cabinet committees, on central departments rather than central agencies, and on broad policy latitude for individual ministers, Lyon operated in a dominant premier mode and was definitely sympathetic to the notion of the unaided cabinet. As far as decision making was concerned, his instincts were closer to those of D. L. Campbell than they were to Duff Roblin's. Under his administration, nonetheless, Lyon was to enjoy only limited freedom to return to the unaided style. In fact, his government accomodated a few tardily-installed cabinet committees as well as the tentative introduction of planning considerations into the budget process.

Whereas many of the department-oriented restraint recommendations of the Riley-Spivak Task Force were adopted, those touching on the central executive were not. The government appreciated the generally managerial tone of the report, but it did not accept some of its more radical ideas, such establishing a Treasury Committee. Consid-

TABLE 7

RILEY-SPIVAK REPORT: SUMMARY OF EXISTING PERSONNEL REPORTING
RELATIONSHIPS, MANITOBA GOVERNMENT, 1977

Activity	Current Reporting Relationship
staff recruitment and selection	Civil Service Commission
staff appeals	Civil Service Commission or Arbitration
training and development	Management Committee
personnel administration (classification, pay research, etc.)	Management Committee
negotiations and collective bargaining	Management Committee

Source: Manitoba. Task Force on Government Organization and Economy, *Report on Government Organization and Economy*, 2 vols., April 1978, p. 44.

ering the *lacunae* evident in the Riley-Spivak Report, it is perhaps not surprising that the premier initially opted instead for something closer to the traditional unaided form of cabinet structure. Yet due to pressure from Finance Minister Don Craik, there was a mid-term restructuring which added new cabinet committees. The committee element of cabinet institutionalization was returning.

Most of the NDP-era cabinet committees and subcommittees were not reappointed. (The one exception was the Provincial Land Use Committee, which continued with roughly the same mandate.) A traditional Treasury Board replaced the Management Committee. By the end of their tenure, the Conservatives had established two more committees—Community Services and Economic Development—and one subcommittee on Federal-Provincial Financial Arrangements. Curiously, the parent committee was not mentioned in the latter's terms of reference; presumably, the subcommittee answered to the Treasury Board.) Cabinet size was reduced, going down to fifteen for the first two years and returning to seventeen and eighteen for the last two.

The authority structure within the Lyon cabinet was reminiscent of his unaided approach to political leadership. Don Craik, a member of the Lyon cabinet, has stated that "Lyon demanded from his ministers the CEO [Chief Executive Officer] model. They were to take full responsibility not only for policy but also for all administration. There was to be no shifting of blame. Anyone who caused the government trouble was your responsibility as minister. Lyon worked it as a tough-minded business operation in the application of discipline. He was the CEO in charge of operations generally. It was a pyramidal system, we realized in retrospect."[18] This dominant premier approach was somewhat unusual for Manitoba, although it was old currency in some provinces.

The Riley-Spivak Treasury Committee idea went nowhere, due to the historical momentum of the Treasury Board concept. Premier Lyon, who had been an important cabinet minister in the Roblin government, felt comfortable with the philosophy, structure, and operation of a traditional Treasury Board. By and large, the Roblin Treasury Board model continued during the Lyon years. The Treasury Board consisted of four to five line ministers, with the premier (and later the finance minister) as chairman. The Board was the most important cabinet committee and wielded tremendous power.

Order in Council 993/78 of 1978 authorized the establishment of a Treasury Board, which had already been operating informally, and detailed what its functions were to be. They were more restricted than those of the Schreyer-era MCC had been, but were generally in line with duties performed by contemporary Treasury Boards across Canada.[19] In November of 1978 D. W. Craik, then finance minister, released Treasury Board guidelines addressed to ministers and deputies.[20] These guidelines had been developed by the Treasury Board over the course of the past year. They showed that the Conservatives were more sensitive, at least in theory, to the danger of overloading the Treasury Board agenda and would allow a measure of financial power to be devolved to ministers and departments.

Intergovernmental relations also affected cabinet structure. Cabinet established the Federal-Provincial Financial Arrangements Subcommittee of Cabinet by Order in Council 567/78 of June 14, 1978, presumably to act as a Treasury Board subcommittee. The job of the subcommittee was to act as a clearing-house for the negotiation of federal-provincial agreements, to focus on federal-provincial matters that affected budget formulation, and to monitor expenditures and program delivery under the agreements.

Despite the care taken to prioritize the Treasury Board's workload, the fact that it was the only standing cabinet committee in the first two years of the Lyon government inevitably meant that it was called upon to decide sectoral policy matters. The agenda of the Board was overloaded and frequently backed up. Some recourse to other cabinet committees proved inevitable. Two cabinet committees — Economic Development and Community Services — were created in April 1979 and November 1979, respectively, two years after the Conservative government had first been elected.[21]

Of the two, Economic Development had de facto priority because it managed the "megaprojects," a generic name given to the plans for major resource development projects, which came to be the Conservatives' most significant plank in the 1981 provincial election. Don Craik, a professional engineer by training, had had lead responsibility for the megaprojects when he was finance minister from 1977 to 1980. It was a responsibility which followed him when he served as minister of the newly created Department of Energy and Mines from 1980 to 1981.

Craik described Economic Development Committee as follows: "I pushed for a Cabinet Committee on Economic Development, but not for an MDA type of Committee. The job of the Economic Development Committee was to promote the megaprojects, —four or five specific projects: Aluminum, Western Power Grid, Potash, Forestry. The gestation period was three to four years for each of these projects, therefore constant attention was necessary . . . The Committee was there to provide first-round examination of the details of each project before it got to Cabinet. We didn't try to give it an MDA-type authority. It was to be a clearing-house."[22]

Besides having a responsibility for reviewing the special development projects, the Economic Development Committee was supposed to develop an economic development strategy, to coordinate economic development departments, and to exchange views with all economic sectors on ways to stimulate the provincial economy.[23] Craik felt the creation of a committee would allow for the talents of ministers with related portfolios to be brought to bear on matters of high political importance. Craik, plainly one of the senior ministers in the government, was chairman of the committee.

Financial control eventually came to act as a factor in cabinet design. The Conservative solution for spiralling costs in social spending at first consisted of an attempt to rationalize delivery of the health, education, and social programs, together with a reliance on the nongovernmental sector to assist or replace government delivery mechanisms. In their first year in government, for example, the Conservatives limited hospital operating budgets to a low 2.9 per cent increase, forced higher tuition fees at post-secondary institutions by subsidizing them below the inflation rate, and initiated a thirty-five-dollar deterrent fee for legal aid services. By 1979 it was becoming evident that a more orderly and politically less troubling process (that would not leave the initiative to individual ministers) should be found. The instrument chosen was the Community Services Committee of Cabinet, installed in November of 1979. The job of this committee was to coordinate the delivery of provincial health; education; social services; consumer services; and leisure, fitness, and cultural services. It was also charged with examining the potential of volunteer services and external agencies as alternatives for provincial delivery.[24]

CENTRAL AGENCIES

The Lyon central staff arrangements were partially reminiscent of the unaided cabinet. They featured a dominant central department (Finance) and only rudimentary ECO central staff assistance. Reflecting the premier's quest for influence, this staff assistance was targeted more at him than at full cabinet. However, the fact that an ECO continued to exist at all and, moreover, that it exercised a modest policy development role indicated a weak element of institutionalization.

One of the recommendations of the Task Force, namely, that there should be a uniting of fiscal and expenditure planning, was put into effect. A Treasury Board support group, the Financial Analysis Branch, was established in the Finance Department as opposed to the Executive Council Office, as in Schreyer's day. The group was lightly staffed in comparison to the MCC organization, and its reviews were not as searching. The deputy minister of finance was secretary to the Board, as in the Roblin era. (In the NDP years Gordon Holland and then Hans Schneider had been the MCC secretaries and had had no structural relationship to the Finance Department.)

This modest change transmitted clear signals of the premier's fondness for the traditional cabinet. It demonstrated, according to one Finance official, "a more important role for Finance and an emphasis on more responsibility and autonomy for departments. There was more leeway for ministers to manage and less second-guessing by central bureaucrats."[25] The reliance on central departments and on departmental autonomy are, of course, characteristics of the unaided cabinet. The shift of Treasury Board support functions to Finance added to the department's prestige and gave it more clout in other areas of the department. Officials in the Federal-Provincial Relations Branch found themselves sought after by economic planners in the departments for policy advice and suggestions on how to work the Treasury Board system. With the assumption of the expenditure planning function and the resumption of the chairmanship of Treasury Board by the finance minister, the era of the strong treasury had returned.

Treasury Board staff operated in a far more restrained role than staff of the old Management Committee had. The emphasis was on ministerial, not bureaucratic, input. As Don Craik has remarked,

We made it the responsibility of Ministers to make recommendations to Treasury Board, not the staff's . . . We did not [as in the NDP era] have the bureaucrats involved in an adversarial role . . . The minister would have to defend his Estimates [before Treasury Board] in the same way he would defend them before the legislature.

173

The bureaucratic staff [aiding Treasury Board] was reduced from 50 to 5. Before [under the NDP] the departments would prepare Estimates of Expenditure and the Management Secretariat would also prepare material. Both would prepare arguments. You had two parts of the bureaucracy in adversarial roles: one defending, one quizzing.

The Premier and myself stripped this down. We decided that the only fights that should take place are in the department. If Treasury Board saw a weakness in a presentation, they might occasionally ask for a special investigation. Previously [under the NDP] the program auditors in Management Committee [Secretariat] did special investigations, but [there was] a high level of gamesmanship at all times. As a result, ministers would get confused at times.[26]

The responsibilities of the Department of Finance were more finely tuned by Order in Council 567/78. The department was ordered to act in a central staff function to the Federal-Provincial Financial Arrangements Subcommittee. It was asked to streamline financial and policy relationships with the federal government, to provide the subcommittee and its secretary with policy overviews, and to identify policy gaps in federal-provincial matters. In conjunction with line departments, it would identify new initiatives and parameters for any new federal-provincial agreements.

With a significant reduction in its mandate and size, the Executive Council Office saw a partial return to an unaided role. The Management Committee Secretariat ceased to exist as a part of the ECO. The Planning Secretariat was "disestablished" (the description is Spivak's) in December 1977, and most of its permanent staff reallocated from the Executive Council Office to departments. For the duration of the Lyon government, ECO staff would function largely in the PMO mode; they were to be principally caretakers, handling correspondence, appointments, and Party relations. With few individuals working in the ECO, no real hierarchy developed in practice, although it existed on paper. Staff tended to specialize.

Derek Bedson continued as the clerk of the executive council, providing yet another example of the momentum factor. The clerk's position in the Schreyer years had mostly entailed protocol, recruitment, and cabinet minute-taking responsibilities. In the Lyon government, Bedson also acted as a general administrative policeman, stopping bureaucratic factions from feuding.

Answering to the clerk, in theory but not in practice, was the special assistant to the premier, who during much of this period was William

R. McCance. An enthusiastic and personable individual with a valuable combination of technical expertise and political instincts, Bill McCance was a chartered financial analyst. He had come to the government after serving as manager of the common stock department of Great West Life Assurance Company. McCance served as secretary of the Task Force on Government Organization and Economy and later as special assistant to the chairman of the Treasury Board, Don Craik.

Technically, McCance was the chief of political staff in the Executive Council Office, although occasionally he also had a policy advisory role. His job entailed the direction of ministerial aides and, if ministers so desired, their selection as well. He arranged the premier's tours and would maintain contact with senior campaign people as the premier's representative. Occasionally he would be the premier's "political policeman" if some politicians or political staff were acting in a way that might embarrass the government.

A third major official in the Lyon era was Don Leitch, the director of the Policy Coordination Group (PCG) and described as the ECO's "ideological policeman." An economist by training, Leitch began his working ties with the Conservatives in 1976, when he became a researcher with the PC caucus. Upon assuming power, Lyon appointed him secretary to the cabinet's Economic Development Committee and assistant to the clerk of the executive council. A journalist recalls that during the Lyon era he was considered to be "the most influential member of Lyon's staff" and was expected to assume the clerk's role but for the defeat of the government in 1981.[27] He was eventually to become the clerk when the Filmon Conservative goverment was formed in May of 1988.

The creation of the Policy Coordination Group can be attributed to the gradual strengthening of the premier's desire for influence. Technically, Leitch reported to McCance but in practice was virtually independent. A person who worked with the ECO during this time has commented on the significance of the creation of the PCG in 1979:

The PCG [creation] was an admission of too much decentralization in government. It was evidence of a need to coordinate activity. Sterling [Lyon] had said "I have chosen the ministers—there should be no second-guessers [central bureaucrats] telling them what they should be doing." The concept of cabinet that predominated was that ministers saw *themselves* as having the primary responsibility for deciding matters.

However, the PCG was *premier oriented* [not cabinet oriented]. Leitch was the "ideological policeman" whose job was to monitor department activity . . . to see that the departments were coordinated with each other. He also saw to the policy development of things that were political in nature.[28]

The Policy Coordination Group did analytical work on the megaprojects, economic development, and some federal-provincial questions. It worked with advertising agencies devising brochures on programs that had been developed out of the PCG. One such program was Shelter Allowances for Elderly Renters (SAFER), which according to a PCG insider, had been "lifted" from a British Columbia model. Although the PCG was on occasion augmented by summer student staff, by 1981 there were no more than four members in the group. "The Premier did not want a large staff," noted one insider.

To round out the story of central staff reorganization, one should mention the re-creation of a central department, the Department of the Civil Service Commission, in 1979. In line with Task Force recommendations, the department added personnel relations, development and training, and staff relations to the existing functions of the CSC and its board. (The Civil Service Board functioned as an appeal body.) Thus there would be two major central departments in the Lyon interlude, Finance and the Civil Service Commission.

BUDGETING

The Riley-Spivak budgeting recommendations gained uneven acceptance. On one hand, the staff function of the Treasury Board was placed in the Department of Finance and the Management Committee Secretariat was disbanded, as the Riley-Spivak Report had wanted. However, the budgeting technique that had been suggested, ZBB, was tried only for a year and in an unenthusiastic fashion. Instead, the modest effects of the momentum factor propelled the tentative reintroduction of planning considerations into the budget process. The Treasury Board included some elementary planning directions in the estimates preparation booklets in the last Conservative years. The directions emphasized the importance of setting objectives as the basis for the preparation of estimates and directed departments to hold specific objectives-setting exercises. They also instructed departments to have their Treasury Board review documents focus upon objectives and outputs. These were to be related to financial and staffing resources.[29] The emphasis on ministerial rather than central agency responsibility for budget adjustments was evident in the estimates directions for fiscal year 1980–81.[30] Treasury Board review packages were submitted by November 1, 1979, underwent a Treasury Board review, and then won cabinet approval. Estimates were ready by February 29 of the next year.

Towards the end of their tenure, in 1981, the Conservatives heightened their planning orientation to budgeting slightly. Unlike planning activities in the Schreyer era, however, the Lyon government's process relied on initial policy direction from the *departments* (and individual ministers) rather than from cabinet. Reviews of policy issues took place at several levels in the system. Departments were expected to define their roles and missions, generate issues, and devise indicators to measure their own success. Cabinet and the Treasury Board then collaborated to produce policy and financial guidelines to be distributed to departments by the Department of Finance. Main Estimates submissions were prepared from July to October; Finance prepared departmental analyses from August to October; departmental reviews by cabinet took place from September to November; and a final summary of decisions was ready by November. Of course, this cycle was abbreviated by the looming of a provincial election in November 1981. (The Lyon government was defeated in the election of 1981. In 1983 Lyon resigned the Tory leadership, and in 1986 the Mulroney government appointed him to the Manitoba Court of Appeal.) Yet the cycle is noteworthy because it demonstrates that Conservative planning activity was occuring, albeit owing mostly to the momentum of planning experiments in the Schreyer era. A planning-budgeting nexus was beginning to take shape, if only at the departmental, not the cabinet, level.

As premier, Lyon was clearly sympathetic to traditional decision-making structures; he employed several elements highly reminiscent of the unaided cabinet. The authority structure of cabinet, as well as the relative autonomy of ministers, stood in contrast to the institutionalized pattern of the Schreyer years. The premier had a dominant role in cabinet, and it was reflected in the central structure. The policy development function was carried out by an official answerable not to cabinet but to the premier. The ECO took on PMO-like qualities in that personal loyalty to the premier was paramount, and the political process was the chief concern of central officials. The premier's drive for influence explains these arrangements.

There was also a marked swing to departmental autonomy in operational and planning matters, reversing a trend evident since the Roblin days. The premier operated largely according to an orthodox unaided theory of ministerial power; consequently, central bodies such as the ECO and the Treasury Board Support Group operated with low personnel complements.

177

Another unaided aspect was the primary reliance on central departments. The dominance of the Finance Department came with the
disappearance of the planning and management central agencies. The
placement of the Treasury Board support function in Finance and the
designation of the finance minister as Treasury Board chairman for
most of this period were signs of Finance's power and a return to the
strong Treasury pattern.

Yet the Lyon cabinet also demonstrated the persistence of some
elements of institutionalization. There was some evidence of collective
efforts in cabinet decision making. Originally there was a simple
cabinet structure; from 1977 to 1979 there were only two committees,
and they were dependent on statute. These were the Treasury Board,
with a cabinet subcommittee, and a land use committee. Two policy
committees were later added after the successful completion of the
government's program demanded it. Ironically, this left Lyon, the
traditionalist, with three major cabinet committees—Treasury, Social,
and Economic—two of them distinctly non-traditional.

The central bureaucracy, although diminished, still bore traces of
institutionalization. The ECO central agency remained, although in a
much reduced state. A planning orientation to government reappeared
in a weakened form with the introduction of departmental role statements in the annual budget process. Lyon thus appeared to have a
limited degree of freedom to establish unaided cabinet governance.
Don Craik (and no doubt other ministers as well) had enough influence
on the premier to resurrect at least some aspects of institutionalization,
such as cabinet committees. The momentum of planning carried on in
weakened form from the Schreyer years. Momentum can also explain
the roles of the Treasury Board and of the clerk of the executive
council. The premier himself found it useful to use the Policy Coordination Group in the Executive Council Office as a monitoring and
control device which effectively extended his authority. Financial control considerations led to the creation of the Social Services Committee.
Under the next premier, a very little of the unaided cabinet pattern
would remain.

Chapter Nine
The Pawley Years

In November 1981 the New Democrats were re-elected to office and began the slow process of reinstitutionalizing cabinet. Surprising, at least to some, was the discontinuity in central government structures and processes between the old (Schreyer-era) and new (first-term Pawley) NDP governments. Unlike the Saskatchewan NDP, which had basically kept the old CCF model intact, the Manitoba NDP of the early eighties did not totally re-adopt the pattern that had marked earlier NDP governance. In fact, much of the system they originally installed seemed quite similar to that of the previous Conservative government. However, during his second government (1986–88) Howard Pawley took steps similar to those of Schreyer; the most notable similarity was his establishment of a Planning and Priorities Committee. Pawley would also centralize Crown corporations supervision, a first for the province.

Despite the difference in particulars, Schreyer and Pawley shared some common influences when it came to designing cabinet. Like Schreyer, Pawley initially emulated his Conservative predecessor; from 1981 to 1986 he demonstrated a commitment to full cabinet priority setting; relative ministerial autonomy; and a trio of treasury, social, and economic committees. Ideology spanned the Schreyer/Pawley years as planning and creation of a planning-budgeting nexus became a focus for the government. (The planning was, however, more project oriented than it had been under Schreyer.) Social science rationalism was apparent in the complexity of Pawley's initial planning and budgeting mechanisms, and in the later use of a consultant to evaluate the decision-making and fiscal frameworks. Like Schreyer, Pawley eventually came to dwell on cabinet financial control as an important design factor; in 1987 he instituted a separate Treasury Board Secretariat with a mandate for long-term expenditure control. The wish to decongest decision making also prevailed, as Pawley explained when he abolished two of the three original major cabinet committees (social and economic).

However, additional factors impinged upon Pawley. The need for cabinet to regain political control of the public agenda was foremost in his second government, in the wake of a Crown corporation scandal and widely observed policy drift. The results were a new cabinet committee on public investments and a new Planning and Priorities Committee which aimed to promote a priority list of cabinet policies. A perceived need to maintain close ties with interest groups resulted in a few specialized cabinet committees. Moreover, it was evident that Pawley wished to distance himself from the more *laissez-faire* aspects of the Lyon cabinet, perceiving it as too shorn of planning capability.

It was not surprising that Howard Pawley accorded importance to collegiality in cabinet. In choosing him as leader in November 1979, the party convention echoed the collectivist perspective of the legislative caucus. Rather than choosing the more dominating and opinionated Sid Green, a Schreyer-era veteran, or political neophyte Muriel Smith, past president of the party, the convention opted for the more team-oriented Pawley. According to one analyst, Pawley was a rarity, "a politician without an ego," chosen for "his record of service and loyalty to the NDP." He immediately vowed to rid the party of the cult of personality that had grown up around Premier Schreyer and to rely instead on social democratic policies to survive.[1]

There was no mistaking his social democratic roots. His maternal grandfather, Henry Madill, "probably the only democratic socialist in [Ontario's] Marlborough County" in the 1920s, sparked his interest in politics. As well, Pawley's father was an CCF activist and sometime candidate in Ontario's Peel County in the 1930s and 1940s.[2] For grades one to eight, Howard attended a one-room schoolhouse near the family farm outside Brampton, a fact that would later earn him the nickname "the Abe Lincoln of the Interlake" in Manitoba law circles.[3] He would later remember visits to the farm by CCF icon J. S. Woodsworth, and counted M. J. Coldwell, T. C. Douglas, and David Lewis as personal influences. The family moved to Winnipeg in 1952 because his father, Russell, had been offered a job there. In succession, young Howard then attended high school, teachers' college, United College, and the Manitoba Law School.

In Manitoba social democratic politics, he opposed the CCF transformation to the NDP and was, in his youth, to the left of centre. He ran unsuccessfully at the federal level in 1957 and 1965, and at the provincial level in 1958. Like others on the left, Pawley learned to live with the transition, and he became an important NDP politician. The 1969, 1973, and 1977 campaigns saw him elected as the member for Selkirk, a citified rural riding outside of Winnipeg. He served as Schreyer's minister of municipal affairs from 1969 to 1976 and as attorney-general from 1973 to 1977. His early cabinet career was highlighted by the successful shepherding of the controversial government automobile insurance plan (Autopac) through the legislature in 1970 and the reform of municipal finance in 1972.

As leader, he won two elections, in November 1981 and March 1986. The second one was a squeaker: a virtual NDP-PC tie in popular vote and a 30–26–1 split in seats for the NDP, PCs, and Liberals, respectively. The first term saw him exercise a shakey hold on power during the debate on French language services; the NDP policy of informal resolution of constitutional rights only inflamed public opinion, and the cabinet was obliged to let the courts set the agenda. In economic matters, the government got better marks from banks and business groups. Bucking national neo-conservative trends in recessionary times, the Pawley government found to its satisfaction that "economic forecast after economic forecast gave the province one of the highest rates of private investment, one of the highest rates of growth, one of the highest rates of job creation and one of the lowest unemployment rates" in the country, albeit at the cost of a half-billion dollar deficit.[4]

However, timing is everything in politics, and a surprise defection by backbencher Jim Walding in 1988 led to a general election which the government lost. After an unsuccessful attempt at winning a federal seat in the 1988 election, Pawley re-entered law and later took up an academic career in political science at the University of Windsor.

CABINET STRUCTURE

There were both continuities and discontinuities between the Lyon and Pawley governments as far as cabinet structure was concerned. Once again an NDP premier emulated the cabinet design of his Conservative predecessor. An official review of Manitoba's central executive in 1986 identified the continuities as a flat authority structure and relatively high ministerial autonomy:

While the pendulum of centralization/decentralization has moved back from the extremes of the mid-1970s (extreme centralization) and the 1978–81 period (extreme decentralization), the [present 1986] system has the same essential logic to its organization [as was] adopted in 1978.

The traditional overall government priority setting process and decision making responsibilities that are delegated to "Priority [*sic*] and Planning" Committees in other Canadian jurisdictions is retained as a responsibility of the full Cabinet in Manitoba. More-over, individual departmental ministers play a more direct and independent role in Manitoba than in some other jurisdictions where "policy committees" have been formalized and entrenched.[5]

Another example of emulation was the tendency to rely on three main cabinet committees: the Treasury Board, a social policy committee, and an economic policy committee. Still another was the practice of having the Treasury Board served by a central department, a special unit of Finance, rather than by a central agency (like the Management Secretariat in the Schreyer ECO) and having it use guidelines virtually identical to those used under Lyon.

Of course, there were discontinuities. Pawley did, after all, come from a more institutionalized tradition. Eventually there were far more cabinet committees under Pawley than under Lyon, and they were used much more as links to interest groups. Pawley also fostered a planning orientation among his cabinet committees and intensified efforts to join planning and budgeting exercises. Cabinet size was also margin-ally larger under Pawley, growing to twenty ministers or more in the mid-1980s.

As in the Lyon years, the Treasury Board was the first committee to be created and it had the highest profile. Its duties were identical to Lyon's version.[6] The NDP generally followed the Conservative pattern of having the minister of finance chair the Treasury Board. From 1981 to 1983, the post of chairman was held by Vic Schroeder, who was finance minister; from 1983 to 1986, however, it passed to Jay Cowan, the minister of cooperative development. The April 1986 post-election cabinet again had a finance minister, Eugene Kostyra, sitting as chairman of the Treasury Board in the traditional arrangement. The board averaged about six members for most of the Pawley years.

The Pawley Treasury Board used approval guidelines similar to those of the Lyon Board.[7] Likewise, the Pawley cabinet seems to have agreed with its predecessor that the Treasury Board should not be loaded down with small items but should be allowed to concentrate on the "big picture" regarding expenditures. Yet a later report by ex-Clerk

Michael Decter was to criticize the Treasury Board's preoccupation with detail to the detriment of close connections between policy and expenditure management.

Like Lyon, Pawley depended on two major ongoing social and economic committees in addition to the Treasury Board, the Social Resources Committee (SRC) and the Economic Resources and Investment Committee (ERIC). Prioritization, consistency, and coordination of activities were their major concerns.[8] In Schreyer's day sectoral committees had been created to allow more ministers to share in central planning; this seems not to have been the case with the SRC and the ERIC, since planning is not even mentioned as a responsibility in internal documents.

Both the social and economic committees had existed informally since the summer of 1982 but were given formal status by order in councils in 1983.[9] The order creating the Social Resources Committee betrayed an additional motivating factor, financial control, when it allocated responsibility for expenditure reprioritization in social departments. Manitoba and Canada at large were experiencing a severe recession, and reprioritization, the government's euphemism for financial restraint, was deemed a necessity. The ERIC emerged from the same context of recesssion. One of its main responsibilities was to run a counter-cyclical job creation fund; in fact, its full title became the ERIC/Jobs Fund Committee when it was created by Order in Council 1234/83 on November 16, 1983. Both the SRC and the ERIC had important de facto decision-making powers in major policy areas.

There were, of course, several other cabinet committees in the Pawley era. They can be divided into two categories: interest group committees and special purpose committees. The Pawley government established special ties to cultural and linguistic interest groups through the cabinet committee mechanism. The French Language Services Committee grew out of the cabinet's abortive attempt in 1983–84 to establish a made-in-Manitoba bilingualism policy. The Ethnocultural Committee, established informally on July 9, 1982 and later by order in council in 1987, was an attempt to heighten the NDP's multiculturalism image. The Native Affairs Committee, informally established on February 10, 1982 and later created by order in council in 1985, provided a forum for discussions between the province's native groups and the federal government. The latter committee had six members, was chaired by the premier at the beginning (and later by Aboriginal cabinet minister Elijah Harper), and had a line department official from Northern Affairs as secretary.

There were also special purpose committees. These were public-sector Compensation, which was at times folded into the Treasury

Board and at other times was left on its own; Strategy, a political committee; Provincial Land Use, which had continued; Joint Council; Communications; and Urban Affairs. The Crown Corporations Reform Committee existed briefly in 1987.

The Pawley cabinet, as will now be apparent, had the largest number of cabinet committees of any government in Manitoba history. In 1985 there were eight committees; after the 1986 election, there were eleven. It is small wonder, with this exponential growth of committees, that some sort of internal hierarchy was established in cabinet to reduce the risk of committees working at cross-purposes. In 1987 a Planning and Priorities Committee of Cabinet was once again operating in the Manitoba NDP cabinet.

CENTRAL AGENCIES AND THE QUESTION OF BALANCE

With the growth of committees, cabinet decision making was becoming more centralized. Realizing this was a general tendency of institution-alized cabinets, Pawley sought to pre-empt negative departmental counter-reaction. He did this by installing hybrid central staff arrange-ments; the aim was to ensure that the organization of the government's central agencies would strike a balance between centralization and decentralization. The government shunned any move that suggested centralization, and as a consequence, there was no strong central planning body in the new NDP government. The lack of a planning secretariat was a marked difference from the pattern of the seventies and signified a change in direction.

Treasury Board Chair Jay Cowan, interviewed in 1985, noted that the gap was partly a matter of resources: "Constraints in the depart-ments led to a dynamic that discouraged it. Everyone felt that a planning secretariat provided another level of decision-making. There were limited resources, so we decided to give the departments a planning role. Planning was non-existent in the departments because of Conservative cutbacks. We literally had to build up a planning mechanism."[10]

A senior Pawley cabinet official, also interviewed in 1985, attributed the lack of central planning to a matter of balance: "The pendulum in Schreyer's era went too far one way, and in Lyon's era it was the same thing [in the other direction]. Schreyer had a bureaucratized centre and Lyon had too little at the centre. The new government feels that deputy ministers must be good managers but that they must also be involved in policy matters. The centre must be more coordination and less direct policy generation . . . The pendulum must be at the centre. There is also a reason for a non-politicized bureaucracy: to return policy generation to the Cabinet . . . It is important that senior officials develop options and advise but do not usurp the role of the ministers."[11]

In the new Pawley government, centralization was considered but avoided, as the same official observed: "Parasiuk [minister of energy and mines, and a former planning secretary to cabinet under Schreyer] wanted a 'heavy centre,' but he did not get it. People realized that the major blunder of the Schreyer era was not to get higher-profile deputies . . . [Because of this] we saw a lack of action in the latter Schreyer era. There was no cooperation from line managers. Roblin's [DM] group went on to greater things . . . but Schreyer did not have notable DMs. Lyon reappointed old DMs. *Now* we have a good team put together."

There was now to be an emphasis on departmental-level planning that responded to central needs. Treasury Board Chairman Cowan noted that by 1981 the

> MCC had been disbanded but no [policy] planning or resource planning had replaced it. One of the first questions we had to ask was "What does the department want to do"? We had to install the basic elements of planning: mission statements, targets for programs . . . We now have departmental planning, but we also have central structural planning to answer central needs. Cabinet committees are now coordinating the planning. We have a decentralized form of planning that fits central requirements. Centrally, we say "we require from you such and such." Later it is used by central people . . . or by departments . . . or by hybrid bodies. We are moving toward this [hybrid model] . . . We are approaching a shared system.[12]

Whereas in the seventies the NDP's planning was expansive and broadly sectoral in nature, it was now done on the basis of projects and issues: for example, daycare, worker co-ops, even Hydro development. Planning activities were conducted in cabinet committee meetings or during the estimates process.[13]

Clerk of the Executive Council Derek Bedson was dismissed by Premier Pawley in 1981. Rumours circulated that the dismissal was an act of retribution for his role in helping weed out and fire civil servants with NDP sympathies in the Lyon years, but the government maintained that it was simply a routine change of top personnel. The whole episode may in fact have been an expedient way of appointing an NDP partisan, Michael Decter, as clerk. A small farewell party held for Bedson in April 1982 as he prepared to leave Manitoba saw three former Conservative premiers in attendance — Weir, Roblin, and

Lyon—who praised his contributions to constitutional wording, Francophone rights, and propriety in official relations.[14]

The operation of the Executive Council Office revealed an attempt at balance. Not all of the cabinet committees depended on the ECO to provide secretariat services; many used relevant departments. The new clerk of the executive council continued to serve as the institutionalized interlocutor between the premier, the cabinet, and the bureaucracy. Decter processed orders in Council and made recommendations to the premier on deputy minister appointments. He supervised cabinet administration and provided staff support to some cabinet committees, such as the Social Resources Committee. Other cabinet committees were serviced by line departments: Municipal Affairs serviced the Provincial Land Use Committee of Cabinet (PLUC); and the Industry, Trade, and Technology Department served the Economic and Resources Investment Committee (ERIC) although Decter served as secretary of ERIC. The Department of Finance provided the secretariat to the Treasury Board.

Staff numbers in the ECO were kept purposely low to prevent an excess of power developing in the hands of central bureaucrats. Following the recommendations of an official communications report, an ECO Communications Secretariat provided central political direction; however, all information officers were ensconced in a line department, Cultural Affairs.[15]

Decter was the clerk of the executive council from December 1, 1981 to May 1, 1986. His experience with Manitoba's central executive had begun in the Schreyer era. After Parasiuk's departure in 1977, he was acting planning secretary to cabinet until the government changed. For a year he acted as a senior advisor to the Conservative government's Riley-Spivak Task Force, in the process helping to "spin-off" several Planning Secretariat officials to line positions. Thereafter he became a consultant and businessman until the NDP government beckoned him in 1981. In 1986 he decided to re-enter the private sector as a consultant and was replaced by George Ford.

Along with the secretariats and the policy group—the PCO side of the central staff—there were others one might expect to find in the Executive Council Office of an institutionalized cabinet: political operatives who constituted the PMO side of the PMO-PCO balance. A principal secretary operated a tactical and strategy-setting group in the Premier's Office called the Policy Coordination Group (PCG). (The Premier's Office was considered part of the Executive Council Office.) From 1981 to 1983 the principal secretary was Bill Regehr and from 1983 to 1986 John Walsh held the post. Regehr came from an Education background, Walsh from Labour. On October 1, 1986 Walsh left for a post with the Yukon government, and Virginia A. Devine assumed the post of principal secretary. Devine had directed the government's policy coordination group from 1984 to 1986 and was also an advisor on health care reform.

Facilitation of interest group input became a factor in the design of ECO functions. The principal secretary himself served as a focal point for interest groups. As well, the principal secretary later initiated and did process work on the Portage Summit, a tripartite government/ business/labour meeting in 1982 which was later institutionalized. The Policy Coordination Group performed functions roughly analogous to those performed by its Lyon-era counterpart but with a lower profile. This group, under the nominal authority of the principal secretary, worked directly for an informal body called the Strategy Committee of Cabinet and also provided input to the Legislative Review Committee of Cabinet. The group organized direct mailings to communicate with interest groups that were perceived as natural supporters of the government: women, labour, and natives. It served as a watchdog over departmental actions and provided occasional political input to the estimates process.

The staff agency serving the Treasury Board was not overly heavy-handed with the departments. The Treasury Board Support Section was located in the Comptroller's Division of the Department of Finance; it coordinated estimates preparation and provided analytical services for the minister of finance, the Treasury Board, and cabinet.[16]

A report commissioned in 1986 noted, however, that Manitoba seemed still not to have reached the correct balance in expenditure matters. The Decter Report noted that "*an excessive tendency to centralize controls* and impose standard measures has removed responsibility and flexibility from managers, effectively releasing them from making judgement calls for which they should be considered accountable."[17] (Emphasis added.) One of Decter's main recommendations was for the "delegation to departmental managers of greater responsibility for expenditure management decisions."[18]

The Treasury Board should give management advice, and policy committees should serve as policy-setting forums with clear mandates; but it was precisely on these points that the Treasury Board, ERIC, and SRC had been disappointing in the first Pawley term, according to Decter. The integrity of the Treasury Board as the main focus of operating decisions had been weakened by its tendency to focus on detailed expenditure issues. The informational role of cabinet committees demanded a strong analytical central staff component, not just the current departmental input.[19]

Despite the concern voiced for central/departmental balance, comparatively little was said in the Decter Report about concrete methods

187

for achieving it. The particular centralized controls and standardized measures that impede departmental responsibilities were never discussed in detail either. Inescapably, one must be vague on the balance question, the report seemed to say. The following except is an interesting summary of the then current state of the art: "There is no known 'correct' balance between centralization and decentralization of planning and expenditure management authorities. Public administration remains well short of a science in its ability to generate universal or absolute truths. The fiscal situation, style and management of the Premier and Cabinet, and priorities of the Government are all factors to be considered in structuring central agencies in any particular jurisdiction."[20]

PLANNING AND BUDGETING

In the fashion of many premiers of institutionalized cabinets, Pawley was interested in the planning implications of the budget process— more so than any previous Manitoba premier. The Pawley cabinet gave much more direct, up-front policy direction (planning) in budgeting than did Lyon's; and Pawley's planning process was, as well, far more intricate. The whole process, by the end, was saturated in rationalist terminology.

The NDP government elaborated its planning-budgeting nexus in three successive stages in 1982, 1984, and 1985. A Treasury Board circular of August 1982 instructed departments to initiate planning processes which would include four components: strategic planning, three to five year planning, resource allocation to approved programs, and operational planning. As before, linkages among objectives, activities, outputs, and resources were to be made explicit.

In June 1984 cabinet approved a revision of the annual estimates process, to take effect in the 1985–86 budget cycle. The most important change was the introduction of "front-end policy direction," which meant that cabinet's policy preferences would be indicated before the preparation of detailed departmental estimates. The mechanism for this front-ending, the Strategic Program Overview (SPO)[21], would be prepared by each department for cabinet review during the late summer or early fall.

Further revisions, decided upon by cabinet in 1985 and implemented during the 1986–87 cycle, also aimed at increasing the front-end aspect of estimates preparation. Whereas the past estimates process had featured three stages (the SPO exercise, then detailed estimates review by the Treasury Board, and lastly cabinet finalization of the main estimates), the 1985 revisions front-ended two more: overall policy development, and strategic policy and resource direction.

Cabinet policy committees, such as the ERIC and Social Resources, and their respective staffs—and the Executive Council Office staff-at-large advising on government-wide issues—were to have a heightened role in helping to define cabinet's priorities at the start of the 1985 changes. The committees and their staffs would prepare high level policy proposals for possible inclusion in the governmental policy statement. The ERIC, SRC, and Treasury Board staffs would review the policy proposals submitted at the strategic policy and resource direction stage and submit their views to cabinet. The appropriate central staff would review and analyze departmental SPO submissions.

The Decter Report

Shortly after the 1986 election, the Decter Report was commissioned. It was, of course, part of a grand Manitoba tradition, being the fourth major "outsider" report by a social scientist to be done on the central executive structure and processes in Manitoba—after those by A. D. Little, Operation Productivity, and T. H. McLeod. It had an impact comparable to or surpassing other similar reports because of the writer and the nature of his support. Not only was it written by the ex-clerk of the executive council, who had just voluntarily resigned, but it also involved two high-level working groups—one for expenditure, and one for taxation—who reported to a Special Ministerial Committee on Tax Reform and Expenditure Management. The Special Ministerial Committee was a blue ribbon one, consisting of the premier, the minister of finance and his deputy, the chairs of the ERIC and SRC committees, the clerk of the executive council, and others. This was plainly no ordinary consultant report.[22] It is therefore safe to assume that Decter's thinking was also an extension of that of cabinet and the senior bureaucracy—and the premier.

The 1986 Decter Report on expenditure management reflected cabinet's continuing commitment to the planning-budgeting nexus. Its preface stated: "This review has focussed on fundamental concerns about 'front-end' issues—in particular, the linkage between policy priorities and expenditure decisions as ensured by an effective operation and support of Cabinet and its committees. In taking the hard decisions it is essential that the context for those decisions has been well and thoroughly established. It is also essential that the expenditure management system deliver on the policy direction and political objectives formulated by the Cabinet. Without this foundation an expenditure management system is simply a process with-outpurpose."[23]

In practice, the union of planning (or front-end policy considerations) and budgeting seemed hard to achieve. The Decter Report stated that policy and expenditure decisions were being undertaken without sufficient linkage to each other. The Treasury Board was not focusing enough on significant issues in giving policy direction to expenditure decisions, and cabinet policy committees were not operating so as to integrate policy and expenditure.[24]

The expenditure management report enunciated a concern with institutionalized cabinet themes, most of which implied heightened political control by cabinet. One theme centred on the need for a planning-budgeting nexus, which was referred to as "the linkage" between policy priorities and expenditure decisions. Another theme was the desirability of balance in central and departmental relations. Other political control themes surfaced, such as the importance of the evaluation function of government and the need for accurate reporting mechanisms. As well, the desire for financial control was apparent in the report's emphasis on restricting external subsidies and narrowing the program base of the provincial government.

Four major recommendations appeared in the report. "The first and most important recommendation," Decter wrote, "is that the role and structure of Treasury Board be altered to further emphasize its primary responsibility for major revenue and expenditure decisions and the management of revenue increase and expenditure reduction issues."[25] His specific recommendations regarding the Treasury Board, which included a request for a full-time secretary to the Treasury Board to be chosen from Finance, called for a strong Treasury and a strong Treasury Board.[26]

A second major recommendation was that the role of cabinet's policy committees be narrowed to an advisory rather than a decision-making focus. This notion stemmed from a simple rationalist principle: the desirability of comprehensive review "to force the competition of all expenditure options in a balanced and comprehensive setting."[27] The committees would offer sectoral considerations during estimates preparation and would also refer to Treasury Board requests for decisions which had expenditure implications.[28]

A third recommendation touched directly on the planning-budgeting nexus. It proposed that the estimates process be simplified and shortened in order to highlight substantive issues and to streamline departmental work.[29] A fourth recommendation, an outline for long-term expenditure reduction, showed that the financial control factor had also played a role in the structural thinking of the premier and cabinet.

The outline consisted of a framework, guidelines, and motivational factors.[30]

THE NEW PAWLEY CABINET

Cabinet's need to assert political control would emerge as a design factor in the second Pawley government (1986–88). Pawley was left with no choice but alteration of the central executive around the time of the March 1986 general election. An unhealthy batch of scandals had occurred in the Crown corporations: these included criminal activities by three executives of McKenzie Seeds; abuse of office by officials in the Manitoba Public Insurance Corporation (Autopac); and serious business mistakes at MTX Telecom Services Inc., a subsidiary of the Manitoba Telephone System (MTS) in Saudi Arabia. In the field of general policy, there were also problems. Several backbenchers felt that cabinet had mismanaged the Manitoba bilingual services issue in 1983–84. Like many other provinces, Manitoba also had a serious deficit situation. The constant adjustment of the expenditure budget process had resulted in an increasingly complex system—one that did not give cabinet a strong enough handle on policy development.

Consequently, it was decided to review the organization of the central executive. The review confirmed the existence of flaws in the central machinery of government and the need for an increased measure of cabinet political control. In 1987 an increased central presence was established for departmental and Crown overview, but the government continued to enunciate the central/departmental balance theme.

Cabinet's need to assert political control continued to affect decision-making structures. The combined effects of the Decter Report, a very slim majority in the 1986 election, a turnover in senior officials, and the political imperatives engendered by the "Crowns Crisis" compelled the premier to make substantial changes in the cabinet. Cabinet would become more hierarchical, have more central staff working directly for it in the Executive Council Office, and emphasize planning and budgeting complementarity to a greater extent. In short, it was to become even more institutionalized, in a manner evocative of the Saskatchewan model with its trinity of important cabinet committees.

The Decter Report had a major impact, doubtless because it reflected a growing consensus to simplify Manitoba's institutionalized cabinet machinery in order to make it more efficient. The Decter recommendations which were adopted were those that called for a stronger and more planning-oriented Treasury Board:

- affirmation of the central role of the Treasury Board in revenue and expenditure management
- appointment of a secretary of the Treasury Board, to be housed in Finance
- amalgamation of central staff
- continuation of the linkage of Finance and Treasury Board functions
- integration of policy and expenditure advice (achieved by integrating the SRC and ERIC into the PPCC and establishing a Treasury Board Secretariat)
- simplification of the estimates process (partly achieved through the development of a priority list)
- projection of expenditures five years into the future
- review of off-budget expenditures by the Treasury Board
- establishment of a framework for long-term expenditure reduction
- movement away from detailed expenditure review by the Treasury Board in favour of a broad management role.

Some of Decter's recommendations were not adopted: for instance, inclusion of the finance deputy on the Treasury Board, establishment of a central agency unit to perform organizational studies, and delegation of greater responsibility for management decisions. These suggestions might have been implemented in the future, but the opportunity was soon lost. The NDP government was defeated in the House on a vote of non-confidence in 1988.[31]

New Cabinet Structures

The new cabinet structures were in keeping with the logic of institutionalization. Most notable was the creation of a Planning and Priorities Committee of Cabinet; not since 1973 had there been such an internal hierarchy in Manitoba's cabinet. There were other cabinet changes as well, elaborated in a news release of February 6, 1987. Two cabinet committees were disbanded, two more were created, and the Treasury Board was strengthened. The wish to decongest cabinet decision making and to widen comprehensive decision making were subsidiary factors in the cabinet design, the premier indicated. A news release dated February 6, 1987, stated that

Premier Howard Pawley has announced significant changes in the committee structure of his cabinet and some changes in the allocation of cabinet portfolios.

"These major cabinet committee changes are intended to streamline and make more efficient the work of cabinet," the premier said. "They should also reduce the growing number of meetings which my cabinet colleagues must attend."

The major changes are the establishment of a Planning and Priorities Committee of Cabinet and a strengthened role for Treasury Board. Treasury Board reviews and makes recommendations to cabinet on all government expenditures.

The Planning and Priorities Committee will assume and incorporate the functions formerly performed by the Economic Resource Investment Committee (ERIC) and the Social Resources Committee (SRC). The two former key committees dealt with recommendations to cabinet in the economic and social policy areas. Their combination in the Planning and Priorities Committee will permit a balanced review and evaluation of government priorities across the whole policy spectrum, integrating both economic and social policies.

The premier announced that he would chair the Planning and Priorities Committee and that Finance Minister Eugene Kostyra would chair the Treasury Board.

Premier Pawley also announced that two new cabinet committees have been established: Crown Reform, chaired by Gary Doer, and River Renewal, chaired by Leonard Harapiak.

Membership of the Crown Reform Committee will include ministers responsible for the major Crown corporations and the Minister of Finance. The Ministers of Natural Resources, Environment, Culture, Heritage and Recreation and Urban and Municipal Affairs will constitute the Cabinet Committee on River Renewal.[32]

Two months later, when making secretarial appointments to Planning and Priorities and to the Treasury Board, the premier elaborated somewhat on the role of these two cabinet committees. The political and financial control motives were more baldly stated: "The Planning and Priorities Committee of Cabinet has been established as a forum for setting directions and monitoring the implementation of priority policies. The Treasury Board has been strengthened to ensure improved management of the province's fiscal resources in the achievement of government priorities. To this end, the board will be charged with responsibility for multi-year fiscal planning, the identification of longer term expenditure reduction possibilities, program and organizational review, and systems for accountability and the delegation of authority.[33]

New Central Agency Arrangements

With the new cabinet structures came new central agency relationships and new personnel. These central agency arrangements were closer to those of a typical institutionalized cabinet than those in place under Pawley. There was now a PPCC Secretariat in the ECO, more central budgeting staff in the Treasury Board Secretariat (TBS), and an extension of the planning-budgeting nexus.

Coincident with the commissioning of the Decter Report, George H. Ford had begun service as the new clerk of the executive council on May 2, 1986. Ford had been deputy minister of employment services and economic security since November 1983 and before this had had about a decade-and-a-half of planning and economic development experience. He had, for example, been secretary to the Manpower and Employment Subcommittee in the former Planning Secretariat. The central policy advice role suggested by the Decter Report made a good fit with the more activist tendencies of Ford.

With the 1987 appointment of a secretary to the Planning and Priorities Committee, on the surface Ford appeared to lose nominal planning duties, but the arrangement in fact only formalized existing arrangements. His responsibility for overall policy coordination had previously been delegated to cabinet committee chairs; this arrangement would continue, but the chairs would have a higher profile. Elizabeth Wagner became the first secretary to Planning and Priorities in a decade-and-a-half. Wagner had at one time been secretary to the Economic and Resources Investment Committee of Cabinet. Michael Mendelson became the secretary to the Treasury Board; previously he had been deputy minister of the Manitoba Community Services Department.[34]

Thus began a substantial build-up of central staff in both planning and budgetary roles. In May of 1987 the Planning and Priorities Committee began advertising for new positions such as executive director of the Health and Social Policy Unit, special projects coordinator, and various policy analysts. The areas of expertise sought were in resource economics, income security, urban planning, and public finance.[35]

The government also began to strengthen its central budgetary staff. Whereas the Treasury Board Support and Financial Analysis group (as it was now called) had previously acted as a branch of the Comptroller's Division, the 1987–88 Estimates created a separate new organization.[36] From now on there would be a Treasury Board Secretariat, headed by a secretary with deputy minister status, in order to enhance the status of expenditure management in the government. The secretariat would be lead agency for coordinating estimates preparation and as well would help fulfil the other new functions outlined for the Treasury Board by the premier.

As before, there was a core Treasury Board support group to coordinate annual estimates and analyze the Province's financial position. The secretariat also included a new type of organization, called Long-Term Expenditure Management and Program Evaluation, with a mandate to achieve the longer-term expenditure reductions the premier had discussed.[37] Staff resources for the Treasury Board function doubled, some of them coming from the former ERIC staff, who had previously been physically located in the Department of Industry, Trade, and Technology (IT & T) but had fallen under the Jobs Fund appropriation. Other ERIC staff went to the Planning and Priorities Secretariat and to IT & T proper.

In terms of process, there were extensions of the institutionalized cabinet as well. These were evident in the role of Planning and Priorities, the operation of the Treasury Board, and the planning-budgeting nexus at the level of central agents. The Planning and Priorities Committee would now give the planning-budgeting nexus a more particular meaning. There was still to be some front-ending of policy in the budgetary process, but increasingly the emphasis would be on specific matters. A senior Treasury Board official noted in June 1987 that this would be accomplished by a "list system":

> Planning is everyone's intent, but the problem is to define planning—What is it? Realistically, in government, the general always gives way to the specific. Specific projects become most important. The problem is to make planning more than generalities [which it tends to be now] and to translate planning intentions into budgetary matters. There are two possible ways to do this: sectoral designations in the envelope system, or a "list system." We believe that the latter is the most effective way.
>
> PPCC's role is, in my view, to drive forward the government's agenda on twenty-three to twenty-four items: a "priority list." The priority list is essentially the NDP platform from the 1986 election. The job of PPCC [and its Secretariat] is to see that they [the items] are implemented. PPCC is *not* a passive organization waiting to react to proposals from departments, like the Planning Secretariat did [in the Schreyer Government]. It is *not* a general vetting body for individual program proposals; Treasury Board is the general vetting body. P and P set up the list and submitted it to Cabinet about two months ago.
>
> Planning and Priorities will work with departments to get the changes effected. It will monitor departments to see that they do

in fact deal with the planning priorities. It will perhaps write to departments to encourage them to deal with priorities — for example daycare.

After this fiscal year, when we have organizational matters sorted out, we will develop a planning and budgeting cycle in which we attempt to integrate the two. Protocols are still being worked out between the planners and budgeters.[38]

As might be expected with two relatively new secretariats, the staff needed time to establish their respective segments of the planning-budgeting nexus. One striking pattern was that of cross-cutting duties. The PPCC staff did not consider themselves to planners only, and TBS staff did not consider themselves only financial analysts." In a holistic fashion, the PPCC Secretariat had authority to make monetary decisions, like the Treasury Board, and its analysts were to do both policy and financial analysis on the priority proposals. The Treasury Board Secretariat planned to do analysis of the fiscal framework in addition to the usual financial analysis of individual proposals. It was expected that the linkage between the PPCC and Treasury Board (TB) would come about in a number of ways: PPCC initiatives would have to go to the Treasury Board for person-year approvals; as a member of both the PPCC and TB, the finance minister would exercise an effective veto in order to ensure financial control; and big decisions would be discussed by both committees before a decision was taken.

Protocols were established to aid cooperation between the two staffs. The Treasury Board secretary attended PPCC meetings, and the PPCC secretary was invited to TB meetings (but could not attend all of them for reasons of time). Contrary to the Decter recommendation, the deputy minister of finance was not to be a member of the Treasury Board due to time constraints.

The Public Investments Corporation of Manitoba

Cabinet's desire for political control was clearly evident in another review or, more precisely, a set of reviews that took place concerning central overview of the Crown corporation sector. A measure of central monitoring and control had taken place in the first Pawley government, but it was not until the second Pawley government that more pervasive central direction was evident. The Lyon government's Task Force on Government Organization and Economy, it will be recalled, had recommended a Treasury Committee with Crown corporations as one of its six functional areas of responsibility; one minister was to be assigned staff coordinating responsibility for the Crowns. Yet it was the Pawley government which first set up a central mechanism to coordinate the "Crowns."

In 1981 the government had established the Department of Crown Investments. It was a small department, never growing larger than about a half-dozen professionals. The purpose of the department was to coordinate and monitor the capital spending, investment, and operation plans of all provincially owned corporations. The government maintained, however, the familiar Canadian practice of not interfering in the specific day-to-day operations of the corporations. By 1986 it was clear that the Manitoba public would no longer accept such a remote relationship with the Crowns if it meant that ministers could not control the types of wrongdoing that were evident at McKenzie Seeds, MPIC, and Autopac. After first looking for answers with consultants,[39] cabinet turned inward, to a cabinet committee.

A strategy for political control of the Crowns sector was considered by a Cabinet Committee on Crown Corporation Reform, established in November 1986 and composed of ministers through whom key Crown corporations reported.[40] The committee suggested a framework for supervision of the corporations which consisted of several elements. The complexity of the framework was indicative of a desire for greater political control over Crown corporations. Among the components suggested in the framework were common financial, planning, and business conduct standards for the Crowns (compliance to be monitored by cabinet committee staff), and submission of detailed corporate business plans to a cabinet committee supervising corporations Crown.[41]

The net result of the committee's work was, in fact, the introduction of new legislation[42] covering sixteen Manitoba Crown corporations, which proposed the initiation of a holding company somewhat in the style of Saskatchewan's Crown Investments Corporation. The Public Investments Corporation of Manitoba, as the holding company was named, would have strong new centralist powers. It could, among other things, control (if desired) all income and profits of the Crowns, as well as review and approve long-term corporate plans and capital expenditure proposals.[43]

The Public Investments Corporation of Manitoba (PIC) was to be managed by a board of directors which was a cabinet committee formed from the previous Cabinet Committee on Crown Reform. The Board, according to the legislation, would consist of three or more members of the Executive Council (s.16[2]). Introducing the Crown corporations legislation, responsible minister Gary Doer noted that there was to be a "streamlining of the former Crown Investments Department and the former ERIC Committee with the holding com-

pany," presumably to establish the staff for the proposed new corporation.[44] He told the Winnipeg *Free Press* that the corporation's board
would consist of "five or six cabinet ministers."[45] There would be only
one political focus on the Crowns at the cabinet level. This essentially
followed the model of the Saskatchewan NDP Crown Investments Corporation.[46] Thus, Manitoba bypassed the more hands-off approach
implied in the Department of Crown Investments arrangement. The
political control slant was implied by Doer's comment that "it [the
Public Investments Corporation of Manitoba] will be a link between
the Crown Corporations and will function like the Treasury Board."[47]
Activism also seemed implicit in the new arrangements.[48]

Given the short length of time they were in effect, one cannot fully
assess the validity of the post-Decter reforms and the Crown sector
changes. Nonetheless, one can observe implicit criticisms of the first
Pawley government in the subtext of the Decter Report. The first
Pawley cabinet had not fully operationalized its commitment to planning and was satisfied with too much administrative centralization.
Even the Schreyer model was criticized implicitly by Decter, as witnessed by his insistence that Finance and Treasury Board functions
continue to be linked.

In his first term Pawley expanded the thin institutionalization of the
Lyon years. Partial emulation, interest groups, social science rationalism, and ideology all appeared to be factors in cabinet design. There
were, first of all, several cabinet committees. Pawley began with the
familiar Lyon-era trio of a Treasury Board with social and economic
committees. Thereafter he created several more committees to give
interest groups favoured by the government a direct line to cabinet.
Central/departmental balance was an article of faith with the government in its first term; this was a weak echo of the departmental
autonomy of the Lyon years. Central staff complements were kept low,
and departments housed some cabinet committee secretariats.

There had been multiple attempts to integrate planning and budgeting. The repeated attempts to institutionalize complementarity
bespoke an overriding dedication to social science rationalism and a
desire to apply NDP ideology to public sector policies. As in NDP
Saskatchewan, there was a collective budget process.

In the Pawley government's abbreviated second term, the Decter
Report, budget problems, and disorganization in the Crowns sector all
played a part in reshaping the central executive. The urge to have
cabinet regain political and financial control made changes in the
machinery of government imperative. A more simplified and purposeful cabinet, along the lines of the Saskatchewan Douglas-Lloyd-
Blakeney model, resulted in strong cabinet committees divided

according to the three major functions of government: policy planning, financial management, and corporate direction. The special purpose committees would continue to exist for the time being, but undoubtedly, the PPCC, TB, and PIC were to become the major workhorses of cabinet.

The clear commitment to political control by cabinet also became evident in the second term with the establishment of new secretariats for Planning and Priorities and for the Treasury Board; presumably, the Public Investments Corporation would later follow suit. Reliance on departments to staff central secretariats, which had characterized the first term, would decrease. Again the similarities to Saskatchewan were evident. As in the Blakeney era, the Pawley government appeared to believe in working out planning-budgeting complementarity at the central agency level. PPCC and TB staff worked on protocols for cooperation. A PCO-PMO split prevailed in the ECO in both terms, with the division between central political and administrative functions well understood by all participants.

In the second Pawley government, central departmental balance was still touted, but there were signs of a slight decrease in departmental autonomy. Sixteen major Crowns were placed under a single cabinet holding company. The long-term expenditure reduction mandate of the Treasury Board and its secretariat had centralist overtones. The PPCC and its secretariat were relatively forceful in pushing its priority list during departmental estimates preparation and in monitoring program implementation. Political and financial control were, in short, strong motivations.

The second Pawley government was to be short-lived. In the general election of April 26, 1988, occasioned by the defection of NDP member James Walding during a vote of non-confidence on March 8, the government suffered a crushing defeat. Public anger over rising taxes and substantially increased public automobile insurance (Autopac) premiums played a crucial role in the defeat, which saw the NDP garner only twelve of fifty-seven seats. Despite sophisticated planning, budgeting, and Crown corporation reforms, the government had become fundamentally out of touch with the electorate. Premier Filmon's minority Conservatives would now attempt, as all governments do, to prove they had a better way.

Part Four

Cabinet Decision Making
in British Columbia

Part Four

Cabinet Decision Making
in British Columbia

CONTINUITY AND REFORM

British Columbia followed a separate road in cabinet decision making for much of its history, only precipitously joining the mainstream in the last decade-and-a-half. The development of B.C.'s central executive has been as insular as its political culture. Indeed, the unaided style of cabinet continued in B.C. long after other provinces had abandoned it. Cabinet organization in other jurisdictions had long been subject to the principle of division of labour, but working cabinet committees became widespread in B.C. only in the W. R. Bennett era. Unlike in Ottawa and many provinces, cabinet was not provided with much staff aid, and this tradition is still comparatively strong. British Columbia did not participate in the budget reform movement until relatively recently and began to coordinate government policy at the cabinet level long after other provinces had initiated institutionalized coordination mechanisms.

Under W. R. Bennett, an unmistakable a sense of political modernization pervaded central executive development; but one should ignore neither the historical precedents to W. R. Bennett's institutionalization, nor the elements of continuity which have been apparent through many governments. In order to trace the steps toward institutionalization, Part IV begins the story with the W. A. C. Bennett era. At that time, there was little analysis, planning, or coordination done for the full cabinet. The elder Bennett was a "fiscally-aided" premier who was dependent on process assistance from the provincial secretary and relied on a comprehensive infrastructural plan dating from the time of World War II. There was even an incipient planning-budgeting nexus at work during his regime. Some of these steps towards institutional-ization—for instance, the provincial secretary model and the fiscally-aided premier style—were continued under Dave Barrett. Rudimentary cabinet committees were formed under both premiers.

True institutionalization came only with W. R. (Bill) Bennett. It featured several operating cabinet committees, the development of central agencies and central departments, and an elaborate budgeting framework. Initially it occurred because of an ideological factor which featured financial control as one of its elements. The populism of the Social Credit Party was oriented towards small government and against big corporations, unions, and civil service power. Accordingly, insti-tutionalization persisted for many reasons. Not the least of these was the premier's quest for influence, as Bennett sought to achieve more personal power through a new Premier's Office and an internal cabinet hierarchy.

The cabinet's wish for collective political and financial control was also instrumental in continuing the logic of institutionalization. Social science rationalism, which at the time was promoting Zero-Base Budg-eting, explained the move to Bennett's new budget infrastructure. British Columbia's new interest in intergovernmental relations, com-bined with emulation of Alberta's intergovernmental machinery, lay behind the establishment of a new Ministry of Intergovernmental Relations separate from the premier's office. (In British Columbia the word *department* was replaced by the word *ministry* for official use in 1979, and for that reason we use "ministry" throughout this chapter.) The wish to cultivate certain interest groups led to the "travelling cabinet committee" mode practiced in the early eighties. The profile of cabinet activity was accordingly heightened in the W. R. Bennett era, but his predecessors had foreshadowed this development.

Chapter Ten
The W. A. C. Bennett Era

The government of Premier William Andrew Cecil Bennett (1952–72) has often been described in extravagant phrases. Observers have viewed him as a brilliant but authoritarian leader who firmly resisted new innovations in cabinet structure, planning, and financial management—in other words, as the quintessential unaided premier. Nonetheless, one should introduce some subtleties into the accounts. It is important to demonstrate the incipient institutionalization of such Bennett practices as process assistance from the provincial secretary ministry, fiscal aid to the premier, and broad planning approaches.

One of the standard descriptions of Bennett, that of Paul Tennant, sees him as the pinnacle of *traditional cabinet* leaders. His successor, David Barrett, was to adopt the same style, minus the authoritarian leader element, in a variant that tennant called the *unaided cabinet*.[1] (Elsewhere in this study, the two italicized terms are used interchangeably, Tennant's distinction notwithstanding.) As Tennant has written,

Under Social Credit the Cabinet had remained entirely traditional—that is, simple in structure and uncomplicated in operation, lacking the committees, staff, staff agencies and extensive paper work which provide planning and coordination capability at the cabinet level in the central government and most of the larger provinces. Aside from changes in the complement of portfolios, the British Columbia Cabinet had changed scarcely at all since Confederation. A few cabinet committees existed but met rarely and played only a rudimentary role. The Treasury Board was completely dominated by the Premier—both ministers and public referred to the Board as "he." The Board had no staff of its own while other committees and the cabinet itself had no staff whatever. There was no clerk to the cabinet and no staff official attended cabinet meetings. For policy advice the cabinet ministers relied largely on senior officials. Individual ministers were allowed wide policy latitude providing that major new expenditures were not involved. Over expenditures the Premier personally exerted minutely-detailed control. The Premier's authoritarian control harmonized with both the attitudes and goals of the government. Financial constraint was highly valued; a balanced budget was seen as the chief indicator of good government; and governmental goals were mainly those of economic development which can be effected on a project basis, rather than those of change in social policy, which require continual and close intergovernmental cooperation. More generally, it would appear that the traditional cabinet is one in which complex planning capability cannot be achieved and in which, at best, coordination may be achieved by an authoritarian leader.[2]

Tennant notes other characteristics of the traditional cabinet. One is that "within the cabinet itself in any policy area there can be no reliable and consistent source of information other than the minister in charge of the area."[3] Another is that "the political entrepreneurship of the more forceful ministers becomes the dominant factor in decision-making."[4]

Young and Morley's review of the elder Bennett's style is surprisingly brief. It stresses his solitary approach:

The W. A. C. Bennett era was characterized by the solitary management of the provincial enterprise by the premier. He did not have an elaborate office staff; indeed he did not even employ an executive assistant. In the latter years of his career, however, that function was performed in large measure by the deputy provincial secretary, L. J. Wallace. Bennett managed the government by exercising strict scrutiny over the minutiae of provincial finance— he met daily with his deputy minister, Gerry Bryson, to review the accounts—and by delegating responsibility to his ministers once the general decisions had been made. It was an effective means of control at a time when the public service was small and malleable. He received his political advice from outside advisors and public relations experts.[5]

Careless's coverage of W. A. C. Bennett is also brief but has the advantage of analyzing his leadership in structural terms. Careless notes that traditional Finance Departments and Treasury Boards were relatively unsophisticated, as was the case in British Columbia; but when they were directly controlled by the premier, serving as responsible minister, they facilitated centralized political control. Careless described this situation as follows:

> Finance Departments were rarely a countervailing force of economic expertise to the narrow interests of departments but were largely an accounting and financial management operation. In fact, so rudimentary were the provincial departments of Finance that very often the premier was also the minister of finance, administering revenues to departments from his own back pocket. British Columbia until 1971 was long representative of this practice, the premier in effect controlled the role of departmental expenditures himself. Because he combined the pinnacles of political and economic power, few departmental changes could be made without his approval, thereby excessively centralizing decision-making. The Treasury Board of British Columbia's Cabinet under Bennett consisted of the premier, deputy minister of Finance, and only two other ministers who sat in judgement upon all the expenditures and management of government services, however small. There was reportedly no planning or priority-setting process outside the premier's mind, no secretary to Treasury Board existed, and there was no use of the more sophisticated and modern techniques of program development and evaluation. Premier Bennett's budgetary control was highly personal and pragmatic, reinforced by the success of his past financial gambles, corrected by his famous "second looks" and made possible by a buoyant and rapidly expanding provincial economy.[6]

Such summaries of the W. A. C. Bennett era are essentially correct but demand qualification since they leave out some elements of incipient institutionalization. The summaries do not, for example, elaborate on the beginnings of a cabinet committee system or acknowledge the planning implications inherent in the development projects launched by the premier. Care should be also taken to explain unaided aspects of his leadership more fully. The summaries reveal that financial control was exercised by means of the premier's vetting of new expenditures but do not mention the additional leverage afforded by his special accounts. Most studies also ignore aspects of the financial management modernization that Bennett introduced. Much of the richness of detail about his premiership is often passed over in favour of more facile generalizations.

In a way, this is understandable since the premier himself never made much of his administrative accomplishments. The emphasis was always on the big picture—even in Bennett's retirement. In 1975, while reminiscing about his accomplishments, he never even mentioned the more prosaic administrative matters, concentrating instead on the building of highways, bridges, and schools; on the "paid off" direct debt; and on the surpluses in perpetual funds and special funds.[7] He could also have mentioned, if he had wanted to, the stunning political coups—almost Gaullist in their imagination and scope—that allowed him to escape narrow ideological classification. Despite a professed faith in free enterprise, he nationalized B. C. Electric and a ferry line, opened the interior with a public railway, and attempted to establish a provincial bank. It was an era of province building, and W. A. C. Bennett was its main architect. Certainly, economic growth in the province was remarkable under his direction; even on the verge of his defeat, the *Financial Post* was forecasting strong increases in the Gross Provincial Product, retail sales, and investment, toasting B.C. as a low-tax province.[8]

Like many other contemporary British Columbians, W. A. C. Bennett had come from elsewhere. He was born in New Brunswick in 1900 and migrated to B.C. as a young man, soon becoming a successful Kelowna hardware merchant. He was elected in 1941 as a Coalition member and remained one for the next ten years. After a year as an independent, he joined the B.C. Social Credit Party ("Socreds" in the political vernacular), realizing it was a likely vehicle for his political ambitions. The provincial general election of 1952 saw an inconclusive result, with the Socreds reaching nineteen seats, the Cooperative Commonwealth Federation (CCF) gaining eighteen seats, and the Liberals and Conservatives winning six and four, respectively. The caucus chose Bennett as the new leader, and the lieutenant-governor asked him to form a new government. He was to govern for the next twenty years by exploiting the polarized politics of the province. "Opposites," Bennett said, "always save each other."[9] A new coalition of labour, public sector workers, environmentalists, and young people formed against him, however, and he lost the 1972 election. Soon after, he abandoned the leadership. W. A. C. Bennett died in 1979.

CABINET STRUCTURE

For most of Bennett's era, the cabinet structure was in the standard unaided form. The Treasury Board was the only working committee, and even it was a shell to be used by Bennett for his own designs. In his last few years as premier, he established a handful of policy committees, but only one — the Environment and Land Use Committee (ELUC) — was at all consequential. Bennett's cabinets were small; in 1953 there were a mere eleven ministers, and in 1972 only seventeen.

The Audit Act of 1913 mentioned the Treasury Board for the first time in British Columbia legislation (ss.3–7) and established the collective nature of financial decision making in the province.[10] Accordingly, the Treasury Board consisted of the minister of finance and three members of the Executive Council. The minister of finance was the ex officio secretary, through whom all internal and external governmental communications were to flow. The Treasury Board was to "act as a committee of the Executive Council in all matters related to finance, revenue, expenditure, or Public Accounts" (s.4). This act remained essentially unchanged for the next seven decades, mandating collective financial decision making for successive governments. Yet financial decision making was not a collective exercise in the Bennett cabinet.

For most of the W. A. C. Bennett era, the Treasury Board remained the only working cabinet committee, however ineffectual it might have been as a collegial body. There was, however, a short period of experimentation with cabinet committees during the late sixties and early seventies. Sidor has noted that "the Bennett government, in 1969, had established several other cabinet committees, [besides Treasury Board] including Land Use; Human Services; Manpower and Employment; and Transportation, Housing and Urban Development. None of these committees, however, not even Treasury Board, had any specifically designated staff.[11] The committees appear not to have had much effect on policy.

One other working policy committee came about at the end of Bennett's tenure. Although its origin owed more to pressure from environmental lobbies than to a desire to shape policy, the creation of the informal Environment and Land Use Committee of Cabinet (ELUC) in 1969 can be seen as a tentative step towards sectoral planning. The Environment and Land Use Act of 1971 later gave a statutory basis to the ELUC and mandated it to study and recommend on any environmental matter. With no membership specified, it allowed the ELUC in turn to create technical committees (again with no specific membership specified). Bennett created one such technical committee, placing on it the deputy ministers of the six departments represented on the ministerial committee. "During the remainder of Bennett's term of office, a narrow interpretation and use was made of the broad policy-making power granted to the [ministerial] committee by the *Act*,"[12] but the die had been cast. In future administrations the ELUC and its secretariat, which was to take the place of the Technical Committee, would undertake important planning efforts.

CENTRAL AGENCIES

W. A. C. Bennett had central staff, but they were characteristic of unaided cabinet arrangements. Such staff assisted the premier mainly in fiscal matters and were situated in central departments. The lack of staff serving cabinet in Bennett's time has been widely noted. The Treasury Board did not have any staff of its own, but relied on the Department of Finance for temporary loans of personnel during the estimates preparation period. With only sporadic use of cabinet committees and a tradition of no staff involvement in cabinet meetings, cabinet paperwork was handled by the deputy provincial secretary, Laurie Wallace.

This is not to say, however, that the premier went unassisted or that there was a lack of central staff. Central staff in the Provincial Secretary Department and the Department of Finance — both central departments — provided analytical and coordinative assistance, primarily to the premier. When he began his premiership, W. A. C. Bennett was probably not markedly out of step with his fellow premiers as far as central assistance went. The Provincial Secretary Department was a surrogate performer of what other provinces would have called the Executive Council Office or the cabinet secretariat function. Historically, this department had always served multifarious duties thrust upon it by the vagaries of provincial development. The need for cabinet record keeping generated just one more duty. Accounts seem to indicate the deputy provincial secretary's role was shaped more to help the premier than to assist full cabinet.[13]

As noted by Young and Morley, Bennett was aided by L. J. Wallace, the deputy provincial secretary. Although they refer to him merely an executive assistant to the premier, starting with the 1970–71 *Public Accounts* of British Columbia (at the end of Bennett's term), Wallace is listed as deputy to the premier. After 1970–71 Wallace was paid out of the Premier's Office appropriation, not through the Department of the Provincial Secretary; this would seem to denote both the beginning of an institutionalized Premier's Office and a higher, "modern" profile for the official performing deputy functions.

During the Bennett era, the British Columbia Department of Finance was also slowly adopting some functions usually associated with mature central bureaucracies. Ritter and Cutt have revealed that as early as 1954 a financial research staff, answering to the assistant deputy minister of finance, was established.[14] In 1964 the research function merited a branch of its own, called the Financial and Economic Research Branch. The branch handled some of the more prosaic duties of the government: preparing prospectuses for borrowing, publishing the annual *Financial and Economic Review*, and monitoring revenue and expenditure performance. However, it also analyzed issues of budget policy, tax policy, and federal-provincial relations—and prepared the budget speech.[15]

Assistance to Bennett from such central departments demonstrated early signs of an aided premiership, if not an aided cabinet. Moreover, such a fiscally-aided premier may be considered a forerunner of the transition to an institutionalized cabinet.

DECISION-MAKING MODES

Financial decision making was not a collective exercise in the Bennett cabinet. Despite the radical growth in revenues and expenditures during Bennett's tenure, there was little growth in central staff aid to the collective cabinet and to the Treasury Board in particular. Instead, it was the premier's power which grew, and he achieved it through four means: the budget process, financial information, special funds, and debt financing procedures. This work will consider these four items together, unlike most reviews that discuss the W. A. C. Bennett era.

However, one must first emphasize that it was Bennett's holding of dual portfolios—those of premier and finance minister from 1953 to 1972—that allowed him the most clout. Former Social Credit Minister Dan Campbell has called Bennett's leadership the "imperial premiership" period in British Columbia history because of this practice.[16]

The first and major source of the premier's leverage was the budget process; here Bennett reigned alone. He described his budget process to his biographer, David Mitchell, in the following revealing account:

Before my administration in 1952, budgeting was very complicated. I developed a system of budgeting so simple that it worked like a charm. The government was divided up into departments, and as premier and minister of finance, I was also chairman of the Treasury Board. Before a department got to Treasury Board to determine their budget, a lot of preliminary work had to be done. So starting in late October, the estimates from all the departments came in from all over the province; they were assembled, and totalled . . . My deputy minister with his staff and the comptroller general would go through the estimates with every department separately in great detail. This was what I called "little treasury board." They would prepare a bare-bones estimate of the programs that were then operating and should be continued: the bare-bones budget. Then they made note of the things that the departments would like to have included in the next budget in addition, and they would place them in order of preference, and the reason why the preference should be given. That bare-bones budget would be really very tough: for argument's sake, $200 million less than I would be prepared to budget for the coming year. Because my finance department officials had already made a study of what the economic conditions were likely to be in the next fiscal year— the rate of expansion we could expect and so forth—I would have a certain amount to allocate over the existing programs of these departments.

Then we would have regular Treasury Board; I was in the chair and we had three ministers there. We'd sit around the table and each person would have the prepared estimates of the department we were dealing with in front of him. The minister in charge of the department and his deputy would appear before us, and we were dealing then with new policies and expansion of present ones. It didn't get into a debating society, but they were arguing why they needed more money and for what reasons . . . If they could convince us, they would get it, because I had my maximum budget I could allow before me at all times, which I didn't disclose. Over a week's time we'd hear from all the departments and I would prepare my budget. That budget was an instrument of government policy to get the province moving and increase the standard of living.[17]

A Finance official of that time noted that Bennett "commanded the government. There was no commitment of money without the Premier's approval. His influence was widespread. Only one or two ministers had any degree of independence of movement."[18] Major spending decisions were planned and executed not within cabinet but within a tiny circle of officials, of which the finance deputy and comptroller general were usually a part. Norman Ruff has observed signs that the Bennett system was beginning to outlive its usefulness as an expenditure forecaster by the end of the 1960s.[19]

A second source of Bennett's financial leverage was the premier's monopolization of financial information. Collective responsibility implies a certain sharing of information within cabinet. However, Bennett's style was to heighten input to the premier and restrict output to cabinet. Daily and monthly financial statements gave him a constant update on the financial status of the province. "Such detailed accounting measures gave Bennett tremendous power and manouverability, especially since these financial statements were for his eyes only. He was fond of saying 'Information is power.' As Premier and Minister of Finance he possessed monopoly control over the financial information relating to his various government departments and agencies. He never made the information public, nor did he share it with his colleagues. Consequently, he usually knew far more about the finances of individual government departments than the ministers in charge."[20]

A third source of Premier Bennett's leverage was the extraordinary leeway given to the executive (and, one presumes, primarily to the premier) to manipulate expenditures through "special purpose funds." This arrangement not only strengthened the hand of the premier over his cabinet but over the legislature as well. According to a financial official of the time, special purpose funds allowed Bennett "to squirrel money away rather than alerting the public to the surpluses—and to [convey] the implication that the tax load was too heavy."[21] Special purpose funds consisted of certain earmarked revenues and various funds set aside over the years using general fund surpluses and current revenue. Furthermore, expenditure from special purpose funds was authorized by the legislation establishing them; annual approval of the legislature for fund expenditures was therefore unnecessary. Special purpose funds evolved in four categories: perpetual funds, project funds, revolving funds, and earmarked revenue funds.[22] The following paragraphs summarize their characteristics.

Perpetual Funds were established to allow expenditures for specified purposes, and financed with transfers from the general fund. The capital balance of the fund could not be touched (hence the name "perpetual") but interest earnings on the assets could be spent for the purpose identified. Between 1967 and 1971 five perpetual funds were established. The First Citizens' Fund, which provided for native education and economic development, was one of the better-known perpetual funds.

Project Funds were generally meant to be one-time or special project expenditures, which were limited to the amount of the original expenditure. They were created with transfers from the general fund. The Burrard Inlet (Third Crossing) Fund was one example of a project fund. The 1972 *Financial and Economic Review* noted that the capital sum for perpetual and special funds amounted to $227 million.[23] In 1971–72 the actual total expenditures of the province, by comparison, were $1.47 billion.[24]

Revolving Funds were transfers from the general fund which enabled investments or loans to be made for provincial programs. They were "revolving" in the sense that repayment of the loans or interest on the investments would be credited back to the individual funds, instead of to the general fund itself. The repayment or interest would in turn be available for further outlay. In contrast, Earmarked Revenue Funds provided for expenditures for purposes defined in enabling legislation, from funds that came not from the general fund, but from specified revenue sources.[25]

Responsible government was damaged by this pattern of special purpose funds. The legislature was denied the opportunity to scrutinize vast areas of government activity because much of the activity was self-sustaining year after year. Furthermore, the range of activity covered by special purpose funds could and did expand after the initial pattern was established. Given the premier's fascination with arcane financial dealings, it is probably safe to assume that the special funds provided Bennett with a method of manipulating fellow cabinet members as well. They were also a kind of incipient planning-budgeting nexus; Bennett planned his projects, then made sure he could fund them. Reform of the special funds structure was not to occur in British Columbia until 1982.[26]

In other respects, Bennett's practices seem similar to those of the later reform era in Canadian public finance. His centralization of financial decision making in the Finance Department has a distinctly contemporary ring to it. Revenues were consistently underestimated from year to year to allow the premier to hobble ministerial ambitions. Technological advances such as computers were introduced in the sixties, bringing daily and monthly financial monitoring to a fine art. Unlike later finance ministers, however, Bennett did not have to struggle for leverage in financial control; expenditures were carefully related to available revenues.

The fourth source of Bennett's leverage was his method of debt financing. Bennett's debt financing can be seen both as an example of lack of candor and as a necessary expedient which provided political leeway for the premier to act. Misrepresentation of the province's public debt situation could be interpreted as lack of candor. The 1952 Budget Speech of the new Social Credit government had placed the net public debt at $190 million; seven years later it was declared nil by the deputy minister of finance and comptroller general of the province. A huge bond-burning ceremony on Okanagan Lake on August 1, 1959 celebrated this feat, flaming its way into political legend. Yet as we saw, Bennett was coincidentally embarking on one of the most ambitious capital expenditure programs in British Columbia history, far beyond the range of current revenues to sustain.

In 1961 Alfred E. Carlsen analyzed the techniques of debt elimination used by the W. A. C. Bennett government.[27] Essentially, the Socred solution consisted of retiring the province's direct debt and expanding its indirect debt (also called "contingent liabilities" or guaranteed debt). To a lesser extent, introducing rigid economies and capitalizing upon buoyant revenues helped to eliminate the debt.

> Yet the considerable budget surpluses achieved through increased revenue and economy of administration do not begin to offset the enormous growth in certain capital outlays—outlays which under earlier regimes would have been classified as budget items. The answer to this apparent anomaly lies in a revised system of bookkeeping. Basically the technique employed has been that of removing from the budget three items of capital outlay which could be considered wholly or partially self-supporting. Thus the debt services for such outlays need not be a significant charge upon the general revenue, and can be disposed of by a "subsidy" or "grant" system. These three items are the Pacific Great Eastern Railway, the Toll Highways and Bridges Authority, and the Provincial Government's share of school construction costs.[28]

British Columbia was not the only province to employ guaranteed debt, but its uniqueness lay in the exclusive use of this category of debt. Ironically, however, the British Columbia government paid off the toll highways and bridges debts, in 1963, and the ferry service debts, in 1966, with current revenues; they had not in fact been self-supporting.

Guaranteed debt, once established as a bookkeeping alternative, could be and was used in other areas. For instance, it was used to finance the public takeover of the British Columbia Electric Company in 1961. The British Columbia Hydro and Power Authority was forced by the premier to borrow $27 million to finance the lion's share of the last of the province's direct debt. Hydro authorities objected, and a full blown controversy led to the establishment of a Royal Commission on B.C. Hydro—The Schrum Commission. The commission vindicated the government's right to do this, but the controversy had made the conversion of direct debt to a contingent liability a politically dangerous action.[29]

In another sense, the debt servicing provisions were necessary expedients. Although they led to confusion in the public mind about the correct debt picture (British Columbia's *total* debt was the highest in Canada in 1965, while the premier maintained the province was debt free)[30] they allowed the government a certain political breathing space to undertake the capital projects. By allowing various authorities to undertake public borrowing and having them levy service charges to cover it, Bennett was distancing himself from the political dangers associated with public finance. It might also be argued that the arrangement gave British Columbians a necessary feeling of self-confidence. History professor Sydney W. Jackman would proclaim proudly in his chapter on Bennett in *Portraits of the Premiers* of B.C. that "W.A.C. Bennett's financial policies have been climaxed by the elimination of the provincial debt."[31] No qualifications were given.

PLANNING

Bennett's planning framework was largely in the unaided mold, but it had some elements of institutionalization to it. True to the unaided style, planning under Bennett remained for the most part at the premier-centered (or personalistic) and project-oriented stage, but occasionally extended to the more ambitious coordinated sectoral and macro investment plan stage. Yet W. A. C. Bennett's planning was by no means a model of thoroughgoing institutionalization. It was comprehensive but not collegial. His *modus operandi* was based too much on intuition and situation-specific solutions. Yet it is important not to lose sight of the seeds of an institutionalized planning approach, even if it was mostly premier based rather than cabinet oriented.

Such a nuanced characterization runs counter to most descriptions of Bennett's activities. Some observers of the W. A. C. Bennett era typify it as being marked by a lack of complex planning capability. If any planning was done, they say, it was simply on a project basis.[32] Again, qualifications are necessary. Indeed, Mitchell goes so far as to say that "W.A.C. Bennett's was the last BC Government to have a clear idea of where it was going and how to get there, all of which was based on the premier's master plan for provincial development— a vision which preoccupied his administration for the greater part of his long tenure . . . With his power, for twenty years he shaped a province and its developing hinterland: he shaped British Columbia."[33]

Mitchell's biography of W. A. C. Bennett, which is based on in-depth interviews with the ex-premier, reveals the personalistic, project-

216

oriented side of Bennett's planning. Bennett took a great deal of satisfaction in devising solutions to policy problems himself, sometimes over the objections of his officials. For example, the homeowner grant—at the time an innovative form of tax relief featuring a rebate on municipal property taxes and administration of the program by municipal governments—had been promised by Bennett in the 1956 election campaign; it was implemented despite the objections of his deputy treasurer.[34]

In the mid-1960s Bennett decided to champion the foundation of a new bank, the Bank of British Columbia, in which the Province would have a minority portion of share capital. The genesis for the idea, Mitchell contends, was the long series of affronts that banks had dealt Bennett in his private and public life.[35] Although the federal government opposed the Bennett-sponsored proposal in 1965, it allowed a totally private proposal to succeed the next year. Mitchell contends that "the Bank of British Columbia certainly differs from W.A.C. Bennett's original vision, but in a real sense it is a product of his initiative."[36]

In transportation policy, Bennett defied advisors who wanted him to sell the money-losing Pacific Great Eastern (later the British Columbia) Railway to the private sector. He cancelled its debts, made himself its president, and planned to extend it even past Prince George to the Peace River country. Mitchell suggests that this urge was partially based on a desire to open up the interior to economic development and partially on a mystical attraction to the area based on relations with his errant father, whom he had last seen there.[37] It was also Bennett who paved the way for what is now the giant B.C. Hydro by deciding to nationalize the B.C. Electric Company, a federally chartered private utility which provided the bulk of electrical service to British Columbians.[38] "Bennett had always advocated an economic system based upon free enterprise and private initiative; therefore it is ironical that he, more than any other BC premier, encouraged the citizenry to rely upon the government to promote their economic well-being. In truth, Bennett was a practising interventionist who taught British Columbians to look to Victoria as the miracle mechanic of the economic machine; and of course the main structural changes in the provincial economy had been engineered in his office."[39]

It may be useful to consider Bennett's interventionism in the context of comparative development planning. Albert Waterston notes that in mixed economies, planning almost always follows a three-stage process.[40] The first stage is the "project-by-project approach," which features public investment projects done on a piecemeal basis with no unifying concept. The next stage is "integrated public investment planning," in which individual projects are prioritized and cumulatively combined into sectoral then macro investment plans for the public sector in order to increase the sum of benefits from the resources available. The last stage, rarely achieved, is "comprehensive planning," which has these characteristics: use of growth models, relating of inputs to outputs, targetting by both public and private sectors, and successive attempts to mesh "top-down" planning by the public sector and "bottom-up" planning by the private sector. Waterston maintains that almost all government planning starts at the project-by-project stage, but that it is preferable to move beyond it.

The rough outlines of integrated public investment planning — Waterston's second stage of planning — can be seen in the policies of W. A. C. Bennett. Mitchell, in fact, goes so far as to imply that a comprehensive macro plan existed for most of the infrastructural improvements Bennett initiated. Bennett helped write the *Interim Report of the Post-War Rehabilitation Council* (1942) for the coalition government in his early days as an M.L.A. The report recommended the extension of the Pacific Great Eastern Railway; the establishment of a publicly owned hydroelectric authority; the development of the agricultural, forestry, and mining industries; and the establishment of a steel industry. Mitchell has noted that

> The scope of the interim report was impressive and, when combined with the Council's final report which was completed, it represented a comprehensive portrait of the hopes and aspirations for the next generation of British Columbians.
>
> W.A.C. Bennett, who put so much of his own time and energy into the report, felt strongly about the council's recommendations and he became frustrated and disillusioned when the government did not enthusiastically endorse them in whole or in part . . .
>
> Interestingly, years later Bennett himself would have the opportunity to fulfill many of the council's recommendations; the little-known report would become a virtual master plan for the development of Canada's west coast province.[41]

At the very least, the master plan seemed to be an example of Waterston's second stage: a prioritized and cumulative development outline which was targetted at a distinct socio-economic category. (This made it unlike most modern plans, which purport to have the general population as the focus for plans.)

There was indeed prioritization. Edwin R. Black has pointed out that "in preferring the individual who owns and operates his own [economic] concern, Social Credit and its supporters are suspicious of big financial interests, big bureaucracies and big integrated development companies."[42] A preference for the owner-operator can be seen in many of Bennett's programs, Black argues. In other matters, "the dovetailing of the interests of Social Credit with those of the support base in the electorate may be seen in a number of policies. The encouragement of property ownership and of the house-building industry, through home-owner grants and home-purchase subsidies, is an excellent example. Another is found in the case of the Bank of British Columbia. Here we see manifestations both of Social Credit's strong distrust of the larger Eastern financial institutions and of its desire to provide better credit facilities for small- and medium-sized business enterprises in the province that are at a disadvantage in competing for capital with the giant corporations.[43]

There was also a sectoral emphasis. Realizing that general economic prosperity and environmental protection dictated reliance on giant industries in forestry, mining, ranching, and fruit farming, Bennett opted to greatly expand the physical communications system. New highways, bridges, ferries, access roads, and a renovated railway would yield benefits to small-scale operators. They promoted social integration, which allowed for rapid economic change, and permitted small cities to act as regional service centres—havens for small businesses. Besides access to resources, access for tourists (attractive to small business) was facilitated by transportation expansion. Such expansion also furthered the fortunes of small-scale contractors.[44] Seen from the perspective of a "state capitalist" seeking to cater to a well-defined clientele, Bennett's planning activity was not so random as it may at first seem. One must ask oneself an important question: faced with the constraints that Bennett faced, would an army of sympathetic public sector planners have devised a much different scenario? They would at least have started where Bennett did.

Bennett's planning therefore contained many unaided elements as well as some hints of the institutionalized style. It was in the unaided style in the sense that it was mostly sporadic, personalistic, and project oriented. There was some extension beyond this, however, in the use of a comprehensive infrastructure plan from the Second World War era and of a prioritized and cumulative approach to project planning (as Waterston would have termed it).

Reviewing the W. A. C. Bennett era, then, one must acknowledge the broad applicability of the terms *traditional* and *unaided* when describing cabinet. Qualifications, however, are necessary. Cabinet was indeed traditional, lacking committees other than the Treasury Board until late in the era (1969), when a handful of committees, subsequently to prove relatively inactive, were created. One of them, the Environment and Land Use Committee, received a statutory foundation only in 1971. Cabinet itself was not provided with staff analytical assistance, and budgeting was rudimentary and premier oriented. Yet Bennett was laying the foundation for future institutionalization. He received fiscal assistance from Treasury officials, process assistance from provincial secretary officials, and practised a form of planning which contained some elements of the institutionalized style.

Bennett's central staff pattern was indeed an unaided cabinet arrangement. Cabinet did lack staff agencies explicity designed to aid collective decision making, but at least the premier himself had help from central departments in fiscal and organizational matters. For more prosaic process assistance regarding cabinet record keeping, Bennett could turn to Provincial Secretary L. J. Wallace, who in the early 1970s was styled the deputy to the premier. It is true that there was not a PCO or ECO model in operation, but perhaps one could call it a "Provincial Secretary model" as far as the clerical function was concerned. Deputy Minister of Finance Gerry Bryson, his staff, and the comptroller general assisted the premier in preliminary estimates review in such detail that Bennett nicknamed them the "little Treasury Board." One might challenge Careless's statement that no secretary to the Treasury Board existed. According to the Audit Act of 1913 the minister of finance was to be secretary to the Treasury Board by virtue of his office. In practice, surely Finance Deputy Bryson acted as a de facto Treasury Board secretary. Ritter has detailed the gradual accretion of functions by Bennett's Finance Department.

The planning implications of the W. A. C. Bennett era have been downplayed, as previously noted. Tennant has observed that, at best, the authoritarian leader (Bennett) can achieve coordination of economic development projects, while Careless has claimed that there was no planning or priority setting outside the premier's mind. Yet planning, even if confined to a premier's mind, *is* planning, and calling the conception of very complex development projects merely "coordination" seems a misuse of words. Much of the process, to be sure, was in the unaided style: sporadic, personalistic, and project oriented. Yet Bennett also relied upon a comprehensive plan for infrastructural improvements put together as a reconstruction exercise during World War II.

As well, evidence of integrated planning might be seen in his combining of sectoral project plans to focus benefits on the Socred electorate of owner-operators and inhabitants of small regional cities. These could be seen as incipient institutionalized planning. Under Bennett, there was even a kind of incipient relationship between planning and budgeting. To finance major projects, the premier constructed special accounts or categorized capital projects as self-supporting entities whose debt charges could ostensibly be disposed of by subsidies.

All of this is not to suggest that Bennett would have considered himself a planner in the modern sense. He often bypassed the conventional wisdom of experts, ignored the niceties of social policy, and imprinted his ideas on the public rather than polling the public for ideas. He was a big dreamer with a hardware merchant's financial common sense.

During W. A. C. Bennett's regime, cabinet and the departmental bureaucracy were plainly dominated by the premier. He centralized financial knowledge in his person, generated major policy decisions for which ministers only filled in details, and controlled new initiatives through the estimates process. Government had been small enough to permit this personalistic style, but toward the end of the era signs of mismanagement began to emerge. When his successor attempted essentially the same style, the results were not salutary.

Chapter Eleven
The Barrett Interlude

David Barrett, like his predecessor, has been characterized in simplistic terms. Few redeeming factors appear in the portrayal of his central executive operation. He is portrayed as the genial but ineffectual leader who allowed his dozen-and-a-half ministers to have free rein in a system devoid of priority setting or planning for most of his time in office (1972–75). This comes closer to a caricature than to a characterization.

The critiques of Barrett have substance, but they are incomplete. They downplay the degree of institutional learning the NDP was assimilating. Barrett was actually drawn in opposite directions: one involved emulation of his unaided predecessor; the other involved institutionalization in the style of other contemporary Canadian cabinets, as promoted by his heavyweight planning advisor to cabinet. There was indeed significant ministerial/departmental autonomy in non-financial matters, combined with a lack of policy coordination by full cabinet: these unaided characteristics persisted for most of the Barrett interlude.

However, some moves in the direction of institutionalization should be noted. First of all, the premier was fiscally aided both by Finance and by a planning advisor housed outside Finance. There was also the belated creation of cabinet committees and a de facto Cabinet Secretariat, both formed as a result of the input from the new planning advisor to cabinet. The government was, in fact, learning that the unaided style was fraught with dangers, but this realization came too late to change most observers' views about the unaided nature of the Barrett cabinet.

Barrett seems only tardily to have admitted the emulation factor in his own psychological make-up. In 1991 he maintained to an interviewer, who questioned him about the effect of W. A. C. Bennett on his own political style, that the insularity of B.C. politics made other role models of premiers hard to come by. "The reality," Barrett explained, "is that I sat across from him [Bennett] for twelve years. I didn't know any other legislature or any other political arena than the one I served in."[1]

Offsetting this emulative factor, however, was a commitment to activist government that grew out of solid socialist roots. The son of a small merchant, Fabian socialist father and a mother on the radical left, Barrett grew up in the working class East End of Vancouver. He studied philosophy at the University of Seattle and later undertook social work studies at St. Louis University. Barrett later attributed his socialist beliefs to a combination of his family background and Catholic encyclicals that had influenced him while at Seattle.[2] Relying on reformist insights he had garnered in his St. Louis education, he went to work for a short stormy period at the B.C. Department of Corrections in 1956. His political career began with election to the provincial legislature in 1960, and he was re-elected in the general elections of 1963, 1966, and 1969. He replaced Tom Berger as party leader in 1969 and went on to form the government in 1972.

Always one to appeal to emotionalism in his listeners—one observer described his pitch as combining "the hypnotic whining of a Sunday morning evangelist with the relentless pace of a Vegematic salesman on late-night television"[3]—he was at first unconcerned about more rationalist organizational concerns. His was a government which undervalued the coordination of the blizzard of reforms it had introduced until the lack of such organization began to have electoral implications. A greater concern for organization followed the politically damaging revelation that there had been a $100 million expenditure overrun in the Department of Human Resources. What better way to solve the government's image problem than to hire Marc Eliesen, who combined socialist conviction and technical smarts, to reinvent the machinery of government in the style of the more advanced social democratic administrations of the day?

CABINET AND CENTRAL AGENCIES

Paul Tennant's view of the NDP government as "unaided politicians in an unaided cabinet" is one which has dominated the literature on the

Barrett interlude.[4] Tennant's view is that Barrett continued the traditional cabinet operation established by W. A. C. Bennett, except that he did not act in the authoritarian style that had allowed Bennett to control the government so completely. Major decisions were taken by dominant ministers, not by cabinet collectively; the NDP cabinet was apparently little more than a "bargaining centre." Financial reporting was not well developed so evaluation of policy proposals was hindered. Legislation was quickly and badly drafted. For most of the Barrett interlude there were no research and support staff reporting to cabinet because of a perceived danger that initiative would be stifled and that party goals would be sabotaged by planners.

Tennant has noted that the government saw a choice between beginning to implement socialism in a series of steps and attending to general matters such as constructing a cabinet bureaucracy. The premier emphasized the former at first, leading to deficiencies in central processes. For example, there was not even a cabinet agenda. The financial system of the B.C. government became the crudest in Canada. To prove how crude the NDP financial system was, Tennant quotes an unnamed Department of Finance economist (appointed to a senior position in the Barrett years), who characterized it as "stop and go. Revenues in, then revenues out. No financial planning. No financial forecasting. No priorities established. They frowned on economists and would wait until the revenue numbers came in and then would draw up their budgets.[5]

Tennant maintains that the situation changed with the belated introduction of a cabinet bureaucracy, but not much. The position of planning advisor to cabinet (PAC) originated in 1974, not from a commitment to planning, but from a desire to balance the budget as a traditional cabinet would. (Of course, a traditional cabinet would have chosen the Finance Department to implement budget balancing, so the choice of the PAC for this purpose is puzzling and is not explained by Tennant.) Appointed as a result of the budgetary crisis of 1974, the PAC's duties were mostly financial control, rather than the officially described duties of policy research, policy coordination, and federal-provincial relations.

There was, Tennant found, widespread bureaucratic resistance to the PAC; not even in the Department of Finance, where Barrett was minister, were there changes made to aid the PAC. The policy process was instead dominated by departmental policy groups—task forces, consultants, and commissions of enquiry—and by extra-departmental agencies. "In all the NDP established some twenty-five new agencies outside the regular departments and completely restructured some half-dozen existing agencies."[6] The ELUC and its secretariat and the Institute for Economic Policy Analysis (IEPA) at the University of Victoria constituted the only attempts (beyond instituting the PAC) to plan and coordinate in a cross-departmental sense, according to Tennant.

Marc Eliesen was the NDP's influential planning advisor to cabinet. He had been hired from Manitoba, where he was secretary to the Planning and Priorities Committee in the Schreyer government. Extremely dissatisfied with the Tennant study, Eliesen has stressed that there were in fact important institutionalized elements in the Barrett machinery of government:

> The [Tennant] article denied the existence of a systematic way of dealing with government policy. The existence of a cabinet structure, of an agenda, of the Environment and Land Use Committee, are denied in the article. [Actually, ELUC is mentioned, but its significance seemed muted.] One established committee, the Environment and Land Use Committee of Cabinet, did exist through the Barrett government, under Bob Williams. I came in with a list of things I wanted to implement. One was a cabinet agenda; another was a cabinet bureaucracy. BC politicians lived in a different era and focussed on different things. That made the system hard to crank up overnight [but we did ultimately derive a system] . . .
>
> There was the Office of the Planning Advisor, which had a coordinating function. We set up the basis of cabinet committees at the centre, following the system of the federal government with its division of cabinet into functional committees. We initiated program evaluation. We introduced minutes of cabinet meetings as well as a Planning and Priorities Committee.[7]

Bryden notes that in the Barrett cabinet "four policy committees were established dealing with the environment and land use, human services, transport and communication, and labour and justice, along with a Legislation Committee."[8] How these matters could have escaped the notice of other commentators is puzzling. They seem to indicate that the government was at least moving toward formalized decision making, if not an all-out planning approach. They also indicate that a new centre of influence had formed in the central executive: Barrett had chosen a new planning advisor and was obviously taking his advice very seriously.[9]

It should also be noted that a Treasury Board did in fact exist. It consisted of the premier; the minister of lands, forests, and water resources, Robert Williams; the minister of transport and communications, Robert Strachan; and the provincial secretary, Ernest Hall.[10]

225

From 1972 to 1974, however, Barrett—emulating Bennett—continued the past practice of "big" and "little" Treasury Boards. This pattern meant that the little Treasury Board (Barrett and Deputy Minister of Finance Gerald Bryson continuing as secretary of the Treasury Board) dominated fiscal decision making, with the nominal Treasury Board effectively rubber stamping the decisions. This was to change somewhat when the PAC was appointed, as noted in another section of this study.

Another aspect of systematized planning and coordination which has often downplayed was the activity of the Environment and Land Use Committee (ELUC) and its secretariat (ELUCS), the NDP replacement for the Technical Committee. A qualification to the Barrett planning record is, of course, that Barrett inherited the ELUC from the previous Bennett government and adapted it to new conditions. He extended the logic of the ELUC far beyond what Bennett had done, however. Sidor's useful graduating essay[11] on British Columbia central agencies in the seventies detailed the growth in both the size and influence of the ELUCS in the Barrett years. To summarize some of its findings, the following observations can be made concerning the ELUCS size, coordination, and ministerial focus.

The Barrett ELUC Secretariat was much larger than W. A. C. Bennett's six-member Environment and Land Use Technical Committee. The ELUCS was constructed in 1973–74 of three units, with the resource analysis unit being the largest at ninety-four persons, and the resource planning unit and special projects unit each having eight. Most of the ELUCS staff were seconded from departments. Of the total of 117 positions, 54 were professional classifications, 42 were technical, and 19 were clerical. The former unit did land inventory work, while the latter two examined and assessed alternatives in resource development. The ELUCS was headed by A. D. Crerar, who was considered an outstanding public servant.[12]

The ELUC and its secretariat specialized in resolving resource disputes where no department had clear jurisdiction or where departments had referred the matter to the ELUC due to an inability to agree. The procedures were evidently successful. Christianna Crook of the Institute for Economic Policy Analysis found "virtually unanimous agreement" among departmental officials interviewed that the ELUC system was "a highly preferable alternative to the 'laissez-faire' resource and land use decision-making of pre-ELUC times."[13] Bob Williams "estimated that fully 25 per cent of all NDP policy concerned itself with matters related to resource development and land use."[14] By 1975 the ELUC had grown to have nine cabinet members out of a total cabinet of nineteen members, making it an important decision-making body.[15]

The ELUCS cabinet staff reported to the chairman of the ELUC (Williams), not to the premier. In a sense, this was an aid to planning because Williams carried weight at the cabinet table.[16] One can imagine that its influence might otherwise have been diluted.

Previous analyses of the Barrett government have downplayed the tentative steps towards institutionalization and the degree to which the government was reacting in a corrective mode to alleged deficiencies in the policy-making structure. There was, in fact, the beginning of a cabinet structure which included a central agency (the Office of the PAC, funded from a provincial secretary appropriation) and a central department (ELUCS). The ELUC itself grew and was successful. Still, it is true that the system was essentially a decentralized one in the unaided cabinet mold: ministers had high status as policy makers, and the recruitment pattern of the government favoured strong departmental influence.

DECISION-MAKING MODES

Even considering the belated bureaucratization of cabinet, the Barrett administration was a heavily decentralized one, in the tradition of unaided cabinets. The aim of central/departmental balance, which had figured relatively strongly in the NDP administration of Saskatchewan, was noticeably absent in British Columbia. Ministers resisted a strong role for central bureaucrats, and the pace of recruitment was most intense at the departmental level. Swainson has noted that Robert Williams, Norman Levi, and Dennis Cocke were the principal change agents in the Barrett ministry. As well as decentralization of authority in cabinet, there was also spatial decentralization: a growth of administrative regions with the concomitant diffusion of authority occurred along with an increased physical dispersion of departmental personnel.[17]

The non-departmental bureaucracy grew markedly during this period as well. "The NDP kept approximately 80% of the boards and commissions they inherited in 1972 and added approximately thirty-nine more, bringing the operative total to about seventy."[18] In addition, "between 1972 and 1975 the NDP government acquired at least a dozen major crown corporations, either creating them *de novo* or acquiring them as going concerns. As well, it purchased at least five small transportation companies and made extensive use of mixed-ownership corporations in the food processing, property development, and forestry industry fields."[19] Because the unaided Barrett government did not establish any major executive or legislative means of coordinating this expansion of non-departmental forms, authority ebbed from the centre.

It was in recruitment patterns that the decentralized bias of the Barrett administration was most evident. The size of the regular public service grew from 30,612 in 1972 to 39,498 in 1976.[20] Still there was no corresponding growth in central agencies (other than in the ELUCS) to deal with the implications of this bureaucratic growth; a formal Treasury Board and a Government Employees' Relations Bureau came into being only in 1976. The growth of the non-careerists among senior civil servants ("senior" meaning deputies, associate deputies, and assistant deputies) was notable. Ruff discovered that "whereas only 15 per cent of the senior bureaucracy could be described as having non-careerist origins [i.e., less than five years employment prior to assumption of a deputy's position] in the pre-1972 period, after 1973 this proportion had reached over 40 per cent under both the NDP and the newly re-elected Social Credit governments."[21] It is evident that the influx of non-careerists was made necessary by the governments' view that its own tenure was shaky and that it had to make progress quickly; to do this, it needed a massive infusion of new talent into the senior provincial bureaucracy. It is also entirely likely that, in turn, the new talent then exacerbated the tendency to decentralize decision making that already existed under Barrett. As Swainson has pointed out,

> When David Barrett and his colleagues assumed office they were strongly conscious of the fact that they may not be in power for long; hence they were determined to move quickly on many fronts to implement a variety of programs which they had endorsed over the years, although these policies had never been formally encapsulated into a planning package . . . The Premier made no effort to emulate his predecessor as a dominant policy initiator. His task was to co-ordinate the march to the new order: policies as varied as pharmacare, radical improvement of public transit, the preservation of agricultural land, the seeking of enhanced economic rents in the production of oil, gas, minerals, and forest products, and the introduction of a new Labour Code, state-run automobile insurance—to name just a few—were introduced by his government.[22]

Young and Morley have commented, more unkindly, that "Barrett . . . delegated authority, but blindly, trusting his ministers to do the right thing."[23] Symbolic of the decentralist slant of the Barrett years was the fact that the appointment of the deputy became an unofficial ministerial prerogative, despite the order in council basis for the appointment. Close minister-deputy relationships developed. This was the case in both the Barrett and William (Bill) Bennett governments.[24]

BUDGETING

The only other major study of the NDP years, that by Kavic and Nixon, also stresses the lack of central planning but does not accept that there was any semblance of financial control. Some characteristics of NDP financial management were in fact examples of Barrett emulating various Bennett-era practices. One of these measures was to have the premier serve as minister of finance (1972–75), which this work has suggested is often the case in unaided cabinets. Revenues were under-estimated as an aid in balancing budgets, a practice that was continued for the first two of the three Barrett budgets. (However, one crucial characteristic apparently not shared by Barrett was an accompanying determination to control expenditures.) Another example of emulation was the continued use of guaranteed debt in financing Crown corporations and agencies. Still another seems to be, from Kavic and Nixon's account, the expanded use of the special purpose funds account, which saw a $210.5 million increase between 1972 and 1975.[25]

The Barrett era was also characterized by a lack of concern with economic planning. According to Kavic and Nixon, "Barrett had neither the upbringing nor the inclination to use the positions of Finance Minister and the chairmanship of the Treasury Board for purposes of economic planning. According to a former provincial secretary of the party, the absence of economic planning characterized not only the approach of the Premier but that of the entire government. 'The problem,' he opined, 'was that the government had no idea of economic priorities. Nobody in the government ever sat down and said what are we trying to do this year and how will we go about it'?"[26]

As in many unaided cabinets, fiscal policy was centralized under the premier. Tax policy was made by him alone. As far as expenditure control went, "Barrett gave his Ministers free rein on the departments, and saw the Finance portfolio as providing the means to keep check on them. He wouldn't fully use this power, but he wouldn't share it either."[27] Even influential ministers couldn't challenge Barrett. "Finance was thus seen even by the influential Williams [Bob Williams, minister of lands and of recreation] as Barrett's prerogative. In the end, though, this power which the Premier was so zealously to guard was to be little used. Expenditures grew almost unchecked while, through ignorance, timorousness or neglect, decisions on fiscal matters in reality went by default to the same senior civil servants Barrett's predecessor relied upon."[28]

Like Bennett, Dave Barrett was his own minister of finance from 1972 until October 3, 1975, at which time Dave Stupich, a cabinet minister with an accounting background, was appointed to the Finance portfolio. A press report of the day noted that Barrett intended to stay on as a member of Treasury Board. It did not explicitly say who was to be the TB chairman, only hinting that Stupich was likely to be, with his general responsibility for a restraint program.[29]

Authors Kavic and Nixon join with many others—notably Tennant—in criticizing Barrett's record of financial management. Barrett and his deputy minister of finance, Gerald Bryson (who was also the finance deputy to both Bennetts), refused to be interviewed for this study, so their side of the story must go unrecorded. The voices of their critics have been numerous, however, denouncing the lack of financial planning and forecasting, the lack of priority setting in budgets, and the poor financial reporting which continued the questionable practices of W. A. C. Bennett.

The net effect of the NDP's financial management was to increase the province's debt and to reverse the budgetary surplus. In 1971–72, according to the Canadian Tax Foundation, the budgetary surplus was $43.5 million.[30] In 1975–76 the budgetary deficit was $139.7 million.[31] Gross contingent liabilities had been $3 billion on March 31, 1972 and were $5 billion on March 31, 1976.[32]

Many of the critiques thus seem to be accurate, but they downplay the improvements that were coming into play at the end of the Barrett interlude. As with the discussion of NDP cabinet bureaucratization, one should be careful to qualify the picture of NDP finances. An implicit indication of NDP concern with the lack of expenditure control came, belatedly, with the creation in 1974 of the Office of Planning Advisor to Cabinet. Although it acted as a central agency, the office was funded out of the Department of the Provincial Secretary. This reinforced the past pattern of having the latter department provide support to the central executive, probably for historical reasons. With this development, Lawrie Wallace returned to the single designation of deputy provincial secretary until 1976–77. A Premier's Office existed, as it had in the Bennett era, but its role was merely clerical.

Marc Eliesen became the PAC and six professional staff were selected. With responsibilities for intergovernmental relations, agenda setting, and budget advice, the PAC staff were clearly overstretched, but they still managed to have some effect. Until this point, Barrett had continued the practice of "big" and "little" Treasury Boards, as in Bennett's day. These bodies had been the loci of financial power.

"Now, in mid-1974 there was evidence of 'another hand' other than those of Bryson and Barrett, in determining the expenditure level" recalled a Finance official of that time.[33] Economies were brought to bear. However, the 1975 election interrupted planning for the 1975–76 budget.

The critiques of Barrett's financial administration are wide ranging. A semi-official history of the British Columbia Ministry of Finance maintains that substantial revenues in 1972 and 1973 gave false assurance to the government. Furthermore,

> the method of providing for capital expenditures was entirely inadequate. At the end of the Treasury Board process each year, amounts were designated for inclusion in capital budgets without any formal evaluation. In addition, capital funding was carried out on an annual basis and was not designed to accommodate projects which involved minimum five year commitments. The large number of capital projects undertaken by the government over this period [1972–75] overwhelmed these antiquated financial mechanisms.
>
> Semi-independent administrative agencies which [were] established and funded by government added to the complexity of financial administration in government. It is noteworthy in this context that at the end of 1975 there were approximately 50% more administrative agencies than in 1971.[34]

Norman Ruff has suggested that the NDP's lack of concern with planning was the major flaw. The government gave priority to departmental aims for social reform and lacked a perception of scarce resources. "By the time of the preparation of the 1975–76 budget, changing economic conditions, revenue shortfalls and over-expenditures by government departments had brought home to the NDP cabinet an awareness of both the capriciousness of natural resource-based tax revenues and the inadequacy of the financial management system."[35] Indicators of the problems with the financial management system were the unprecedented size of special warrant expenditures on human resource programs and a 1974–75 cost overrun of nearly $200 million which necessitated retroactive approval in Schedule A of the 1976–77 Estimates.[36]

A senior finance official with first-hand knowledge of the era has given a number of reasons why NDP finances were poorly administered:

> You can't undertake social legislation without attention to cost projections three to five years ahead. The NDP downplayed projections.

The social attitude of the population can also influence the level of government expenditure. We noticed that a substantial drop in the welfare rolls followed the election of the new Socred government.

Strong ministers in that government were hard to control. For example Bob Williams and Norm Levi would appeal attempts to control their expenditures.

Agricultural programs were significant for expenditure growth . . . You just have to look at the 1973–74 sessions to get a flavour of the attention paid to agriculture . . .

But commitment is the major item. W.A.C. Bennett had control [and Barrett did not].[37]

Barrett's silence on the subject will allow many of the charges to pass with few offsetting comments. The chief standard bearer for the NDP era's record seems to be Dave Stupich, who was finance minister for only three months before the government's defeat at the polls. In 1979, for example, Stupich answered Socred overspending accusations in a detailed way before the legislature's Committee of Supply. He also levelled an accusation himself, arguing that the new 1976 Social Credit government had made new expenditures and then charged the NDP with overspending.[38]

Marc Eliesen's version of the NDP budgeting procedures blunts the force of the critiques about special funds, lack of priority setting, and the dearth of financial planning. He has maintained that there was in fact cabinet priority setting and central analysis.

The old system of financial planning [in Bennett's time] was that expenditures were overestimated always and revenues were underestimated always . . . [so] there would be a small surplus if possible. The new system we established contained more elements. We would not have special funds as a source of expenditure. Departmental proposals would have to be submitted to expenditure analysis, so that there would be a rational basis for expenditure. Guidelines were established, emanating from the first minister and Government: priorities were identified for the coming years . . . The duty of Finance was to submit a revenue framework and to suggest a fiscal stance; it was something like the Ottawa model. And something like an ABX format [for expenditure planning] existed.[39]

Finance was no longer the centre of expenditure planning. Another central body—a de facto Treasury Board secretariat located outside the Finance Department—was beginning to assume responsibility for expenditure analysis and long-term fiscal planning.

> We took away the expenditure analysis function from Finance. The arrangement was the same as with the Federal Government [where expenditure review was moved from Finance to another department]. Bryson had previously had a "yes" or "no" stamp for government expenditures; now there was a delegation of this power to the Secretary [the Planning Advisor]. The Deputy Minister of Finance had to submit to the Planning Advisor. Now planning and budgeting would be done with a view to the next three to four years [not just a year ahead as in the traditional budget]. My Finance background [Eliesen had worked with the federal Finance Department] also helped me to deal with the brushfires that came up. I was tossed into fiscal policy decision-making on occasion.[40]

One cannot help but notice that Eliesen's cumulative central executive experience affected the B.C. machinery of government. First he had reshaped cabinet in the Ottawa/Manitoba mold and now he was recasting financial management in the Ottawa style as well.

It may thus be overstating the case to say that there was little financial planning and analysis in the later Barrett period. To be sure, there was precious little manpower with a only half-dozen people to do the analytic work. Yet in effect, the Office of the Planning Advisor had become a nascent Treasury Board secretariat. Power politics may have prevented the "secretariat" from joining Finance, which was the general pattern in many other provinces. Eliesen may have also felt more comfortable having the expenditure analysis function in the Executive Council Office. This was, after all, the pattern he had just left in Manitoba. (A Management Committee Secretariat in the Executive Council Office had done expenditure review in the Schreyer government.)

A harsh evaluation of the Barrett government views it as an undisciplined group of independent souls in control of government. A more charitable interpretation sees it as a group of traditionalists who had just begun to learn the imperatives of power in the modern age when the electorate gave them the harshest lesson of all. When the political environment dictated a more conservative stance in expenditure policy, they were ready to adapt: the PAC was instituted, and expenditure cutbacks became more commonplace at the end. The NDP may not have been good planners, but they were fairly good politicians: their popular vote held rock solid in 1975, and most of the important programs they initiated are still in existence.[41]

To summarize, the Barrett government has been described by Tennant as "unaided politicians in an unaided cabinet." This was essentially accurate for most of the Barrett period, but weak movement toward institutionalization did occur towards the end. Consider the cabinet committees. Unaided cabinets are said to be reluctant to establish cabinet committees to perform detailed policy examination. Observers have generally ignored Eliesen's contention that committees were in fact developing in the last part of the Barrett interlude. It is true that only a nominal Treasury Board as well as the Environment and Land Use Committee (ELUC) existed for most of the Barrett years, but at the end a Priorities and Planning Committee and some functional cabinet committees had been established. The role and influence of the ELUC expanded during these years, and with at least half of the cabinet membership involved in the ELUC early on, the growth of cabinet committees was on its way.

Another attribute of the unaided cabinet is the lack of staff and agencies available to perform cross-departmental analysis, planning, and coordination. Tennant has implicitly admitted that the inauguration of a PAC was a move away from the unaided cabinet, but says that the combination of narrow PAC concentration on financial control, bureaucratic resistance to the PAC, and domination of departmental policy groups prevented fundamental change in the uncoordinated nature of B.C. policy development.

Yet Tennant has downplayed developments that supported a fiscally-aided premier, which can be a signal of transition to an institutionalized cabinet. The early Barrett years featured the continued practice of the "big" and "little" Treasury Boards, which meant that Finance Deputy Bryson continued to advise the premier (who was at first also the finance minister) on broad financial matters. Beginning in 1974 the premier received a wider gamut of policy advice. The Office of the PAC, situated in the Provincial Secretary Department, became a de facto Treasury Board and cabinet secretariat. Finance continued to provide the fiscal framework and revenue forecasts, but the PAC was moving towards expenditure analysis (assumed from Finance) and long-term fiscal planning. Thus, the premier essentially had two central bodies advising him (and in the case of PAC, ostensibly advising the full cabinet) on fiscal matters.

It is true that the continuation of the provincial secretary model, in which a special minister with a line department provided staff support to cabinet, meant that the Premier's Office would continue its narrow clerical role. Yet the logic of institutional development in the B.C. central executive under Barrett was that a full-fledged institutionalized central agency—a cabinet secretariat—would have ultimately come about in the Premier's Office (or an Executive Council Office). Already the PAC officials were recording cabinet minutes, establishing cabinet agendas, and engaging in some program evaluation; and Eliesen himself was pushing for a full-fledged cabinet bureaucracy. A move beyond mere financial control to policy coordination also seemed imminent, because the NDP had not only an economic policy but also a social and environmental policy agenda. A kind of central department—the ELUCS under Williams—was already actively coordinating environmental policy. A cabinet secretariat performing policy coordination is, of course, a sign of an institutionalized cabinet.

These developments in the central executive must be kept in perspective. There were powerful centrifugal forces at work in financial and policy matters which made the Barrett cabinet a predominantly unaided one. Barrett, like Bennett, was his own finance minister and dominated tax policy, but Barrett did not exercise the tight-fisted expenditure control role that his predecessor had. There was a significant degree of ministerial autonomy in general policy matters, and it was even said that ministers had the informal prerogative of choosing their own deputies. There was spatial decentralization and growth in administrative regions; a rapid growth in the number of boards, commissions, and Crown corporations; and a burgeoning of the non-careerist civil service; but there was no concomitant growth of coordination mechanisms in the central executive.

In the final analysis, Barrett can be seen as drawn in two directions during his mandate. On the one hand, he displayed disguised admiration for his predecessor by emulating his largely unaided structural arrangements in the central executive. Barrett continued the Bennett practice of the "big" and "little" Treasury Boards from 1972 to 1974 and adopted his predecessor's general approach to financial management, acting as his own finance minister and using innovative funding methods. The ELUC was continued and expanded. The contemporary dynamic elsewhere in the West was for an *institutionalized* premier to emulate an *institutionalized* predecessor, but here both premiers were largely in the unaided mold. This emulative effect clearly slowed cabinet modernization in British Columbia. On the other hand, the planning advisor to cabinet had appeared, representing and reinforcing the conventional wisdom of the NDP about the need for central planning and priority setting, and bringing the weight of considerable federal and provincial central executive experience. Weak moves toward institutionalization were accordingly taken, but they came too late to make a major impact on the direction of the Barrett government.

Chapter Twelve
The W. R. Bennett Years

With his surprise resignation in 1986, William R. Bennett brought to an end a full decade of experimentation in central public administration. For a premier with a reputation as a conservative in social and economic policies, Bennett had a remarkable tendency to experiment in matters of public finance and with the machinery of government. Writers still concentrate on his social and economic policies, so his administrative changes have received little attention. This is ironic, since it was Bill Bennett who initiated true cabinet institutionalization in British Columbia.

Bennett initiated the new cabinet structure for an essentially ideological reason, but one which had the motive of financial control at the base. The younger Bennett shared with his father a Social Credit populism which amounted to distrust of big government, big business, and big unions—especially public sector unions. In practice, this populism translated into a preoccupation with controlling provincial government expenditure and a sympathy for deregulation and privatization. It also involved substantial government participation and direction in major economic development projects, and cabinet domination of public sector collective bargaining. Bennett quickly realized that such an ambitious agenda would necessitate control and coordination mechanisms at the centre. He therefore initiated new cabinet committees and central agencies as well as new processes for financial management and control of the public service.

Bennett's populistic impulse was bolstered by various factors which ensured the persistence of institutionalization. An important one was the premier's own desire for influence, which he perceived could be heightened by a cabinet hierarchy. A new Premier's Office, with talented individuals working to further his personal agenda, came to serve the same end. Cabinet, too, sought influence over politics and finances, and collective decision making became the practice rather than the exception. Other factors influencing the central organization were social science rationalism, reflected in a new budgeting process; the pressure of contemporary intergovernmental relations, which resulted in a new Ministry of Intergovernmental Relations; and openness to certain interest groups, which resulted in cabinet committees conducting hearings across the province. Full cabinet now acted more purposefully and as more of a unit.

To some extent, cabinet experimentation and attempts at control were extensions of Bennett's search for himself. He had the difficult job of living up to the reputation of a famous father (W. A. C. Bennett), a challenge which he met like most others in his life, with quiet and uncomplaining determination. He had, in fact, displayed no political ambitions early in life: he had graduated from high school and together with his brother, Russell, built up the family hardware chain in the Okanagan Valley. They also undertook various successful land development projects together. By the time his father was defeated, Bennett was a millionaire.[1]

Despite the apparent lack of a political streak, he sought the Social Credit nomination in Okanagan South and thereafter became party leader. He then undertook a masterful process of coalition building under the Social Credit umbrella, attracting prominent Conservatives Hugh Curtis and Peter Hyndman, and Liberals William Vander Zalm, Garde Gardom, Patrick McGeer, and Allan Williams. After a surprise election call in late 1975, Bennett led the Socreds to a convincing victory by garnering forty-nine per cent of the popular vote (it had been thirty-one per cent in 1972) and thirty-five seats versus the thirty-nine per cent for the NDP, who slid from thirty-eight to eighteen seats.

Governing was a more difficult venture for Bennett. A person "once paralyzed by stage fright in public and painfully shy in public," he was curiously out of place in the provincial capital; he had few trusted political friends and lived while premier as a "recluse" in Victoria's Harbour Towers Hotel.[2] Maintaining a coalition meant that influence was spread relatively widely throughout the cabinet, especially after the premier became the scapegoat for the poor showing of the party in the 1979 election. He took the opportunity of a stronger Socred showing in the 1983 election (fifty per cent versus forty-five per cent for the NDP) to construct a tough new approach to public policy, something which in retrospect he seemed to have always been seeking throughout his public life. He left public life three years later, after achieving a number of large scale projects, such as the northeast coal development in the Peace River, the Skytrain mass rapid transit in Vancouver, the Expo 86 World's Fair, and a host of highway projects.

CABINET STRUCTURE

The first major sign of institutionalization in the Bill Bennett era was the changing of cabinet structure and processes to heighten collective decision making. The collective approach was evident with cabinet committees in general and with financial administration in particular.

Bennett's was a truncated kind of collective decision making, because much power was centralized in an unofficial inner cabinet consisting of a Planning and Priorities Committee of Cabinet and a Treasury Board with virtually similar memberships. It did, however, entail some heightening of cabinet control over matters for which it was ultimately held responsible. The expansion and institutionalization of central agencies also facilitated collective decision making.

Collective decision making was further strengthened by both informal and formal measures which expanded cabinet's effective control. Informally, Premier Bill Bennett's decision-making style resulted in a more collegial approach in cabinet. This was due as much to political necessity as to personal preference. Not until his third general election in 1983 did Bennett perceive a personal mandate to govern. Previously he had occasionally even been criticized in public by M.L.A.s. The premier gained badly needed prestige in 1983, but the residual effect was a relatively egalitarian pattern of influence. A senior cabinet official commented in August of 1983 that "the Premier calls the shots on about five to ten percent of the issues—a couple of issues. The rest are done by the whole Cabinet."[3] The 1983 decision on downsizing the public service was a Bennett initiative, but even here cabinet support of the policy was important.

Cabinet Committees

Formally, Bennett introduced a number of institutionalized cabinet mechanisms which bolstered cabinet's collective decision making and the range of decision points available to it. The first set of mechanisms involved cabinet committees. By 1977 there were eleven cabinet committees (both standing and special); in 1983 the number was nine, the same as in 1986 after the cabinet shuffle of February 11. (This is a rather large number for a small cabinet; in 1976 cabinet numbered fifteen ministers and in 1986 twenty-one.) The committees were considered important elements in the systematic management of cabinet decision making. A 1986 pamphlet issued by the Ministry of Intergovernmental Relations said they were used for:

- informing Ministers of their colleagues' activities;
- permitting early, in-depth debate of matters before they reach full Cabinet;
- determining financial and economic feasibility;
- reconciling short term and long term goals in various policy fields;
- providing a sense of balance in the advice Ministers may receive from their colleagues; and
- [ensuring] efficient use of Minister's time.[4]

An authority structure outlined a hierarchy of cabinet committees. The effect was to place significant authority in the hands of the premier and a small group of fellow ministers. The earliest division between cabinet committees was between standing and special committees. Shortly after the Bennett government assumed office, it established four standing committees: Planning and Priorities, Treasury Board, Economic Development, and Social Services. These were to remain the principal policy committees throughout the Bennett era. A chart of the 1975–76 cabinet committee structure shows that the membership of Planning and Priorities and the Treasury Board were virtually synonymous, denoting a small inner core of powerful ministers. In the late seventies the powerful inner core was to consist of Bill Bennett, Grace McCarthy, Pat McGeer, Evan Wolfe, and Don Phillips, with alterations made later as a result of retirement and new assignments.

Linkage between committees was aided by the fact that those for Social Services and Economic Development were chaired by members of the Planning and Priorities Committee. Planning and Priorities would determine priorities and approve new programs. The Treasury Board would be active in the areas of the budgetary process, personnel matters, and expenditure proposal approvals. The majority of the other ministers were put on the functional Economic Development and Social Services committees to coordinate policy. In late 1976 cabinet created a Cabinet Legislation Committee, bringing the number of standing committees to five.

There were six special committees by 1977. These were Environment and Land Use, Urban Affairs, Coal, Anti-Inflation, Constitution, and Energy,[5] encapsulating the major policy concerns of the time. A cabinet hierarchy was evident in the fact that committees other than Priorities and Planning and the Treasury Board did not have a wide sphere of independent decision making. Most committee recommendations were ultimately channelled through Planning and Priorities. Often submissions travelled between special and standing committees before reaching Planning and Priorities.[6]

The most important committee of all in the late seventies, except for full cabinet, was Planning and Priorities (P&P). Analogous to the Ottawa model of the time, P&P was chaired by the premier. It considered all proposals for new programs before the Treasury Board would consider funding questions. Proposals ended up before P&P as a result of references from other cabinet committees, except in the case of submissions from Evan Wolfe (Finance) and Grace McCarthy (provincial secretary), which went directly to P&P.[7] P&P could send the matter to full cabinet, or back to the committee or the department, or to the Treasury Board, depending on the nature of the proposal and the state of its preparation.

After the 1979 general election and a change of ministerial responsibilities, Bennett introduced a three-part hierarchy in cabinet whereby responsibilities were even more finely tuned. The November 1979 changes set up a cabinet with coordinating committees below it on the hierarchy, followed by standing and special committees. The special committees included Confederation, Urban Transit, and others. The 1986 version of cabinet structure was to be only marginally different, with management and coordinating committees (Treasury Board, P&P, and Legislation) on the highest rung and the names of special committees (B.C. Transit, Cultural Heritage, and Expo Legacy) changed. The standing committees (Economic Development, Environment and Land Use, and Social Services) continued.

Accordingly, the cabinet decision-making pattern after 1979 featured three levels of review: policy review and approval by a standing or special committee, then coordination by a management and coordinating committee, and finally cabinet discussion and approval. Depending on the nature of the issue, the first two steps could be bypassed and the decision sent to the implementation phase, or the first step need not entail the next two, or step two could be bypassed.

In the course of the Bennett decade, the functions of the Planning and Priorities Committee changed; a progressive narrowing of duties is apparent in official literature on the subject. The 1976 functions of P&P—political strategy, priorities determination, new program approval, and intergovernmental relations policy—were apparently modified. A 1986 draft pamphlet prepared by the cabinet secretariat made no reference to its earlier functions of vetting proposals for new initiatives or of coordinating intergovernmental relations policy.[8] Presumably, it now set only general priorities and policies.

Planning and Priorities Committee authority seems to have waned over the course of the Bennett government to the benefit of full cabinet and other committees—in other words, in the direction of even more collective authority. A senior official in Intergovernmental Relations noted in April 1984 that "a lot of 1977–79 policy issues were handled by Planning and Priorities. After 1979 a Catch-22 situation developed. P and P stopped meeting because the Premier was away a lot of the time, so full Cabinet began to take more of the decisions."[9]

Despite the plethora of cabinet committees, there were no definitive rules about what matters were appropriate to discuss at full cabinet level and what was suitable for committee discussion. However, the standing committees evolved roles as windows on decision making, allowing the public and interest groups to have access to part of the cabinet decision-making process. As one official observed at the time, "Economic Development is well known as the main focus for interest groups. Social Services takes the heat off Cabinet in social policy matters; it does a lot of travelling and people can give [committee members] their views. ELUC's major concern is the 'politics of scarcity.' They get more demands and more groups seeking to meet with them all the time."[10]

Cabinet Financial Decision Making

A second set of institutionalized cabinet mechanisms used to bolster collective decision making involved financial administration. These included a legislative change and an expanded list of financial decision makers. The major legislative change was the clarification of Treasury Board responsibilities in the new Financial Administration Act of 1981. One of the stated purposes of the Act was to clarify responsibilities between the minister of finance and the Treasury Board. The responsibilities of the Board are set out in some detail in the Act; the Board, rather than the minister of finance, was to be the chief financial manager of the government.

An unforeseen series of complications muddied the role of the British Columbia Treasury Board. One factor was the ongoing jockeying between cabinet bodies. A branch head in the Ministry of Finance noted in 1984 that "the relationship [of the Treasury Board] to Social Services and Economic Development and other major cabinet committees is not clear. What is to go to a cabinet committee? Sometimes financial things are referred to Treasury Board *after* they have been to cabinet committees. So is it a management committee of cabinet with responsibility for the expenditure side of budget implementation rather than policy issues? Or is it a super policy committee with responsibility for any policy issue with significant financial implications? And most do [have such implications]."[11]

The role of cabinet itself was another complicating factor for the Treasury Board. A senior Finance official noted that the details of the 1983 Restraint Program and those of the 1984 budget spending plans — which for the first time in thirty-one years featured a *reduction* in provincial government spending — were effected by cabinet. The cuts were accomplished "by collegiality in Cabinet, by peer group pressure for reductions. There were essentially eighteen envelopes, but tradeoffs within the departments, not groups of ministers . . . Full Cabinet, rather than Treasury Board, made the most important budget decisions. Treasury Board was essentially bypassed this time . . . If more cuts are needed, cabinet will probably be the essential tool. If you have a bureaucratic approach to budget making, you won't be able to do what BC did here."[12] Whether this implies that treasury boards are inherently unequal to the task of restraining expenditures is a moot point. It does show full cabinet insisting on collective decision making when it came to matters of crisis budget preparation.

Collective decision making in financial management was also heightened by the fact that the budget decision-making timetable now featured an expanded list of participants, in the fashion of insitutionalized cabinets. The list was not dissimilar to ones in other provinces, but the expansion of influence was significant when contrasted to the W. A. C. Bennett years. The first step in the annual budget cycle was cabinet consideration of the fiscal framework. Both medium-term (five-year) and current year projections were considered. This usually took place in the early summer. A memorandum from the chairman of the Treasury Board gave ministers a feeling for the relative tightness of the budget and indicated whether expansion or restriction was preferable. Using this input, cabinet selected a surplus or deficit target and made rough allocations of resources between ministries.

Based on this target, a booklet entitled "Budget Estimates: Policy and Procedures" was written in Finance and sent to departmental financial officers. Within each department, a number of budget committees ranked program packages and a "super budget committee" consisting of the D.M.s, A.D.M.s, and important financial officers did the total aggregation. This formed the basis for departmental briefing books, which went to the Treasury Board to be reviewed in the late Fall. The final package went back for final cabinet review in January, and the estimates were tabled in the legislature in February. Cabinet, accordingly, was more meaningfully involved in budgeting matters than it had been twenty years before.

Of course, there was not a complete collectivization of financial decision making; individual ministerial decision making was also honoured. Decentralization of certain types of decision making evolved during the post-1976 Social Credit era. By the early eighties the aim was to present Treasury Board and ultimately cabinet with time to concentrate on "big ticket" items and major policy issues. Such willingness to avoid excessive monitoring did not always prevail. A senior Treasury Board official of the early W. R. Bennett era commented that "prior to 1976, there was no *effective* Treasury Board Committee [although one existed in name] . . . The Socreds in 1976 found little control over expenditures. The first thing they did was put out a directive . . . not to spend any money of any sort without coming to Treasury Board. There was a freeze on hiring. The system was changed. Treasury Board evaluated ministries more; there was more emphasis on policies and implications of *not* undergoing certain expenditures."[13]

The new enthusiasm for central monitoring of expenditures brought about bottlenecks. By 1981–82 the Treasury Board was processing about 2,000 submissions a year. By 1982–83 the number was down to about 660, largely due to suggestions made by David Emerson, the new secretary of the treasury board.[14] Devolution of signing authority to ministers and deputies allowed for more policy analysis in the Treasury Board context. The new approach facilitated increased concentration on matters such as hospital costs, computer utilization, and government loans.

CENTRAL AGENCIES AND DEPARTMENTS

A second major indicator of cabinet institutionalization under Bennett was the development of central agencies and central departments. The Bennett government greatly increased the number of central agency staff. It also institutionalized a number of central positions to aid collective cabinet decision making and to give the premier some political control over the bureaucracy and his party. Central agencies and central departments were created to provide cabinet services, to monitor personnel policy, and to support the Treasury Board. The premier was now to be served by his own central agency, the Premier's

Office, not by central departments as in his father's day. The following sections will examine cabinet services, the Treasury Board Secretariat, and the Premier's Office.

Cabinet Services

Under Bill Bennett, cabinet received institutionalized secretariat services, first from a central office and then from a full-fledged central department. The Office of the Planning Advisor to Cabinet was disestablished, and in the Premier's Office a new central body called the Office of Intergovernmental Relations (OIR) came into being. The OIR coordinated intergovernmental policy, showing the new importance of this policy area, and provided some of the secretariat assistance accorded to cabinet committees from 1976 to 1979. However, not only OIR staff but also some departmental staff provided aid to cabinet. Originally, three of the ten individuals serving cabinet—G. B. Bryson, Mark Krasnick, and Mel Smith—were from departments, although Krasnick and Smith of the Attorney General's Department later came to work directly for the OIR.[15]

The Premier's Office was renamed the Executive Council Office (ECO) in the years 1976–77 to 1979–80. The ECO grouped together the Premier's Office staff and the newly formed Office of Intergovernmental Relations. From 1976 to 1979, somewhat confusingly, there continued to be a small organizational entity called the Premier's Office within the ECO, which provided personal service to the premier.

The Ministry of Intergovernmental Relations (IGR) provided secretariat services to cabinet after 1979; its founding legislation was passed in August of 1980. The IGR was to be a central department, meaning that it was a body serving the cabinet decision-making process but was accountable to a line minister, not to the premier. A news release of November 23, 1979 that outlined cabinet changes announced the formation of the new ministry and noted that its main functions were to oversee intergovernmental relations and constitutional matters, and to facilitate the operation of the cabinet committee system. The Premier's Office would now be a separate organization, free to concentrate on policy development.[16] The IGR was at the time the only intergovernmental department among the provinces that housed a cabinet secretariat.

The cabinet secretariat handled the consultations and coordination relating to cabinet submissions. It also serviced the committees of cabinet, establishing their agendas and recording their decisions. The secretaries were process oriented, ensuring that submissions were routed correctly and were complete. In 1984 the ministry inaugurated a computer-based information system for managing cabinet committee records.

As instruments of central/departmental balance, deputy minister committees were introduced. These were something like the now-defunct D.M. "mirror committees" in Ottawa that would vet proposals before they reached cabinet committees. In Victoria, deputy minister committees examined submissions before they were sent to the standing committees of cabinet. The cabinet secretariat provided support services for D.M. committees as well.

It was widely suspected that an additional reason for separating the cabinet secretariat from the old ECO was merely symbolism—a means of semaphoring to the public the *appearance* of achieving economies in a setting where the total costs of the central agencies actually went up. The authorized vote for the Office of the Planning Advisor had been $276,000; in 1977–78 there was a $713,648 authorized vote for the Premier's Office[17] (as the premier himself was still, confusingly, calling the Executive Council Office in Supply debates) and in 1978–79 it was $753,760.[18] The splitting of the IGR from the Premier's Office allowed British Columbia to reduce the costs of the Executive Council Office (Premier's Office) to $551,612.[19] However, the NDP Opposition criticized a special warrant passed on February 11, 1982 authorizing additional spending of $150,000 in the Premier's Office,[20] indicating that the Office was not immune to the bureaucratic tendency of incremental expansion.

The Treasury Board Secretariat

The Treasury Board Secretariat (TBS) in the Ministry of Finance was created in December 1976; Bennett had observed that no effective central body had hitherto existed with expenditure control as its main aim. TBS analysts attended not only Treasury Board meetings but also those of cabinet and its major committees. The potential for impact was significant. The TBS, in the words of one official, "shadowed" the cabinet committees; it reviewed submission requests for all expenditures with major fiscal and economic implications and provided a one-page "briefing note" summary on these to the minister of finance. For full cabinet, the same briefing notes would be made available to the Premier's Office.

The Treasury Board and the Public Service Commission (PSC) shared responsibility for personnel duties under the Public Service Act of 1976.[21] Like its counterpart federally, the main duties of the PSC were recruitment and selection, appeals, and training. The Public Service Act gave the Treasury Board wide powers, to be exercised with the

245

assistance of the Government Employee Relations Bureau (GERB) in the Ministry of the Provincial Secretary. These encompassed tasks performed as the government bargaining agent, classification and job evaluation, compensation for "in-scope" and excluded employees, and conditions of employment for the latter. The Financial Administration Act of 1981[22] gave the Treasury Board the power to act as a committee of the Executive Council in matters relating to "government personnel management that it does not have power to deal with under the Public Services Act."

Part of the growing pains of the Ministry of Finance during the early part of the W. R. Bennett years involved dealing with two of its increasingly restive divisions. Ritter and Cutt summarized the first few years of the history of the TBS as well as the recent history of the comptroller general position (created in 1917):

> The other central agencies [TBS, Comptroller General's Office] . . . enjoyed considerable operational autonomy. They appeared to be moving toward an institutional model similar to that in the Government of Canada where the Treasury Board Secretariat and the Office of the Comptroller General were institutionally separate from the Department of Finance. This trend was abruptly halted in 1980 when, shortly after changes at the Minister and Deputy Minister level, Treasury Board Staff and the Office of the Comptroller General were drawn into the Ministry of Finance reporting structure. It was argued that independence was unnecessary for the Comptroller General since an independent Auditor General had been established. Further, it was argued that agency autonomy had contributed to loss of expenditure control in the federal government, and had led to coordination problems among central agencies and communication problems with the ministries in the Government of BC.[23]

Over time the TBS became more and more cognizant of revenue constraints and general economic policy in its review of departmental expenditure proposals. This tendency became even more pronounced after 1982 when the Economic and Policy Division, which handled the financial forecasting and revenue functions, was amalgamated into the Treasury Board staff.

In 1983 the Treasury Board Secretariat gained new power and prestige with the cabinet's introduction of a wide-ranging restraint program which convulsed both the B.C. government and provincial society. The restraint package was first introduced in the budget of

July 7, 1983 by Finance Minister Hugh Curtis. An internal memorandum circulated to Treasury Board staff in August of 1983 identified "higher order policy issues" that would comprise a "mental check list" for analysts reviewing submissions in a restraint context. The issues would form the substance of a Ministry of Finance briefing note which would be circulated to politicians. Some issues the TBS was to deal with were unsurprising, such as identification of cost drivers and revenue potentials. Other issues made it clear, however, that the TBS was the cutting edge for implementation of the restraint program. One of the directives asked, "Is the proposal consistent with current budget themes, i.e., program capping, deregionalization, downsizing, deregulation and privatization"? Surprisingly, the analysts were also expected to make a form of political assessment. "It is also important to highlight the likely political implications of various options, i.e., the likely response of the public and interest groups."[24]

It was partially to deflect hostility from Finance (both before and after restraint) that central/departmental consultation was necessary. The deputy minister of finance said in a March 1984 interview that

> It is necessary to be careful about how power is exercised. Otherwise cycles appear and the amplitude is greater. Power is taken, but power is also taken away if one does not understand how to use it and too many overt decisions are taken. The classic case is D'Arcy McKeough in Ontario.
>
> The techniques I use are these. Before I took the job, Treasury Board Secretariat used to brief Treasury Board before the Ministry would come in for policy review. I changed this. If there were disagreements, they were open—and in writing. Also, options and consequences are put in papers to Treasury Board, sometimes *without* recommendations. And analysts share comments on all legislation and financial proposals with the departments.[25]

The Premier's Office

Another notable sign of institutionalization was the creation of a Premier's Office. Whereas the IGR Cabinet Secretariat and the TBS were central departments which tended to strengthen collective decision making, the premier gradually built up his own central agency, the Premier's Office, to bolster his personal influence and to serve as a counterweight to his collective ministry. Coincident with the creation of the IGR in 1979, the name of the Executive Council Office was changed back to the Premier's Office. The Premier's Office would eventually contain a deputy minister to the premier, a principal secretary, some special purpose assistants, and secretarial help.

There was an institutionalization of important positions in the Premier's Office: the position of deputy minister to the premier was one example. The deputy minister's function was to ensure that the government bureaucracy responded appropriately to political direction. The position had actually existed, in all but name, with PAC Marc Eliesen and OIR Director Dan Campbell (who had been minister of municipal affairs under W. A. C. Bennett). Lawrie Wallace, deputy provincial secretary, served briefly in a deputy-like function in 1980–81. For a time (1980–81) Bennett also had an executive director of the premier's office, W. A. R. (Tony) Tozer, a close friend from Kelowna. In April 1981 the post of deputy minister to the premier was created for the first time, and its first incumbent was Patrick Kinsella, an ex-political operative from Ontario's "Big Blue Machine." In March 1982 Dr Norman Spector replaced Kinsella as deputy minister to the premier, serving until July 1986. A newspaper report said this of Spector in August 1983:

His rise to power has been rapid.
- In early 1981, he arrived from the Ontario Civil Service as part of a staff-exchange program, joining the intergovernmental affairs ministry as an assistant deputy minister, where he played a key role in BC's participation in conferences leading to the new Constitution.
- In August 1981, he joined Bennett's office as assistant deputy minister in charge of policy.
- In March 1982, he became a full deputy. At the time Bennett said he liked Spector's aggressive manner.
- In December 1982, Spector's role was expanded to include deputy provincial secretary.

Bennett has since made it clear to deputy ministers in all government departments that their prime allegiance is to him—through Spector—and not to their ministers.[26]

On November 16, 1983 Robert Plecas replaced Spector in the deputy provincial secretary position.

Spector's activities can be considered a surrogate for those of Premier Bennett, given the close consultative relationship that existed between the two. Spector is considered to have been the main de facto government representative in the public employee collective bargaining negotiations of 1982 and the 1983. In the 1983 confrontation with Operation

Solidarity public sector union representatives over the Restraint Program, he was a major actor in reaching the Kelowna Accord which ended the strife. He was one of the few non-elected officials to work on the legislative restraint package of the summer of 1983 and one of about five non-elected officials to stage manage its implementation. Even with the loss of his deputy provincial secretary role, Spector still wielded a great deal of influence, largely due to his close relationship with the premier. The premier, moreover, had his own prestige heightened by the political effectiveness of his deputy minister.

The principal secretary was the other major position in the Premier's Office. Bennett believed that a PCO-PMO split—a common trait of institutionalized cabinets—should characterize his Premier's Office. The deputy minister to the premier would have the PCO function—the policy coordination role—and there would be a principal secretary to perform the PMO function, namely, partisan input. However, the partisan role developed much later than the policy role, and its continuation seemed due to the personal success of the first two incumbents in extending the premier's influence in party and electoral affairs. The principal secretary handled electoral strategy and party-government relations. Before 1982 the position did not exist in British Columbia. In March of 1982 Patrick Kinsella became principal secretary to the premier after relinquishing the post of deputy minister (which Norman Spector then obtained).

Kinsella attempted to reverse the foundering support for the Social Credit Party. A January 1984 article stated that "Kinsella has brought to BC politics a new faith in the powers of mass persuasion: images, advertising and polling. The NDP claims that the Socreds spend $700,000 to $800,000 a year on polls and surveys. During the last election [1983], the Social Credit Party, using the same firm the Ontario Tories favoured—Allan Gregg's Decima Research, run in the West by Ian McKinnon, son of Victoria Conservative MP Allan McKinnon—polled public views on prospective party candidates, major issues and responses to individual TV ads. If the ads got a bad rating, they were pulled. It was Patrick Kinsella who knew how to turn poll results into adroit shifts in the campaign."[27]

In the spring of 1984 Kinsella was replaced by lawyer S. Douglas (Bud) Smith as principal secretary. A newspaper article described Bud Smith's rise to his position:

Smith teamed up with the late Hugh Harris, then executive-director of the party, in an effort to modernize the party.

The two looked at political organizations across Canada and the US to serve as models. In the process, Harris persuaded members of Ontario's Big Blue Machine to come to BC and help turn the Socreds from a back-of-the-napkin party into a modern machine.

Smith's and Harris' work was put to the test in the 1981 byelection in Kamloops. Socred Claude Richmond was trailing the local New Democrat by 19 points at the beginning of the race.

New canvassing techniques, polling and attention to detail paid off. Richmond managed a stunning upset.

The techniques used in the byelection served as a model for the 1983 provincial election. During that campaign, Smith was wagon master, in charge of the premier's tour. He preferred jeans, plaid shirts and cowboy boots to three-piece suits . . .

During the campaign, Smith won the admiration of Bennett. The two, both competitive, shared an affinity for the Interior. Bennett found in Smith a person he could trust.

Smith was urged to join Bennett as his principal secretary. He took the job in April 1984 and set about attempting to revitalize the party grassroots. He encouraged MLAs and cabinet ministers to visit small communities, the idea being to convince people the government had not become distant.[28]

Bud Smith spent much of 1985 in an energetic membership drive throughout the province. In early 1986 he left the deputy's post and later that year ran for the Social Credit leadership, coming a respectable fourth.

By 1986 the utility of the principal secretary role had been firmly demonstrated by Kinsella and Smith. The W. R. Bennett government in its later days had a definite reputation for reliance on polls, and this was due in no small part to the influence of the principal secretaries.

Ultimately an institutionalized staff arrangement, with both a central agency as well as central departments, made a difference. The Premier's Office allowed for the advancement of the premier's influence; Barrett had shown that without an autocratic personality (like that of W. A. C. Bennett) one could not dominate the system, even if one combined both the premier and Finance portfolios. Bennett, the son, knew he must have surrogates to achieve the influence his father had enjoyed.

BENNETT'S REFORMS

The ebb and flow of reform measures in Bennett's central executive of the late seventies and early eighties may appear puzzling. British Columbia engaged in one of the most thoroughgoing budget reforms of any provincial government—the high-profile introduction of modified Zero-Base Budgeting (ZBB)—only to withdraw from it partially half a decade later. After budget reform there was a sudden preoccupation with financial administration legislation. Then there was a sudden attack, first on the salary levels and then on the very jobs of many public servants.

This course of reform probably only makes sense if viewed from the perspective of budgeting in an institutionalized cabinet. Institutionalized cabinets feature budgeting which often has multiple aims and uses means such as political controls taken in an off-budget context. Social Credit budgeting originally featured the narrow aim of financial control, but by 1983 expanded to include ideological aims as well. The means used to fulfill budgeting aims also expanded in complexity.

The quest for financial control was first sought through reform of the regular expenditure budget. ZBB offered Social Credit politicians the chance to set financial priorities and to avoid manipulation by the bureaucracy. However, when ZBB became too concerned with marginal expenditures and too detailed to be useful to politicians, it was made optional and its impact gradually faded. Budget reform had failed the one primary aim set for it, namely, financial control. In the fashion of institutionalized cabinets, the premier and his cabinet then turned to a series of off-budget means to achieve the financial control aim. (The term *off-budget* refers to political control measures applied outside the regular budgetary process.) When the financial situation worsened despite these measures, the premier and cabinet decided to pursue the financial control ideological aims by a set of even wider-ranging means included in provincial revenue budgets. Accordingly, this study's review of financial control mechanisms is in two parts: expenditure budget reform and off-budget financial control measures included in revenue budgets.

Expenditure Budget Reform

Expenditure budget reform in the W. R. Bennett era meant the movement to more rational and comprehensive budgeting. It was signalled by the introduction of Zero-Base Budgeting, later to be called "modified ZBB" because of departures from the general ZBB model. ZBB was made optional in 1984–85 because cabinet found it too detailed for its purposes, and because other more efficacious means were available to achieve the traditional Social Credit program of financial control.

It is instructive to trace the steps by which ZBB was introduced and modified in British Columbia because they reveal the drift from political to bureaucratic utility. ZBB was introduced as a result of direct political input from the Premier's Office. The premier, in turn, appears to have been influenced by the current social science of the late seventies. As the former Treasury Board official who managed the introduction of ZBB has explained,

> There was a lot of pressure from the Premier's Office. Someone showed the Premier an article. He showed it to the Finance Minister. I was asked to comment. I thought it was an old story. I thought it should be introduced slowly, if at all. I sent staff to Georgia, Washington, D.C., Ontario and the Federal Government [to study ZBB]. They went to a seminar given by Peter Pyhrr.
>
> I recommended a modified form of ZBB. We would do it in two ministries at first, one in the social services—the AG's [Attorney-General's] Department—and one in an economic-related ministry—Forestry. The system would be not from zero. There would be two cuts: an 85% base, and show packages above that, and 95%.
>
> The first ZBB was in 1978, for the 1979–80 budget. We backed the other ministries into it. With the other ministries we didn't call it ZBB. We just said rank priorities [like in] A, B and X budgets . . . The priority fights went all the way down.[29]

Dan Campbell of the Premier's Office (part of the Office of Intergovernmental Relations at the time) has noted the Finance Department was asked to study ZBB because "we saw from the Premier's Office that it was a matter of public discussion."[30] The ZBB reference was one of a number of initiatives, such as government communications policy, which stemmed from the OIR.

The objectives of ZBB enunciated by Premier Bennett on April 19, 1978 gave precedence to cabinet financial control and implied that social science rationalism had found a new home in the B.C. government. ZBB was to "permit a detailed analysis and justification of budget requests which will enable one to identify, evaluate, and rank in order of importance, all functions and operations of a ministry."[31]

However, when the first formal statement of objectives appeared in the 1981–82 budget procedures manual, the objectives were diffuse. Instead of the simple ranking justification for the ZBB system, which is after all its essence, the new objectives did not directly mention prioritization or ranking.[32] (ZBB theory states that "decision packages" should be ranked on the basis of resources available.) Other than mentioning an attack on incrementalism in budgeting, most of the items seemed to indicate that ZBB was chiefly an information system and strongly hinted that bureaucratic needs were foremost. The objectives of B.C.'s ZBB, as later described in a historical monograph by Ritter and Cutt, were broader still.[33]

The manuals outlining budget estimates preparation procedures became increasing complex, a sign of the growing effect of social science rationalism. Ritter and Cutt have noted that "the first two manuals described a model which was similar to the traditional ZBB model established by Peter Pyhrr. The two subsequent manuals reflected various adaptations and modifications. The process which evolved in BC came to be referred to as 'Modified ZBB' because of its many differences from the conventional ZBB model."[34]

The manuals show the system's concern with financial control slipping away in 1981–82 and 1982–83, when the "operational minimums" (bare necessities) were defined at higher levels. This shows the politicians effectively losing faith in the system. They downplayed it in 1983–84 to place more faith in an envelope system to achieve financial control, and then in 1984–85 they made the ZBB system "optional" (effectively dead) by calling simply for a broad expenditure target below the previous year's figure. The reasons for the switch from mandatory to optional ZBB vary, yet two have been identified by Ritter in his historical review of the Ministry of Finance. One reason was that the Treasury Board could not deal with the excessive information generated. The other was that modified ZBB, with its emphasis on levels above the base, became less useful during restraint, which "made the levels above the base irrelevant."[35]

Finance officials agree that ZBB information was far too detailed and bureaucratic to be of political utility. A senior Treasury Board staff official told the author in September 1983 that "cabinet doesn't relate to the 'analytic' budget preparations of the budget professionals. Now there is a clear separation between information for bureaucrats and information for politicians. We package data so as to make policy issues transparent and unmistakable . . . We force politicians to think about subsidization questions as well as traditional policy questions."[36]

Information for bureaucrats was detailed. Treasury Board staff received reams of paper generated by the ZBB system from the departments. Information for politicians was relatively more succinct. Cabinet, finding departmental ZBB material obtuse, got only "sets of interesting statistics" — information which could have been generated without structuring a complicated ZBB system. The instructions for the 1986–87 Budget informed departments that "since the Deputy Ministers and Cabinet review will concentrate only on *major* operational and policy issues, detailed budget data at the program or activity level is not necessary and can be prepared at a later date."[37] ZBB was mentioned only in passing as one possible method of building budgets.

The switch from mandatory to optional ZBB also stemmed from the failure to eradicate incrementalism from the expenditure budget, as was noted by a senior Finance official with responsibilities in estimates preparation. The problem of defining the status quo—the operational minimum—was a recurring one, with upward pressure always exerting itself.[38] Certainly, the cabinet acted upon this perception when it began to use off-budget instruments of financial control in the early eighties. With the ZBB system failing at the task, it did not make sense to demand it as a mandatory exercise.

When one considers the range of objectives that had been sought with ZBB in B.C., some disappointment might seem inevitable. The bureaucratic actors lost sight of the objectives first sought for the ZBB system, namely, cabinet political and financial control. Yet the balance of the experience with ZBB was positive: in 1984, in the optional phase, more than half of the ministries were still using the system.[39] A 1985 evaluation found that there was an increase in the number of resource trade-offs, and the government could increasingly juxtapose resource requests and their impact on specific objectives.[40]

Off-budget Financial Control

In the early eighties it became apparent that the financial control aim was not going to be achieved merely by using the expenditure budget process. Social expenditures were locked in by social expectations, demographic factors, inflation, and intergovernmental agreements. As well, public bodies with a degree of independence (such as hospitals and school divisions) were not susceptible to control by the normal expenditure review process. The answer was to move to the off-budget means sometimes associated with institutionalized cabinet budgeting. These off-budget political control measures included legislation to give cabinet more control over the levers of expenditure in public bodies and public salaries, as well as ministerial initiatives to cut public jobs. These off-budget instruments would work alongside the traditional expenditure budget.

Like many academics, B.C. Finance officials were not of one mind regarding the causes of expenditure growth. One official spoke in 1983 of a "pass-through" mentality (that is, pass on costs without attempting to control them) which had made control of public bodies difficult in the late seventies and early eighties.[41] Another blamed widespread complicity within the Treasury Board and cabinet for lack of control. Special warrants could be considered as indicators of the faulty assumptions of cabinet expenditure planning, and they were substantial.[42]

254

Still another official stated that the "demand driven" nature of British Columbia spending programs made for difficulty in achieving leverage in expenditure control. He cited a 1983 analysis by an investment house which showed the problem to be a general one provincially, but especially severe in B.C.'s case. Social contract expenditures[43]— that is, social expenditures—had become increasingly burdensome because of population growth and inflation, enhancement of per capita service levels, and faulty original assumptions about federal funding, problems that were especially acute in the three westernmost provinces. A chart done by the investment firm showed B.C. social contract spending,[44] a net of related federal transfer payments, to be 65.5 per cent of provincial source revenue in the fiscal year 1982, 79.3 per cent in the fiscal year 1983, and in the 83–86 per cent range in the fiscal year 1984. This was the highest rate in Canada.[45] Such a percentage could not but fail to alarm the B.C. finance minister and cabinet.

In view of the many causes offered for expenditure growth, it is not surprising that the measures taken to achieve financial control were broadened to include varied political control measures in the institutionalized cabinet style. Beginning in 1980 a number of steps were taken to control the so-called cost-drivers within the immediate provincial jurisdiction.

The strategy of restraint was gradually revealed in a series of off-budget documents, events, and speeches. Following the evolution of these measures allows one to reconstruct the reasoning behind cabinet's decision making. At first cabinet was apparently swayed by single-cause explanations of financial growth (loss of control over public bodies, public service wages, and the size of the public service establishment). Later it would be persuaded that the issue of public sector growth was connected to a complex web of factors, only some of which were susceptible to regular expenditure budget solutions. Off-budget political control means are summarized below under the following headings: Public Bodies and the Financial Administration Act, Public Sector Compensation and Staffing Levels, The 1983 Provincial Revenue Budget, and Post-1983 Provincial Revenue Budgets.

Public Bodies and the Financial Administration Act Finance Minister Hugh Curtis unveiled the first draft of a proposed Financial Administration Act in August 1980. Officials acknowledge that this was the first flowering of an attempt to curb government expenditure growth. "It was more an information-gathering aspect" than a full-fledged program, said one important central official in 1984. There is a surprising amount of analysis of public bodies in the 1980 *Discussion Paper on a New Financial Administration Act* which contained the draft act. This emphasis on identifying, classifying, and suggesting controls for public bodies is puzzling unless viewed as an extension of budgetary political controls taken in an off-budget context. Cabinet realized that it had a variety of means available to achieve its financial control aim, and it was beginning to act on them. The draft Financial Administration Act would replace the currently existing Revenue Act, the Financial Control Act, and the Financial Information Act.[46]

Much of the analysis in the discussion paper concerned the need for classification and financial control of public bodies. A public body, as defined in the draft act, included Crown corporations as well as several varieties of municipalities, school trustee boards, higher education institutions, and hospitals and regional hospital districts. The government later waffled on including municipalities.[47] The report distinguished between bodies that received minimal public revenue and those that received substantial public revenue. For those highly dependent on public funds, a high degree of control by cabinet and the finance minister would have been necessary. Such control ranged from capital budgeting curbs to collective bargaining on behalf of the Crowns (S.66).

The discussion paper was in fact a kind of Green Paper released to generate discussion and to help prepare a bill in 1981. However, what it generated was active opposition from a wide variety of bodies. In the face of this, the finance minister had to devise a second consultative measure. In October 1980 Curtis appointed nine individuals, predominantly from the British Columbia senior civil service, to form the Task Force on the Financial Administration Act. Hearings were slated for the end of November 1980.

Opponents of the proposed legislation perceived its financial control implications immediately. Centralized cabinet control over labour matters under the proposed S.66 was considered especially troublesome. The Employers Council feared public-sector-wide strikes,[48] Labour, the effect of master contracts on regional needs,[49] the Vancouver *Sun*, and the repetition of federal-style labour relations.[50] Even some Social Credit cabinet members—Rafe Mair of Health and Education's Brian Smith—opposed the proposed cabinet control over specific categories of public bodies, demonstrating Bennett's tenuous hold on cabinet solidarity.[51]

The report of the Task Force presented to the public in March 1981 was sensitive to fears about extending cabinet's labour relations power. It recommended, perhaps predictably, that public bodies not be included within a revised act. The Task Force suggested the removal of the public bodies section of the draft and continuing review of proper accountability and control systems.[52] Accordingly, the resultant legislation—the Financial Administration Act (FAA) of 1981—did not include references to public bodies, even in the Interpretation section. "We realized that we would have to draw back," acknowledged a Finance official involved in the analysis of the legislation, "We didn't think through the politics of the thing."[53] Instead, cabinet and the Ministry of Finance obtained rather more oblique controls over public bodies through Crown corporation submissions to the Treasury Board, Memoranda of Agreement stipulating external financial matters, and the use of conditions in grants to public bodies.[54] In other respects, however, the FAA of 1981 was a major improvement over previous legislation which had been vague or silent on other major issues.

Cabinet decided against direct control of staffing and pay for public bodies, but it could not ignore the question of financial control. Economic imperatives were to cause rapid changes in policy in the near future. In the words of the provincial Finance ministry, the first half of the eighties were turbulent. In particular, "there was a sudden and sustained change in export market conditions which threatened to destabilize the provincial government's finances."[55] The response of the Province would be to limit expenditures by a public sector compensation program and cut staffing levels. The financial control aim was still being sought, but off-budget means other than legislative reform were being used to achieve it.

Public Sector Compensation and Staffing Levels The clear turning point for restraint policies came in February 1982. Facing a deepening structural deficit, Premier Bennett revealed in a televised address a multifaceted program for controlling the growth of public expenditures and the public service. The program called for three measures of a financial control nature; two of them were off-budget in character. As his first measure, Bennett announced a provincial government "compensation stabilization program," with former Labour Relations Board Vice-Chairman Ed Peck appointed to rule on public sector wage restraints. Free collective bargaining would continue, but within limits. The limit would be a basic ten per cent ceiling on public sector wage increases, with variations to be allowed between eight and fourteen per cent. Secondly, government spending would be limited to a twelve per cent increase in 1982–83, presumably from cuts in the regular expenditure budget. Lastly, guidelines would be set for limiting the size of the public service. Other initiatives relating to job creation and capital investment were also announced, seemingly to offset the bad news.[56]

Intergovernmental relations may have had some effect on the Bennett program. British Columbia Senator Jack Austin opined that Bennett was "responding to the federal government's position outlined at the first minister's conference on the economy, on the problem of inflation and the need for restraint in the Canadian community."[57] The thrust of the announcement was however roundly condemned by a vast cross-section of British Columbia labour. .

A few months later the government introduced Bill 28, the Compensation Stabilization Act. Minister of Finance Hugh Curtis, moving its second reading, revealed what was "free" about collective bargaining under this wage restraint program by advising workers to "jump safely or be pushed."[58] The Bill's two enforcement mechanisms (the first voluntary and the second regulatory) were similar to the federal government's Anti-Inflation Act pattern of the mid- to late seventies. The bill received assent on June 25, 1982.

The next off-budget development in financial restraint concerned staffing levels. Early in 1982 Provincial Secretary James Chabot began to hint that there would be a twenty-five per cent reduction in the provincial civil service. In spring of 1983 Chabot sent an internal letter to the departments outlining an attrition approach to reduction. Staff who retired or resigned would not be replaced.

On May 5, 1983 British Columbia voters returned the Social Credit to power in an election many political experts had expected them to lose. The Socreds even gained seats relative to the 1979 election, climbing from thirty-one to thirty-four; the NDP dropped from twenty-six to twenty-three. The Social Credit popular vote rose from 48.2 to 49.8 per cent. On the night of the election, the premier said the reason for the surprising turn-about was voter preference for the Social Credit stand on restraint. "I think the people of this province believe in hearing the truth. The truth was the restraint program."[59] He attributed the increase in the popular vote to people "voting for restraint."[60]

In the months to come, the political and administrative managers of restraint were to interpret the 1983 election results as a clear mandate for a new, expanded restraint program. A more accurate interpretation seems to be that the electorate voted for the *existing* compensation stabilization program. The Social Credit Party gave little if any public indication during the election of plans for a broad-ranging plan of restraint.[61] Now a fresh electoral cycle was beginning, and Bennett showed every indication of having contemplated a combined financial and ideological program for some time. Allan Garr has cited a fascinating speech by Patrick Kinsella which attributed Bennett's restraint program to his personality traits and to traditional Social Credit populism. Bennett had longed for some time to return to the

1975 populist Social Credit platform of "less government," from which he had reluctantly strayed.[62]

The 1983 Provincial Revenue Budget The B.C. provincial revenue budget of July 7, 1983 signalled the continued expansion of budgeting in the institutionalized cabinet mode. On the one hand, there were signs that cabinet was continuing and redoubling its former efforts to achieve its financial control aim. On the other, there was evidence of a broadening of budgetary aims beyond that of mere financial control. Cabinet would also target an ideological aim—the elaboration of the Social Credit populist tendency of hostility to big, interventionist government. As cabinet had learned more about the complex causes of public-sector expansion, its susceptibility to a multifaceted ideological response rose.

In keeping with the broadened aims, there were broadened means of budgeting: not only were there guidelines obviously intended to help shape future expenditure budgets, but there were also some policy directives meant to apply in an off-budget context. In addition to the budget measures *per se*, there were other measures included in the several legislative bills that were tabled at the same time as the July 7 budget. Even though simultaneously presented, the bills were additional off-budget measures in the sense of not being integrated into the regular budget cycle within the departments.

Normally due in February, the 1983 budget address (referred to here as the "revenue budget" for the sake of clarity) had been delayed for months. Doubtless, this was because an election was pending, and the message it would contain could have dampened the electorate's enthusiasm for the ruling party. To general surprise, the July 7 budget was accompanied by twenty-six bills which revealed a broad governmental program with neo-conservative tendencies. Left-wing analysis in British Columbia would subsequently attribute the neo-conservative elements of the government program to the influence of the B.C.-based Fraser Institute, a right-wing think tank. A senior civil servant intimately involved with the implementation of Bennett's 1983–84 restraint program denies this; the premier and cabinet, he has asserted, had always thought this way.[63]

Finance Minister Hugh Curtis made it unmistakable that financial control was the main aim. He stated the basic rationale for the budget and accompanying bills as "a simple truth that bears repeating": government had grown too large and was experiencing the law of diminishing returns in service to the public. The minister indicated that a major expenditure restraint program was necessary to relieve taxpayers and to sustain economic recovery. The 1983–84 expenditure was $8.4 billion—12.3 per cent higher than in 1982–83. The deficit was forecast to be $1.6 billion. This could be compared to a $542 million *surplus* in 1979–80, a $257 million deficit in 1980–81, a deficit of $184 million in 1981–82, and a $978 million deficit in 1982–83.[64]

The budget speech, written largely by Deputy Minister of Finance Larry Bell, also showed the unmistakable influence of Social Credit ideology. None of the budget's themes would have been out of place at a Social Credit convention and, in fact, they received tremendous applause at the Fall convention later that year.[65] The budget themes (to use the terminology of Finance Ministry officials) were "program capping, downsizing, deregionalization, deregulation, and privatization."[66] The first three can be considered as guidelines intended to direct the preparation of future expenditure budgets. The deregulation and privatization themes could have served the same purpose but seem to have been mentioned with an off-budget context in mind.

Some of the legislative bills accompanying the July 7, 1983 budget can also be considered as off-budget financial control measures. The proposed legislation covered a wide variety of policy fields. Some of the bills implied long-term, recurring savings or revenue enhancement to a greater degree than did others. These were:

- Bill 3: The Public Sector Restraint Act. This act would permit dismissal without cause of public-sector employees when collective agreements had expired. Public-sector employees were defined broadly in the Bill, ranging from direct government employees to those in hospitals, universities, and others.
- Bill 6: The Education (Interim) Finance Amendment Act. This act would permit the minister to supervise each school board's budgets and expenditures.
- Bill 11: The Compensation Stabilization Amendment Act. This act would put into effect the budget's promise to extend the compensation stabilization program (CSP) indefinitely. It now would allow wage *reductions*. As well, the public sector wage increases would be tied to productivity and the employers' ability to pay.

These budget and off-budget measures did not, of course, go unchallenged. A broad common-front movement named Operation Solidarity, together with an NDP opposition that confined itself to parliamentary tactics, fought the passage of several of the bills unsuccessfully for the next four months. On November 1, 1983 the British Columbia Government Employees' Union (BCGEU) sent forty thousand of its workers on a legal strike. They were joined by forty thousand members of the Teachers' Federation on November 8. Other civil servants—transportation and municipal workers—threatened to walk out as well. The issue was Bill 3 and its destruction of seniority rights. On November 13, in what became known as the Kelowna Accord, a modified seniority system and consultation on social programs were agreed to by Premier Bennett and Solidarity spokesman Jack Munro.

The agreement removed the traditional job tenure of civil servants, but required that layoffs for economic reasons be done in the reverse order of seniority. The BCGEU and other public-sector unions were to be exempt from the dismissal provisions of the Public Sector Restraint Act. The agreement contained other items as well. Bill 2, The Public Sector Labour Relations Amendment Act, which would have reduced the range of bargainable items, was scuttled. Consultation between cabinet ministers and Solidarity leaders on various social service program changes was to proceed. Amnesty for participating unions and the return of lost teachers' wages to the education system were to be negotiated. As well, nominal wage increases were to be allowed the BCGEU.[67]

Post-1983 Provincial Revenue Budgets The budgets for 1984, 1985, and especially 1986 brimmed with optimism, but even here one could find signs of both expenditure budget and off-budget financial control. The government noted in 1984 that its expenditure budget had actually decreased by 6.2 per cent (excluding a one-time resource fund payment); it was the first time in twenty years that a federal or provincial government had achieved this.[68] In the 1985 budget, the schools fiscal framework provided no funding for negotiated salary increases in 1985."[69] The Compensation Stabilization Program was the major continuing off-budget element of expenditure control.[70] Finance Minister Curtis emphasized in the 1986 budget that "the government intends to use any additional funding available to improve public services and create jobs, not to increase compensation for those already employed."[71]

The lengthy restraint program had ambiguous results. A government sourcebook of British Columbia facts noted in January 1986 that "an average of 33,960 employees were employed (full-time equivalent basis) in British Columbia services during the 1984/85 fiscal year."[72] One will recall that the figure had been 47,000 full-time equivalent in April 1982. The government claimed that its economic program had resulted in B.C. "avoiding the accumulation of excessive government debt and beginning the process of reducing the deficit."[73] In fact, the B.C. deficit had stayed at high levels. The 1984 budget revised the

1983–84 deficit to a $1.307 billion forecast. The 1985 budget said the 1984–85 revised deficit was $970 million. The 1986 budget set the 1985–86 revised deficit at $948 million and estimated the 1986–87 deficit at $875 million. Expenditures increased, however, by 3.5 per cent over 1984–85 revised forecasts to $9.056 billion in 1985–86, and by 5.7 per cent over 1985–86 revised forecasts to $9.643 billion in 1986/87.

DECISION-MAKING MODES

One of the distinctive characteristics of the W. R. Bennett era was the regime's concern that central departmental relations should be balanced or even interactive. In the Bennett government, central agencies had definite areas of policy hegemony, but in general the actors sought balance between the central executive and the departments. Balance was achieved by various patterns of devolution of authority, consultation, and selective specialization.

In its relations with departments, the Bennett government displayed a pattern often found in institutionalized cabinets. Decision making in such cabinets usually becomes more centralized, but a fairly constant tension develops between centralization and departmental autonomy as ministers assert their natural tendencies toward independence. Premiers ease this tension by enunciating specific policies promoting balance in central/departmental relations. Examples of such balance were evident in the functioning of three important central departments/central agencies: Treasury Board activities in the Ministry of Finance, intergovernmental activities in the Ministry of Intergovernmental Relations, and personnel management in the new Government Personnel Services Division. Each of these will now be examined in turn.

Treasury Board Activities

Ritter and Cutt reviewed the activities of the Treasury Board as well as the Treasury Board Secretariat and the Comptroller General's Office in the Ministry of Finance. They found evidence of strong initial centralization under the Social Credit but noted some efforts at balance (devolution) taking place in the early eighties.

> There was . . . a perception at the senior level that constraints on ministries should be reduced. In 1981, the FAA [Financial Administration Act] provided the basis for a devolution of authority to the ministries for their own financial affairs subject to the general

direction of Treasury Board. The devolution of authority has been a gradual process which is very detailed, reflecting the view that guidelines must be prepared to ensure that financial control is not sacrificed through the devolution . . . Devolution of authority in the budget area included reduction in the need for ministries to obtain Treasury Board approval. This involved restructure of the Estimates to allow greater flexibility within Votes, and restructure of STOB [Standard Object of Expenditure] codes to allow greater flexibility within codes. Other major areas of devolution of authority were voucher processing, internal audit in the larger ministries, SFO [Senior Financial Officers] bank accounts for payments not exceeding $100, and ministry accounting systems.[74]

The results were less paperwork and a clearer focus for ministers: in 1983 the number of Treasury Board submissions was down 70 per cent from 1981, and the Board was dealing with fewer but more substantial items.[75] The pace was uneven due to fiscal restraint and downsizing, but the focus was progressive.[76]

Consultation between ministries, the staff of the Treasury Board, and the Office of the Comptroller General (OCG) proceeded as a direct result of the councils of executive finance officers and senior finance officers. In 1983 the OCG undertook a client evaluation of its services.[77] Yet these semi-official declarations of consultation and devolution of authority should be balanced with reference to the restraint program and its aftermath, to which the study makes only oblique reference. While there may have been real cooperation between the centre and departments previous to the July 1983 budget, afterwards there was massive policy confusion, job insecurity, and ill will. Part of the bureaucratic paranoia reflected back on central departments such as Finance and the provincial secretary, which were the lead agencies for implementation of the program.

Intergovernmental Activities

The intergovernmental activities (as distinct from cabinet secretariat activities) of the Ministry of Intergovernmental Relations (IGR) also show the search for central/departmental balance. This was achieved by selective specialization, the practice of picking and choosing only a relatively few matters on which to pre-empt the departments. The Ministry of Intergovernmental Relations Act, with its general wording, may give the impression that the ministry, a central department, coordinated most intergovernmental matters. Yet IGR specialized in relatively few matters and thus bypassed the initial "centralization" stage of institutionalization and proceeded directly to the "balance" stage.

The Act is significant as much for what it does not say as for what it does say. Unlike the corresponding Alberta Act, which established a powerful, interventionist Department of Federal and Intergovernmental Affairs, there is no legislative provision for mandatory channelling of intergovernmental arrangements through the B.C. Ministry of Intergovernmental Affairs.

A senior cabinet official has described how the Ministry of Intergovernmental Relations got started; his story demonstrates how intergovernmental relations can affect the structure of the central executive:

> Brown and Campbell [David Brown, the communications planning advisor, and Dan Campbell, the premier's principal secretary until 1979] went to Alberta to see what they were doing. Their report to the Premier said the Alberta model was good but not suitable to BC. A smaller one would be better.
>
> The 1979 first ministers' meeting had convinced Bennett of the need to get the Province's act together. The creation of IGR would allow for specialized work to be done. It would also allow for Mel Smith [of the Ministry of the Attorney-General, the province's main constitutional expert] and Matkin [Jim Matkin, deputy in Labour and later IGR's first deputy minister] to be brought under one roof. The turf wars would be done before they came to the Premier.[78]

The reason for the particular form of B.C. intergovernmental institutionalization was explained by an experienced Finance official interviewed for this study in early 1984. The federal-provincial network within the British Columbia government was, as he pointed out, influenced by the gains possible through one-to-one provincial relationships with federal counterparts:

> Tight control is manifested in Alberta but in BC there is not strong central control over Federal-Provincial matters. Things are left to the ministries. This is because there is generally a dislike of outsiders, a feeling that specifics are better left to the experts. As well, the advantages of tight control have not been demonstrated. For example, BC gets more CAP [Canada Assistance Plan] money per capita than any other province in Canada. People in the Human Resources Ministry have a special relationship with Ottawa . . . The big money ones are EPF [handled by Ministry of

Finance under the Established Programs Financing Act] and CAP and a bunch of little ones. On the other hand, things like Indian education funds have been underendowed. All things considered, however, our interests may balance out.[79]

The respondent listed a number of similar structural disincentives discouraging Alberta-style centralization of intergovernmental affairs within the British Columbia government.

The Feds give out their money according to certain criteria which don't change — whether or not you have a "FIGA" . . .

The Young Offenders cost-sharing issue is a demonstration that political negotiating can be done without a ministry.

Most programs [of a federal-provincial nature] are small.

Most programs [of a federal-provincial nature] are established and long-lasting.

The existence of central agencies is a sign of mistrust and hostility. Also, FIGA has to prove its existence and proves itself by showing how adversarial it is to departments.[80]

According to a senior IGR official, the ministry's major problem was "trying to figure out a role within a government which has no tradition of central agencies." Within this context, an accomodating game plan was established. It was restrained by the B.C. tradition of ministerial autonomy as well as by the fact that it was not a central agency *per se*: "The *modus operandi* is to pick areas you know best, then branch out. You try to build up credibility with the departments. *The problem in BC is that you have strong ministers with strong departments*. The PCO/IGR difference [referring to Ottawa-Victoria differences] is that the [federal] PCO is the PM's ministry, headed by people with clout; in BC this is less the case [Intergovernmental Relations has been headed by a line minister since 1980]."[81] (Emphasis added.)

The most intensive activity was on the constitutional/intergovernmental side of the department, with the cabinet secretariat eschewing any active policy formulation role. Organizational adaptability seemed to be the key to IGR's success. According to the aforementioned official, "We watch issues only for a month or so, then switch. We do things like the Compensation Stabilization Program on a task force basis. The range of issues calls for flexibility. It's the opposite of Ottawa, which is heavy on committees [so that a flexible response is not as easy to achieve]."[82]

It appears that there were many intergovernmental policy areas that IGR did not directly control or, for that matter, even attempt to control.

An intergovernmental network spread throughout the bureaucracy depending on the issue, as a respondent in the ministry noted in September 1983. "On constitutional questions, IGR is predominant but [Norman] Spector is the final say on most items. For General Development Agreements, the Ministry of Industry and Small Business Development and its deputy are the main players. For health and medicare positions it's the top end of the [Health] Ministry. In Natural Gas, the [provincial] Ministry of Energy, Mines and Petroleum Resources interacts with the federal Department of Energy, Mines and Resources. In some matters of international involvement, Industry and Small Business Development has traditionally interacted with External Affairs [the federal department]."[83]

IGR had some notable successes thoughout its history, but it suffered from structural impediments. It is above all the deputy ministers of IGR who had successes in the selective specializations of the ministry. The deputy's position in Intergovernmental Relations was held briefly by Dan Campbell in 1979–80 before he left under a cloud in a series of political scandals. It was then vacant for a short time. Melvin Smith became deputy minister (Constitutional Affairs) in 1981, and later that year James G. Matkin also became deputy minister. (The ministry had legislated permission to have two deputies.)

Matkin had had a long and illustrious history in the B.C. service. He had been deputy minister of labour since 1973 and had drafted the NDP government's Labour Code. He played an important role in drafting the new Canadian Constitution and was, along with Spector, one of Bennett's key political advisors.[84] Matkin was apparently the instigator of the 1982 compensation program.[85] In 1983 he left to be president of the Employer's Council of British Columbia. After a year-long power vacuum, Melvin Smith became simply deputy minister, shedding his qualifying title. Smith himself had played a key role in other intergovernmental talks of the early 1980s.

Outside the realms of constitutional affairs and general policy, Michael Howlett has noted two structural impediments to IGR influence. One is simply the matter of scarce resources:

> Between 1979 and 1983, fewer than a dozen personnel in the Ministry actually worked on intergovernmental relations. Most of the staff employed by the Ministry performed clerical or secretarial duties. In fact, the Ministry only began to receive the personnel and funding necessary to allow it to perform any kind of effective intergovernmental role in 1981–1983. Senior staff were appointed to the Ministry after 1979 who had a major impact on the constitutional negotiation process, but these officials had little day-to-day

responsibility for the running of the Ministry. Instead they worked almost exclusively on projects assigned to them by the Premier. Most of these staff had left the Ministry by 1983. The remaining staff managed in 1983 to institute for the first time the monitoring function originally assigned to the Ministry in 1979.[86]

Another reason for IGR's limitations was the competition from line departments and especially from Treasury Board staff in the early eighties:

It is also important to recognize that even the advisory function performed by the Ministry of Intergovernmental Relations was limited. The Ministry played an important role in developing the province's Senate reform proposals and in rationalizing its overall intergovernmental policy, but had only a minor role to play in the development of the provincial trade liberalization proposal. That proposal was developed in the Economic Analysis and Planning Division of the Ministry of Economic Development, which itself coordinated British Columbia's interaction with the federal government concerning DREE programs. This Division was later transferred from the Ministry of Industry and Small Business Development to the Ministry of Finance. The Ministry also suffered from the increasing attention paid by the executive to the internal development of the provincial economy throughout the early 1980's. This has worked to the disadvantage of the Ministry of Intergovernmental Relations at the same time that it worked to the advantage of the Ministry of Finance and its Treasury Board Staff division. The Treasury Board Staff had always retained control over the negotiation of the Federal-Provincial Fiscal Arrangements and Established Programs Financing Act and with the transfer of the Economic Analysis and Planning Division began to take on extensive policy evaluation and development functions. The Treasury Board Staff has grown quickly in terms of administrative resources, jumping from expenditures of $1,187,519 in 1981–1982 to an estimated expenditure budget of $3,179,666 in 1983–1984. In fact, the Treasury Board Staff has assumed much of the coordinating role originally assigned to the Ministry of Intergovernmental Relations in 1979.[87]

Personnel Management

Another and even more explicit attempt to solidify central/departmental balance was the establishment of the Government Personnel

267

Services Division (GPSD). By establishing the Division, the Bennett government hoped to centralize collective bargaining and personnel management but decentralize the application of the merit principle. The GPSD was to absorb the collective bargaining functions of the Government Employee Relations Bureau (GERB), and the departments would adopt some functions previously performed by the Public Service Commission (PSC). The GERB and PSC had until then replicated the centralized version of public personnel management then current in Ottawa.

In February 1985 legislation was introduced which had been the better part of a year in gestation. The Public Service Act created a new central agency with centralized personnel responsibilities, the GPSD of the Provincial Secretary Department. The GERB would no longer exist; instead, the GPSD would develop labour relations strategy in concert with departments. The Act also changed the role of the Public Service Commission (PSC) from providing redress and monitoring the application of the merit principle to merely providing redress. This was a decentralizing move, reflecting the pressure from ministers for more autonomy in personnel matters. Dual responsibilities, as in the Ottawa PSC model, were unsatisfactory.

The GERB had existed from 1976 to 1984. Although nominally placed for most of that period under the provincial secretary, in practice it seems to have had a high degree of operational autonomy. Operating under the authority of an amendment made in 1976 to the Public Service Act, the GERB had a dual role. On the one hand, it served as the industrial relations arm of the Treasury Board; it represented the Board at the negotiating table and administered public service collective agreements. On the other hand, it was the central personnel agency in the government, establishing personnel policy and setting up and maintaining systems of job evaluation and classification for unionized public servants. For excluded employees (those not subject to collective bargaining), it was responsible for establishing salary rates, benefits, and other terms and conditions of employment.

The Public Service Commission was responsible for both administering the staffing process and policing it, but a central agency was an inefficient means for making day-to-day personnel decisions.[88] Transfer decisions could only be made by the commission, which had no first-hand knowledge of departmental situations. As well, classification decisions had been made by the GERB based on second-hand information from ministries. Shared responsibilities were clouding the proper accountability of both managers and central agencies.[89] In sum, a decade of experience with the personnel controls of both the PSC and GERB had convinced ministers that there was too much centralization.

In keeping with the general tendency in institutionalized cabinets, strong initial centralization was to be followed by an attempt at central/ departmental balance.

Provincial Secretary James Chabot noted that internal studies of the government had brought about the same conclusion as that reached by the federal D'Avignon Committee in its report.[90] He asserted that "we need a strong central focus in government to set goals for personnel management, create policies and monitor actual practices. The [proposed] organization structure . . . will clearly define responsibilities and properly assign accountabilities for personnel management in the public service."[91]

The strong central focus was to be the Government Personnel Services Division, operating under the general umbrella of the department. New centralized personnel management responsiblities were to be balanced against new decentralized arrangements for application of the merit principle. "The bill permits the centralization of policy development in collective bargaining authority . . . In this respect, personnel management in the BC government will parallel our system of financial management. The Treasury Board will continue to act as a committee of the executive council in matters relating to government of personnel management. Just as directives respecting accounting policies and practices are issued through the Ministry of Finance, directives respecting personnel management will be issued through the Ministry of Provincial Secretary and Government Services."[92]

The Public Service Commission would no longer have formal authority for appointment and promotions; ministries would. "Accountability for the proper application of the merit principle [is] to be clearly assigned to ministries."[93] The independent Public Service Commission would hear appeals of job applicants "who feel the principle of merit has not been followed in specific appointments."[94]

The Ministry intended central/departmental balance (or what it called the "corporate" approach) to guide future policy making in labour relations and personnel management. According to an internal document, policies and procedures would generally be the result of work by joint GPSD branch ministry teams.[95] Labour relations strategy was a case in point: branch staff would lead the government negotiating team, but the team would have ministry representatives, and the strategy would be jointly determined.[96]

The New Democrat Opposition did not take kindly to the new personnel arrangements. They saw departmental control of the merit system as an invitation to ministerial interference and patronage. Yet both they and the government agreed about the decentralized implications of the new legislation.

Premier Bill Bennett ushered in the institutionalized age for the British Columbia central executive. The innovations he introduced were similar to those being tried or extended in other Canadian jurisdictions: Zero-Base Budgeting, a Planning and Priorities Committee of Cabinet, and a Ministry of Intergovernmental Relations. Yet it was not "faddism" which compelled Bennett and the B.C. Cabinet to adopt these changes, although there appears to have been an element of that. Above all, the premier seems to have been influenced by the populist roots of the Social Credit Party in his decision to institutionalize the B.C. cabinet. Socred populism involved antagonism to large government expenditure, public sector unionism, and the regulatory state. Yet to control these, Bennett decided that new cabinet committees, central agencies, and financial legislation were necessary. Ironically, he sought to control big government with a big central executive.

The persistence of Bennett's institutionalized reforms can be ascribed to a number of factors. The premier's quest for political influence led him to expand his own Premier's Office and to institute a cabinet hierarchy. Moreover, because ministers other than the premier acquired political power resources, Bennett had to strengthen collective decision making. Cabinet's desire for political and financial control influenced cabinet organization, central agency formation, and budgeting matters. However, there was still attention to central/departmental balance because of a respect for ministerial autonomy and because of its obvious administrative benefits. Intergovernmental relations and social science rationalism also favoured the persistence of the institutionalized approach.

The effects of these factors on the B.C. cabinet were wide ranging. First of all, multiple committees were formed or continued over the Bennett decade. Planning and Priorities and the Treasury Board were the two most powerful. The similarity of P&P and Treasury Board membership meant that the circle of powerful ministers was not too large. The fact that there was a hierarchy of cabinet committees in what was, after all, only a small provincial cabinet (in the fifteen to twenty minister range) meant that a minority of powerful ministers had successfully executed a drive for political control. Other cabinet committees (i.e. Treasury Board and the functional committees) saw elaboration of their roles. In this, the influence of the financial control and interest group factors was apparent.

The elaborate development of central agencies and central departments is another striking institutionalized characteristic of the Bennett government. The creation of such agencies and departments can be traced to the desire to give cabinet political control over the bureaucracy and to give the premier more influence *vis-à-vis* the rest of the central executive. Two characteristics marked the ascendancy of these central bodies.

Firstly, the more haphazard provincial secretary model was dropped and replaced by something that approximated the PCO-PMO model. Now the premier had a deputy and cabinet had its own secretariat, which was, however, placed in a central department, the Ministry of Intergovernmental Relations.

Secondly, there was a growth of influential central departments, including the OIR, TBS, GERB, GPSD, and a restructured PSC. Political and financial control by cabinet seemed to be factors in the creation of such central departments. The TBS and GERB both grew out of a similar context, arising from a perceived lack of central controls over the various objects of provincial expenditure. Clearly, the major reason for creating the GPSD and restricting the merit role of the PSC was to enhance the political control of individual ministers over their own departments and to thus achieve a balance between centralization and departmental autonomy.

The course of budgeting history under Bennett shows the combined effect of social science rationalism, the quest for financial control, and an ideological predisposition. The premier seems to have introduced ZBB because of its current respectability in the social sciences. The quest for financial control then seems to have become a factor around 1980–81, as Canada began to slip into a recession. Cabinet seemed convinced at first by single-cause explanations for public-sector growth and then later adopted multiple-cause explanations. Evidence seems to reveal that cabinet thought that government growth was caused, in succession, by outdated budgeting frameworks, poor monitoring, extravagant wages, and too many public servants. Single-factor explanations were apparently rejected in the 1983 budget, which revealed that cabinet saw public-sector growth as having many causes.

As cabinet's working explanation for public-sector expansion grew more complex, populist ideology seemed to offer supplementary assistance in the design of appropriate aims and means for the budgeting exercise. The appropriate aims were traditional financial control, mixed with an ideological determination to reduce government size and reverse government interventionism. The appropriate means were available on several planes: they involved expenditure reductions, staff reductions, privatization, and deregulation, to name a few. An ideological agenda had become intermeshed with the fiscal agenda.

There was an attempt at greater central/departmental balance to offset the centralization that is associated with the installation of an institutionalized cabinet. W. R. Bennett's institutionalized cabinet therefore attempted to balance collective and individual ministerial

271

decision making. It expanded collective decision making to the extent of creating more cabinet committees, giving cabinet's coordinating committees special powers, and occasionally including full cabinet in "crisis budget preparation" that would ordinarily be the province of the Treasury Board. Yet it honoured ministerial decision making by applying the concept of central/departmental balance, devolving signing authority from the Treasury Board to ministers, and in general sheltering significant spheres of power for ministers. Strong personalities dictated that the premier would not monopolize power within cabinet, but self-interest and administrative common sense combined to limit the collective sharing of what remained.

Bennett's predecessors had done enough prepatory work for the institutionalized cabinet to make its final installation seem a natural end. Ideological reasoning had preceded the initiation of institutionalization; building up the central executive was deemed a necessary forerunner to implementing the Social Credit vision. However, once installed, institutionalization persisted due to many of the usual factors, extending the premier's influence, ensuring cabinet's political and financial control, following social science teaching, and responding to other governments and to interest groups. These factors were potent, for Bill Bennett changed the face of B.C. public administration in less than ten years.

Part Five

Changing Cabinet's Design

Chapter Thirteen
Evolution of the Institutionalized Cabinet

At the provincial no less than the federal level in Canada, the unaided cabinet has given way. It has been replaced by the institutionalized cabinet, which features a more complex cabinet structure and important new roles for central agencies. The institutionalized cabinet also heralds the advent of a new prime ministerial role as organizational architect. Both the initiation and the persistence of the structured cabinet in Saskatchewan, Manitoba, and British Columbia in the postwar period were due to a complex web of factors other than the growth of cabinet size. The effects of the institutionalized cabinet in these provinces were manifest on three levels: the political, the bureaucratic, and the functional. Examination of this limited range of cabinet histories may provide grist for a wider theory of provincial cabinets in Canada.

Each of these cabinet models has recognizable key features. The unaided cabinet is simple in structure, with few standing committees, and features restricted collegiality, that is, limited collective decision making and power sharing as regards departmental policy. The premier is the architect of personnel choice and is usually, but not always, the dominant politician. There are central departments which perform technical services but which undertake little planning or policy analysis. Such a department performs a service-wide facilitative and coordinating role but is headed by a minister other than the premier. There are few, if any, cabinet level staff. For an unaided cabinet, budgeting has narrow aims—usually fiscal control predominates—and employs limited means. Planning is seen as an optional function of government, and when used it tends to be sporadic, personalistic, project oriented, and coordinating in nature. The unaided cabinet promotes a decision-making style which is hierarchical in financial matters, features few sources of alternative advice to cabinet other than deputy ministers, and is decentralized in non-financial matters. Restricted collegiality is the order of the day.

The institutionalized cabinet, on the other hand, has a complex cabinet structure with many standing committees and expanded collegiality, that is, greater collective decision making and power sharing as regards departmental policy. The premier's role is expanded to include the responsibilities of organizational architect as well as architect of personnel choice. There are both central departments and central agencies, and cabinet receives both partisan (PMO-type) and technocratic (PCO-type) input. Central agencies are those service-wide facilitative and coordinating bodies directly responsible to the premier.[1] As well, cabinet-level staff are relatively numerous.

Under an institutionalized cabinet, budgeting features wider aims and means than the control-oriented budget process of the traditional cabinet. Planning is still considered optional by cabinet, but there is generally more recourse to it; it is both project oriented and comprehensive. A planning-budgeting nexus, an explicit link between the two functions, is common. There are alternative sources of information to cabinet other than the responsible minister and his or her deputy. Decision making is more centralized in the structured cabinet. Cabinet makes a wider range of decisions, and central bureaucrats monitor departments to a greater extent. Not surprisingly, there is almost constant tension between the centre and the departments.

It is useful at this point to recall some nuances. There is not one basic form of institutionalized cabinet. Structured cabinets can be more or less collegial, more or less hierarchical, or more or less centralizing. Their common feature is that institutionalizing premiers are actively engaged in a persistent search to make decision making more manageable. J. S. Dupré has likened this search to the quest for the Holy Grail, and the analogy is apt.[2]

Another nuance involves *central departments* and *central agencies*. It is uncommon, at least in Canadian political science, to draw a distinction between central agencies and central departments. The distinction is useful, however, because of the implications arising from the fact that institutionalized cabinets have both. To foreshadow the analysis a bit: a cabinet having only central departments such as

Finance or a Treasury Board Secretariat (TBS) will be subject to the reactive, budget-balancing input of Finance officials. When the premier is also finance minister and the TBS is in effect the premier's department, the influence of Finance officials may be magnified. Central agencies make a difference. A well-staffed Premier's Office can bolster the influence of a premier who is not concurrently the finance minister. Central agencies can also keep planning tasks on the government's agenda.

The specific task of this study is to review the forces that underlie the initiation, persistence, and effects of cabinet institutionalization in the postwar period in Saskatchewan, Manitoba, and British Columbia. To a lesser extent, this study also assesses the potential for applying these experiences to other governments organized along the Westminster model.

THE INITIATION OF CABINET INSTITUTIONALIZATION

The factors promoting initial cabinet institutionalization in the three provinces under investigation were a mixture of ideology, pragmatism, and historical precedent peculiar to each province. Only in Saskatchewan was an institutionalized cabinet devised by a premier writing on a clean slate, and he was influenced by a left-wing ideology from which subsidiary considerations flowed. Current thought about the planning infrastructure in the Tommy Douglas/Woodrow Lloyd years (1944–64) is that its genesis lay in socialist literature on central planning.[3] Douglas's wish to steer public policy led him to favour rationalistic (as opposed to intuitive) decision-making processes, such as year-round in-depth budget preparation spearheaded by the Budget Bureau and the amelioration of departmental work plans.[4] Budgeting became a function dependent upon the prior establishment of philosophical and operational objectives by cabinet.

In Manitoba the structural adaptations of the Roblin-Weir era indicate that institutionalization can be a gradual, trial-and-error process based on a unique mixture of ideology, pragmatism, and management. The ideological element was Roblin's predilection for government-led economic development and industrial modernization. It led to the formation of both the interventionist Manitoba Development Authority (MDA), a cabinet committee established in 1959 to provide leadership in economic development planning, and the Manitoba Development Fund, a government lending agency established in 1958. There was an element of pragmatism as well. Manitoba's Treasury Board borrowed liberally from Ontario, Saskatchewan, and Ottawa, adopting those elements that had been most successful for them. Even the

Conservatives' indicative planning model was borrowed, this time from France.[5]

As regards cabinet assistance, the MDA and its successor, the Planning and Priorities Committee, were not wedded to a single model, to say the least. In the short space of ten years, Roblin had given the cabinet's primary committee three completely different types of support: a deputy minister committee, a committee of private sector officials to promote indicative planning, and a group of central agency officials. If an agency did not work as expected—as with the Manitoba Economic Consultative Board's private sector officials—it was fairly quickly dispatched. Roblin's respect for management was evident in the radically broadened mandate of the Treasury Board at the very beginning of his government.

In British Columbia W. R. (Bill) Bennett stands out as an organizational architect who started off with right-wing ideological premises, a relatively unusual genesis for cabinet institutionalization. Bennett sought fiscal control to achieve populist checks on big government through a variety of means: reform of financial legislation in 1981, restriction of public sector compensation in 1982, and implementation of a broad restraint program in 1983. Cabinet and central agencies were also operated with this primary aim of fiscal control in mind. Bennett's Treasury Board and Priorities Committee had virtually identical membership, so fiscal considerations were given special treatment. The government operated on a strong Treasury model, giving the Ministry of Finance a predominant role among central agencies.

However, historical precedent also played a role. Contrary to the impression left by Tennant,[6] who has painted both W. A. C. Bennett and Dave Barrett as having largely traditional cabinets, Bennett's predecessors had taken enough steps along the way to institutionalization to ensure that Bennett himself did not begin with a blank slate. W. A. C. Bennett was a fiscally-aided premier whose technical finance assistance proved to be the germ of a later Treasury Board Secretariat function. Process assistance from the Provincial Secretary Department to the premier (and later to the cabinet) in the senior Bennett and Dave Barrett years would in Bill Bennett's time be elaborated by a Premier's Office proper. In both the senior Bennett and the Barrett years, there were incipient planning approaches. W. A. C. Bennett worked from a comprehensive reconstruction plan for infrastructural improvements, which he had helped to write in 1942 (the *Interim Report of the Post-War Rehabilitation Council*. His biographer has called his encompassing vision of hinterland development "the premier's master plan for provincial development."[7] Dave Barrett, for his part, inherited a shell for environmental planning called the Environment and Land Use Committee of Cabinet, expanded its role, and gave it a formal secretariat. His planning advisor to cabinet was important.

THE PERSISTENCE OF CABINET INSTITUTIONALIZATION

There are both endogenous and exogenous factors common to more than one province which affect the persistence of institutionalized cabinets. Their relative weight differs from one premier to another. Some factors are particularly useful in explaining why even those premiers who were less enamoured of the institutionalized model — for example, Thatcher and Lyon — nevertheless carried over some of the model's elements into their own public administration. Their successors, in turn, reacted against the effects wrought by premiers less prone to institutionalization.

Endogenous Factors

Endogenous factors are those that grow from within the government. Several of them will now be discussed.

The Premier's Quest for Influence This explains, at least in part, a great many structural elements in central executives. One reason for the growth of central agencies in addition to central departments is to bolster the premier's power. Ross Thatcher continued the Budget Bureau and kept the positions of secretary to cabinet, which Douglas had established in 1948, and clerk of the executive council so that the incumbents could help him maintain financial control and personal scrutiny over certain key policies. In Manitoba Roblin achieved control by chairing his only two cabinet committees — the Treasury Board and MDA — and by holding the Treasury portfolio from 1958 to 1966, almost every year of his time as premier. Lyon had a policy coordination group responsible to him and not to cabinet *per se*. Under Bill Bennett, various senior officials of the Premier's Office demonstrated, by their own usefulness, the political value of having a premier's staff. The popularity of PMO-type bureaus among modern premiers — Blakeney, Devine, Schreyer, Lyon, Pawley, and Bill Bennett all had them — points to a desire to manage party relations in a closer fashion. Cabinet hierarchies — such as the priorities and/or coordinating committees found in the cabinets of Blakeney, Devine, the early Schreyer, Pawley, and Bill Bennett — can be attributed in part to the premier's desire for personal power.

Unsatisfactory Aspects of the Unaided Cabinet Premiers who follow those who have partially deinstitutionalized cabinet typically find some of the results unsatisfactory. Blakeney thought that an inadequate number of planning people in the Thatcher years (1964–71) had put too much pressure on deputies and key ministers;[8] the clear implication was that there should be more central officials, more cabinet committees, and a greater division of labour. Pawley and his colleagues disliked Lyon's de-emphasis of planning but, in contrast to Blakeney, chose to "work from the departments up" in reinstituting it. Ultimately, however, the structural results were quite similar.

Emulation of Predecessors Not all premiers find the central executive model used by their predecessors deficient. Policy- or ideology-oriented premiers such as Schreyer and Barrett, who did not have a tradition of administrative experience to guide them, implicitly tended to rely on their predecessors for structural direction. Schreyer continued to depend upon a great many Roblin-Weir senior officials. From 1969 to 1973, fully half his time in office, he maintained the Conservatives' dual model of two main anchor committees—Planning and Priorities and the Management Committee—as well as the development agencies pioneered by Roblin. Pawley, like Lyon, declined to institute a priorities committee in his first government (1981–86) and emphasized for nearly half-a-decade the same three main cabinet committees—Treasury, Social, and Economic—as had his predecessor. Barrett initially continued the budgeting style he inherited from W. A. C. Bennett. For most of his tenure (1972–75), he acted as his own finance minister and kept a "little" Treasury Board (Barrett and Finance Deputy Gerald Bryson) as well as a big Treasury Board (the statutory entity) to review expenditures. As well, he continued and elaborated the ELUC mechanism for environmental planning and coordination. Devine came as a novice to the machinery of government, found the existing design convenient, and adopted the traditional outlines of Saskatchewan institutionalization. This outline consisted of functional cabinet committees, cabinet staff, collective planning and budgeting, and a planning-budgeting relationship.

Cabinet's Quest for Political Control An enduring theme in provincial executive government is the political tug of war between cabinet and bureaucracy. The desire to wrest the function of effective prioritization from the hands of departmental officials and to return it to cabinet is a potent motivating force in structuring both the departmental and non-departmental executive. Blakeney fought for the return of a regularized budget process to keep priority setting within cabinet. Roblin created the Operation Productivity task force in 1967 to suggest methods of political control over the bureaucracy; a dual cabinet committee structure for planning and management resulted. Schreyer eliminated the Planning and Priorities Committee in 1973 and gradually created more cabinet committees in order to expand the collective aspects of cabinet political control. Pawley used a priority list as a policy control innovation in his second government (1986–88) and engaged a Planning and Priorities Committee as the main means of pushing those priorities through the departmental system. Both Saskatchewan and Manitoba—the former early (1947) and the latter late (1987)—adopted a cabinet committee on Crown corporations as a prerequisite for political control of the Crown sector.

Cabinet's Quest for Financial Control A related factor in structuring provincial executive government is cabinet's desire for cost containment. This desire ebbs and flows with the relative health of the provincial finances. Under Blakeney, cabinet's wish to assert financial control after the 1975 election provoked the resurrection of the Cabinet Planning Conference, a Douglas-era mechanism which had been revived in 1971 but was then inoperative for two years. Devine's 1987 restraint program led to a short-term centralization of power in government. In Manitoba concern over the adequacy of budget control led Roblin and Weir to introduce program budgeting and a dualist cabinet structure—a Planning and Priorities Committee for priority setting and a Management Committee for expenditure control—in the late sixties. In the health and education area, rising costs convinced Schreyer, Lyon, and Pawley to establish social committees of cabinet. Schreyer's Management Committee sought to contain costs through detailed review of new expenditures. Financial control needs forced Pawley to institute a separate Treasury Board Secretariat with a mandate for long-term expenditure control. Fiscal concerns in British Columbia led to the introduction of Zero-Base Budgeting (ZBB) in 1978 and the rise in status of fiscal conservatives in the central agencies. As deficits grew to alarming heights despite the apparent sophistication of ZBB, and cabinet grew more receptive to the New Right interpretations of government growth, B.C. sought financial control through a variety of means first introduced in the famous 1983 restraint budget. Some of these measures were expenditure reduction, staff reduction, privatization, and deregulation.

Decongestion The urge to free key decision makers from overload, time-consuming meetings, or bottlenecked decision points occasionally leads to structural innovations. Blakeney thought that departments were

281

seeking Treasury Board approval for overly detailed matters, and in 1977 he initiated reviews which ultimately led to the streamlining of the Board's agenda. Schreyer created several cabinet committees, which he called "cluster" committees, in part to save his own time as well as that of cabinet. In 1979 Bill Bennett transferred the cabinet secretariat and intergovernmental functions to a newly created Ministry of Intergovernmental Relations, ostensibly to leave the Premier's Office free to concentrate on policy development.

Ideology The ideological factor affects not only the initiation of cabinet institutionalization but its persistence as well. Most NDP governments have a commitment to planning as a basic ideological cornerstone, and consequently their planning committees play a central role. Douglas, Blakeney, Schreyer, and Pawley, for example, established planning committees. Barrett lacked an ideological commitment to planning but in a sense imported it in 1974 when he hired a mainstream NDP official, Marc Eliesen. Right-wing governments tend to emphasize fiscal control or economic development, or both, and consequently tend to emphasize the Treasury Board or an economic development committee, or both. Devine, Roblin, Lyon, and Bennett all established economic development committees in name or in effect.

The Internal Logic of Structural Reforms Finally, the institutionalized cabinet tends to persist because of the internal logic of structural reforms. A function will tend to continue to be exercised, and indeed to flourish, until it is countered by an equal and opposite tendency. The Douglas government invested so much psychic energy into its management seminars and its annual budget decision-making process that its rationalism entered into the mainstream of Saskatchewan's politico-bureaucratic thought. Detailed planning and budgeting attained a momentum that kept it going through later governments. Roblin put great stock in making business people part of the actual governmental decision-making structure. Schreyer tried similar approaches with his Economic Development Advisory Board and Manitoba Development Corporation, which were successors to the Manitoba Economic Consultative Board and the Manitoba Development Authority, respectively. Lyon also relied in a major way on business input to his Riley-Spivak Task Force on Government Organization and Economy. The use of a traditional Treasury Board, a clerk of the executive council, and a modest planning element in budgeting in the Lyon years can be attributed to momentum from the Roblin, Weir, and Schreyer years. The financial function has tended to dominate all others in British Columbia largely, one suspects, through the cumulative efforts of each succeeding premier.

Exogenous Factors

Exogenous factors are those that are imposed on government from the outside. There are fewer exogenous factors promoting the institutionalization of cabinet, but they are not to be overlooked. The most important is the impact of other governments, most importantly the federal government. Significant factors are outlined in the following sections.

The Necessity for Policy Coherence vis-à-vis other Governments Provincial governments across Canada have entered a new era in which jurisdictional and constitutional questions are more focused and hold greater implications. The influence of these developments on the structure of central executives is apparent in all three of the provinces examined. Blakeney saw to it in 1972 that an intergovernmental support function was included in his new central agency, Planning and Research. This function then gestated into a full-fledged central department in 1979, only to be placed once again in a central agency by Devine in 1982.

In Manitoba intergovernmental relations have long affected the structure of cabinet. Roblin added a youth and manpower function to the MDA in 1966 to react to new federal manpower activism. Schreyer's Manpower and Employment and his Resource and Economic Development subcommittees owed their origins partly to the need to coordinate federal-provincial agreements. His Intergovernmental Affairs Subcommittee performed an analogous function with matters affecting Aboriginal people. The Urban Affairs Committee was formed to coordinate provincial policy *vis-à-vis* the newly amalgamated City of Winnipeg. Lyon created a Federal-Provincial Financial Relations Subcommittee of Cabinet.

Barrett's planning adviser to cabinet had intergovernmental responsibilities which were later passed to Bennett's Office of Intergovernmental Relations. The profile of the intergovernmental function in the Bill Bennett government grew steadily at this central agency level, culminating in the creation of a separate central department, the Ministry of Intergovernmental Relations, in 1979. However, intergovernmental responsibilities were spread throughout Bennett's government departments so as to maximize revenue from federal sources (some departments had special relationships with their Ottawa counterparts, which resulted in relatively lucrative federal transfers).

Cabinet Structure as Semaphore The organizing of the public sector to signal messages of reassurance has a long history in government.[9] Symbolic messages are also used in the specific realm of the central executive. By reorganizing cabinet, governments implicitly or explicitly declare that a matter of public concern is being dealt with within the inner sanctums of power. In a province victimized by the economy, Douglas emphasized economic planning. At the height of a prairie farm crisis, Devine established the Special Cabinet Committee on Farm Input Costs. As well, private-sector membership on his Crown Management Board symbolized the opening of the Crowns sector to business influence. Roblin established a Manitoba Development Authority in a chronically underdeveloped Manitoba. W. A. C. Bennett established a pro forma environmental committee of cabinet to signal his apparent sensitivity to the newly influential environmental movement. His son, Bill Bennett, placed the cabinet secretariat in the intergovernmental ministry rather than in his ECO to allow for appearances of economy. Reviewing a list of cabinet committees is one way to get a fix on the relative priorities of the government in question. If the government wants to emphasize the message even more, it enshrines the cabinet structure in legislation, as did premiers Blakeney, Roblin, and Schreyer.

The Rationalism of Social Scientists One factor which cannot be overlooked as a spur to institutionalization is the kind of rationalism brought to bear on government by postwar social scientists versed in political science, law, economics, and management studies. The social science of the day held that governing was just as much a matter of designating correct procedures as it was of political will. It promoted a so-called rationalism which involved establishing primary objectives, then designing structures and processes to move the system towards achieving them, and finally providing for feedback and evaluation. Government was rational inasmuch as it was purposeful and self-correcting.[10] Senior public servants Tommy Shoyama, and A. W. Johnson, as well as Premier Blakeney, were explicit about the academic rationalist assumptions of the CCF-NDP planning machinery. Rationalist assumptions can also explain the importance which Blakeney's central executive accorded to the Program-based Management Information System, a budget and management improvement system which was culled from a literature search,[11] and to the Bureau of Management Improvement which ran it. Rationalism also explains the introduction of ZBB in Devine's government. Successive Manitoba regimes have relied heavily on outside experts from academe and on consulting firms when tracing the *grandes lignes* of budget systems and cabinet

284

restructuring. British Columbia politicians and senior officials seized eagerly at the prevailing notions of budget reform when modernizing provincial financial processes in the 1970s.

Facilitation of Interest Group Input Governments occasionally use cabinet committees as direct two-way conduits of information and opinion between the Executive Council and politically significant interest groups. The Pawley government had cabinet committees which facilitated input from Franco-Manitobans, Native peoples, and various other ethno-cultural groups. A major role of the standing committees of Bill Bennett's government was to tour the province and sound out public opinion on their respective policy areas. Occasionally the input function becomes a major role to be played by central agents and agencies as well, as was the case with Pawley's principal secretaries and his policy coordination group in the Executive Council Office.

THE EFFECTS OF CABINET INSTITUTIONALIZATION

Not surprisingly, the institutionalization of provincial cabinets has had a major effect on political actors in the three provinces studied. This is evident at the level of cabinets, premiers, individual ministers, central agents, and some of the central processes of government.

Cabinet structure is a partial indication of how power is shared within cabinet. If there is no priorities committee or its equivalent, the authority structure will tend to be rather flat; with one, it tends to be more hierarchal. Priorities committees were, in fact, the dominant pattern by the mid-1980s. Bill Bennett had one since 1979, and Devine and Pawley both introduced them in 1986. Weir and Schreyer had experimented with a Planning and Priorities Committee earlier.

A related observation is that, with certain exceptions, full cabinet appears to have been overshadowed as a decision-making centre. With Douglas, Lloyd, and Blakeney, the Treasury Board appears to have been the workhorse of cabinet. There was a tendency under Blakeney for smaller groups of ministers in formal and informal committees— such as those on potash, gas, and constitutional policy—to set the broad parameters of public policy. The overshadowing of cabinet in Saskatchewan is underscored by the observation that cabinet commit-tees, rather than full cabinet, were most heavily aided in the CCF-NDP years. Devine, who drifted towards use of full cabinet in his uncertain first years, created an inner cabinet hierarchy with treasury and pri-orities committees in his second government (1986–91). In Manitoba Roblin atomized cabinet with the creation of the MDA as the high command of cabinet, and both Schreyer and Pawley extended this atomization with the creation of multiple committees. In British Columbia Planning and Priorities appear to have had almost equivalent status with cabinet under Bill Bennett.

At first glance, J. R. Mallory's comment about the role of the federal cabinet also seems apropos to the western provincial cabinets: "The Cabinet has become simply a meeting at which members may be informed about major policy issues decided elsewhere, about which they can complain to a limited degree. In other words, Cabinet is a mini-caucus, not a decision-making body."[12] But these provincial cabinets, although frequently overshadowed, are decidedly more than mere mini-caucuses. Premiers can and sometimes do have recourse to full cabinet as a collective decision-making instrument. The relatively small size of the provincial cabinets studied has permitted the use of full cabinet for decision making at certain times and in certain circumstances. Devine used full cabinet and de-emphasized cabinet committees as an election loomed at the end of his first government. Lyon and Pawley preferred full cabinet to perform those functions usually allocated to priorities and planning committees in other Canadian jurisdictions. Full cabinet proved particularly useful to both Bennett and Devine in the initial planning stages of their restraint programs.

Premiers must share power more widely in the institutionalized cabinet. In the unaided cabinet, with some exceptions, there is a tendency for restricted collegiality and a dominant premier. In the new context, the premier shares power with

- the chairs of influential cabinet committees;
- the finance minister, since there is more of a tendency for the finance function and that of premier to be separated;
- the members of inner cabinets (priorities committees) if such there be; and
- in a few cases, deputy premiers.

Accordingly, premiers must search for new and more subtle ways to exercise power. In the unaided cabinet, the premier had available to him such traditional means of influence as the conventional appointive power and his capacity, when heading a majority government, to determine the timing of elections. He could also aggrandize his position through information control (like W. A. C. Bennett), the tenure of dual finance/premier portfolios (as with Thatcher, W. A. C. Bennett, and Barrett), and the determination of cabinet's agenda. In the institutionalized cabinet, the premier searches for new means of influence, namely:

286

- chairmanship of, or at least membership on, key cabinet committees,
- establishment of central agencies to counter-balance the influence of central departments, and
- the use of powerful central officials to act as surrogates for him.

For individual ministerial autonomy, the effects of the institutionalized cabinet have been ambiguous. In the unaided cabinet, ministerial autonomy and influence were favoured in relative terms over the power of the collective central executive. In the institutionalized cabinet, many methods are employed to bolster the power of the central executive. The increasing collectivization of the revenue and expenditure budget processes, the expansion of decision making by cabinet committees, and the use of full cabinet during restraint exercises are but a few of these methods. However, ministers have not been passive in the face of such developments and a certain central/departmental tension has developed.

Like premiers, individual ministers have had to seek more subtle ways of exerting influence in the era of the institutionalized cabinet. They tend to do it by proxy. They request and support measures which give more voice to their departmental officials. Some of these measures are:

- the deletion of a control orientation by cabinet and its central agencies, and its replacement by management systems and standards which require only occasional monitoring;
- a general emphasis on allowing flexibility for line managers in program implementation;
- departmental preparation and delivery of the main estimates material submitted to Treasury Board, and
- the establishment of specialized mandates for central agencies, which leaves the lead responsibility for some important functions (e.g., specific intergovernmental matters, protection of the merit principle, and so forth) in departmental hands.

The central bureaucracy of government has been deeply marked by the emergence of institutionalization. Unaided cabinets generally depended on central departments for whatever help they needed; usually the aid was of a clerical or technical/financial nature and was directed more at the premier than at full cabinet. However, a small Executive Council Office might occasionally be used to provide the required clerical assistance; the individuals providing the assistance did not use the position to achieve further power. In the transitional period between the two types of cabinet, quasi-central agencies — development agencies performing roles somewhat analogous to regular central agencies but staffed by private sector people — were sometimes developed in order to coordinate private sector development.

In contrast, there are both central departments and central agencies in the institutionalized cabinet. This dualist central bureaucracy has both administrative and political implications. The administrative implications are, of course, an increase in the size of central establishments and more bureaucratized cabinet procedures. The political implications are discussed in the following three paragraphs.

Premiers may use the central agencies to put certain types of issues on the provincial policy agenda. A Premier's Office will be used to put the premier's personal agenda forward, and a planning agency will be employed to put complicated issues before the public in as comprehensive and succinct a manner as possible. Bill Bennett's deputy, Norman Spector, stage-managed much of the premier's 1983 restraint package, for instance; and Schreyer's Planning Secretariat forecast the government's general intentions in the planning document, *Guidelines for the Seventies (1973)*.

The development of a PMO-PCO split in the ECOs of the eighties has brought political realism to planning orientations, and vice versa. Pawley's policy coordination group infused political considerations into the planning-budgeting process, Patrick Kinsella's polling as W. R. Bennett's principal secretary influenced policy directions, and Devine's principal secretaries appear to have acted a conduits for Conservative Party influences on Saskatchewan public policy.

The individuals who have senior positions in the central agencies amass personal influence as a result of their connection with premier and cabinet. This enables them, effectively, to become lead actors in some of the most important policy issues of the day, such as constitutional and fiscal matters. The fact that names like George Cadbury, Tommy Shoyama, and Norman Riddell in Saskatchewan, Rex Grose and J. C. Weldon in Manitoba; and Marc Eliesen, Pat Kinsella, and Norman Spector in British Columbia are well known is testimony to the heightened role of central agents in provincial politics.

Of course, the growth of central agencies affected central departments, of which the most notable are departments of Finance. In creating new central agencies, premiers sometimes discontinued the tradition of the strong treasury and sometimes left it intact. The term *strong Treasury* means that the Treasury or Finance Department has a relatively large staff, especially in those divisions that interact

288

directly with cabinet (such as the Treasury Board staff); that Finance controls both the fiscal policy and expenditure management processes; and that Finance has primacy among central agencies.

Changes affected the various Finance departments unevenly. J. Stefan Dupré has described the traditional Finance Department in the following manner. "The taxing, spending and borrowing activities of government have always given a special status to Department of Finance (or Treasury). Long before the rise of the institutionalized cabinet and the coining of the term 'central agency,' Finance Departments stood out as horizontal portfolios whose government-wide scope made them readily available adjuncts of first ministers."[13]

Dupré indicates that the growth of other competing central agencies in the federal government and the waning of the fiscal relations model (essentially, trust-based negotiation networks between like-thinking federal and provincial finance ministers and officials) led to the attenuation of the hegemony of the federal Finance Department. While this has been true at the federal level, at least until the apparent post-Trudeau resurgence of Finance, the pattern in provincial governments is more uneven.

The British Columbia Finance Department did indeed have a special status under W. A. C. Bennett. Bennett had been its responsible minister and used its senior officials as extensions of his authority. The next two premiers did not change the status of Finance appreciably in spite of their creation of new central agencies. Finance introduced ZBB in 1978, spearheaded the establishment of a new centralist Financial Administration Act in 1981, and gained a high profile when it was used as the principal mechanism to implement the restraint program in 1983. Meanwhile the other central agencies had not been competitive. The Office of Intergovernmental Relations, then the Ministry of Intergovernmental Relations, was lightly staffed, had ill-defined responsibilities, and tended to specialize in constitutional matters. The Government Employee Relations Bureau (GERB) in the Public Service Commission had to share jurisdiction over collective bargaining with the Treasury Board (effectively, Finance) until the GERB was abolished in 1984. The Premier's Office was definitely powerful, but it specialized so much that it left much for Finance to control.

Saskatchewan's Department of Finance was relatively powerful until the Devine era. The Douglas CCF cabinet placed much emphasis on the budgeting function, and Treasury controlled most of the aspects of budgeting. Thatcher destroyed the central planning bureaucracy but left Finance, and especially the Budget Bureau, relatively intact. In the Blakeney years, Finance did not even have to share the budgeting process with the central planning body, as had been the Douglas-Lloyd pattern. In the Devine years, Finance's status began to wane, and the Executive Council Office demanded at least equal status. Even program evaluation, formally spearheaded by the Department of Finance, was shared with a deputy minister-level body.

In Manitoba Finance's profile was on the decline from about 1968 until a change of direction in the mid-1980s. When the Operation Productivity report (1968) led to the creation of a new cabinet management committee which undertook budgeting, management improvement, and personnel responsibilities, Finance was eclipsed. The Secretariat of the Management Committee, a central agency, was placed in the Executive Council Office, so the finance minister did not control it. Finance became principally preoccupied with revenue and taxation matters. In the Lyon era (1977–81), Management Committee and secretariat responsibilities were folded back into Finance but with only a small staff. However, since the Pawley government continued to build the Treasury Board support role of Finance, by the mid-1980s Finance had regained many of the attributes of a strong treasury. In 1987 a separate and distinct Treasury Board achieved even greater status with the disestablishment of two policy committees of cabinet.

Clearly, institutionalized cabinets affect the nature of planning and budgeting. As cabinets become more complex, these functions themselves become more complex, as might be expected in a central executive which involves more people, more talent, more ambition, and more rewards. Complexity marks the evolution of planning, which, where it is attempted, appears to develop along a continuum.

At one end of the continuum, in the unaided cabinet, planning will be sporadic, project oriented, coordinative, and personalistic (i.e. done by the premier and/or outside consultants). Thatcher's economic development planning followed this pattern. W. A. C. Bennett's development planning can perhaps best be described as integrated, being a kind of ambitious project planning which featured prioritization and cumulative investment plans aimed especially at resource infrastructure development, with a special concern for the needs of the B.C. interior.[14]

There may be a transitional kind of planning that mixes characteristics of both unaided and institutionalized cabinet planning. Like unaided planning, it would feature involvement by outsiders; but like institutionalized planning, it would involve comprehensive as well as project planning. Roblin practised what might be called an advanced form of transitional planning, with outsiders performing both project and comprehensive planning: witness the reports of the Committee on Manitoba's Economic Future (1963), the Manitoba Commission on

290

Targets for Economic Development (1969), and the work of the Manitoba Economic Consultative Board from 1963 to 1966.

⟨At the other end of the continuum is the comprehensive planning favoured by institutionalized cabinets. Such planning may be comprehensive in regard to public objects or to both public and private objects. Douglas and Schreyer fostered comprehensive planning, at least in intent. Planning is considered optional in both unaided and institutionalized cabinets,⟨but there is a stronger tendency to engage in it as one moves towards the institutionalized cabinet.⟩

Like planning, the planning-budgeting nexus is not automatically present when a cabinet begins to institutionalize. However, there is a strong tendency for it to develop in an institutionalized cabinet. The nexus idea may sometimes be expressed as the tension/competition between planning and budgeting, as was the case in Devine's system. Of course, an elemental planning-budgeting nexus was practised by Thatcher and W. A. C. Bennett; both dominated the budget process and cached finances in special funds to be used later for development projects. However, the connections become much more explicit and detailed in the institutionalized cabinets. There is a growing consensus that the budgeting process is the central planning focus of government. Nevertheless, incrementalism lasted a longer time in provincial budgeting.[15]

CONCLUSION

This study, based on a small sample of provinces, will not make hard and fast statements about the possibility of applying these experiences to other Westminster-type jurisdictions. Rather, these final offerings are more tentative and suggestive. For example, it may be that a premier's needs and perceptions should receive relatively less priority in the design of the central executive, given what has been learned about the needs of full cabinet, party ideologists, and interest groups. The multiplicity of factors that affect the persistence of the institutionalized cabinet—and there may be more than have been uncovered with these three provinces—may be of use in building the expanding field of transition literature.[16] In-house assessments of the central executive may also use some of these factors as points of departure in establishing evaluation criteria.

This study also suggests further areas of research and raises as yet unanswered questions. Given the less dominant premier this investigation has discovered, is it still accurate to say that "provincial government is Premier's government"?[17] Has there been a relationship between the strong treasury and fiscal responsibility? What functions should be included under central departments and which under central agencies?[18] Are the mechanisms of central/departmental balance sufficient to compensate for the possible weakening of individual ministerial responsibility in the institutionalized cabinet? Is a new philosophy of cabinet government being born? From this relatively modest overview, some interesting questions emerge.

One question concerns the matter of teleology versus evolution in provincial cabinet decision making. It may appear that this review assumes that the institutionalized cabinet is the natural end, the final destination and final shape of the central executive, and that further structural change will be minor at most. Such a conclusion cannot be drawn from the data available. The value of this study, then, lies in its implicit encouragement of inductive logic in the examination of the central executive. It examines the exogenous and endogenous factors impinging on cabinet design, as well as the designs themselves, and tries to establish whether there are commonalities or differences in the patterns of these central structures and processes.

It is not unrealistic, for example, to suggest that a post-institutionalized cabinet may emerge in the provinces. The factors impinging on cabinet design cannot be perceived of as unchanging. On the cusp of a new millennium, a qualitatively different order of political forces may come to bear. A new sense of crisis in many provincial capitals surrounds the problems of efficiency, downsizing, empowerment of public sector employees, burgeoning deficits, the crisis of the welfare state, ecological challenges, and international competitiveness. A political response could include, among other measures, smaller and more powerful cabinets, fewer cabinet committees, fewer and larger departments (which assume some of the policy coordination role previously performed by cabinet committees), a more strictly facilitative role for central agencies involving fewer overhead costs, and greater emphasis on strategic planning. It could be that the institutionalized cabinet has been a whistle stop on the way to a new destination.

Whatever the future pattern or patterns may be, this book has never intended to paint a static picture of the modern provincial cabinet. As the initial chapter indicated, its main job has been to review the factors leading to the initiation and persistence of cabinet institutionalization in the postwar period. In the future inductive empirical research will no doubt find new patterns developing in cabinet governance.

As it stands, the institutionalized cabinet is a fixture in Saskatchewan, Manitoba, and British Columbia. It has owed its introduction to province-specific mixtures of ideology and pragmatism and its continuance to internal and external factors common to more than one province. Its existence has profoundly affected how power is wielded and who wields it. Certainly, the premier's role has been significantly broadened. Understanding the history of the initiation and persistence of the institutionalized cabinet is a prerequisite to adapting it to the needs of future decades, as premiers pursue the Grail-like quest to make decision making manageable.

Notes

ABBREVIATIONS

SAB Saskatchewan Archives Board
PAM Public Archives of Manitoba

INTRODUCTION

1 One notable exception is Careless, *Initiative and Response*, which deals mostly with the initiation of planning systems and not their persistence.

2 Chandler and Chandler, *Public Policy*, p. 98. For similar descriptions, see Bryden, "Cabinets," pp. 310–11; White, "Governing from Queen's Park," pp. 174–75; and French, *How Ottawa Decides*, pp. 18–19.

3 Simeon, *Federal-Provincial Diplomacy*, pp. 35–38. See also McAllister, *The Government of Edward Schreyer*, p. 27.

4 Aucoin, "Organizational Change," p. 26. See also Smith, "Ruling Small Worlds," pp. 128–29; and Maslove, ed., *Budgeting in the Provinces*, pp. 38–40, 115, 127, and 138–39.

5 White, "Big is different from little," p. 535.

CHAPTER 1

1 Canada. Royal Commission on the Economic Union, *Report*, p. 45.

2 Canada. Privy Council Office, *The Office of Deputy Minister*, p. 8–9.

3 Tennant, "The NDP Government of British Columbia." An explanation of the term is found in the chapter on W. A. C. Bennett in this book.

4 This description of traditional, departmentalized, and institutionalized cabinets can be found in Dupré, "Executive Federalism," pp. 3–4.

5 The Queen's Privy Council for Canada is established by virtue of section 11, "to aid and advise in the Government of Canada." The main difference between federal and provincial executives is that federal ministers do not relinquish membership in the Queen's Privy Council for Canada upon resignation from cabinet, although for reasons of convention ex-ministers do not participate in actual executive power. In the provinces, membership in cabinet and membership in the executive council are synonymous.

6 The purposes of the expenditure budget are discussed in Kroeker, "The Expenditure Budgetary Process," p. 144.

7 Wilson, *Canadian Public Policy*, p. 274.

PART 2

1 Brownstone, "The Douglas-Lloyd Governments."

2 Ibid., p. 66.

3 Ibid., pp. 69–70.

CHAPTER 2

1 Eager, *Saskatchewan Government*; la Pierre et al, eds., *Essays on the Left*; Johnson, "Biography of a Government"; and McLeod and McLeod, *Tommy Douglas*. This names only a few.

2 SAB, Blakeney Papers, III 27. T. K. Shoyama, "Planning in the Government of Saskatchewan," Regina, n.d. (probably 1958).

3 Ibid.

4 McLeod and McLeod, *Tommy Douglas*, p. 127. This echoes Johnson's earlier view that the mandate of the EAPB derived largely from CCF ideology and to some extent from the erratic performance of departments in the early Douglas government. See Johnson, "Biography of a Government," pp. 299–303.

5 Ibid., pp. 27–28.

6 Cadbury, "The Saskatchewan Experiment," p. 6. Cadbury stood like a collossus across the planning framework of the Douglas government. He brought discipline and sophistication to the EAPB's analytic work. He would later go on to become a senior UN official and planning advisor to several developing countries.

7 Ibid.

8 Ibid.

9 The CCF annual seminar material includes reviews by deputies and planning officers testifying to the high level of planning activity in their departments.

10 Saskatchewan *Commonwealth*, July 7, 1943, quoted in McLeod and McLeod, *Tommy Douglas*, p. 128.

11 Ibid., p. 128.

12 Cadbury, "The Saskatchewan Experiment," p. 6.

13 Mitchell, "The Executive Council," p. 6.

14 SAB, Blakeney Papers, III 27. "Summary: Research and Planning in the Provincial Government," Regina, n.d. The summary noted that present planning activities were deficient because of outdated economic data, lack of a central program evaluation structure, and lack of a systematic approach to economic

planning. Eight departments were said to have research and planning units and together employed nineteen economists.

15 Quoted in Saskatchewan. Planning Bureau, "Central Planning in Saskatchewan," p. 2.

16 Ibid., p. 3.

17 Cadbury, "Planning in Saskatchewan," p. 56.

18 SAB, Blakeney Papers, V 63. "Notes for Remarks by Wes Bolstad to Treasury Board Seminar, July 14–15, 1977," p. 8.

19 Johnson, Presentation, pp. 34–41.

20 Ibid., pp. 35–37.

21 SAB, Blakeney Papers, V 63. Correspondence from D. D. Tansley to A. W. Johnson, Regina, April 25, 1960.

22 SAB, Blakeney Papers, III 27. D. Levin (director of research and planning, Department of Social Welfare and Rehabilitation), "An Approach to Planning," Regina, n.d. (probably 1958).

23 Ibid. Quotation from Millett, *Management in the Public Service*, p. 55.

24 SAB, Blakeney Papers, III 27. T. K. Shoyama, "Central Administrative Processes in Policy Formulation and Control," Lecture 6, Regina, Jan. 21, 1960.

25 Ibid.

26 SAB, Blakeney Papers, III 27. D. Levin, "A Concept of Planning," Regina, 1960.

27 Ibid.

28 McLeod and McLeod, *Tommy Douglas*, pp. 169–70.

29 Ibid., pp. 170–71.

30 SAB, Blakeney Papers, III 27. T. K. Shoyama, "Central Administrative Processes." See note 24, above.

31 Johnson, "Planning and Budgeting," pp. 145–53.

32 Ibid., p. 149.

33 SAB, Blakeney Papers, V. 44. D. D. Tansley, "Budgeting in the Government of Saskatchewan," Regina, May 1958.

34 Ibid.

35 Ibid., section by Wakabayashi.

36 Cadbury, "Planning in Saskatchewan," p. 56.

37 Careless, *Initiative and Response*, p. 136.

38 Johnson, "Planning and Budgeting," p. 146.

39 Ibid., p. 150.

40 Ibid., pp. 152–53.

41 Saskatchewan, Planning Bureau, "Central Planning in Saskatchewan," p. 4.

42 SAB, Blakeney Papers, III 27. T. K. Shoyama, "Central Administrative Processes."

43 Cadbury, "The Saskatchewan Experiment," p. 7.

44 McLeod and McLeod, *Tommy Douglas*, p. 174.

CHAPTER 3

1 Eisler, *Rumours of Glory*, p. 9.

2 Ibid., p. 42.

3 Saskatchewan, Crown Investments Corporation, *Public Enterprise in Saskatchewan*.

4 Eager, *Saskatchewan Government*, pp. 137 and 144.

5 Confidential interview.

6 Confidential interview.

7 Saskatchewan. *Public Accounts*, 1964–65 to 1968–69.

8 Steuart, interview. Senator David Gordon Steuart was the former provincial treasurer of Saskatchewan (December 25, 1967 to June 30, 1971). For a review of Moore's background see Eisler, *Rumours of Glory*, pp. 120–21.

9 Saskatchewan. *Public Accounts*, 1969–70.

10 Saskatchewan. Legislative Assembly, *Debates and Proceedings*, April 26, 1972.

11 Saskatchewan. Executive Council, *Saskatchewan into the Eighties*, p. 25.

12 Steuart, interview.

13 Saskatchewan. Crown Investments Corporation, *Public Investment in Saskatchewan*.

14 Steuart, interview.

15 Ward, "The Contemporary Scene," p. 297.

16 Saskatchewan. Royal Commission on Government Administration, *Report*, pp. 142–43. (Hereafter cited as the Johnson Commission Report.)

17 Confidential interview.

18 Saskatchewan. Johnson Commission Report, pp. 189–92.

19 Ibid., pp. 204–5.

20 Ibid., pp. 548–49.

21 Ibid., pp. 555–56.

22 Steuart, interview. Fred Johnson was a lawyer and past Liberal candidate; Lloyd Barber was dean of administration, University of Saskatchewan; and John Rowand was a Regina businessman.

23 Wallace, "Budget Reform in Saskatchewan."

24 Ward, "Saskatchewan," p. 162.

25 Confidential interview.

26 Ibid.

27 Steuart, interview.

28 Hayden, *Seeking a Balance*, p. 254.

29 Ibid., p. 256.

30 Steuart, interview.

31 Dyck, *Provincial Politics in Canada*, p. 399.

32 Richards and Pratt, *Prairie Capitalism*, p. 201.

33 Eager, *Saskatchewan Government*, p. 144.

34 Confidential interview.

35 Eisler, *Rumours of Glory*, p. 158.

36 Confidential interview.

37 Confidential interview.

38 Confidential interview.

39 Eager, *Saskatchewan Government*, pp. 137–38.

40 Steuart, interview.

41 Ibid.

42 Ibid.

43 Eisler, *Rumours of Glory*, pp. 48–49, 51–52, 139, 158–59, 211.

44 Eisler, *Rumours of Glory*, p. 159.

CHAPTER 4

1 One notable one is Blakeney and Borins, *Political Management in Canada*, 1992.

2 Conway, "The End of the Blakeney Era," 7–8 at 7.

3 Gruending, *Promises to Keep*, pp. 242–43.

4 Ibid., p. 240.

5 Saskatchewan. Government Information Services, News Release, October 27, 1971.

6 SAB, Blakeney Papers, IV 67a. "Progress Report to Cabinet by Task Force on Planning Organization," Regina, September 17, 1971.

7 Saskatchewan. Premier's Office, News Release, April 13, 1972.

8 SAB, Blakeney Papers. Minutes of the first meeting of the Planning Committee to the cabinet, Regina, September 14, 1972.

9 Saskatchewan. The Executive Council Act, 1972, Cap. 40, SS.5 and 6.

10 Saskatchewan. Legislative Assembly, *Debates and Proceedings*, April 26, 1972.

11 Saskatchewan. The Legislative Assembly and Executive Council Act, 1979, Cap. L–11.1, S.72(1).

12 SAB, Blakeney Papers, III 249. Memo from the premier to all cabinet ministers re the "Role of Treasury Board," Regina, September 15, 1971.

13 Ibid.

14 Ibid.

15 SAB, Blakeney Papers, III 249. D. M. Wallace (deputy minister of finance), "The Treasury Board in Saskatchewan—1972–1977."

16 Ibid.

17 MacLean, *Public Enterprise in Saskatchewan*, p. 13.

18 SAB, Blakeney Papers, III 247(b). Cabinet agenda item from W. A. Robbins to Allan Blakeney and all cabinet ministers re "Mid-year Treasury Board Submissions," Regina, April 18, 1974.

19 SAB, Blakeney Papers, III 249. D. M. Innes (director, Budget Bureau), "The Treasury Board Process—A Look Ahead," presented at the Treasury Board seminar, Regina, 1977.

20 SAB, Blakeney Papers. Information is excluded in order to protect confidentiality.

21 SAB, Blakeney Papers, III 249. "Suggested Topics for Premier to Cover in Remarks to Treasury Board Seminar."

22 SAB, Blakeney Papers. Wallace, "The Treasury Board in Saskatchewan." See note 15, above.

23 SAB, Blakeney Papers. Innes, "The Treasury Board Process." See note 19, above.

24 Saskatchewan. Department of Finance, *PMIS Orientation and Procedures Manual*, pp. 4–2–1 to 4–2–2.

299

25 Patriquin, "Presentation on the Planning Bureau." Patriquin was the deputy secretary of the Saskatchewan Planning Bureau. The 1973–75 figures are from internal documents, as is much of what follows.
26 Romanow, interview. Roy Romanow was the former attorney-general of Saskatchewan.
27 Ibid.
28 Ibid.
29 Cowley, interview. Elwood Cowley was the former minister of finance, minister of mineral resources, and provincial secretary in the Blakeney government.
30 Romanow, interview.
31 Cowley, interview.
32 Lloyd, interview. Roy Lloyd was the former chief planning officer in the Blakeney government.
33 Cowley, interview.
34 Saskatchewan. The Executive Council Act, 1972, Cap. 40, S.7.
35 Saskatchewan. The Legislative Assembly and Executive Council Act, 1979, Cap. L–11.1, S.74.
36 SAB, Blakeney Papers, IV 67b. Memo from Planning and Research to Allan Blakeney, re "Development of Planning and Research Office," Regina, June 22, 1972.
37 Saskatchewan. Planning Bureau, "Central Planning in Saskatchewan," p. 5.
38 Saskatchewan. Premier's Office, News Release 73–519, May 31, 1973.
39 Saskatchewan. Planning Bureau, "Central Planning in Saskatchewan," p. 6.
40 Blakeney, letter to the author. Blakeney was then Leader of the Opposition.
41 Ibid.
42 Saskatchewan. Planning Bureau, "Central Planning in Saskatchewan."
43 Blakeney, letter to the author.
44 Saskatchewan. Planning Bureau, "Function and Operation of the Planning Bureau."
45 SAB, Blakeney Papers, "Suggested Topics." See note 21, above.
46 SAB, Blakeney Papers, IV 67a. Memo from Planning and Research, Executive Council, and Department of Finance to Premier Allan Blakeney, Elwood Cowley, minister of finance, re "Organization and Operation of the Central Machinery," Regina, August 23, 1972.
47 SAB, Blakeney Papers, V 66(a). J. E. Sinclair, "Cabinet Planning Conferences on the Budget," Regina, September 4, 1979.
48 Ibid.
49 SAB, Blakeney Papers, IV 67a. "Organization and Operation of the Central Machinery." See note 46, above.
50 SAB, Blakeney Papers, V 63. "Notes for Remarks by Wes Bolstad to Treasury Board Seminar, July 14–15, 1977," p. 13.

CHAPTER 5

1 Eisler, "The Rise of an Invisible Man," p. 26.
2 Bott, "Hard Times," p. 10.

3 For an examination of the populist theme in Saskatchewan politics and how it relates to the political economy of the province, see Dunn and Laycock, "Saskatchewan," pp. 207–42.

4 Hardy, interview. Neil Hardy was then Saskatchewan's minister of the environment and a member of both the Treasury Board and the Planning Committee.

5 Saskatchewan. Government Information Services, News Releases, (Agriculture 86–021) January 16, 1986; and (Rural Development 86–455) June 19, 1986.

6 S.S. 1983 c.D–15.1.

7 Saskatchewan. Crown Investments Review Commission, *Report*.

8 Saskatchewan. Crown Investments Corporation, "Crown Corporations," pp. 3–4.

9 Saskatchewan. Legislative Assembly, *Debates and Proceedings*, Committee of Finance, Regina, June 17, 1985, pp. 3464–79.

10 Ibid., p. 3477.

11 Confidential interview.

12 Saskatchewan. Legislative Assembly, *Debates and Proceedings*, Committee of Finance, Regina, June 17, 1985, pp. 3464–79.

13 Robin Schiele, "Saskatchewan Pension Plan Sets Precedent," *Financial Post*, June 28, 1986, p. 6.

14 Confidential interview.

15 Confidential interview.

16 Riddell, letter to the author. Norman Riddell was then deputy minister to the Saskatchewan premier and cabinet secretary.

17 Confidential interview.

18 Lane, interview. Gary Lane was then the minister of finance of Saskatchewan.

19 Saskatchewan. Department of Finance, "Purpose and Scope of Zero-Base Reviews."

20 Lane, interview.

21 Saskatchewan. Department of Finance, "The Budget Planning Process," pp. 2–3.

22 Lane, interview.

23 Confidential interview.

24 Throne speech quoted in Saskatchewan. Government Information Services, News Release, "Throne Speech Opens New Session," (Executive Council 86–772) December 3, 1986, p. 5.

25 Saskatchewan. Department of Finance, *Saskatchewan Economic and Financial Position*, p. 8.

26 Ibid., p. 2.

27 Ibid., p. 12.

28 Ibid., pp. 14–15.

29 Saskatoon *Star-Phoenix*, May 4, 1987.

30 Saskatchewan. An Act respecting the Organization of the Executive Government of Saskatchewan, Bill 5 of 1986–87, introduced in December of 1986.

31 Smith, "The Parliamentary Tradition in Saskatchewan," p. 31. Smith reviewed the debate on second reading of the Bill and found four major Opposition

objections to it: it would delegate the power to make rules, which would in effect amend or repeal existing legislation; it would narrow the function and power of the Assembly, leaving scrutiny to the regulations committee only (which had narrow terms of reference); it would, in part, change the party which makes the law, contrary to what the Judicial Committee said in the "initiative and referendum reference"; and, lastly, it would close to the Opposition "its window on the operation of Government."

32 "Bill Expanding Cabinet's power slammed by NDP's Romanow," Regina *Leader Post*, December 16, 1986.

33 Saskatchewan. Government Information Services, News Release, "Departments Reorganized" (Finance 87–136) March 26, 1987.

34 Ibid.

35 Saskatchewan. Government Information Services, News Release, "Review to Begin Immediately" (Executive Council 87–041) January 30, 1987.

36 Saskatchewan. Government Information Services, News Release, "Public Service Reductions" (Public Service Commission 87–121) March 20, 1987.

37 Ibid.

38 Saskatchewan. Minister of Finance, Budget Address, June 1987, p. 4.

39 Bill Allan, "Government Lists 2,267 jobs chopped during past year," Regina *Leader-Post*, June 18, 1987.

40 Saskatchewan. Minister of Finance Budget Address, June 1987, p. 8.

41 Cited in Johnstone, "Deficit 'Reduction' called into question," Regina *Leader-Post*, June 18, 1987.

42 Ibid.

43 Confidential interview.

44 Allan, "Government Lists 2,267 jobs" see note 39, above. Allan cites documents showing that the ECO lost only 2.4 person-years in the 1987 cuts, leaving it with 82 person-years.

CHAPTER 6

1 This theme is elaborated in Dunn, "The Manitoba Cabinet," pp. 85–102.

2 The descriptions are attibuted to Roblin by a one-time political opponent, former CCF leader Lloyd Stinson, in "The Roblin Decade," Winnipeg *Free Press*, February 27, 1971.

3 Duart Farquharson, "Duff Roblin: he continues to await and assess," Winnipeg *Tribune*, June 6, 1967.

4 Richard Purser, "Duff Roblin in Business," Winnipeg *Tribune*, July 4, 1975.

5 Chorney, "The Political Economy," pp. 85–86.

6 Bracken had been both premier and treasurer from 1925 to 1932; Garson from 1943 to 1948, his entire period as premier; and Campbell from November to December 1948 and from February 1950 to December 1951. Garson had actually been treasurer since 1936. Even Schreyer, a premier of an institutionalized cabinet, was to perform brief stints as finance minister.

7 Walter C. Newman alleges that it was Industry and Commerce Deputy Minister Rex Grose who persuaded the Liberal cabinet to hire A. D. Little to

undertake the studies. Newman, *What Happened When Dr Kasser Came*, p. 9.

8 The Gordon Commission, as quoted in Little, *Economic Survey of Northern Manitoba, 1958*, p. iii.

9 Little, *Economic Survey of Northern Manitoba*, p. 163.

10 Ibid., p. 163.

11 Ibid., p. 164.

12 PAM, Gurney Evans Papers, MG 14 B27 Box 9, "Meeting Re Manitoba Development Authority and Business Development Corporation."

13 PAM, Gurney Evans Papers, MG 14 B27, Box 9, "Memorandum on the Proposal to Establish a Manitoba Development Authority, November 26, 1958." A. D. Little consulted political scientist Marven A. Bernstein of Princeton University for this draft.

14 Ibid., p. 1–2.

15 Ibid., p. 3.

16 Ibid., p. 7.

17 Poyser, interview.

18 Careless, *Initiative and Response*, p. 146.

19 Manitoba. Treasury Board, Operation Productivity *Report*, pp. A-2 to A-3. (Hereafter cited as the Operation Productivity Report). (Author's collection).

20 McLeod, "Planning Organization." (Author's collection).

21 S.M., 50 Vic. 1887, c. 20.

22 S.M., 1 Edward VIII 1936, c. 45.

23 Donnelly, *The Government of Manitoba*, p. 100.

24 Roblin, interview. Dufferin Roblin was premier of Manitoba from 1958 to 1967.

25 Ibid.

26 PAM, Gurney Evans Papers, MG 14 B27 Box 13. Minutes of a meeting of the Treasury Board, July 16, 1958; and a letter from Roblin to Evans "Re: Treasury Board," October 17, 1958.

27 PAM, Gurney Evans Papers, MG 14 B27 Box 13. Untitled pages recording meeting with Johnson and Watters.

28 Anderson, interview. J. S. Anderson was once Manitoba's deputy treasurer and later served as deputy finance minister.

29 PAM, Gurney Evans Papers, MG 14 B27 Box 13. "Treasury Board Direction #1: Treasury Board, Composition, Function," March 18, 1959.

30 Ibid. The 1959 listing of Treasury Board functions read as follows:

a) To review the annual current and capital budgets of the Government and to make recommendations in this connection to the full Cabinet; and generally to oversee the controlling of revenue and expenditure within the limits of legislation.

b) To establish uniform regulations for governmental matters and activities which involve expenditures and which may cut across departmental lines and to coordinate where necessary.

c) To direct research and investigation necessary to deal with all government matters having financial implications, and to dispose of these matters either finally, where they lie within the Board's sole responsibility, or to recommend for the consideration of full Cabinet appropriate courses of action.

In carrying out these functions it is not intended that the Treasury Board will interfere in any way with departmental administration. As a committee of the Executive Council it is the principal duty of Treasury Board to make recommendations to Cabinet and, accordingly, any decision of the Board may be reviewed by the Executive Council.

31 Manitoba. Treasury Board, *Minutes* 8/59, 10/59, 15/59, 27/59, 7/60, 22/60, and 31/60.

32 See, for example, Stinson, *Political Warriors*, p. 196; and Careless, *Initiative and Response*, p. 146.

33 Roblin, interview.

34 Bedson, interview. Derek Bedson was clerk of the Manitoba Executive Council, for the years 1958–81.

35 PAM, Gurney Evans Papers, MG 14 B27 Box 39. Submission to Cabinet from the Treasury Board re "Proposed Study of the Administration of the Government of Manitoba," March 9, 1967.

36 Holland, interview. Gordon W. Holland was secretary to the Management Committee of Cabinet in Manitoba for 1968–74.

37 PAM, finding-aid to Operation Productivity papers. The projects covered government organization, financial management, personnel management, systems, materials management, highways, and telecommunications.

38 Manitoba. Treasury Board (Operation Productivity), *Report*, pp. A–2 to A–3.

39 Ibid., p. A–4.

40 Ibid., p. A–4.

41 Ibid., pp. 9–10.

42 Manitoba. Government News Service, News Releases, "Cabinet Committees are Key to Control," "Major Shifts in Departmental Duties," and "Statement by Premier Weir," September 25, 1968.

43 Ibid. (All three news releases.)

44 PAM, Gurney Evans papers, MG 14 B27 Box 27. "Terms of Reference—Management Committee—October 3, 1968," taken from the agenda for the Management Committee meeting of October 4, 1968, prefaced "Mr Evans: Suggested items for informal discussions."

45 Submission to the Planning and Priorities Committee of Cabinet re "Integrated Planning-Programming Budgeting System (PPBS) for Manitoba." February 24, 1970.

46 PAM, Gurney Evans Papers, MG 14 B27 Box 39. Memo from C. H. Witney to all ministers and deputies, October 10, 1968.

47 Manitoba. Planning and Priorities Committee of Cabinet, *Minutes*, (PPCC 8/68) November 29, 1968.

48 Careless, *Initiative and Response*, p. 146.

49 Manitoba. Government News Service, News Release, "Bedson is Chairman of Centennial Corporation," November 2, 1973.

50 Bedson, interview.

51 Stinson, *Political Warriors*, p. 196.

52 Bedson, interview.

53 Byfield, "He who made history live," p. 52.

54 Ibid., p. 52.

55 Ibid., p. 52.

56 Ibid.

57 PAM, Gurney Evans Papers, MG 14 B27 Box 9. Memo from Grose to Evans re "Manitoba Development Authority," November 27, 1958.

58 Ibid.

59 PAM, Gurney Evans Papers, MG 14 B27 Box 13. Letter from Grose to Evans, September 3, 1958. This shows him proffering advice as a consultant to Evans on items such as the development corporation, A. D. Little, and tourism development.

60 Biographical information on Grose's career is taken from Manitoba. The CFI Inquiry *Report*, pp. 87, 99, 131–32, 1635–38 and 1652–53.

61 S.M., The Development Authority Act, 1959.

62 PAM, Gurney Evans Papers, MG 14 B27 Box 9. Memo from Grose to Evans re the "Manitoba Development Authority," November 16, 1959.

63 Manitoba. The CFI Inquiry *Report*, pp. 1636–38.

64 S.M. The Development Authority Act, 1963, Cap. 23.

65 PAM, Gurney Evans Papers, MG 14 B27 Boxes 9 and 13, respectively. Memo from Grose to Evans, May 29, 1963, re "Manitoba Development Authority/ Manitoba Economic Consultative Board"; and minutes of the meeting of the Manitoba Development Authority, May 31, 1963.

66 Ibid.

67 Manitoba. Government News Service, News Release, "Economic Consultative Board is Appointed," Aug. 1, 1963. By development work, the news release was probably referring to projects he had been involved with in Iran and Tanzania.

68 S.M., An Act to Amend the Development Authority Act, 1966. C.16.

69 Manitoba. Treasury Board, Operation Productivity *Report*, p. A–4.

70 Ibid., p. A–5.

71 PAM, Gurney Evans Papers, MG 14 B27 Box 13. Untitled work descriptions. This quotation and subsequent descriptions are taken from that paper.

72 Ibid.

73 PAM, Gurney Evans Papers, MG 14 B27 Box 13. "Department of the Provincial Treasurer, Province of Manitoba" Review of Treasury functions.

74 Holland, interview.

75 PAM, Gurney Evans Papers, MG 14 B27 Box 36. Memos from Stuart Anderson, secretary of the Treasury Board, to Treasury Board members and senior governmental staff re "Treasury Board Review of Departmental Estimates," 1966 and 1967.

76 Figures derived from Table 1 of McAllister, *The Government of Edward Schreyer*, p. 37.

77 PAM, Gurney Evans Papers, MG 14 B27 Box 36. "Memorandum to Cabinet from Treasury Board" re Treasury Board meeting 7/67, May 19, 1967.

78 PAM, Gurney Evans Papers, MG 14 B27 Box 36. Memo from Stuart Anderson to Duff Roblin, May 19, 1967, re "Aide-Memoire for Deputy Ministers' meeting May 24th."

79 Manitoba. Treasury Board, Operation Productivity, *Report*, pp. A–2 to A–3.

80 Ibid. pp. 9–10.

81 Manitoba. Submission to the Planning and Priorities Committee of Cabinet re "Integrated Planning-Programming Budgeting System (PPBS) for Manitoba." February 24, 1970.

82 Morton, *Manitoba: A History*, p. 501.

83 Manitoba. The CFI Inquiry *Report*, pp. 1636–38.

CHAPTER 7

1 Schreyer admitted as much in the Manitoba Legislative Assembly a year after the 1969 election. See Manitoba, Legislative Assembly, *Debates and Proceedings*, July 20, 1970, p. 3945.

2 Words to this effect were stated to the author in interviews by Ed Schreyer and by Sidney Green, one of his main ministers. Schreyer, interviews; and Green, interview.

3 Susan Riley, "What exactly is a morning suit?: The Schreyers prepare for Rideau Hall," Winnipeg *Tribune*, January 13, 1979.

4 Tim Harper, "For third time, Schreyer to be youngest ever," Winnipeg *Tribune*, December 6, 1978. Schreyer served in the Manitoba Legislative Assembly from 1958 to 1965 and in the federal House of Commons from 1965 to 1969. Weir called an election for June 25, 1969, in the middle of the provincial NDP's leadership race, obviously hoping to score a political advantage. The ploy backfired when the media gave wide coverage of the leadership convention on July 7, and Schreyer gave an uncharacteristically impassioned speech, probably the best in his life. The speech is widely regarded as an element in the NDP electoral success.

5 Franklin, "Meet the Schreyers of Manitoba," p. 64.

6 Susan Riley, "What exactly is a morning suit"? see note 3, above.

7 Franklin, "Meet the Schreyers of Manitoba," p. 62.

8 See, for example, an interview conducted with Premier Schreyer on July 5, 1969, within days of his government's taking office, reprinted from the Winnipeg *Tribune* in Beaulieu, *Ed Schreyer*, pp. 187–211.

9 Schreyer interview.

10 S.M. The Financial Administration Act, 1969, c.8.

11 S.M. The Executive Government Organization Act, 1970, c.17.

12 Manitoba, Legislative Assembly, *Debates and Proceedings*, April 30, 1970, p. 1433.

13 Ibid., p. 1434.

14 Ibid., p. 1433.

15 Schreyer, interview.

16 Green, interview.

17 PAM, Schreyer Papers, Box 228, various files. The NDP cabinet decided at

a cabinet seminar in Nov. 1969 to query McLeod to see if he wanted the position of secretary to cabinet; in a cabinet meeting on January 28, 1970, it was decided to ask him to serve on the staff of the PPCC. His associate on the study, Professor Meyer Brownstone, was asked to suggest policy objectives for the government and was also to be approached for temporary government employment.

18 Internal papers in author's collection. Hereafter, the reports will be cited without notes.

19 Schreyer, interview.

20 PAM, Schreyer Papers, Box 228, memo from Edward Schreyer to all ministers, in the cabinet material for September 17, 1969.

21 Confidential interview.

22 Brownstone and Plunkett, *Metropolitan Winnipeg.*

23 Ibid., pp. 19–47, especially pp. 34–47.

24 Manitoba. *Proposals for Urban Reorganization*, p. 27.

25 Ibid., p. 28.

26 Schreyer, interview.

27 *The Financial Post*, March 28, 1970, and May 16, 1970.

28 Ted Allan, "A workaholic about politics," Winnipeg *Free Press*, February 13, 1982, p. 3. In a nice piece of political irony, he handed in his resignation to Industry and Commerce Minister Len Evans, to whom he had once offered a job (in 1953) in the very same department that Evans was now heading. (Evans did not take it.) Recalling the resignation scene some years later, Evans said Grose accused him of "compromising his reputation."

29 Newman, *What Happened When Dr Kasser Came*, p. 83.

30 Ibid., pp. 85–86.

31 Ibid., pp. 98–99.

32 Ibid., p. 99.

33 "Miller Chairman of Group," Winnipeg *Free Press*, October 29, 1971.

34 Schreyer, interview.

35 Manitoba. Cabinet Committee on Health, Education, and Social Policy, *White Paper on Health Policy.*

36 Ibid., p. 1.

37 Ibid., p. 4.

38 Manitoba. Task Force on Post-Secondary Education in Manitoba, *Report.*

39 Memo from Premier Schreyer to all ministers, deputy ministers, and cabinet committee secretaries, September 6, 1973 re the "Reorganized Central Planning Structure." (Author's collection.)

40 Schreyer, interview.

41 Ibid., and Green, interview.

42 Frances Russell, "Cabinet Growth Reflects Electorate's Wants," Winnipeg *Tribune*, December 7, 1971. At the beginning of December, Schreyer hinted at the creation of two new committees: one joining justice, consumer affairs, human rights, and labour; and the other combining mines and resources, and industry and commerce.

43 Manitoba. Government Information Services, News Release, September 1, 1972.

44 See, for example, his essay, "On the Economics of Social Democracy," in

the seminal New Party collection edited by fellow academic Michael Oliver, *Social Purpose for Canada*, pp. 171–97.

45 Weldon, "What is Planning"? pp. 1–13.

46 Fenichel and Ingerman, eds., *On the Political Economy of Social Democracy*, pp. xviii–xxiii.

47 Memo from E. Petrich, Planning Secretariat, to all deputy ministers and agency heads, Aug. 6, 1971, re "Breakfast Meeting: Planning Secretariat," pp. 5–6. (Author's collection.)

48 Ibid., p. 10.

49 PAM, Schreyer Papers, Boxes 229 and 231. The Northern Working Group, for example, was discussed in the PPCC meetings of Nov. 26, 1970; Jan.21, 1971; and May 17, 1971.

50 Manitoba. Planning Secretariat, *Report of the Manpower Working Group*, p. 58.

51 Richard Purser, "Restructured Body Finally Gains Recognition," Winnipeg *Tribune*, December 18, 1971.

52 PAM, Schreyer Papers, cabinet material for September 6, 1972. Submission to cabinet from the PPCC chairman, re "Functional Reorganization of PPCC Secretariat."

53 Malcolm Gray, "The NDP ace who's gone to aid Barrett," *Globe and Mail*, October 5, 1974.

54 In doing so, Eliesen endured some flak when a draft chapter of the plan proposing a more interventionist industrial policy was leaked to the Winnipeg *Tribune*. Susan Hoeschen, "Public Corporations proposed in Province," Winnipeg *Tribune*, November 14, 1972.

55 Ingeborg Boyens, "From log cabin to the cabinet," Winnipeg *Free Press*, January 9, 1983; Wendy Stevenson, "Minister still a farmboy at heart," June 21, 1987; and "Manitoba, Government Information Services, News Release, "Parasiuk appointed Planning Secretary," June 21, 1974.

56 Schreyer, interview.

57 Seidman and Gilmour, *Politics, Position and Power*.

58 Wiseman, *Social Democracy in Manitoba*, p. 36.

59 League For Social Reconstruction, *Social Planning for Canada*, ch. IX.

60 It was not so much the character of the premier *per se* that alarmed business; it was a persistent fear that others—radicals, such as Sidney Green—lurked ready to influence the premier or cabinet unduly or even to take over should the premier resign. A newspaper article of the era (Steven Kerstetter, "Bogeyman or Benefactor: A Portrait of Sidney Green," Winnipeg *Free Press*, Jan. 19, 1976) is instructive:

> Few political observers would be surprised if Mr Green eventually decides to try again for the party leadership. Fewer still would be surprised if his opponents don't try to brand him as the dangerous radical who lurked in the shadows of a "moderate" NDP government.
>
> When a Winnipeg newspaper editorial espoused such a view during the 1973 provincial election campaign, however, Mr Green was quick to respond.

"They're saying if Ed Schreyer leaves, the bogey-man will get you," he told a political meeting.

After a pause, he grinned and announced: "Here I am."

61 Schreyer, interview.

62 Schreyer, interview.

63 Manitoba. Government Information Services, News Release, November 14, 1969.

64 The EDAB recommended priorities in its first report, but not thereafter. See Manitoba, Economic Development Advisory Board, "Report to the Standing Committee on Economic Development," pp. 1–4.

65 Confidential interview with a former EDAB member. The premier tended to refer little directly to the Board but had Board *members* investigate matters for him.

66 Schreyer, interview.

67 Confidential interview with a former EDAB member.

68 McAllister, *The Government of Edward Schreyer*, p. 71.

69 Ibid., p. 72.

70 Ibid., p. 29.

71 Schreyer, interview.

72 Kierans, *Report on National Resources Policy*.

73 Barber, *Welfare Policy in Manitoba*.

74 Green, interview. It should be noted that Mr Green left the NDP to found the right-wing Progressive Party of Manitoba.

75 Schreyer, interview.

76 Schreyer, interview.

77 Manitoba. *Guidelines for the Seventies*, 3 vols.

78 McAllister, *The Government of Edward Schreyer*, p. 72.

79 Careless, *Initiative and Response*, p. 146.

80 Manitoba. Planning and Priorities Committee of Cabinet, *Minutes*, January 27, 1970.

81 Eliesen, interview. Marc Eliesen was the former planning secretary of the Manitoba cabinet.

82 Schreyer, interview.

83 Holland, interview. Gordon W. Holland was the former secretary to the Management Committee of the Manitoba cabinet.

84 Schreyer, interview.

85 Schreyer, interview.

86 Manitoba, Task Force on Government Organization and Economy, *Report* p. 57. (Hereafter referred to as the Riley-Spivak Report.)

87 Brownstone, "The Douglas-Lloyd Governments," pp. 69–70. See also ch. 2 of this book, on the Douglas-Lloyd era.

88 Schreyer, interview.

89 McAllister, *The Government of Edward Schreyer*, p. 159.

90 Schreyer, interview.

91 Memo from Marc Eliesen, PPCC secretary, to all deputy ministers, May 14,

1973 (revised July 10, 1973) re "Government Decentralization," pp. 10, 15, and 33. (Author's collection.)

92 McAllister, *Report on Management Committee of Cabinet*. (Hereafter referred to as the "McAllister Report.")

93 Ibid., p. 1.

94 *The General Manual of Administration* of the Schreyer-era Manitoba government outlined a very detailed list of personnel responsibilities for the Management Committee of Cabinet. See Manitoba, *General Manual of Administration*, 1974, page IV, A.1–(3)(b).

95 Schreyer, interview.

96 Ibid.

CHAPTER 8

1 Sterling Lyon, as quoted in Mary Ann Fitzgerald, "Lyon: Two People in One," Winnipeg *Free Press*, Dec. 3, 1983, p. 47.

2 Jenni Morton, "Manitoba Mean," *The Canadian* (supplement to the Winnipeg *Tribune*), September 30, 1978, p. 4; Manitoba, Government Information Services, News Release, "Sterling R. Lyon, Premier-designate," October 14, 1977; and Fitzgerald, see note 1, above.

3 A notable example was Deputy Minister of Education Lionel Orlikow, whose progressive education philosophy was devastatingly targetted by the Opposition in the period leading up to the provincial election of 1977.

4 Fred Cleverley, "I'd rather be right than premier: Lyon," Winnipeg *Free Press*, September 29, 1982, p. 7.

5 Catherine Bainbridge, "Lyon's colourful career filled with controversy," Winnipeg *Free Press*, December 20, 1986.

6 Jenni Morton, "Manitoba Mean."

7 Joan Sadler, "A little help from his friends."

8 Ibid., p. 6.

9 Manitoba. Task Force on Government Organization and Economy, *Report*, vol. 1, p. 25. (Referred to in other chapters as the Riley-Spivak Report).

10 Ibid., p. 58.

11 Ibid., pp. 61–62.

12 Ibid., p. 66.

13 Ibid., p. 64.

14 Ibid., pp. 41–42.

15 Ibid., pp. 43–44.

16 Ibid., p. 45.

17 Ibid., p. 45.

18 Craik, interview. Don Craik, former minister of finance for Manitoba, unfortunately passed away a few weeks after this interview.

19 Order in Council 993/78 listed the duties of the Treasury Board. They included policy setting for central systems and operations; coordination of the budget process and recommendations to cabinet thereon; making changes in staff complements and levels of program delivery; reviewing requests for expansion of programs beyond approved appropriations; reviewing departmental financial status

reports; conducting program reviews; providing direction for fiscal planning; recommending on departmental organization; setting levels of expenditure by classification or amount, and other duties as charged by the LGIC.

20 Memo from Don Craik, chairman of the Treasury Board, to ministers, deputy ministers, and directors of administration re "Treasury Board—Functions/ Guidelines," November 9, 1978. (Author's collection.)

21 The Economic Development Committee was created by O/C 348/79, dated April 4, 1979; the Community Services Committee was created by O/C 1086/79, dated November 21, 1979.

22 Craik, interview.

23 Order in Council 1100/79, November 21, 1979, outlined the purposes and objects of the Committee on Economic Development.

24 Order in Council 1086/79, dated November, 21, 1979, outlined the purposes and objects of the Community Services Committee of Cabinet.

25 Confidential interview.

26 Craik, interview.

27 Pauline Comeau, "Former Lyon advisor named top civil servant," Winnipeg *Free Press*, May 12, 1988.

28 Confidential interview.

29 Manitoba. Department of Finance, *Preparation of Estimates, 1980–81* p. 1.

30 Ibid., p. 1.

CHAPTER 9

1 John Drabble, "Pawley: He *is* the NDP," Winnipeg *Tribune*, May 31, 1980.

2 Mary Ann Fitzgerald, "Howard Pawley's Secret Desire," Winnipeg *Free Press*, January 2, 1982, p. 1L.

3 "Howard Pawley," *Winnipeg Sun*, November 27, 1983.

4 Smith, "Pawley's Progress," p. 29.

5 Decter, *Expenditure Management*, p. 15. (Hereafter referred to as the Decter Report.)

6 Order in Council 993/81 listed responsibilities for the Treasury Board, which were exactly identical to those outlined for the Board in the Lyon years. See note 11, chapter 8.

7 Manitoba. Department of Finance, "Treasury Board."

8 From an internal Finance Department document, "The Government of Manitoba: Cabinet and Central Agencies, 1984," forwarded to the present author by a Department of Finance official in 1985.

9 Order in Council 201/83 outlined the functions of the SRC. Order in Council 1234/83 created the ERIC/Job Funds Committee.

10 Cowan, interview. Jay Cowan was minister of Cooperative Development and chairman of the Manitoba Treasury Board.

11 Confidential interview.

12 Cowan, interview.

13 Ibid.

14 Fred Cleverly, "Goodbye to Faithful Servant of Manitoba," Winnipeg *Free Press*, April 12, 1982.

15 Weppler et al., "Monologue vs. Dialogue," pp. 93–101.

16 Manitoba, Department of Finance, *Supplementary Information*, p. 38.

17 Decter, *Report*, p. ii.

18 Ibid., p. ii.

19 Ibid., p. 9.

20 Ibid., p. 5.

21 SPOs were beefed-up versions of the mission statement seen in the early eighties in the Lyon government. They included a departmental overview (departmental role statement, environmental analysis, and statement of major departmental objectives), a program display of current operations, a review of opportunities for trade-offs in the coming year, a review of new initiative proposals, and a review of non-discretionary programming.

22 Decter, *Report*, p. i.

23 Ibid., pp. 29–30.

24 See the sessional paper tabled by Kostyra in the Manitoba Legislative Assembly, May 21, 1986, re contract for services between the Province of Manitoba and the October Partnership regarding assessment of tax reform and expenditure management reform.

Ultimately two reports were submitted by Decter: "Expenditure Management" and "Taxation."

This chapter will concentrate on the former as being more germane, and, as noted previously, will refer to it as the Decter Report.

25 Decter, *Report*, p. 49.

26 Ibid., p. 49–50.

27 Ibid., p. 33.

28 Ibid., pp. 50–51.

29 Ibid., pp. 51–52

30 Ibid., pp. 54–57.

31 See the end of the section entitled "Conclusion" in this chapter.

32 Manitoba. Government Information Services, News Release, "Cabinet Committee Changes Announced," February 6, 1987.

33 Ibid., News Release, "Secretaries Appointed to Key Cabinet Bodies," April 3, 1987.

34 Ibid.

35 Manitoba. Civil Service Competitions 1151, 1152, and 1153 (1987), as advertised in the Toronto *Globe and Mail*, May 30, 1987, p. B16.

36 Manitoba. Department of Finance, *Supplementary Information*, pp. 66–73.

37 Ibid.

38 Confidential interview.

39 Stevenson Kellogg Ernst and Whinney produced a report late in 1986 for the government. See Don Benham "Stable Shut Too Late to Stop the Triple Crown," Winnipeg *Sun*, December 1, 1986. NDP government officials refused to release the consultants' report to the present author.

40 Manitoba. Government Information Services, News Release, "Premier Details Reforms for Crown Corporations," November 28, 1986.

41 Ibid.

42 S.M. An Act respecting the Accountability of Crown Corporations, 1987–

88, Cap. 55. Introduced June 3, 1987; received Royal Assent July 17, 1987.

43 See Ibid., ss.22(1) and 21(2), for a full list of powers.

44 Manitoba. Legislative Assembly, *Debates and Proceedings*, June 3, 1987, p. 2700.

45 Winnipeg *Free Press*, June 4, 1987.

46 Confidential Interview, Department of Crown Investments, June 1987. Order in Council 1298/87 disestablished the Crown Corporation Reform Committee and all appointments thereto.

47 Winnipeg *Free Press*, June 4, 1987.

48 As if to symbolize the new-found determination to become active in the Crown corporation sector, in June of 1987 the Manitoba government decided to acquire ICG Utilities—Greater Winnipeg Gas, a subsidiary of Inter-City Gas Corporation of Toronto. This was the first effective nationalization since the government had taken over auto insurance in 1970–71. On June 10, 1987, the Hon. Wilson Parsiuk introduced An Act to Govern the Supply of Natural Gas in Manitoba. (Bill 68). Bill 68 proposed a new Crown corporation, the Manitoba Consumers Gas Company, with the power to expropriate any land or corporation in Manitoba. Another stated purpose was to give Manitobans the benefits of earlier deregulation by giving the province the power to regulate the price of gas in the province. (See Winnipeg *Free Press*, June 11, 1987; and Manitoba, Legislative Assembly, *Debates and Proceedings*, June 10, 1987, p. 1941.) Ultimately, however, the government called off the deal for intergovernmental and financial reasons.

CHAPTER 10

1 Tennant, "The NDP Government of British Columbia," pp. 489–503.

2 Ibid., pp. 491–92.

3 Ibid., p. 492.

4 Ibid., p. 492.

5 Young and Morley, "The Premier and the Cabinet," p. 63.

6 Careless, *Initiative and Response*, p. 124.

7 "Interview with W. A. C. Bennett," *Maclean's*, p. 4.

8 Hyman Solomon, "Belling the cat easier said than done," *Financial Post*, August 5, 1972.

9 "Interview with W. A. C. Bennett," *Maclean's*, p. 12.

10 S.B.C. 1913, ch. 5.

11 Sidor, "The Structure of Policy Planning," p. 18.

12 Ibid., p. 20.

13 Young and Morley, "The Premier and the Cabinet," p. 63.

14 Ritter and Cutt, *The Evolution of Central Financial Administration*.

15 Ibid., p. 20.

16 Campbell, interview. Dan Campbell was the former Social Credit minister of municipal affairs in the W. A. C. Bennett government.

17 Mitchell, *W. A. C.*, pp. 275–76.

18 Confidential interview.

19 Ruff, "Administrative Styles," p. 9.

20 Mitchell, *W. A. C.*, p. 273.

21 Confidential interview.

22 British Columbia, Ministry of Finance, *Background Papers to the 1982 Budget*, p. 64.

23 Ibid.

24 British Columbia, Department of Finance, *Financial and Economic Review*, p. 14.

25 Ibid., pp. 51–52.

26 Ritter and Cutt, *The Evolution of Central Financial Administration*, pp. 51–52.

27 Carlsen, "Public Debt Operations," pp. 64–71.

28 Ibid., p. 65. Carlsen goes on to describe the three items.

29 Sherman, *Bennett*, pp. 197–202.

30 Ibid., p. 207.

31 Jackman, *Portraits of the Premiers*, p. 262.

32 Tennant, "The NDP Government of British Columbia," pp. 491–92; and Careless, *Initiative and Response*, p. 124.

33 Mitchell, *W. A. C.*, p. 423.

34 Ibid., pp. 282–83.

35 Ibid., p. 327.

36 Ibid., p. 331.

37 Ibid., p. 24.

38 Ibid., p. 290.

39 Ibid., p. 422.

40 Waterston, *Development Planning*, pp. 63–64.

41 Mitchell, *W. A. C.*, p. 74.

42 Black, "British Columbia," p. 260.

43 Ibid., p. 262.

44 Ibid., p. 261.

CHAPTER 11

1 Trevor Lautens, "No Regrets" [interview with Dave Barrett], Vancouver *Sun*, July 27, 1991, p. B5.

2 Allan Fotheringham, "A socialist in the land of plenty," *Maclean's*, pp. 65–66. The main encyclicals were Pope Leo XIII's *Rerum Novarum* of 1891 and Pope Pius XI's *Quadragesimo Anno* of 1931. He was also affected by Pope John's *Pacem in Terris*.

3 Vaughan Palmer, "It's difficult to be kind about Mr Barrett's political life," Vancouver *Sun*, May 31, 1984, p. A4.

4 Tennant, "The NDP Government of British Columbia, pp. 489–503. Refer back to the previous chapter for a detailed description of the attributes of an unaided cabinet, according to Tennant.

5 Ibid., pp. 493–94.

6 Ibid., p. 495.

7 Eliesen, interview. Marc Eliesen was the ex-Planning Advisor to the cabinet of British Columbia.

8 Bryden, "Cabinets," p. 319.

9 Malcolm Gray, "The NDP ace who's gone to aid Barrett," *Globe and Mail*, October 10, 1974, p. 10.

10 Sidor, "The Structure of Policy Planning," p. 29.

11 Ibid.

12 Ibid., p. 21.

13 Christianna Crook, quoted in Sidor, "The Structure of Policy Planning." p. 24.

14 Ibid., p. 24.

15 Ibid., p. 26.

16 Ibid., pp. 27–28.

17 Swainson, "The Public Service."

18 Ibid., p. 149.

19 Ibid., p. 151.

20 Sidor, "The Structure of Policy Planning," p. 4, derived from British Columbia Public Service Commission *Annual Reports*.

21 Ruff, "Administrative Styles," p. 14.

22 Swainson, "Governing Amid Division," pp. 199.

23 Young and Morley, "The Premier and the Cabinet," p. 68.

24 Ruff, "Administrative Styles," p. 13.

25 Kavic and Nixon, *The 1200 Days*, p. 87. The figure is from an address by Premier W. R. Bennett, February 20, 1976.

26 Ibid., p. 85.

27 Ibid., p. 85.

28 Ibid., p. 86.

29 Vancouver *Province*, October 4, 1975, pp. 1 and 27.

30 Canadian Tax Foundation, *Provincial and Municipal Finances* 1973, p. 25.

31 Canadian Tax Foundation, *Provincial and Municipal Finances*, 1977, p. 29.

32 Canadian Tax Foundation, *Provincial and Municipal Finances*, 1973, p. 46; and 1977, p. 61. The 1972 figure was offset by sinking funds of $257.6 million, and the 1976 figure was offset by sinking funds of $472.8 million.

33 Confidential interview.

34 Ritter and Cutt, *The Evolution of Central Financial Administration*, p. 15. This was semi-official in the sense that the project was initiated by the Ministry of Finance itself and relatively open access to ministry staff and information was accorded. However, the publishing authority for the study was the University of Victoria's School of Public Administration.

35 Ruff, "Managing the Public Service," p. 181.

36 Ibid., pp. 181–82.

37 Confidential interview.

38 British Columbia, Legislative Assembly, *Debates*, June 22, 1979, pp. 345–46; see also pp. 324–27.

39 Eliesen, interview.

40 Ibid.

41 The NDP popular vote was close to forty per cent in 1972 and close to thirty-nine per cent in 1975.

CHAPTER 12

1 "Retiring Bennett a believer in hard work," Vancouver Sun, May 23, 1986.

2 Newman, "The personal legacy of the Bennett era," p. 22.

3 Confidential interview.

4 British Columbia. Ministry of Intergovernmental Relations, "Cabinet Secretariat."

5 Sidor, "The Structure of Policy Planning," pp. 61–65, 104–7.

6 Ibid., p. 63.

7 Ibid., p. 62.

8 British Columbia. Ministry of intergovernmental Relations. "Cabinet Secretariat."

9 Confidential interview.

10 Ibid.

11 Confidential interview.

12 Confidential interview.

13 Confidential interview.

14 Emerson, interview. David Emerson was secretary to the British Columbia Treasury Board.

15 Sidor, "The Structure of Policy Planning," pp. 104–7, discusses the background of Krasnick and Smith. The present author's research revealed that from 1976 to 1979 Planning and Priorities was served by Dan Campbell, director of the OIR; Treasury Board by Bryson, the finance deputy; Economic Development by Peter Jull, OIR; Social Services by Don Axford, OIR; Legislation by Mark Krasnick, Attorney-General (AG) Department; Urban Affairs by Laura Anderson, OIR; Coal by Peter Jull; Anti-Inflation by Bill Neilson, a special consultant to the premier; Constitution by Mel Smith, AG; and Energy by Michael Randall of the OIR.

16 British Columbia. Press Release, "Reorganization Highlights: A summary of New Cabinet Responsibilities and Changes in Organization of Government Ministries," November 25, 1979.

17 British Columbia. Legislative Assembly Debates, February 18, 1977, p. 1073. The speaker is W. R. Bennett.

18 British Columbia. Legislative Assembly Debates, May 2, 1978, p. 976. (W. R. Bennett).

19 British Columbia. Legislative Assembly Debates, April 10, 1980, pp. 1925–26. (W. R. Bennett).

20 British Columbia, Legislative Assembly Debates, April 6, 1982, p. 6886; and April 8, 1982, p. 6959.

21 R.S.B.C. 1976, Chap. 343, S.54.

22 S.B.C. 1981, Chap. 15, S.4(e).

23 Ritter and Cutt, The Evolution of Central Financial Administration, pp. 120–21.

24 British Columbia. Department of Finance, internal memorandum, August 1983.

25 Bell, interview. Larry Bell was B.C.'s deputy minister of finance.

26 Eli Sopow, "Power Behind Bill Bennett's Throne," *The Province*, Sunday, August 7, 1983, p. 21.

27 Ladner, "Who are Those Masked Men"? p. 38. In August 1986 Spector was appointed secretary to the cabinet for Federal-Provincial Relations in the federal government; it seems that he was hired largely on the basis of his performance with the B.C. government during the Canada-U.S. Free Trade talks.

28 Gary Mason, "Bud Smith: Unknown Wages Bid with Grassroots Ties, Skills as an Organizer," Vancouver Sun, July 8, 1986.

29 Confidential interview.

30 Campbell, interview.

31 Ritter and Cutt, *The Evolution of Central Financial Administration*, p. 45.

32 1981–82 Treasury Board staff presentation.

33 Ritter and Cutt, *The Evolution of Central Financial Administration*, p. 46.

34 Ibid., p. 45.

35 Ritter, in an early draft of the Ritter and Cutt report, p. 43.

36 Confidential interview.

37 British Columbia. 1986–87 Budget Instructions.

38 Confidential interview.

39 Ritter, in early draft of the Ritter and Cutt report, p. 42.

40 Ritter and Cutt, *The Evolution of Central Financial Administration*, p. 46.

41 Confidential interview.

42 Confidential interview.

43 McLeod Young Weir, *Review of Fiscal 1984 Provincial Budgets*, pp. 11–12.

44 Ibid., p. 11. McLeod Young Weir explained the term as follows: "The restraints on growth of government overhead generally, and labour compensation in particular, are most visible in the labour-intensive areas of health and education. These functions, together with the social services, public protection, and recreation and culture, make up a block of activity to which provincial governments are committed by 'Social Contract'."

45 Ibid., p. 12.

46 British Columbia. Ministry of Finance, *A New Financial Administration Act*.

47 Vancouver *Province*, September 18, 1980. Hospital and school boards were also to decry the threat to local autonomy during the Bill-related hearings. See the Vancouver *Province*, November 6, 1980.

48 Vancouver *Province*, October 24, 1980.

49 Vancouver *Province*, October 27, 1980.

50 Vancouver *Sun*, December 2, 1980.

51 "Oak Bay and Victoria: Two Faces of Politics in B.C.," Vancouver *Sun*, May 20, 1981.

52 British Columbia. *Report of the Task Force on the Financial Administration Act*, p. 5.

53 Confidential interview.

54 Ritter and Cutt, *The Evolution of Central Financial Administration*, p. 35.

55 British Columbia. *The Economy in a Changing World*, pp. 12–13.

56 Vancouver *Sun*, February 19, 1982.

57 Ibid.

58 British Columbia. Legislative Assembly Debates, May 3, 1982, p. 7341.

59 Vancouver *Sun*, May 6, 1983, p. B9.

60 Ibid.

61 Vancouver *Sun*, Final Edition, April 21, 1983; Vancouver *Sun*, April 22, 1983; May 4, 1983, p. C8.; and May 4, 1983, p. B3.

62 Garr, *Tough Guy*, pp. 47–50.

63 Confidential interview.

64 These figures are found in the 1985 Budget, p. 3.

65 Marjorie Nichols, "A Disconnected Convention," Vancouver *Sun*, October 15, 1983, p. A4. See also "Socreds Veto Rentalsman Bid," Vancouver *Sun*, October 15, 1983, p. A12.

66 British Columbia. Ministry of Finance, internal memorandum, 1983.

67 The details of the Kelowna accord are taken from *Globe and Mail*, November 15, 1983; and the Vancouver *Sun*, November 17 and 18, 1983.

68 British Columbia. Ministry of Finance. *Budget*, 1984, p. 8.

69 British Columbia. Ministry of Finance. *Budget*, 1985, p. 16.

70 British Columbia. Ministry of Finance. *Budget*, 1986, p. 8.

71 Ibid., p. 9.

72 British Columbia. Ministry of Industry and Small Business Development, "British Columbia Facts and Statistics," p. 32.

73 British Columbia. Ministry of Finance, *The Economy in a Changing World*, p. 15.

74 Ritter and Cutt, *The Evolution of Central Financial Administration*, p. 122.

75 Ibid., p. 54.

76 Ibid., p. 123.

77 Ibid., pp. 123–24.

78 Confidential interview.

79 Confidential interview.

80 Ibid.

81 Confidential interview.

82 Ibid.

83 Confidential interview.

84 Rod Mickleburgh, "Bennett Aide Expected to Head Employers' Group," Vancouver *Province*, May 9, 1983.

85 Allen Garr, *Tough Guy*, p. 55.

86 Howlett, "The Development of Intergovernmental Relations," pp. 58–59.

87 Ibid, pp. 59–61.

88 British Columbia. Legislative Assembly, *Debates*, February 18, 1985, p. 5007.

89 Ibid., p. 5008.

90 See Canada, Special Committee, *Report*, especially chapters 5, 6, and 13.

91 British Columbia. Legislative Assembly, *Debates*, February 18, 1985, p. 5009.

92 Ibid., p. 5008.

93 Ibid., p. 5009.

94 Ibid., p. 5007.

95 British Columbia. Ministry of Provincial Secretary and Government Services, *Statement of Branch Roles*.

96 Ibid., p. 3.

CHAPTER 13

1 The general description of the role of central staff bodies is reminiscent of Wilson, *Canadian Public Policy and Administration*, p. 274. It should also be noted that one may refer to a *part* of a department as a central department—like the Treasury Board Secretariat in a Finance Department.

2 Dupré, "Reflections on the Workability of Executive Federalism" p. 4. Dupré initiated the term *institutionalized cabinet* in this article. The term *unaided cabinet* was first used by Paul Tennant in "The NDP Government of British Columbia," pp. 489–503. We use the term *unaided* rather than the older term *departmentalized* cabinet simply because the former describes characteristics that are particularly appropriate to provincial cabinet history, whereas the latter tends to be associated with the development of federal cabinets.

3 McLeod and McLeod, *Tommy Douglas*, p. 127. See also Richards and Pratt, *Prairie Capitalism*, especially pp. 129–30.

4 Johnson, Presentation, pp. 34–41.

5 Manitoba. Legislative Assembly, *Debates and Proceedings*, April 29, 1963, pp. 1787–90.

6 Tennant, "the NDP Government of British Columbia," pp. 491–3.

7 Mitchell, *W. A. C.*, p. 423.

8 Saskatchewan. Legislative Assembly, *Debates and Proceedings*, April 26, 1972, pp. 1988–89.

9 Trebilcock et al., *The Choice of Governing Instrument*; Edelman, *The Symbolic Uses of Politics*.

10 This general approach to rationalism has been the subject of a revisionist critique by an older Aaron Wildavsky, and others. See, for example, Wildavsky, *Speaking Truth to Power*, pp. 1–40, 62–85, and 114–41; and Gustafsson and Richardson, "Concepts of Rationality and the Policy Process," pp. 415–36. Richard French suggests that rationalist social scientists had an impact on early Trudeau federal cabinet design. See French, *How Ottawa Decides*.

11 Wallace, "Budget Reform in Saskatchewan," pp. 586–91.

12 Mallory, "The Continuing Evolution of Canadian Constitutionalism", p. 67.

13 Dupré, "Executive Federalism," p. 4.

14 Black, "British Columbia," pp. 260–62.

15 See, for example, Dunn, "The Manitoba Cabinet," pp. 97–100.

16 The idea would be to develop a Canadian literature of the breadth and scope of some American examples: Carl M. Brauer, *Presidential Transitions: Eisenhower Through Reagan* (New York and Oxford: Oxford University Press, 1986); and James P. Pfiffner, *The Strategic Presidency: Hitting the Ground Running* (Chicago: The Dorsey Press, 1988). A useful beginning is the 1993 collection edited by Donald Savoie, *Taking Power*.

17 The expression is from Young, "The Premier and the Cabinet," p. 54. It

is quoted in White, "Big is different from little," pp. 535–36. It should be noted that many Atlantic political scientists consider premiers in the Atlantic provinces to be "dominant premiers." This raises interesting questions about the stages of executive development in Canadian provinces.

18 Howard Leeson, for example, considers the appropriate home for the inter-governmental function to be the Premier's Office. See Leeson, "The intergovern-mental affairs function," pp. 399–420.

Bibliography

ARCHIVAL SOURCES

Blakeney Papers, Saskatchewan Archives Board. (Premier Allan Blakeney of Saskatchewan)
Bracken Papers, Public Archives of Manitoba. (Premier John Bracken of Manitoba)
Garson Papers, Public Archives of Manitoba. (Premier Stuart Garson of Manitoba)
Personal Papers of Gurney Evans, Public Archives of Manitoba.
Personal Papers of Edward Schreyer, Public Archives of Manitoba.

PUBLISHED AND UNPUBLISHED SOURCES

Anderson, J. S. Interview with the author. Winnipeg, June 1984.
Arthur D. Little, Inc. *Economic Survey of Northern Manitoba, 1958*. Report prepared for the Ministry of Industry and Commerce, Province of Manitoba. Sessional Paper #5, Second Session. Winnipeg, 1958.
Aucoin, Peter. "Organizational Change in the Management of Canadian Government: From Rational Management to Brokerage Politics." *Canadian Journal of Political Science* 19, no. 1 (March 1986): 3–27.
Baker, William V. "Evaluation in Saskatchewan: A Working System." Paper presented at the Canadian Evaluation Society Annual Conference, held at Banff, Alberta, April 19, 1986.
Barber, Clarence L. *Welfare Policy in Manitoba*. Report submitted to the Planning and Priorities Committee of Cabinet Secretariat, Province of Manitoba. Winnipeg, December 1972.
Beaulieu, Paul. *Ed Schreyer: A Social Democrat in Power*. Winnipeg: Queenston House, 1977.
Bedson, Derek. Interview with the author. Winnipeg, August 16, 1988.

Bell, Larry. Interview with the author. Victoria, March 1984.

Black, Edwin R. "British Columbia: The Politics of Exploitation." In *British Columbia: Patterns in Economic, Political and Cultural Development*. Victoria: Camosun College, 1982.

Blakeney, Allan. Letter to the author, April 4, 1986.

Blakeney, Allan and Sanford Borins. *Political Management in Canada*. Toronto and Montreal: McGraw-Hill Ryerson, 1992.

Bott, Robert. "Hard Times." *Saturday Night* 101, no. 4 (April 1986): 10.

British Columbia. Department of Finance. Internal Memorandum, August 1983.

– Legislative Assembly. *Debates*, 1977–80, 1982, and 1985.

– Ministry of Finance. *A New Financial Administration Act: Discussion Paper*, August 1980.

– Ministry of Finance. *Background Papers to the 1982 Budget*, 1982.

– Ministry of Finance. *Budget*, 1984, 1985, and 1986.

– Ministry of Finance. *Financial and Economic Review*, July 1972.

– Ministry of Finance. *The Economy in a Changing World*, budget paper, 1985.

– Ministry of Industry and Small Business Development. *British Columbia Facts and Statistics*, January 1986.

– Ministry of Intergovernmental Relations. "Cabinet Secretariat," draft pamphlet, 1986.

– Ministry of Provincial Secretary and Government Services. "Statement of Branch Roles and Operating Philosophy," mimeo, n.d. (c. 1984).

– Press Release, 1979.

– Public Service Commission. *The Organization of the Public Service of the Province of British Columbia*, 1982.

– Statement by Premier Bill Vander Zalm, November 6, 1986.

– Task Force on the Financial Administration Act. *Report*, March 1981.

– Treasury Board. "Budget Estimates Policy and Procedures for Fiscal Year 1982–83," April 1981.

– Treasury Board. "Budget Estimates Policy and Procedures for Fiscal Year 1983–84," July 1982.

– Treasury Board. "Budget Estimates Preparation Procedures: Zero Base Budgeting Process for Fiscal Year 1979–80," April 1978.

– Treasury Board. "Budget Estimates Preparations Procedures: Zero Base Budgeting Process for Fiscal Year 1980–81," May 1979.

– Treasury Board. "Out-line zzb Estimates Preparation Process for Fiscal Year 1981–82," 1981.

– Treasury Board, "Zero-Base Budgeting Process for Fiscal Year 1981–82," staff presentation, c.1981.

Brownstone, Meyer. "The Douglas-Lloyd Governments: Innovation and Bureaucratic Adaptation." In *Essays on the Left*, edited by Laurier la Pierre *et al.* Toronto: McClelland and Stewart, 1971: 65–80.

Brownstone, Meyer and T.J. Plunkett. *Metropolitan Winnipeg: Politics and Reform of Local Government*. Berkeley: University of California Press, 1983.

Bryden, Kenneth. "Cabinets." In *The Provincial Political Systems: Comparative Systems*, edited by David J. Bellamy, Jon H. Pammett, and Donals C. Rowat. Toronto: Methuen, 1976.

Byfield, Ted. "He who made history live now lives in Manitoba history." *Western Report* (May 29, 1989): 52.

Cadbury, George. "Planning in Saskatchewan." In *Essays on the Left*, edited by Laurier la Pierre *et al.* Toronto: McClelland and Stewart, 1971: 51–64.

– "The Saskatchewan Experiment." *NeWest Review* 12 (May 1987): 6–8, 11.

Campbell, Daniel. Interview with the author. Victoria, October 27, 1983.

Canada. Privy Council Office. *The Office of Deputy Minister*, March 1987.

– Royal Commission on the Economic Union and Development Prospects for Canada *Report*, vol. 3, 1985.

– Special Committee on the Review of Personnel Management and the Merit Principle, *Report*, September 1979.

– Canadian Tax Foundation. *Provincial and Local Finances*, 1973.

– *Provincial and Municipal Finances*, 1977.

Careless, Anthony. *Initiative and Response: The Adaptation of Canadian Federalism to Regional Economic Development*. Montreal and London: McGill-Queen's University Press, 1977.

Carlsen, Alfred E. "Public Debt Operations in British Columbia Since 1952." *Canadian Journal of Economics and Political Science* 27 (February 1961): 64–71.

Chandler, Marsh A. and William M. Chandler. *Public Policy and Provincial Politics*. Toronto: McGraw-Hill Ryerson, 1979.

Chorney, Harold Ross. "The Political Economy of Provincial Economic Development Policy: A Case Study of Manitoba." Master's thesis, University of Manitoba, 1970.

Clark, Ian. *Recent Changes to the Cabinet Decision—Making System*. Ottawa: Privy Council Office, December 3, 1984.

Conway, J. F. "The End of the Blakeney Era: An Assessment." *NeWest Review* 13, no. 3 (November 1987): 7–8.

Corpus Information Services. *Corpus Administrative Index: April-May-June 1984*. Don Mills: Southam Communications, 1987.

Cowan, Jay. Interview with the author. Winnipeg, June 11, 1985.

Cowley, Elwood. Interview with the author. Saskatoon, November 6, 1985.

Craik, Donald. Interview with the author. Winnipeg, June 11, 1985.

Decter, Michael *et al.* ("The October Partnership" consultants). *Expenditure Management: A Review and Recommendations for Reform*. Report commissioned by the Province of Manitoba. Winnipeg, November 19, 1986.

– *Taxation: A Review and Recommendations for Reform*. Report prepared for the Province of Manitoba. Winnipeg, November 19, 1986.

Doern, Russell. *Wednesdays Are Cabinet Days*. Winnipeg: Queenston House, 1981.

Donnelly, M. S. *The Government of Manitoba*. Toronto: University of Toronto Press, 1963.

Dunn, Christopher. "Changing the design: cabinet decision making in three provincial governments." *Canadian Public Administration* 34, no. 4 (Winter 1991): 621–40.

– "The Manitoba Cabinet in the Liberal-Progressive Era." *Prairie Forum* 15, no. 1 (Spring 1990): 85–102.

Dunn, Christopher and David Laycock. "Saskatchewan: Innovation and Competition in the Agricultural Heartland." In *The Provincial State: Politics in Canada's Provinces and Territories*, edited by Michael Howlett and Keith Brownsey. Toronto: Copp Clark Pitman, 1992.

Dupré, J. Stefan. "Reflections on the Workability of Executive Federalism." In *Intergovernmental Relations*, coordinated by Richard Simeon. Study 63 of the Macdonald Royal Commission. Toronto: University of Toronto Press, 1985.

Dyck, Rand. *Provincial Politics in Canada*. Scarborough, Ontario: Prentice-Hall, 1986.

Eager, Evelyn. *Saskatchewan Government: Politics and Pragmatism*. Saskatoon: Western Producer Prairie Books, 1980.

Edelman, Murray. *The Symbolic Uses of Politics*. Urbana: University of Illinois Press, 1964.

Eisler, Dale. "The Rise of an Invisible Man." *Maclean's* 10 (May 1982): 26.

– *Rumours of Glory: Saskatchewan and the Thatcher Years*. Edmonton: Hurtig, 1987.

Eliesen, Marc. Interview with the author. Winnipeg, August 14, 1985.

Emerson, David. Interview with the author. Victoria, 1983.

Fenichel, Allen and Sidney H. Ingerman, eds. *On the Political Economy of Social Democracy: Selected Papers of J. C. Weldon*. Montreal and Kingston: McGill-Queen's University Press, 1991.

Financial Post. Toronto, 1986.

Fotheringham, Allan. "A Socialist in the land of plenty." *Maclean's* (June 1973): 65–66.

Franklin, Stephen. "Meet the Schreyers of Manitoba." *Chatelaine* (April 1970): 34, 60, 62, and 64.

French, Richard. *How Ottawa Decides*. Toronto: James Lorimer and Company, 1980.

Garr, Allen. *Tough Guy: Bill Bennett and the Taking of British Columbia*. Vancouver: Key Porter Books, 1985.

Gibbins, Roger. *Prairie Politics and Society*. Toronto: Butterworths, 1980.

Globe and Mail. Toronto, 1974.

Green, Sidney. Interview with the author. Winnipeg, September 6, 1988.

Gruending, Dennis. *Promises to Keep: A Political Biography of Allan Blakeney*. Saskatoon: Western Producer Prairie Books, 1990.

Gustafsson, Gunnel and J. J. Richardson, "Concepts of Rationality and the Policy Process." *European Journal of Political Research* 7 (1979): 415–36.

Hagan, Matthew. "Interview with W. A. C. Bennett," *Maclean's* (December 1, 1975): 4, 8, 10, and 12.

Hardy, Neil. Interview with the author. Saskatoon, October 22, 1985.

Hayden, Michael. *Seeking a Balance: University of Saskatchewan, 1907–1982*. Vancouver: University of British Columbia Press, 1983.

Holland, Gordon W. Interview with the author. Winnipeg, August 8, 1988.

Howlett, Michael Patrick. "The Development of Intergovernmental Relations in the Province of British Columbia." Masters thesis, Department of Political Science, University of British Columbia, March 1984.

Jackman, S. W. *Portraits of the Premiers*. Sidney, B.C.: Gray's Publishing, 1969.

Jackson, James A. *The Centennial History of Manitoba*. Toronto: McClelland and Stewart, 1970.

Johnson, A. W. "Biography of a Government: Policy Formation in Saskatchewan 1944–1961." Ph.D. diss., Harvard University, 1963.

– "Planning and Budgeting." *Canadian Public Administration* 2 (1959): 145–53.

– Presentation. Paper given at the Fourth Annual Conference of the Institute of Public Administration of Canada, held at Montreal, October 23–25, 1952.

Kavic, Lorne J. and Gary Brian Nixon. *The 1200 Days: A Shattered Dream, Dave Barrett and the NDP in BC, 1972–1975*. Coquitlam, B.C.: Kaen Publishers, 1979.

Kendle, John. *John Bracken: A Political Biography*. Toronto: University of Toronto Press, 1979.

Kierans, Eric. *Report on National Resources Policy in Manitoba*. Prepared for the Secretariat of the Planning and Priorities Committee of Cabinet, Province of Manitoba. Winnipeg, February 1973.

Kroeker, H. V. "The Expenditure Budgetary Process." In *Public Policy in Canada*, edited by G. Bruce Doern and Peter Aucoin. Toronto: Macmillan, 1979.

Ladner, Peter. "Who are Those Masked Men?" *Vancouver* (magazine) (January 1984): 38.

Lane, Gary. Interview with the author. Saskatoon, February 20, 1986.

League for Social Reconstruction. *Social Planning for Canada*. Toronto: Thomas Nelson and Sons, 1935.

Leeson, Howard. "The Intergovernmental Function in Saskatchewan, 1960–1983." *Canadian Public Administration* 30, no. 3 (Fall 1987): 399–420.

Lloyd, Roy. Interview with the author. Saskatoon, June 18, 1985.

Loxley, John. "The 'Great Northern' Plan." In *Studies in Political Economy, A Socialist Perspective* 6 (Autumn 1981): 151–82.

Mallory, J. R. "The Continuing Evolution of Canadian Constitutionalism." In *Constitutionalism, Citizenship, and Society in Canada*, compiled by Allan Cairns and Cynthia Williams. Study 33 of the Macdonald Royal Commission. Toronto: University of Toronto Press, 1985.

Manitoba. An Act to Govern the Supply of Natural Gas in Manitoba and to Amend the Public Utilities Board Act, 1987.

– The Development Authority Act, 1959.

– The Executive Government Organization Act, 1970.

– The Financial Administration Act, 1969.

– Cabinet Committee on Health, Education and Social Policy. *White Paper on Health Policy*, July 1972.

– Commission of Inquiry into The Pas Forestry and Industrial Complex at The Pas, Manitoba. *Report*, several volumes, submitted by commissioners Hon. C. Rhodes Smith (Chairman); Murray S. Donnelly, Ph.D.; and Leon Mitchell, Q.C., ("CFI Inquiry"), 1974.

– Commission on Targets for Economic Development. *Manitoba to 1980*, ("TED Report"), March 1969.

– Committee on Manitoba's Economic Future. *Manitoba 1962–75*, ("COMEF Report"), March 6, 1963.

- Department of Finance. *Preparation of Estimates, 1980–81*, n.d. (c.1980).
- Department of Finance. *Supplementary Information for Legislative Review, 1986–87 Estimates*, c.1986.
- Department of Finance. "The Government of Manitoba: Cabinet and Central Agencies, 1984," 1984.
- Department of Finance. "Treasury Board," n.d. (c.1984 or 1985).
- Economic Development Advisory Board. *Report to the Standing Committee on Economic Development*, June 10, 1971.
- *General Manual of Administration*, 1974.
- *Guidelines for the Seventies*. Vol. 1, *Introduction and Economic Analysis*; vol. 2, *Social Goods and Services*; vol. 3, *Regional Perspectives*. March 1973.
- Government Information Services. News Releases, 1963, 1968, 1972, 1973, 1974, 1977, and 1989.
- Legislative Assembly. *Debates and Proceedings*, 1970.
- *Manitoba 1962–75*. Report of the Committee on Manitoba's Economic Future, ("COMEF Report"), March 6, 1963.
- *Manitoba to 1980*. Report of the Commission on Targets for Economic Development. ("TED Report.") Winnipeg, March 1969.
- Planning and Priorities Committee of Cabinet. *Minutes for meeting #4/70*, January 27, 1970.
- Planning Secretariat. *Report of the Manpower Working Group*. Submitted to the Planning and Priorities Committee of Cabinet, February 29, 1972.
- Postwar Reconstruction Committee. *Report*. Submitted to Premier Stuart Garson by Chairman W. J. Waines, 1945.
- *Proposals for Urban Reorganization in the Greater Winnipeg Area*, n.d. (Said to be December 23, 1970.)
- Provincial Municipal Committee. *Report and Memorandum of Recommendations and the Statement of Government Policy with Respect to Provincial-Municipal Relations*, 1953.
- *Public Accounts*, 1959–60 to 1967–68.
- "Reorganized Central Planning Structure," memorandum from Premier Schreyer to all ministers, September 6, 1973.
- Task Force on Government Organization and Economy. *Report on Government Organization and Economy*, 2 vols., April 1978.
- Task Force on Post-Secondary Education in Manitoba. *Report*, 1973.
- Treasury Board. *Minutes*, 1959–60. Treasury Board (Operation Productivity). *Government Organization*, June 1968.
Maslove, Allan M., ed. *Budgeting in the Provinces: Leadership and the Premiers*. Toronto: Institute of Public Administration of Canada, 1989.
McAllister, James A. *The Government of Edward Schreyer: Democratic Socialism in Manitoba*. Kingston and Montreal: McGill-Queen's University Press, 1984.
- *Report on Management Committee of Cabinet: Its Functions, Organization and Operation*. Submitted to the Planning Secretariat of Cabinet, Province of Manitoba. Winnipeg, November 8, 1974.
McLeod, T. H. "Planning Organization." Memoranda to S. M. Cherniak. Winnipeg, September 12, 1969.

McLeod, T. H. and Ian McLeod. *Tommy Douglas: The Road to Jerusalem*. Edmonton: Hurtig, 1987.

McLeod Young Weir. Government Finance Department. *Review of Fiscal 1984 Provincial Budgets*. Toronto, September 1983.

Michell, David. *W. A. C.: Bennett and the Rise of British Columbia*. Vancouver: Douglas and McIntyre, 1983.

Michelmann, Hans J. and Jeffrey S. Steeves. "The 1982 Transition in Power in Saskatchewan: The Progressive Conservatives and the Public Service." *Canadian Public Administration* 28 (Spring 1985): 1–23.

Millett, John D. *Management in the Public Service*. Toronto: McGraw-Hill, 1954.

Mitchell, Grant C. "The Executive Council." Paper presented at the "Symposium on the Policy Process in Saskatchewan: An Overview of the Principal Actors," held at St Thomas More College, University of Saskatchewan, March 27, 1981.

Morley, J. Terrence *et al*. *The Reins of Power: Governing British Columbia*. Vancouver: Douglas and McIntyre, 1983.

Morton, Jenny. "Manitoba Mean." *The Canadian* (September 30, 1978): 4.

Morton, W. L. *Manitoba: A History*. Toronto: University of Toronto Press, 1967.

Newman, Peter C. "The personal legacy of the Bennett era." *Maclean's* (June 2, 1986): 22–24.

Newman, Walter C. *What Happened When Dr. Kasser Came to Manitoba*. Winnipeg: Newmac Publishing Company, 1976.

Oliver, Michael. *Social Purpose for Canada*. Toronto: University of Toronto Press, 1961.

Patriquin, D. S. "Presentation on the Planning Bureau." Paper presented at the "Symposium on the Policy Process in Saskatchewan: An Overview of the Principal Actors," held at St Thomas More College, University of Saskatchewan, March 27, 1981.

Poyser, Ted. Interview with the author. Winnipeg, October 1988.

Ramesh, M. "The Role of Intergovernmental Agencies in Canada: The Case of the Saskatchewan Department of Intergovernmental Affairs." Master's thesis, Department of Economics and Political Science, University of Saskatchewan, 1982.

Regina *Leader-Post*. 1986 and 1987.

Richards, John and Larry Pratt. *Prairie Capitalism: Power and Influence in the New West*. Toronto: McClelland and Stewart, 1979.

Riddell, Norman. Letter to the author, November 25, 1986.

Ritter, Richard and James Cutt. *The Evolution of Central Financial Administration in the Government of British Columbia*. Report prepared for the Ministry of Finance, Province of British Columbia. Victoria, B.C.: University of Victoria Institute for Research on Public Policy, April 1985.

Roblin, Dufferin. Interview with the author. Winnipeg, December 13, 1983.

Romanow, Roy. Interview with the author. Saskatoon, June 21, 1985.

Ruff, Norman J. "Administrative Styles in the British Columbia Public Service." Paper presented at the "Reflections on a Decade: B.C. Politics in the Seventies" symposium of the Canadian Political Science Association, held at University of British Columbia, Vancouver, June 5, 1983.

- "Managing the Public Service." In *The Reins of Power*, edited by J. Terence Morley *et al*. Vancouver: Douglas and McIntyre, 1983: 161–98.
Sadler, Joan. "A little help from his friends." Trib Magazine (March 1, 1980): 6.
Saskatchewan. An Act respecting the Organization of the Executive Government of Saskatchewan, 1987.
- The Executive Council Act, 1972.
- The Legislative Assembly and Executive Council Act, 1979.
- Crown Investments Corporation. "Crown Corporations: Background and New Organizational Structure," June 29, 1983.
- Crown Investments Corporation. *Public Investment in Saskatchewan*, rev. ed. prepared by Gordon W. MacLean, 1981.
- Crown Investments Review Commission. *Report to the Government of Saskatchewan*, December 28, 1982.
- Department of Finance. *The Budget Planning Process*, n.d. (c.1985).
- Department of Finance. *An Evaluation of the Saskatchewan Program-Based Management Information System*, prepared by David Anderson, Budget Bureau, June 1976.
- Department of Finance. *PMIS Manual of Instructions*, 1977.
- Department of Finance. *PMIS Orientation and Procedures Manual*, May 1982.
- Department of Finance. "Purpose and Scopy of Zero-Base Reviews," n.d. (c.1985).
- Department of Finance. *Saskatchewan Economic and Financial Position*, March 1987.
- Executive Council. *Saskatchewan into the Eighties*, (rev. ed., 1980).
- Executive Council. Planning Bureau. "Central Planning in Saskatchewan: 1944 to Present," mimeo, prepared by Wendy MacDonald, June 26, 1980.
- Executive Council. Planning Bureau. "Function and Operation of the Planning Bureau," June 1980.
- Government Information Services. News Releases, Oct. 27, 1971; April 13, 1972; Dec. 3, 1986; Jan. 30, 1987; March 20, 1987; March 26, 1987.
- Legislative Assembly. *Debates and Proceedings*, 1972 and 1985.
- Minister of Finance. Budget Address, June 1987.
- *Public Accounts*, 1964–65 to 1969–70.
- Royal Commission on Government Administration. *Report*, June 15, 1965.
Saskatoon *Star-Phoenix*. 1987.
Savoie, Donald. *Taking Power: Managing Government Transitions*. Toronto: Institute of Public Administration of Canada, 1993.
Schreyer, Edward. Interviews with the author. Winnipeg, September 21 and 22, 1988.
Scott, F. R. *et al. Social Planning for Canada*. Reprint (original by League for Social Reconstruction Research Committee). Toronto and Buffalo: University of Toronto Press, 1975.
Seidman, Harold and Robert S. Gilmour. *Politics, Position and Power: From the Positive to the Regulatory State*. 4th ed. Oxford and New York: Oxford University Press, 1986.
Sherman, Paddy. *Bennett*. Toronto: McClelland and Stewart, 1966.
Sidor, Nick. *The Structure of Policy Planning and Financial Management in British*

Columbia, 1972–1977: A Province in Transition. Graduating essay, Department of Political Science, University of Victoria, April 18, 1977.

Simeon, Richard. *Federal-Provincial Diplomacy: The Making of Recent Policy in Canada*. Toronto: University of Toronto Press, 1972.

Smith, David E. "The Parliamentary Tradition in Saskatchewan: Approximating the Ideal." Paper presented at the conference on "Parliamentary Tradition in Canada," held at Quebec City, March 1987.

Smith, Douglas. "Pawley's Progress." *This Magazine* 21 no. 7 (Dec. 1987–Jan. 1988): 27–30.

Smith, Jennifer. "Ruling Small Worlds: Political Leadership in Atlantic Canada." In *Prime Ministers and Premiers: Political Leadership and Public Policy in Canada*, edited by Leslie A. Pal and David Taras. Scarborough, Ontario: Prentice-Hall, 1988.

Steuart, Senator David Gordon. Interview with the author. Regina, July 4, 1986.

Stinson, Lloyd. *Political Warriors: Reflections of a Social Democrat*. Winnipeg: Queenston House, 1975.

Swainson, Neil. "Governing Amid Division: The Premiership in British Columbia." In *Prime Ministers and Premiers: Political Leadership and Public Policy in Canada*, edited by Leslie A. Pal and David Taras. Scarborough, Ontario: Prentice-Hall, 1988.

– "The Public Service." In *The Reins of Power: Governing British Columbia*, edited by J. Terence Morley *et al.* Vancouver: Douglas and McIntyre, 1983.

Tennant, Paul. "The NDP Government of British Columbia: Unaided Politicians in an Unaided Cabinet." *Canadian Public Policy* 3 (Autumn 1977): 489–503.

Thomas, Clive Y. *Dependence and Transformation: The Economics of the Transition to Socialism*. New York: Monthly Review Press, 1974.

Thorburn, H. G. *Planning and the Economy*. Ottawa: Canadian Institute for Economic Policy, 1984.

Trebilcock, Michael J. *et al*. *The Choice of Governing Instrument*. Ottawa: Supply and Services Canada, 1982.

Vancouver *Province*. 1975, 1980, and 1983.

Vancouver *Sun*. 1980, 1982, 1983, 1984, 1986, and 1991.

Wallace, D. M. "Budget Reform in Saskatchewan: a new approach to program-based management." *Canadian Public Administration* 17 (1974): 586–99.

Ward, Norman. "Saskatchewan," In *The Canadian Annual Review for 1969*, edited by J. Saywell. Toronto: University of Toronto Press, 1970.

– "The Contemporary Scene." In *Politics in Saskatchewan*, edited by Norman Ward and Duff Spafford. Don Mills: Longmans, 1968.

Waterston, Albert. *Development Planning: Lessons of Experience*. Baltimore: Johns Hopkins University Press, 1979.

Weldon, J. C. "What is Planning?" in *Democratic Planning: A Symposium*. Toronto: Ontario Woodsworth Memorial Foundation, 1962.

Weppler, Murray *et al*. *Monologue vs. Dialogue: A Review of Manitoba Government Communications*. N.p., June 1982.

White, Graham. "Big is different than little: on taking size seriously in the analysis of Canadian government institutions." *Canadian Public Administration* 33, no. 4 (Winter 1990): 526–50.

– "Governing from Queen's Park." *In Prime Ministers and Premiers: Political Leadership and Public Policy in Canada*. edited by Leslie A. Pal and David Taras. Scarborough, Ontario: Prentice-Hall, 1988.

Wildavsky, Aaron. *Speaking Truth to Power*. New Brunswick: Transaction Books, 1989.

Wilson, V. Seymour. *Canadian Public Policy and Administration: Theory and Environment*. Toronto: McGraw-Hill Ryerson, 1981.

Winnipeg *Free Press*. 1971, 1976, 1982, 1983, 1984, 1986, and 1988.

Winnipeg *Sun*. 1986.

Winnipeg *Tribune*. 1971, 1972, 1975, and 1980. / *The Canadian* (supplement). 1978. / *Trib Magazine*. 1980.

Wiseman, Nelson. *Social Democracy in Manitoba*. Winnipeg: University of Manitoba Press, 1983.

Young, Walter D. and J. Terence Morley. "The Premier and the Cabinet." In *The Reins of Power: Governing British Columbia*, edited by J. Terence Morley *et al*. Vancouver: Douglas and McIntyre, 1983.

Note: More than two hundred interviews were conducted with politicians and officials influential in the development of cabinet systems in the western provinces. Since most of the interviews were conducted with the explicit or implicit understanding of confidentiality, many of the interviewees have not been listed.

Index

Riddell, Norman, 88–89, 92–93, 96, 102–3, 284
Roblin, Dufferin (Duff), 105–6: biography, 107–9; budget reform, 127–29; cabinet structure 110–17; central agencies and staff, 120–27; Operation Productivity, 117–20; planning, 129–30
Royal Commission on Government Administration (Johnson Commission), 48–50

Schreyer, Edward (Ed), 131: biography, 132–33; cabinet structure, 134–46; central agencies, 146–50; central planning, 153–54; decision-making modes, 157–59; planning and budgeting, 154–57; planning traditions, 150–52
Shoyama, T. K. (Tommy), 27–28, 32, 37–38, 44, 280, 284
special purpose funds, 209–10, 225
Spector, Norman, 244–45, 262, 284
Steuart, David (Davie), 42, 43, 45, 47, 49, 51, 53, 54–55

Tennant, Paul, 11, 201–2, 216, 219–21, 226, 230, 274
Thatcher, Ross, 4, 23–24, 35, 275, 276, 282, 285, 286, 287: biography, 41–43; budgeting, 45–52; cabinet structure and central agen-

cies, 43–45; decision-making modes, 52–55
Treasury, strong, 136, 142, 171, 176, 188, 274, 284, 286, 288

Wallace, D. M. (Murray), 50, 62, 70–71
Wallace, L. J., 202, 206–7, 216, 226, 244
Wallace, Robert A., 120, 125, 147
Weir, Walter, 5, 106, 107, 109–10, 111, 114, 118–19, 122, 125, 127, 129–30, 134, 136, 146–47, 151, 154, 159–60, 162, 183, 273
Weldon, J. C., 147–48

unaided cabinet, 3, 5, 11–12, 20, 23–24, 276: Barrett, 219–21, 223, 225; Blakeney, 62; defined and compared with institutionalized cabinet, 13–16, 271–72, 282–84, 286–87; Lyon, 161, 164, 167–69, 171, 175–76; Roblin, 107, 110, 121–22, 129; Shreyer, 160; Tennant theory, 221–23, 230; Thatcher, 41–42, 48, 50, 52, 55–56; W. A. C. Bennett, 201–3, 206, 215–16

Zero-Base Budgeting (ZBB), 94–95, 96, 103, 166–67, 174, 246–50, 266–67, 277, 280, 285